Daniel Wight
2nd hand, Glasgow, N

PENGUIN BOOKS

THE FOUCAULT READER

Michel Foucault was one of the most influential thinkers in the contemporary world. Social scientist and historian of ideas, Michel Foucault was Professor of History of Systems of Thought at the Collège de France. He wrote frequently for French newspapers and reviews, and edited *Critique*. Among his many other publications are *Madness and Civilization* (1961), *The Archaeology of Knowledge* (1972), *The Birth of the Clinic* (1973), *Discipline and Punish* (1975, Penguin 1979), and *The History of Sexuality*, Volume I (Penguin 1981), Volume II (Penguin 1987) and Volume III (Penguin 1990). Professor Foucault died in 1984.

Paul Rabinow is currently Professor of Anthropology at the University of California at Berkeley. He is the author of *French Modern: Norms and Forms of the Social Environment*.

The
FOUCAULT
Reader

Edited by
Paul Rabinow

Penguin Books

PENGUIN BOOKS

Published by the Penguin Group
Penguin Books Ltd, 27 Wrights Lane, London W8 5TZ, England
Penguin Books USA Inc., 375 Hudson Street, New York, New York 10014, USA
Penguin Books Australia Ltd, Ringwood, Victoria, Australia
Penguin Books Canada Ltd, 10 Alcorn Avenue, Toronto, Ontario, Canada M4V 3B2
Penguin Books (NZ) Ltd, 182–190 Wairau Road, Auckland 10, New Zealand

Penguin Books Ltd, Registered Offices: Harmondsworth, Middlesex, England

First published in the USA by Pantheon Books, a division of
Random House, Inc., New York, and simultaneously in
Canada by Random House of Canada Ltd, Toronto 1984
Published in Peregrine Books 1986
Reprinted in Penguin Books 1991
3 5 7 9 10 8 6 4 2

Printed in England by Clays Ltd, St Ives plc

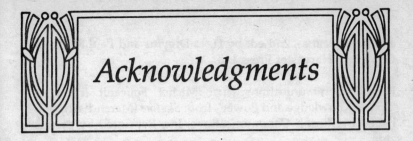

Acknowledgments

Grateful acknowledgement is made to the following for permission to reprint previously published material:

Methuen & Co Ltd:
Michel Foucault, 'What is an author?' translated from the French by Josué V. Harari, in *Textual Strategies: Perspectives in Post-Structuralist Criticism*, edited by J. Harari, pp. 141–160. Copyright Methuen & Co. Ltd.

Basil Blackwell Publishers:
Michel Foucault, 'Nietzsche, Genealogy, History' in *Language, Counter-Memory, Practice: Selected Essays and Interviews* by Michel Foucault, translated from the French by Donald F. Bouchard and Sherry Simon, and edited by Donald Bouchard. Copyright Basil Blackwell Publishers.

Tavistock Publications:
Michel Foucault, *The Order of Things: An Archaeology of the Human Sciences*, translated from the French by Alan Sheridan-Smith. Copyright Tavistock Publications.

Michel Foucault, *Madness and Civilization*, translated by Richard Howard. Copyright Tavistock Publications.

Harvester Press Ltd:
Michel Foucault, *Power/Knowledge: Selected Interviews and Other Writings, 1972–1977*, edited by Colin Gordon. Copyright Harvester Press Ltd.

Michel Foucault, 'On the Genealogy of Ethics: An Overview of Work in Progress', from *Michel Foucault: Beyond Structuralism and Hermeneutics*, 2nd ed. by H. L. Dreyfus and Paul Rabinow. Copyright Harvester Press Ltd.

Rizzoli Communications, Inc: Michel Foucault interview, 'Space, Knowledge and Power', from *Skyline* (March 1982), published by Rizzoli Communications, Inc. Reprinted by permission.

Contents

———————————————○○———————————————

The
FOUCAULT
Reader

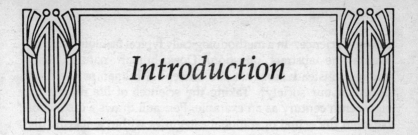

Introduction

Michel Foucault and Noam Chomsky appeared, some years ago, on a Dutch television program for a debate on the topic "Human Nature: Justice versus Power." The two thinkers never quite engaged in the agonistic sparring that such occasions are ideally supposed to produce, but some striking differences were clearly articulated. Although both men are highly critical of the current social and political order, their fundamental assumptions about the nature of human beings, about power and justice, and about how to understand such matters differ radically. Let me use this exchange as a means of introducing some of the elements of the work of Michel Foucault.

For Noam Chomsky, there is a human nature. This point is fundamental: unless there is some form of relatively fixed human nature, true scientific understanding is impossible. Starting from his own research, Chomsky asked: How is it that on the basis of a partial and fragmentary set of experiences, individuals in every culture are able not only to learn their own language, but to use it in a creative way? For Chomsky, there was only one possible answer: there must be a bio-physical structure underlying the mind which enables us, both as individuals and as a species, to deduce from the multiplicity of individual experiences a unified language. There must be, Chomsky insists, a "mass of schematisms, innate governing principles, which guide our social and intellectual and individual behavior . . . there is something biologically given, unchangeable, a foundation for whatever it is that we do with our mental capacities." [1] Chomsky's scientific career has been devoted to uncovering these structures. His aim: a testable mathematical theory of mind. His lineage: Cartesian rationality.

Michel Foucault rejects Chomsky's view of both human na-

3

ture and science. In a methodologically typical fashion, Foucault avoids the abstract question: Does human nature exist?, and asks instead: How has the concept of human nature functioned in our society? Taking the sciences of life during the eighteenth century as an example, Foucault draws a distinction between the actual operational categories within a specific discipline at a particular historical moment and those broad conceptual markers such as "life," or "human nature," which, in his opinion, have had very little importance in the internal changes of scientific disciplines. According to Foucault, "It is not by studying human nature that linguists discovered the laws of consonant mutation, or Freud the principles of the analysis of dreams, or cultural anthropologists the structure of myths. In the history of knowledge the notion of human nature seems to me mainly to have played the role of . . . designat[ing] certain types of discourse in relation to or in opposition to theology or biology or history." Foucault is highly suspicious of claims to universal truths. He doesn't refute them; instead, his consistent response is to historicize grand abstractions. In the last analysis, he doesn't take a stand on whether or not there is a human nature. Rather, he changes the subject and examines the social functions that such concepts have played in the context of practices "such as economics, technology, politics, sociology which can serve them as conditions of formation, of models, of place, etc. . . . what [it is] in social forms that makes the regularities of science possible." [2]

For Foucault, there is no external position of certainty, no universal understanding that is beyond history and society. His strategy is to proceed as far as possible in his analyses without recourse to universals. His main tactic is to historicize such supposedly universal categories as human nature each time he encounters them. Foucault's aim is to understand the plurality of roles that reason, for example, has taken as a social practice in our civilization not to use it as a yardstick against which these practices can be measured. This position does not entail any preconceived reduction of knowledge to social conditions. Rather, there is a consistent imperative, played out with varying emphases, which runs through Foucault's historical studies: to discover the relations of specific scientific disciplines and particular social practices.

A parallel set of differences between Chomsky and Foucault emerges in their discussion of politics. The interviewer asks each man why he is interested in politics. Chomsky answers by returning to other dimensions of universal human nature and reason. In his opinion, there is a universal human need for creative work and free inquiry. The possibility of satisfying this need is stifled in our society. Given modern technology and science, Chomsky argues, the means are currently available to overcome the alienation and drudgery of labor. If this has not been accomplished, the fault lies not in science but in the social and political organization of our society. The real problem we must confront, therefore, is a political one: how to bring about the just society in which creativity and reason would reign. Our job is to "try to create the vision of a future just society; that is to create, if you like, a humanistic social theory that is based, if possible, on some firm and humane concept of the human essence or human nature." [3] For Chomsky, the end of political action is clear—or will become so—because it is guided by reason and human nature. The task of intellectuals is to use the concept of human nature as a standard against which to judge society and to use their reason to formulate a precise conceptualization of a more humane and just social order. Our political tasks can be coherently informed by the universals of reason and justice.

Foucault, typically, refuses to answer why he is interested in politics. He finds this both trivial and self-evident. Instead, he shifts the "why" question to a "how" question—how am I interested in politics? Certainly not, he parries, "by imagining an ideal social model for the functioning of our scientific or technological society." One of the hallmarks of Western political philosophy, in Foucault's interpretation, has been its devotion to such abstractions, first principles, and utopias—i.e., theory. In the West we have consistently approached the problem of political order by building models of the just social order or searching for general principles by which to evaluate existing conditions. But, Foucault claims, it is exactly this emphasis, this "will to knowledge," that has left us almost totally in the dark about the concrete functioning of power in Western societies. Our task is to cast aside these utopian schemes, the search for first principles, and to ask instead how power actually operates in our society. "It seems to me," Foucault expounds, "that the real political task in a society such as ours is to criticize the working of institutions which appear to be both neutral and independent; to criticize them in such a manner that the political violence which has always exercised itself obscurely through them will be unmasked, so that one can fight them."[4]

But why should we fight against political violence? Again, Chomsky and Foucault differ. For Chomsky, we must struggle against the injustices of our current society in the name of a higher goal—justice. Surely, Chomsky argues, unless we have a guiding principle, we will have no way of judging the actions of others. It is perfectly possible that we may find ourselves in a situation in which a revolution turns out to be worse than the regime it replaces. Unless we have some fixed and rational standards for judging what constitutes a better society, we will be lost. This does not mean, Chomsky adds, that we have to achieve a perfect enactment of these standards, but unless we have them we will have no way to act or judge.

Foucault disagrees. And it is in this disagreement that Foucault is his most radical and disconcerting. He says: "I will be a little bit Nietzschean about this . . . it seems to me that the idea of justice in itself is an idea which in effect has been invented and put to work in different types of societies as an instrument of a certain political and economic power or as a weapon against that power . . . one can't, however regrettable it may be, put these notions forward to justify a fight which should . . . overthrow the very fundaments of our society."[5] Foucault is being consistent here. He is not saying that the idea of justice should never be invoked in a political struggle. But his basic metaphor is one of battle and not conversation. The point of engaging in political struggles—and Foucault thinks we are engaged in them all the time, hence his disdain for the question about the importance of politics—is to alter power relations.

For Foucault, knowledge of all sorts is thoroughly enmeshed in the clash of petty dominations, as well as in the larger battles which constitute our world. Knowledge is not external to these fights; it does not constitute a way out of, or above, the fray in the way Chomsky views it. Rather, for Foucault, the "will to knowledge" in our culture is simultaneously part of the danger and a tool to combat that danger. Following Nietzsche, Foucault asserts that knowledge did not "slowly detach itself from its empirical roots, the initial needs from which it arose, to become pure speculation subject only to the demands of reason. . . . Where religions once demanded the sacrifice of bodies, knowledge now calls for experimentation on ourselves, calls us to the sacrifice of the subject of knowledge."[6] Foucault confronts this challenge, this threat, by refusing to separate off knowledge from power. His strategy has been to focus his work, both political and intellectual, on what he sees as the greatest threat— that strange, somewhat unlikely, mixing of the social science and social practices developed around subjectivity.

Foucault calls this attempt to locate historically and analyze the strands of discourse and practices dealing with the subject, knowledge, and power "the genealogy of the modern subject." What is distinctive about Western culture is that we have given so much importance to the problem of the subject in our social, political, economic, legal, philosophical, and scientific traditions. Foucault's most general aim is to "discover the point at which these practices became coherent reflective techniques with definite goals, the point at which a particular discourse emerged from these techniques and came to be seen as true, the point at which they are linked with the obligation of searching for the truth and telling the truth."[7]

The Problem of the Subject

Let us follow Foucault in a recent self-characterization in which he says, "the goal of my work during the last twenty years has not been to analyze the phenomena of power, nor to elaborate the foundations of such an analysis. My objective, instead, has been to create a history of the different modes by which, in our culture, human beings are made subjects."[8] His schema of three modes of objectification of the subject provides a convenient means to present briefly the main themes of his work.

The first mode of objectification of the subject is somewhat cryptically called "dividing practices." The most famous examples from Foucault's work are the isolation of lepers during the Middle Ages; the confinement of the poor, the insane, and vagabonds in the great catch-all Hôpital Général in Paris in 1656; the new classifications of disease and the associated practices of clinical medicine in early-nineteenth-century France; the rise of modern psychiatry and its entry into the hospitals, prisons, and clinics throughout the nineteenth and twentieth centuries; and finally the medicalization, stigmatization, and normalization of sexual deviance in modern Europe.

In different fashions, using diverse procedures, and with a highly variable efficiency in each case, "the subject is objectified by a process of division either within himself or from others." [9] In this process of social objectification and categorization, human beings are given both a social and a personal identity. Essentially "dividing practices" are modes of manipulation that combine the mediation of a science (or pseudo-science) and the practice of exclusion—usually in a spatial sense, but always in a social one. These dividing practices form a substantial part of the subject matter of Foucault's earlier books, *Madness and Civilization* and *The Birth of the Clinic*, as well as later ones like *Discipline and Punish*. The main topics here are: the objectification of individuals drawn first from a rather undifferentiated mass (e.g., the vagabond populations in Paris in the seventeenth century), and later from more highly preselected populations (delinquents from working-class quarters); the interconnections of dividing practices with the formation and increasingly sophisticated elaboration of the social sciences; the historical relationship of these modes of classification, control, and containment to a distinctive tradition of humanitarian rhetoric on reform and progress; the increasingly efficient and diverse applications of these combined procedures of power and knowledge mainly, although not exclusively, to dominated groups or to groups formed and given an identity through the dividing practices.

The second mode for turning human beings into objectified subjects is related to, but independent from, the first. Let us call it "scientific classification." It arises from "the modes of inquiry which try to give themselves the status of sciences; for example, the objectivizing of the speaking subject in *grammaire générale*, philology, and linguistics . . . [or] the objectivizing of the productive subject, the subject who labors, in the analysis of wealth and of economics. Or . . . the objectivizing of the sheer fact of being alive in natural history or biology." [10] This list constitutes a concise summary of the contents of Foucault's most controversial but also most well-received book, *The Order of Things*. In this dense and erudite study, Foucault shows how the discourses of life, labor, and language were structured into disciplines; how in this manner they achieved a high degree of internal autonomy and coherence; and how these disciplines of life, labor, and language—which we tend to view as dealing with universals of human social life and as therefore progressing logically and refining themselves in the course of history (as in the natural sciences)—changed abruptly at several junctures, displaying a conceptual discontinuity from the disciplines that had immediately preceded them.

The historical breaks that set off the classical age (roughly from the middle of the seventeenth century to the French Revolution) are characteristic hallmarks in all of Foucault's writings. Given French history, there is nothing particularly surprising about this chronology. Indeed, Foucault has often mistakenly been seen as a philosopher of discontinuity. The fault is partially his own; works such as *The Archaeology of Knowledge* and *The Order of Things* certainly do emphasize abrupt changes in the structures of discourse of the human sciences. But Foucault has also stressed, in other contexts, the longer-range continuities in cultural practices. The sharp lines of discursive discontinuity in the human sciences and the longer lines of continuity in non-discursive practices provide Foucault with a powerful and flexible grid of interpretation with which to approach relations of knowledge and power. It should be underlined, however, that this is not a philosophy of history which for some mysterious reason glorifies discontinuity.

In both *The Order of Things* and in *The Archaeology of Knowledge* (Foucault's only attempt at a systematic theoretical analysis abstracted from the historical dissection that constitutes the subject matter of his other books), discourse is bracketed off from the social practices and institutions in which it is embedded. This bracketing has also caused some confusion. Although

Foucault was temporarily caught up in some of the structuralist vocabulary of the moment, he never intended to isolate discourse from the social practices that surround it. Rather, he was experimenting to see how much autonomy could legitimately be claimed for discursive formations. His aim, then as now, was to avoid analyses of discourse (or ideology) as reflections, no matter how sophisticatedly mediated, of something supposedly "deeper" and more "real." In this sense, Foucault has been consistently materialist. In asking, "How does discourse function?," his aim has been to isolate techniques of power exactly in those places where this kind of analysis is rarely done. But to achieve this, he at first overemphasized the inner articulations and seemingly self-enclosed nature of social scientific discourses. Although Foucault has preserved the majority of his "archaeological" systematizations of the formation of concepts, objects, subjects, and strategies of discourse in the human sciences, he has now explicitly widened his analysis to show how these disciplines have played an effective part in a historical field that includes other types of nondiscursive practice.

Foucault has been consistently interested in the shifting ways that the body and the social institutions related to it have entered into political relations. In the first mode of objectification (the dividing practices), the constituted subject can be seen as a victim caught in the processes of objectification and constraint—most obviously the case for prisoners and mental patients. Although there are parallel developments associated with the second mode of objectification (scientific classification), the relation to domination is more oblique. For example, in *The Birth of the Clinic* Foucault demonstrates how the body was increasingly treated as a thing during the nineteenth century, and how this objectification was paralleled and complemented by the dividing practices instituted in the clinic's spatial, temporal, and social compartmentalizations. But the two dimensions—dividing practices and scientific classification—are not the same thing; nor are they orchestrated together by some unseen actor. Foucault offers no casual explanations for these changes, leaving his readers somewhat at sea with regard to how he evaluates the interplay of intentional action, socioeconomic changes, particular interests, and accidents.

Foucault's third mode of objectification represents his most original contribution. Let us call it "subjectification." It concerns the "way a human being turns him- or herself into a subject." [11] This process differs in significant ways from the other two modes and represents an important new direction in Foucault's work. The dividing practices, broadly speaking, are techniques of domination and have been applied mainly to vagabond populations, the working classes, those defined as marginal, etc. The interplay between these modes of domination and various social scientific forms of classification, although given new clarity and power by Foucault's analysis and historical studies, has been recognized by other thinkers. In both instances, the person who is put into a cell or whose dossier is being compiled is basically in a passive, constrained position. In contrast, with the third mode—"subjectification"—Foucault looks at those processes of self-formation in which the person is active. His published analyses have focused on the dominant classes, in particular the nineteenth-century French bourgeoisie; work in progress examines Greek citizens and the early Christian ascetics and Church Fathers. In these analyses, Foucault is primarily concerned with isolating those techniques through which the person initiates an active self-formation. This self-formation has a long and complicated genealogy; it takes place through a variety of "operations on [people's] own bodies, on their own souls, on their own thoughts, on their own conduct." [12] These operations characteristically entail a process of self-understanding but one which is mediated by an external authority figure, be he confessor or psychoanalyst. Foucault shows us, for example, how during the nineteenth century there was a vast proliferation of scientific discourses about "sex," in part because sex was seen as holding the key to self-understanding; this line culminated in Freud. Foucault also points to a growing obsession with sexuality, the health of the individual and the race, the growth of medical discourses about sexuality, and so forth. The individual and the race were thereby joined in a common set of concerns. It is important here not to draw too sharp a line between these processes of subjectification and, say, dividing practices. As Foucault shows in *The History of Sexuality* and in *Discipline and Punish*, the two can be effectively combined, although they are analytically distinguishable.

The Problem of Power/Knowledge

Taken together, the three modes of objectification of the subject (those that categorize, distribute, and manipulate; those through which we have come to understand ourselves scientifically; those that we have used to form ourselves into meaning-giving selves) designate the problematic of Foucault's inquiries. Yet it soon becomes apparent that if the most general theme of Foucault's work has been the problem of the subject, an understanding of this investigation requires the arsenal of subsidiary concepts and concerns he has forged along the way. Clustered tightly around the problem of the subject are the twin terms of power and knowledge. Their importance has already been well situated by Colin Gordon in his anthology of Foucault's essays, *Power/Knowledge*. Although there is no need to rehearse the arguments in any detail here, several points deserve to be underlined.

During most of the 1960s, Foucault sought, in a variety of ways, to isolate and analyze the structures of the human sciences treated as discursive systems. It is important to stress that Foucault did not see himself as a *practitioner* of these human sciences. They were his object of study. Foucault never took these discourses from the inside. That is, he never posed the question of the truth or falsity of the specific claims made in any particular discipline. Although he traced with great patience the discursive systems of the sciences of life, language, and labor, his aim was not to unveil the truths they had discovered or the falsities they had propounded. Rather, once again, it was the effective operation of these disciplines—how and around what concepts they formed, how they were used, where they developed—that was Foucault's prey. The problem became how to analyze the statements of the social sciences without judging their "progress" or lack of it, and without reducing their relative discursive and conceptual autonomy to something else seen to be more basic. As Colin Gordon puts it: "How are the human sciences historically possible, and what are the historical conditions of their existence?" [13] Parallel, although not identical, questions have obviously been raised before, most notably in Nietzsche's *Genealogy of Morals*, but Foucault has pursued the consequences of these questions with unparalleled systematicity and vigor.

Foucault is resolutely and consistently anti-Hegelian and anti-Marxist in this area. The search for a general theory of history is not on his agenda. In fact, it is, in Foucault's diagnosis, part of the problem. Foucault seems to be identifying with the critique of theory initiated in modern times by Nietzsche and pursued by Heidegger. Yet Foucault's situating himself within this lineage does not entail the rejection of reason. He is adamant that he is not—as Jurgen Habermas, among others, has charged—an "irrationalist." [14] Nor has he abandoned sustained critical argument in the public arena. He simply refuses to see reason as either our hope or our nemesis. Foucault puts it this way: "The relationship between rationalization and excesses of political power is evident. And we should not need to wait for bureaucracy or concentration camps to recognize the existence of such relations. But the problem is: What to do with such an evident fact? Shall we try reason? To my mind, nothing would be more sterile. First, because the field has nothing to do with guilt or innocence. Second, because it is senseless to refer to reason as the contrary entry to nonreason. Lastly, because such a trial would trap us into playing the arbitrary and boring part of either the irrationalist or the rationalist." [15]

This anti-metaphysical and anti-ontological strain in Foucault's work is a powerful one. But questions—both philosophical and political—remain about the exact status of reason in Foucault's work. He seems to set himself close to, but apart from, a line of thinkers stretching from Max Weber to Martin Heidegger through Theodor Adorno and Max Horkheimer. Each of these men, in different ways, recognized both a centrality and a danger in the processes of increasing rationalization and technological development of the world. Each also differentiated between types of reason or thinking—instrumental, substantive, formal, critical, etc.—and attempted to separate out those dimensions and consequences of rational activity which were pernicious and those which in some form or other could serve as instruments of resisting or overcoming the destructive functioning of reason in Western culture.

Foucault's work is itself a testament to sustained critical rationality with political intent. However, we have only the beginnings of a critical assessment of the positive functions of reason for Foucault. His is a constant pluralizing and decapitalizing of all the great concepts, first principles, and fundamental grounds that our tradition has produced. The problem of reason is not a juridical or ontological one; it is historical and political. As Foucault explains: "The central issue of philosophy and critical thought since the eighteenth century has always been . . . *What* is this Reason that we use? What are its historical effects? What are its limits, and what are its dangers? . . . [If] philosophy has a function within critical thought, it is precisely to accept this sort of spiral, this sort of revolving door of rationality that refers us to its necessity, to its indispensability, and at the same time to its intrinsic dangers." [16]

The Problem of Government

Just as Foucault innovatively sought to isolate and analyze a schema for understanding how our culture has produced different types of subjects, so too, his more recent work has thematicized power in a new way. In his words: "Since the sixteenth century, a new political form of power has been continuously developing. This new political structure, as everyone knows, is the state. But most of the time, the state is envisioned as a kind of political power which ignores individuals, looking only at the interests of the totality, or, I should say, of a class or a group among the citizens. That's quite true. But I'd like to underline the fact that the state's power (and that's one of the reasons for its strength) is both an individualizing and a totalizing form of power. Never, I think, in the history of human societies—even in the old Chinese society—has there been such a tricky combination in the same political structures of individualization techniques, and of totalization procedures." [17]

We have already looked at these "individualization techniques" in relation to the objectification of the subject. Now let us turn briefly to the "totalization procedures"—first, with a brief outline of Foucault's analysis of key historical changes in the state's relation to the individual.

With the Renaissance, new links between the state (formed by the great territorial monarchies that arose in Europe from the fragments of feudal estates) and the individual (whose soul and salvation were given renewed prominence as a political issue in the Reformation and Counter-Reformation) gave rise to a new type of political reflection. From the middle of the sixteenth century, a series of treatises on the "art of government" began to appear. They were not concerned with the traditional questions of the nature of the state, nor even with problems of how the prince could best guard his power (although these topics were not entirely absent). Their scope was much wider. In fact, they covered almost everything. These treatises spoke directly of the "governing of a household, souls, children, a province, a convent, a religious order, or a family." Political reflection was thereby tacitly broadened to include almost all forms of human activity, from the smallest stirrings of the soul to the largest military maneuvers of the army. Each activity in its own specific way demanded reflection on how it could best be accomplished. "Best," Foucault tells us, meant "most economical." "The art of government . . . is concerned with . . . how to introduce economy, that is the correct manner of managing individuals, goods and wealth within the family, . . . how to introduce this meticulous attention of the father towards his family, into the management of the state." [18]

The first major shift, therefore, is from a concern with the nature of the state and then the prince and his concerns per se, to a broader and more detailed consideration of how to introduce economy and order (i.e., government) from the top of the state down through all aspects of social life. Society was becoming a political target.

Once one grasps Foucault's conceptualization of this shift, many seemingly mundane statements by minor administrators take on a new significance. For example, Foucault quotes a philosopher, Guillaume de la Perriere, in his treatise *Miroir de la politique* (1567): "government is the right disposition of things arranged so as to lead to a convenient end." The phrasing seems innocuous. Foucault, however, reads it as indicating a major shift in political thinking. He points out that for traditional theories of sovereignty there was a fundamental link between the sovereign and a territory. Granted, the sovereign also ruled all those who lived in that territory and controlled its resources. But the fundamental tie, the source of the sovereign's legitimacy, was his connection to a realm. In Guillaume de la Perriere's definition, there is no mention of territory. Rather, a complex relationship of men and things is given priority. "Consequently," Foucault concludes, "the things which the government is to be concerned about are men, but men in their relations, their links, their imbrication with those other things which are wealth, resources, means of subsistence, the territory with its specific qualities, climate, irrigation, fertility, etc.; men in their relation to other kinds of things which are customs, habits, ways of doing and thinking, etc.; lastly, men in their relation to that other kind of things which are accidents and misfortunes such as famine, epidemics, death, etc." [19] The concerns of a well-governed polity (or, as it would be called in the eighteenth century, a well-policed state) now extend from the prince and his conduct down through the customs of the people to the environment itself.

These treatises on government were more than merely academic exercises. In France, from the middle of the sixteenth century on, they are linked directly to the rise and growth of centralized state administrative apparatuses. In fact, it was only slightly later, in the seventeenth century, that detailed knowledge of the disposability of the things available—the different "elements, dimensions and factors of the state's power"—was christened "statistics": the science of the state. The art of government and empirical knowledge of the state's resources and condition—its statistics—together formed the major components of a new political rationality. A rationality, Foucault assures us, from which we have not yet emerged.

The attention to population, family, and economy during the classical age is related to well-studied historical events which the *Annales* school has made famous: "the demographic expansion of the eighteenth century, connected with historical monetary abundance, which in turn was linked to the expansion of agricultural production through a series of circular processes." [20] Foucault's contribution has been to extend the links between these long-term changes and certain political processes which have been systematically underplayed by the *Annales* historians. Specifically, he has helped to explain economic, demographic, and political patterns of the classical age in a manner which reveals conscious decisions being made by administrators regarding the supposedly unconscious forces analyzed by the "long durée" historians.

As the fostering of life and the growth and care of population becomes a central concern of the state, articulated in the art of government, a new regime of power takes hold. Foucault calls this regime "bio-power." He explains that bio-power "brought life and its mechanisms into the realm of explicit calculations and made knowledge-power an agent of the transformation of human life. . . . Modern man is an animal whose politics places his existence as a living being in question." [21] Bio-power coalesces around two distinct poles at the beginning of the classical age. One pole is the human species. For the first time in history, scientific categories (species, population, fertility, and so forth), rather than juridical ones, become the object of systematic, sustained political attention and intervention.

The other pole of bio-power is the human body: the body approached not directly in its biological dimension, but as an object to be manipulated and controlled. A new set of operations, of procedures—those joinings of knowledge and power that Foucault calls "technologies"—come together around the objectification of the body. They form the "disciplinary technology" that Foucault analyzes in detail in *Discipline and Punish*.

The aim of disciplinary technology, whatever its institutional form—and it arose in a large number of different settings, such as workshops, schools, prisons, and hospitals—is to forge a "docile body that may be subjected, used, transformed and improved." [22] This is done in several related ways: through drills and training of the body, through standardization of actions over time, and through the control of space. Discipline proceeds from an organization of individuals in space, and it requires a specific enclosure of space. Once established, this grid permits the sure distribution of the individuals who are to be disciplined and supervised. In a factory, the procedure facilitates productivity; in a school, it assures orderly behavior; in a town, it reduces the risk of dangerous crowds, wandering vagabonds, or epidemic diseases.

Disciplinary control—and the readings included in this collection specify its complexity and variety in detail—is unquestionably linked to the rise of capitalism. But the relationship between the economic changes that resulted in the accumulation of capital and the political changes that resulted in the accumulation of power remains to be specified. Foucault argues that the two are mutually dependent: "Each makes the other possible and necessary; each provides a model for the other." For instance, "the massive projection of military models onto industrial organization was an example of [the] modeling of the division of labor following the model laid down by the schemata of power." [23] Disciplinary technologies, in other words, preceded modern capitalism. In Foucault's argument, they are among its preconditions. Without the availability of techniques for subjecting individuals to discipline, including the spatial arrangements necessary and appropriate to the task, the new demands of capitalism would have been stymied. In a parallel manner, without the fixation, control, and rational distribution of populations built on a statistical knowledge of them, capitalism would have been impossible. The growth and spread of disciplinary mechanisms of knowledge and power preceded the growth of capitalism in both the logical and temporal sense. Although these technologies did not cause the rise of capitalism, they were the prerequisites for its success.

The growth of capitalism, however, is not Foucault's focus. His concern is the subject and power, as well as the political rationality which has bound them together. We can draw these themes together with an example, perhaps the most famous one from Foucault's repertoire. Foucault selects Jeremy Bentham's plan for the panopticon as the paradigm of a disciplinary technology. And his analysis of this apparatus serves as a shorthand for the other technologies that he analyzes.

The panopticon offers a particularly vivid instance of how political technologies of the body function. It is "a generalizable model of functioning; a way of defining power relations in terms of the everyday life of men. . . . [I]t is the diagram of a mechanism of power reduced to its ideal form . . . it is in fact a figure of political technology that may and must be detached from any specific use." [24] It is also a particular organization of space and human beings, a visual order that clarifies the mechanisms of power which are being deployed.

The panopticon consists of a large courtyard, with a tower in the center, surrounded by a series of buildings divided into levels and cells. In each cell there are two windows: one brings in light and the other faces the tower, where large observatory windows allow for the surveillance of the cells. The cells become "small theatres, in which each actor is alone, perfectly individualized and constantly visible." [25] The inmate is not simply visible to the supervisor; he is visible to the supervisor alone—cut off from any contact. This new power is continuous and anonymous. Anyone could operate the architectural mechanisms as long as he was in the correct position, and anyone could be subjected to it. The surveillant could as easily be observing a criminal, a schoolboy, or a wife (Bentham suggests, apparently without humor, that the panopticon would be an extremely effective arrangement for a harem, since it would cut down the number of eunuchs necessary to watch the women in the cells).

The architectural perfection is such that even if there is no guardian present, the power apparatus still operates effectively. The inmate cannot see whether or not the guardian is in the tower, so he must behave as if surveillance were perpetual and total. If the prisoner is never sure when he is being observed, he becomes his own guardian. As the final step in architectural and technological perfection, the panopticon includes a system for observing and controlling the controllers. Those who occupy the central position in the panopticon are themselves thoroughly enmeshed in a localization and ordering of their own behavior. "Such is perhaps the most diabolical aspect of the idea and of all the applications it brought about," Foucault comments. "In this form of management, power is not totally entrusted to someone who would exercise it alone, over others, in an absolute fashion; rather, this machine is one in which everyone is caught, those who exercise this power as well as those who are subjected to it." [26]

Thus, through spatial ordering, the panopticon brings together power, control of the body, control of groups and knowledge (the inmate is observed and examined systematically in his cell). It locates individuals in space, in a hierarchical and efficiently visible organization. Although Bentham's scheme was never fully implemented, nor (as we shall see) did the numerous adaptations ever operate as effectively as Bentham intended them to, it is nonetheless a crucial development for Foucault. As he explains: "The automatic functioning of power, mechanical operation, is absolutely not the thesis of *Discipline and Punish*. Rather, it is the idea, in the eighteenth century, that such a form of power is possible and desirable. It is the theoretical and practical search for such mechanisms, the will, constantly attested, to organize this kind of mechanism which constitutes the object of my analysis." [27]

A particular rationality accompanies the panoptic technology: one that is self-contained and nontheoretical, geared to efficiency and productivity. For Bentham, the panopticon had the advantage of being utilitarian, capable of service in a multitude of settings for a multitude of purposes. It seemed to pose no standard of judgment or to follow any particular program. It aimed to be a tool for distributing individuals in space, for ordering them in a visible way. Hence its potential for generalization.

Foucault, however, points to an additional rationality built into the project of the panopticon. It offered a logic not only of efficiency but also of normalization. By "normalization," Foucault means a system of finely gradated and measurable intervals in which individuals can be distributed around a norm—a norm which both organizes and is the result of this controlled distribution. A system of normalization is opposed to a system of law or a system of personal power. There are no fixed pivot points from which to make judgments, to impose will. Normative, serialized (to use the Sartrean term) order is an essential component of the regime of bio-power, for "a power whose task is to take charge of life needs continuous regulatory and corrective mechanisms. . . . Such a power has to qualify, measure, appraise, and hierarchize, rather than display itself in its murderous splendor . . . it effects distributions around the norm. . . . [The] juridical institution is increasingly incorporated into a continuum of apparatuses (medical, administrative, and so on) whose functions are for the most part regulatory." [28]

This normative rationality has gradually undermined and "invested" (like a parasite invests a body) both the excesses of sovereign power and, more important, the procedures of the law (without eliminating either, again like a parasite). The entry of medicine, psychiatry, and some social sciences into legal deliberations in the nineteenth century led in the direction of what Foucault calls a systematic "normalization" of the law—that is, toward an increasing appeal to statistical measures and judgments about what is normal and what is not in a given population, rather than adherence to absolute measures of right and wrong. Under the regime of bio-power, neither the sovereign nor the law—*ni roi, ni loi*—escapes the spread of normative rationality. "There are two meanings of the word *subject*," Foucault writes, "subject to someone else by control and dependence, and tied to his own identity by a conscience or self-knowledge. Both meanings suggest a form of power which subjugates and makes subject to." [29]

An essential component of technologies of normalization is the key role they play in the systematic creation, classification, and control of "anomalies" in the social body. Their *raison d'être* comes from two claims of their promoters: first, that certain technologies serve to isolate anomalies; and second, that one can then normalize anomalies through corrective or therapeutic procedures, determined by other related technologies. In both cases, the technologies of normalization are purportedly impartial techniques for dealing with dangerous social deviations. However, as Foucault shows in great detail in *Discipline and Punish* and in *The History of Sexuality*, the advance of bio-power in the nineteenth century is in fact contemporary with the appearance and proliferation of the modern categories of anomaly—the delinquent, the pervert—which the technologies of discipline and confession are supposedly designed to eliminate, but never do. In Foucault's reading: "The implantation of perversions in an instrument effect: it is through the isolation, intensification, and consolidation of peripheral sexualities that the relations of power to sex and pleasure branched out and multiplied, measured the body, and penetrated modes of conduct." [30] The end of good government is the correct disposition of things—even when these things have to be invented so as to be well governed.

With the nineteenth century, the possibility of knowledge about and control over the most minute aspects of behavior in the name of the population's welfare is at least present in principle, although never fully realized. A vast documentary apparatus becomes an essential part of normalizing technologies. Precise *dossiers* enable the authorities to fix individuals in a web of objective codification. More precise and more statistically accurate knowledge of individuals leads to finer and more encompassing criteria for normalization. This accumulation of documentation makes possible "the measurement of overall phenomena, the description of groups, the characterization of collective facts, the calculation of the gaps between individuals, their distribution in a given 'population.' " [31] The power of the state to produce an increasingly totalizing web of control is intertwined with and dependent on its ability to produce an increasing specification of individuality.

Foucault does not claim that this totalizing and individualizing power has empirically taken hold of everything, nor that it is ineluctable. And yet this increasing subjection is not a mere dream. One can fairly ask of Foucault: What is to be done in the face of this spreading web of power? Yet he has been in general highly reticent about the role of advocate. All the same he does, from time to time, offer general evaluations. Here is one: "Maybe the target nowadays is not to discover what we are, but to refuse what we are. We have to imagine and to build up what we could be to get rid of [a] political 'double bind,' which is the simultaneous individualization and totalization of modern power structures. The conclusion would be that the political, ethical, social, philosophical problem of our days is not to try to liberate the individual from the state, and from the state's institutions, but to liberate us both from the state and from the type of individualization which is linked to the state. We have to promote new forms of subjectivity through refusal of this kind of individuality which has been imposed on us for several centuries." [32]

The general practical implications of this challenge have not been explored by Foucault in his writings, at least not to any great extent. If one were to analyze Foucault's political activities over the last twenty years, one would gain an indication of the scope of fights against totalization and objectification of the subject. But in these struggles he has been a citizen like any other, claiming no special rights for himself, nor any direct and privileged relationship between his intellectual work and his actions.

The Location of the Author

Indeed, one encounters great difficulty in trying to situate Foucault as an intellectual spokesman with a particular message to propound. He is not an intellectual prophet. Unlike Jean-Paul Sartre, he does not take it upon himself to speak in the voice of Reason, Justice, Progress, Objectively Better Positions, or even Futility. On several occasions (e.g., in "Truth and Power"), Foucault has pronounced, in the most reluctant of prophetic voices, the end of intellectual prophecy. But that is the extent of his Delphic statements. In his opinion, the universal intellectual, whose task was to speak the truth to power in the name of universal reason, justice, and humanity, is no longer a viable cultural figure; the reign of that individual is over. Sartre was the last incumbent. (Of course, there is a certain contradiction in Foucault's assuredness in offering such predictions. On the basis of what privileged position, what sources of certain knowledge, can he be sure that the figure of the universal intellectual has passed from the historical scene?)

But Foucault is not a biologist or a physicist, a man of science, either. Such scientists occupy the key positions of the "specific intellectual" (Foucault's term for those sectorial specialists on whom our future depends and who must speak to us from their laboratories). Their voices are given an authority because their work and our fate are intertwined, not because they have any special claim to represent reason. The specific intellectual is "he who, along with a handful of others, has at his disposal, whether in the service of the state or against it, powers which can either benefit or irrevocably destroy life. He is no longer the rhapsodist of the eternal, but the strategist of life and death." [33] As a professor who holds the Chair of the History of Systems of Thought at the Collège de France, Foucault is clearly not without a certain prestige, yet he is obviously not a "strategist of life and death"—even if he has become their historian.

Nor has Foucault been willing to play the Parisian game of

the "writer" as it has been defined in recent years. The "writer" has now replaced the universal intellectual. Although such figures no longer wield the power and influence of Emile Zola, Victor Hugo, or even André Gide, they are nonetheless persons of influence and visibility in contemporary France. In fact, the new socialist regime, highly self-conscious about its relations with intellectuals and its place in history, has chosen to give prominence to two types of intellectuals: writers and technocrats. Among his first acts, in the name of French universalism, President François Mitterrand granted French citizenship to two writers exiled from totalitarian regimes; his highly influential and ambitious minister of research has chosen to lionize French technocrats, declaring that nuclear power and bio-engineering are the key sectors for socialism to develop.

How, then, to situate Foucault? From whence does his authority flow—if not from Reason and Justice, if not from Science, if not from courtly Art? In his essay "What Is an Author?" Foucault provides us with some elements of an answer. He makes a distinction, for instance, between the changing historical importance of the author in literature and science. He points out that in the West, until the seventeenth century, the scientific text was the one more closely associated with and legitimated by the celebrity and authority of the author: "Those texts that we now would call scientific—those dealing with cosmology and the heavens, medicine and illnesses, natural sciences and geography—were accepted in the Middle Ages, and accepted as 'true' only when marked with the name of their author." [34] This situation has obviously changed today. Once these disciplines crossed the scientific threshold of "formalization" and succeeded in developing procedures of concept formation, evidence, verification, etc., then the name of the author was no longer central to the authority of the text. Truth became more anonymous.

In literature, schematizing broadly, we find the opposite trajectory. During the Middle Ages, "the texts that we today call 'literary' (narratives, stories, epics, tragedies, comedies) were accepted, put into circulation, and valorized without any question about the identity of their author; their anonymity caused no difficulties since their ancientness, whether real or imagined, was regarded as a suffecient guarantee of their status." [35] Since the beginning of the nineteenth century, however, literature with a capital *L* has emerged as an autonomous and highly valued activity, with a place for itself on the intellectual scene (see Roland Barthes's *Writing Degree Zero*). And the authority of the author has continued to grow in literary productions. The identification and evaluation of a literary work are intimately linked to the fame, standing, and reputation of its author, and from the intellectual world that gravitates toward those in power.

Foucault then briefly alludes to a third type of authorial location. These are the rare figures, social thinkers it seems, whom he calls "founders of discursivity." Specifically, he mentions Karl Marx and Sigmund Freud. What Foucault describes are figures who provide a paradigmatic set of terms, images, and concepts which organize thinking and experience about the past, present, and future of society, doing so in a way which enigmatically surpasses the specific claims they put forth. This status is particular to the human sciences. Whereas in the biological or physical sciences the original texts, say James Clerk Maxwell's equations or those of Albert Einstein, are fully absorbed and surpassed by the scientific work that follows them, this is not the case in the human sciences.

Foucault is not implying that progress is unilinear in the harder sciences, only that one type of discursive system is characteristic of these disciplines, and another is characteristic of the contemporary human sciences. In the latter case, one finds a constant return to the texts of certain "founders of discursivity," despite advances in factual content, verification of hypotheses, and method. Showing the inconsistencies in Freud or the failure of Marx's predictions has not destroyed either Freudian psychoanalysis or Marxism. Foucault observes: "To expand a type of discursivity, such as psychoanalysis as founded by Freud, is not to give it a formal generality that it would not have permitted at the outset, but rather to open it to a certain number of applications . . . . In addition, one does not declare certain propositions in the work of these founders to be false: instead . . . one sets aside those statements that are not pertinent . . . reexamining Freud's texts modifies psychoanalysis itself, just as a reexamination of Marx's would modify Marxism." [36] Foucault is not endorsing, celebrating, or lamenting this curious discursive formation in the human sciences; he is indicating its existence, and in that he is, again, highly original.

My wager is that Michel Foucault himself may well be one of these "founders of discursivity." The judgment having been made, it must be immediately modified. If Foucault's work does indeed function in the future as a central organizer of social discourses, it will do so in a way radically different discursively, institutionally, politically, and—dare I say—psychologically from the work of Marx and Freud.

Nor do I see Foucault as the sole figure with such a status. Two figures with whom interesting comparisons might be made are Thomas Kuhn and Max Weber (neither of whom has had any direct influence on Foucault).

Taking Kuhn first, there are of course striking parallels in the content of Foucault's and Kuhn's work, in their emphasis on how scientific reflection and research are organized, operate, and change.[37] Moreover, both have been received enthusiastically, yet both have shunned the empire-building that has been opened to them. At the same time a flurry of negative reviews and hostile, petty corrections has accompanied the growing influence of and the new inquiries stemming from both men's work. This reaction seems to indicate an important shift in our contemporary discursive style, and perhaps the emergence of a radically different manner of inquiry for research. The questions both men ask extend from the human sciences across to the supposedly solid, unbiased, hard sciences. What is most infuriating to fact-oriented, feet-on-the-ground empiricists is that Foucault's and Kuhn's thinking has evolved from a systematic ability to comprehend exactly those phenomena of "shared practices," "disciplinary matrices," "petty malices" which partially constitute scientific activity, although they don't exhaust it.

Still, whatever the impact of Kuhn's work in the long run, its scope and subject matter are more limited than and inherently different from those of Foucault. And so the comparison with Max Weber suggests itself. For Foucault and Weber share a clarity about our historical nightmare—in Weber's terms, the "mighty cosmos of the modern economic order . . . the iron cage [in which] specialists without spirit, sensualists without heart,

[are] caught in the delusion that [they] have achieved a level of development never before attained by mankind." [38] That Weber came from the liberal nationalist tradition of the German academy and Foucault from the radical splinters of the French intelligentsia is of course historically significant, but it is not an impediment to the comparison, for neither man can be captured by or reduced to these characterizations. Weber, although often cast as a conservative, offers a devastating account of modern capitalism which certainly does not suggest that he wished to preserve it whole. Foucault has been cast as a conservative by some, in the sense that he has consistently opposed much of modern French Marxism, "existing socialism," and those utopias and nightmares associated with this tradition. But such labels tell us little. What both Weber and Foucault proffer—in a pessimistic and dour mode in Weber's case, and an elusive and joyous one in Foucault's—is a heroic refusal to sentimentalize the past in any way or to shirk the necessity of facing the future as dangerous but open. Both have committed their lives to a scrupulous, if unorthodox, forging of intellectual tools for the analysis of modern rationality, social and economic organization, and subjectivity. Both see a form of critical historicism as the only road to preserving reason and the obligation—differently understood by Weber and Foucault—to forge an ascetic ethic of scientific and political responsibility as the highest duty of the mature intellectual.

—Paul Rabinow

[Editor's note: The choice of texts is always an arbitrary one. Given the wealth of Foucault's past writings and the new directions his work is currently taking, the task is doubly hard. I have chosen to emphasize the political and social dimensions of his work in which practices and discourses intertwine. The main sacrifice this choice has occasioned is the absence of texts from Foucault's rich and important "archaeological period" during the 1960s—*The Birth of the Clinic*, *The Order of Things*, *The Archaeology of Knowledge*. It seemed better to concentrate on those texts in which power, discourse, and the subject were related to non-discursive practices in a sustained manner than to try to include everything. The resultant distortion is duly noted and responsibility accepted.]

Notes

[1] Noam Chomsky, in "Human Nature: Justice versus Power," in *Reflexive Water: The Basic Concerns of Mankind*, ed. Fons Elders (London: Souvenir Press, 1974), pp. 136, 140.

[2] Michel Foucault, in "Human Nature," pp. 140, 160.

[3] Chomsky, in "Human Nature," p. 172.

[4] Foucault, in "Human Nature," p. 171.

[5] Ibid., p. 187.

[6] Michel Foucault, "Nietzsche, Genealogy, History" (1971), in *Language, Counter-Memory, Practice: Selected Essays and Interviews*, ed. D. F. Bouchard (Ithaca: Cornell University Press, 1977), p. 163. (See also this volume, p. 95.)

[7] Michel Foucault, "Howison Lectures," Berkeley, 20 October 1980.

[8] Michel Foucault, "The Subject and Power," in *Michel Foucault: Beyond Structuralism and Hermeneutics*, by Hubert Dreyfus and Paul Rabinow (Chicago: University of Chicago Press, 1982), p. 208.

[9] Ibid.

[10] Ibid.

[11] Ibid.

[12] Foucault, "Howison Lectures."

[13] Colin Gordon, "Afterword," in *Power/Knowledge*, ed. Colin Gordon (New York: Pantheon Books, 1980), pp. 230–1.

[14] See Jurgen Habermas, "Modernity versus Postmodernity," *New German Critique*, No. 22 (Winter 1981), p. 13.

[15] Foucault, "Subject and Power," p. 210.

[16] Michel Foucault, "Space, Knowledge, and Power: An Interview with Michel Foucault by Paul Rabinow," *Skyline* (March 1982), p. 19. (See also this volume, p. 239.)

[17] Foucault, "Subject and Power," p. 213.

[18] Michel Foucault, "On Governmentality" (1978), *Ideology and Consciousness*, No. 6 (Autumn 1979), pp. 8, 10.

[19] Ibid., pp. 10, 11.

[20] Ibid., p. 11.

[21] Michel Foucault, *The History of Sexuality*, Vol. I (1976; New York: Pantheon, 1978), p. 143. (See also this volume, pp. 264–65.)

[22] Michel Foucault, *Discipline and Punish* (1975; New York: Vintage Books, 1979), p. 198.

[23] Ibid., p. 221. (See also this volume, pp. 209–10.)

[24] Ibid., p. 205.

[25] Ibid., p. 200.

[26] Michel Foucault, "The Eye of Power" (1977), in *Power/Knowledge*, p. 156.

[27] Michel Foucault, in *L'Impossible prison*, ed. Michelle Perrot (Paris: Editions du Seuil, 1980), p. 37.

[28] Foucault, *History of Sexuality*, p. 144. (See also this volume, pp. 266–67.)

[29] Foucault, "Subject and Power," p. 212.

[30] Foucault, *History of Sexuality*, p. 48. (See also this volume, pp. 327–28.)

[31] Foucault, *Discipline and Punish*, p. 190. (See also this volume, pp. 202–03.)

[32] Foucault, "Subject and Power," p. 216.

[33] Michel Foucault, "Truth and Power," in *Power/Knowledge*, p. 129. (See also this volume, p. 70.)

[34] Michel Foucault, "What Is an Author?" (1969), in *Textual Strategies* ed. Josue V. Harari (Ithaca: Cornell University Press, 1979), p. 149. (See also this volume, pp. 108–09.)

[35] Ibid.

[36] Ibid., pp. 156–7. (See also this volume, pp. 116–17.)

[37] For a more detailed discussion of these questions, see Dreyfus and Rabinow, *Michel Foucault: Beyond Structuralism and Hermeneutics*.

[38] Max Weber, *The Protestant Ethic and the Spirit of Capitalism* (New York: Scribner's & Sons, 1948), p. 182.

Part

I

Truth and Method

What Is Enlightenment?

(Was ist Aufklärung?)

I.

Today when a periodical asks its readers a question, it does so in order to collect opinions on some subject about which everyone has an opinion already; there is not much likelihood of learning anything new. In the eighteenth century, editors preferred to question the public on problems that did not yet have solutions. I don't know whether or not that practice was more effective; it was unquestionably more entertaining.

In any event, in line with this custom, in November 1784 a German periodical, *Berlinische Monatschrift*, published a response to the question: *Was ist Aufklärung?* And the respondent was Kant.

A minor text, perhaps. But it seems to me that it marks the discreet entrance into the history of thought of a question that modern philosophy has not been capable of answering, but that it has never managed to get rid of, either. And one that has been repeated in various forms for two centuries now. From Hegel through Nietzsche or Max Weber to Horkheimer or Habermas, hardly any philosophy has failed to confront this same question, directly or indirectly. What, then, is this event that is called the *Aufklärung* and that has determined, at least in part, what we are, what we think, and what we do today? Let us imagine that the *Berlinische Monatschrift* still exists and that it is asking its readers the question: What is modern philosophy? Perhaps we could respond with an echo: modern philosophy is the philosophy that is attempting to answer the question raised so imprudently two centuries ago: *Was ist Aufklärung?*

* * *

Translated by Catherine Porter.

Let us linger a few moments over Kant's text. It merits attention for several reasons.

1. To this same question, Moses Mendelssohn had also replied in the same journal, just two months earlier. But Kant had not seen Mendelssohn's text when he wrote his. To be sure, the encounter of the German philosophical movement with the new development of Jewish culture does not date from this precise moment. Mendelssohn had been at that crossroads for thirty years or so, in company with Lessing. But up to this point it had been a matter of making a place for Jewish culture within German thought—which Lessing had tried to do in *Die Juden*— or else of identifying problems common to Jewish thought and to German philosophy; this is what Mendelssohn had done in his *Phädon; oder, Über die Unsterblichkeit der Seele*. With the two texts published in the *Berlinische Monatschrift*, the German *Aufklärung* and the Jewish *Haskala* recognize that they belong to the same history; they are seeking to identify the common processes from which they stem. And it is perhaps a way of announcing the acceptance of a common destiny—we now know to what drama that was to lead.

2. But there is more. In itself and within the Christian tradition, Kant's text poses a new problem.

It was certainly not the first time that philosophical thought had sought to reflect on its own present. But, speaking schematically, we may say that this reflection had until then taken three main forms.

• The present may be represented as belonging to a certain era of the world, distinct from the others through some inherent characteristics, or separated from the others by some dramatic event. Thus, in Plato's *The Statesman* the interlocutors recognize that they belong to one of those revolutions of the world in which the world is turning backwards, with all the negative consequences that may ensue.

• The present may be interrogated in an attempt to decipher in it the heralding signs of a forthcoming event. Here we have the principle of a kind of historical hermeneutics of which Augustine might provide an example.

• The present may also be analyzed as a point of transition toward the dawning of a new world. That is what Vico describes in the last chapter of *La Scienza Nuova*; what he sees "today" is "a complete humanity . . . spread abroad through all nations, for a few great monarchs rule over this world of peoples"; it is also "Europe . . . radiant with such humanity that it abounds in all the good things that make for the happiness of human life." [1]

Now the way Kant poses the question of *Aufklärung* is entirely different: it is neither a world era to which one belongs, nor an event whose signs are perceived, nor the dawning of an accomplishment. Kant defines *Aufklärung* in an almost entirely negative way, as an *Ausgang*, an "exit," a "way out." In his other texts on history, Kant occasionally raises questions of origin or defines the internal teleology of a historical process. In the text on *Aufklärung*, he deals with the question of contemporary reality alone. He is not seeking to understand the present on the basis of a totality or of a future achievement. He is looking for a difference: What difference does today introduce with respect to yesterday?

3. I shall not go into detail here concerning this text, which is not always very clear despite its brevity. I should simply like to point out three or four features that seem to me important if we are to understand how Kant raised the philosophical question of the present day.

Kant indicates right away that the "way out" that characterizes Enlightenment is a process that releases us from the status of "immaturity." And by "immaturity," he means a certain state of our will that makes us accept someone else's authority to lead us in areas where the use of reason is called for. Kant gives three examples: we are in a state of "immaturity" when a book takes the place of our understanding, when a spiritual director takes the place of our conscience, when a doctor decides for us what our diet is to be. (Let us note in passing that the register of these three critiques is easy to recognize, even though the text does not make it explicit.) In any case, Enlightenment is defined by a modification of the preexisting relation linking will, authority, and the use of reason.

We must also note that this way out is presented by Kant in a rather ambiguous manner. He characterizes it as a phenomenon, an ongoing process; but he also presents it as a task and an obligation. From the very first paragraph, he notes that man himself is responsible for his immature status. Thus it has to be supposed that he will be able to escape from it only by a change that he himself will bring about in himself. Significantly, Kant says that this Enlightenment has a *Wahlspruch*: now a *Wahlspruch* is a heraldic device, that is, a distinctive feature by which one can be recognized, and it is also a motto, an instruction that one gives oneself and proposes to others. What, then, is this instruction? *Aude sapere*: "dare to know," "have the courage, the audacity, to know." Thus Enlightenment must be considered both as a process in which men participate collectively and as an act of courage to be accomplished personally. Men are at once elements and agents of a single process. They may be actors in the process to the extent that they participate in it; and the process occurs to the extent that men decide to be its voluntary actors.

A third difficulty appears here in Kant's text, in his use of the word "mankind," *Menschheit*. The importance of this word in the Kantian conception of history is well known. Are we to understand that the entire human race is caught up in the process of Enlightenment? In that case, we must imagine Enlightenment as a historical change that affects the political and social existence of all people on the face of the earth. Or are we to understand that it involves a change affecting what constitutes the humanity of human beings? But the question then arises of knowing what this change is. Here again, Kant's answer is not without a certain ambiguity. In any case, beneath its appearance of simplicity, it is rather complex.

Kant defines two essential conditions under which mankind can escape from its immaturity. And these two conditions are at once spiritual and institutional, ethical and political.

The first of these conditions is that the realm of obedience and the realm of the use of reason be clearly distinguished. Briefly characterizing the immature status, Kant invokes the familiar expression: "Don't think, just follow orders"; such is, according to him, the form in which military discipline, political power, and religious authority are usually exercised. Humanity will reach maturity when it is no longer required to obey, but when men are told: "Obey, and you will be able to reason as much as you like." We must note that the German word used here is *räsonieren*; this word, which is also used in the *Critiques*, does not refer to just any use of reason, but to a use of reason in which reason has no other end but itself: *räsonieren* is to reason for reasoning's sake. And Kant gives examples, these too being perfectly trivial in appearance: paying one's taxes, while being able to argue as much as one likes about the system of taxation, would be characteristic of the mature state; or again, taking responsibility for parish service, if one is a pastor, while reasoning freely about religious dogmas.

We might think that there is nothing very different here from what has been meant, since the sixteenth century, by freedom of conscience: the right to think as one pleases so long as one obeys as one must. Yet it is here that Kant brings into play another distinction, and in a rather surprising way. The distinction he introduces is between the private and public uses of reason. But he adds at once that reason must be free in its public use, and must be submissive in its private use. Which is, term for term, the opposite of what is ordinarily called freedom of conscience.

But we must be somewhat more precise. What constitutes, for Kant, this private use of reason? In what area is it exercised? Man, Kant says, makes a private use of reason when he is "a cog in a machine"; that is, when he has a role to play in society and jobs to do: to be a soldier, to have taxes to pay, to be in charge of a parish, to be a civil servant, all this makes the human being a particular segment of society; he finds himself thereby placed in a circumscribed position, where he has to apply particular rules and pursue particular ends. Kant does not ask that people practice a blind and foolish obedience, but that they adapt the use they make of their reason to these determined circumstances; and reason must then be subjected to the particular ends in view. Thus there cannot be, here, any free use of reason.

On the other hand, when one is reasoning only in order to

use one's reason, when one is reasoning as a reasonable being (and not as a cog in a machine), when one is reasoning as a member of reasonable humanity, then the use of reason must be free and public. Enlightenment is thus not merely the process by which individuals would see their own personal freedom of thought guaranteed. There is Enlightenment when the universal, the free, and the public uses of reason are superimposed on one another.

Now this leads us to a fourth question that must be put to Kant's text. We can readily see how the universal use of reason (apart from any private end) is the business of the subject himself as an individual; we can readily see, too, how the freedom of this use may be assured in a purely negative manner through the absence of any challenge to it; but how is a public use of that reason to be assured? Enlightenment, as we see, must not be conceived simply as a general process affecting all humanity; it must not be conceived only as an obligation prescribed to individuals: it now appears as a political problem. The question, in any event, is that of knowing how the use of reason can take the public form that it requires, how the audacity to know can be exercised in broad daylight, while individuals are obeying as scrupulously as possible. And Kant, in conclusion, proposes to Frederick II, in scarcely veiled terms, a sort of contract—what might be called the contract of rational despotism with free reason: the public and free use of autonomous reason will be the best guarantee of obedience, on condition, however, that the political principle that must be obeyed itself be in conformity with universal reason.

Let us leave Kant's text here. I do not by any means propose to consider it as capable of constituting an adequate description of Enlightenment; and no historian, I think, could be satisfied with it for an analysis of the social, political, and cultural transformations that occurred at the end of the eighteenth century.

Nevertheless, notwithstanding its circumstantial nature, and without intending to give it an exaggerated place in Kant's work, I believe that it is necessary to stress the connection that exists between this brief article and the three *Critiques*. Kant in fact describes Enlightenment as the moment when humanity is going to put its own reason to use, without subjecting itself to any authority; now it is precisely at this moment that the critique is necessary, since its role is that of defining the conditions under which the use of reason is legitimate in order to determine what can be known, what must be done, and what may be hoped. Illegitimate uses of reason are what give rise to dogmatism and heteronomy, along with illusion; on the other hand, it is when the legitimate use of reason has been clearly defined in its principles that its autonomy can be assured. The critique is, in a sense, the handbook of reason that has grown up in Enlightenment; and, conversely, the Enlightenment is the age of the critique.

It is also necessary, I think, to underline the relation between this text of Kant's and the other texts he devoted to history. These latter, for the most part, seek to define the internal teleology of time and the point toward which history of humanity is moving. Now the analysis of Enlightenment, defining this history as humanity's passage to its adult status, situates contemporary reality with respect to the overall movement and its basic directions. But at the same time, it shows how, at this very moment, each individual is responsible in a certain way for that overall process.

The hypothesis I should like to propose is that this little text is located in a sense at the crossroads of critical reflection and reflection on history. It is a reflection by Kant on the contemporary status of his own enterprise. No doubt it is not the first time that a philosopher has given his reasons for undertaking his work at a particular moment. But it seems to me that it is the first time that a philosopher has connected in this way, closely and from the inside, the significance of his work with respect to knowledge, a reflection on history and a particular analysis of the specific moment at which he is writing and because of which he is writing. It is in the reflection on "today" as difference in history and as motive for a particular philosophical task that the novelty of this text appears to me to lie.

And, by looking at it in this way, it seems to me we may recognize a point of departure: the outline of what one might call the attitude of modernity.

II.

I know that modernity is often spoken of as an epoch, or at least as a set of features characteristic of an epoch; situated on a calendar, it would be preceded by a more or less naive or archaic premodernity, and followed by an enigmatic and troubling "postmodernity." And then we find ourselves asking whether modernity constitutes the sequel to the Enlightenment and its development, or whether we are to see it as a rupture or a deviation with respect to the basic principles of the eighteenth century.

Thinking back on Kant's text, I wonder whether we may not envisage modernity rather as an attitude than as a period of history. And by "attitude," I mean a mode of relating to contemporary reality; a voluntary choice made by certain people; in the end, a way of thinking and feeling; a way, too, of acting and behaving that at one and the same time marks a relation of belonging and presents itself as a task. A bit, no doubt, like what the Greeks called an *ethos*. And consequently, rather than seeking to distinguish the "modern era" from the "premodern" or "postmodern," I think it would be more useful to try to find out how the attitude of modernity, ever since its formation, has found itself struggling with attitudes of "countermodernity."

To characterize briefly this attitude of modernity, I shall take an almost indispensable example, namely, Baudelaire; for his consciousness of modernity is widely recognized as one of the most acute in the nineteenth century.

1. Modernity is often characterized in terms of consciousness of the discontinuity of time: a break with tradition, a feeling of novelty, of vertigo in the face of the passing moment. And this is indeed what Baudelaire seems to be saying when he defines modernity as "the ephemeral, the fleeting, the contingent." [2] But, for him, being modern does not lie in recognizing and accepting this perpetual movement; on the contrary, it lies in adopting a certain attitude with respect to this movement; and this deliberate, difficult attitude consists in recapturing something eternal that is not beyond the present instant, nor behind it, but within it. Modernity is distinct from fashion, which does

no more than call into question the course of time; modernity is the attitude that makes it possible to grasp the "heroic" aspect of the present moment. Modernity is not a phenomenon of sensitivity to the fleeting present; it is the will to "heroize" the present.

I shall restrict myself to what Baudelaire says about the painting of his contemporaries. Baudelaire makes fun of those painters who, finding nineteenth-century dress excessively ugly, want to depict nothing but ancient togas. But modernity in painting does not consist, for Baudelaire, in introducing black clothing onto the canvas. The modern painter is the one who can show the dark frock-coat as "the necessary costume of our time," the one who knows how to make manifest, in the fashion of the day, the essential, permanent, obsessive relation that our age entertains with death. "The dress-coat and frock-coat not only possess their political beauty, which is an expression of universal equality, but also their poetic beauty, which is an expression of the public soul—an immense cortège of undertaker's mutes (mutes in love, political mutes, bourgeois mutes . . .). We are each of us celebrating some funeral." [3] To designate this attitude of modernity, Baudelaire sometimes employs a litotes that is highly significant because it is presented in the form of a precept: "You have no right to despise the present."

2. This heroization is ironical, needless to say. The attitude of modernity does not treat the passing moment as sacred in order to try to maintain or perpetuate it. It certainly does not involve harvesting it as a fleeting and interesting curiosity. That would be what Baudelaire would call the spectator's posture. The *flâneur*, the idle, strolling spectator, is satisfied to keep his eyes open, to pay attention and to build up a storehouse of memories. In opposition to the *flâneur*, Baudelaire describes the man of modernity: "Away he goes, hurrying, searching. . . . Be very sure that this man . . . —this solitary, gifted with an active imagination, ceaselessly journeying across the great human desert—has an aim loftier than that of a mere *flâneur*, an aim more general, something other than the fugitive pleasure of circumstance. He is looking for that quality which you must allow me to call 'modernity.' . . . He makes it his business to extract from fashion whatever element it may contain of poetry within history." As an example of modernity, Baudelaire cites the artist Constantin Guys. In appearance a spectator, a collector of curiosities, he remains "the last to linger wherever there can be a glow of light, an echo of poetry, a quiver of life or a chord of music; wherever a passion can *pose* before him, wherever natural man and conventional man display themselves in a strange beauty, wherever the sun lights up the swift joys of the *depraved animal*." [4]

But let us make no mistake. Constantin Guys is not a *flâneur*; what makes him the modern painter *par excellence* in Baudelaire's eyes is that, just when the whole world is falling asleep, he begins to work, and he transfigures that world. His transfiguration does not entail an annulling of reality, but a difficult interplay between the truth of what is real and the exercise of freedom; "natural" things become "more than natural," "beautiful" things become "more than beautiful," and individual objects appear "endowed with an impulsive life like the soul of [their] creator." [5] For the attitude of modernity, the high value of the present is indissociable from a desperate eagerness to imagine it, to imagine it otherwise than it is, and to transform it not by destroying it but by grasping it in what it is. Baudelairean modernity is an exercise in which extreme attention to what is real is confronted with the practice of a liberty that simultaneously respects this reality and violates it.

3. However, modernity for Baudelaire is not simply a form of relationship to the present; it is also a mode of relationship that has to be established with oneself. The deliberate attitude of modernity is tied to an indispensable asceticism. To be modern is not to accept oneself as one is in the flux of the passing moments; it is to take oneself as object of a complex and difficult elaboration: what Baudelaire, in the vocabulary of his day, calls *dandysme*. Here I shall not recall in detail the well-known passages on "vulgar, earthy, vile nature"; on man's indispensable revolt against himself; on the "doctrine of elegance" which imposes "upon its ambitious and humble disciples" a discipline more despotic than the most terrible religions; the pages, finally, on the asceticism of the dandy who makes of his body, his behavior, his feelings and passions, his very existence, a work

of art. Modern man, for Baudelaire, is not the man who goes off to discover himself, his secrets and his hidden truth; he is the man who tries to invent himself. This modernity does not "liberate man in his own being"; it compels him to face the task of producing himself.

4. Let me add just one final word. This ironic heroization of the present, this transfiguring play of freedom with reality, this ascetic elaboration of the self—Baudelaire does not imagine that these have any place in society itself, or in the body politic. They can only be produced in another, a different place, which Baudelaire calls art.

I do not pretend to be summarizing in these few lines either the complex historical event that was the Enlightenment, at the end of the eighteenth century, or the attitude of modernity in the various guises it may have taken on during the last two centuries.

I have been seeking, on the one hand, to emphasize the extent to which a type of philosophical interrogation—one that simultaneously problematizes man's relation to the present, man's historical mode of being, and the constitution of the self as an autonomous subject—is rooted in the Enlightenment. On the other hand, I have been seeking to stress that the thread that may connect us with the Enlightenment is not faithfulness to doctrinal elements, but rather the permanent reactivation of an attitude—that is, of a philosophical ethos that could be described as a permanent critique of our historical era. I should like to characterize this ethos very briefly.

A. *Negatively*

1. This ethos implies, first, the refusal of what I like to call the "blackmail" of the Enlightenment. I think that the Enlightenment, as a set of political, economic, social, institutional, and cultural events on which we still depend in large part, constitutes a privileged domain for analysis. I also think that as an enter-

prise for linking the progress of truth and the history of liberty in a bond of direct relation, it formulated a philosophical question that remains for us to consider. I think, finally, as I have tried to show with reference to Kant's text, that it defined a certain manner of philosophizing.

But that does not mean that one has to be "for" or "against" the Enlightenment. It even means precisely that one has to refuse everything that might present itself in the form of a simplistic and authoritarian alternative: you either accept the Enlightenment and remain within the tradition of its rationalism (this is considered a positive term by some and used by others, on the contrary, as a reproach); or else you criticize the Enlightenment and then try to escape from its principles of rationality (which may be seen once again as good or bad). And we do not break free of this blackmail by introducing "dialectical" nuances while seeking to determine what good and bad elements there may have been in the Enlightenment.

We must try to proceed with the analysis of ourselves as beings who are historically determined, to a certain extent, by the Enlightenment. Such an analysis implies a series of historical inquiries that are as precise as possible; and these inquiries will not be oriented retrospectively toward the "essential kernel of rationality" that cán be found in the Enlightenment and that would have to be preserved in any event; they will be oriented toward the "contemporary limits of the necessary," that is, toward what is not or is no longer indispensable for the constitution of ourselves as autonomous subjects.

2. This permanent critique of ourselves has to avoid the always too facile confusions between humanism and Enlightenment.

We must never forget that the Enlightenment is an event, or a set of events and complex historical processes, that is located at a certain point in the development of European societies. As such, it includes elements of social transformation, types of political institution, forms of knowledge, projects of rationalization of knowledge and practices, technological mutations that are very difficult to sum up in a word, even if many of these phenomena remain important today. The one I have pointed out and that seems to me to have been at the basis of an entire form of philosophical reflection concerns only the mode of reflective relation to the present.

Humanism is something entirely different. It is a theme or, rather, a set of themes that have reappeared on several occasions, over time, in European societies; these themes, always tied to value judgments, have obviously varied greatly in their content, as well as in the values they have preserved. Furthermore, they have served as a critical principle of differentiation. In the seventeenth century, there was a humanism that presented itself as a critique of Christianity or of religion in general; there was a Christian humanism opposed to an ascetic and much more theocentric humanism. In the nineteenth century, there was a suspicious humanism, hostile and critical toward science, and another that, to the contrary, placed its hope in that same science. Marxism has been a humanism; so have existentialism and personalism; there was a time when people supported the humanistic values represented by National Socialism, and when the Stalinists themselves said they were humanists.

From this, we must not conclude that everything that has ever been linked with humanism is to be rejected, but that the humanistic thematic is in itself too supple, too diverse, too inconsistent to serve as an axis for reflection. And it is a fact that, at least since the seventeenth century, what is called humanism has always been obliged to lean on certain conceptions of man borrowed from religion, science, or politics. Humanism serves to color and to justify the conceptions of man to which it is, after all, obliged to take recourse.

Now, in this connection, I believe that this thematic, which so often recurs and which always depends on humanism, can be opposed by the principle of a critique and a permanent creation of ourselves in our autonomy: that is, a principle that is at the heart of the historical consciousness that the Enlightenment has of itself. From this standpoint, I am inclined to see Enlightenment and humanism in a state of tension rather than identity.

In any case, it seems to me dangerous to confuse them; and further, it seems historically inaccurate. If the question of man, of the human species, of the humanist, was important throughout the eighteenth century, this is very rarely, I believe, because the Enlightenment considered itself a humanism. It is worthwhile, too, to note that throughout the nineteenth century, the historiography of sixteenth-century humanism, which was so important for people like Saint-Beuve or Burckhardt, was always distinct from and sometimes explicitly opposed to the Enlightenment and the eighteenth century. The nineteenth century had a tendency to oppose the two, at least as much as to confuse them.

In any case, I think that, just as we must free ourselves from the intellectual blackmail of "being for or against the Enlightenment," we must escape from the historical and moral confusionism that mixes the theme of humanism with the question of the Enlightenment. An analysis of their complex relations in the course of the last two centuries would be a worthwhile project, an important one if we are to bring some measure of clarity to the consciousness that we have of ourselves and of our past.

B. *Positively*

Yet while taking these precautions into account, we must obviously give a more positive content to what may be a philosophical ethos consisting in a critique of what we are saying, thinking, and doing, through a historical ontology of ourselves.

1. This philosophical ethos may be characterized as a *limit-attitude*. We are not talking about a gesture of rejection. We have to move beyond the outside-inside alternative; we have to be at the frontiers. Criticism indeed consists of analyzing and reflecting upon limits. But if the Kantian question was that of knowing what limits knowledge has to renounce transgressing, it seems to me that the critical question today has to be turned back into a positive one: in what is given to us as universal, necessary, obligatory, what place is occupied by whatever is singular, contingent, and the product of arbitrary constraints? The point, in brief, is to transform the critique conducted in the form of necessary limitation into a practical critique that takes the form of a possible transgression.

This entails an obvious consequence: that criticism is no

longer going to be practiced in the search for formal structures with universal value, but rather as a historical investigation into the events that have led us to constitute ourselves and to recognize ourselves as subjects of what we are doing, thinking, saying. In that sense, this criticism is not transcendental, and its goal is not that of making a metaphysics possible: it is genealogical in its design and archaeological in its method. Archaeological—and not transcendental—in the sense that it will not seek to identify the universal structures of all knowledge or of all possible moral action, but will seek to treat the instances of discourse that articulate what we think, say, and do as so many historical events. And this critique will be genealogical in the sense that it will not deduce from the form of what we are what it is impossible for us to do and to know; but it will separate out, from the contingency that has made us what we are, the possibility of no longer being, doing, or thinking what we are, do, or think. It is not seeking to make possible a metaphysics that has finally become a science; it is seeking to give new impetus, as far and wide as possible, to the undefined work of freedom.

2. But if we are not to settle for the affirmation or the empty dream of freedom, it seems to me that this historico-critical attitude must also be an experimental one. I mean that this work done at the limits of ourselves must, on the one hand, open up a realm of historical inquiry and, on the other, put itself to the test of reality, of contemporary reality, both to grasp the points where change is possible and desirable, and to determine the precise form this change should take. This means that the historical ontology of ourselves must turn away from all projects that claim to be global or radical. In fact we know from experience that the claim to escape from the system of contemporary reality so as to produce the overall programs of another society, of another way of thinking, another culture, another vision of the world, has led only to the return of the most dangerous traditions.

I prefer the very specific transformations that have proved to be possible in the last twenty years in a certain number of areas that concern our ways of being and thinking, relations to authority, relations between the sexes, the way in which we perceive insanity or illness; I prefer even these partial transformations that have been made in the correlation of historical analysis and the practical attitude, to the programs for a new man that the worst political systems have repeated throughout the twentieth century.

I shall thus characterize the philosophical ethos appropriate to the critical ontology of ourselves as a historico-practical test of the limits that we may go beyond, and thus as work carried out by ourselves upon ourselves as free beings.

3. Still, the following objection would no doubt be entirely legitimate: if we limit ourselves to this type of always partial and local inquiry or test, do we not run the risk of letting ourselves be determined by more general structures of which we may well not be conscious, and over which we may have no control?

To this, two responses. It is true that we have to give up hope of ever acceding to a point of view that could give us access to any complete and definitive knowledge of what may constitute our historical limits. And from this point of view the theoretical and practical experience that we have of our limits and of the possibility of moving beyond them is always limited and determined; thus we are always in the position of beginning again.

But that does not mean that no work can be done except in disorder and contingency. The work in question has its generality, its systematicity, its homogeneity, and its stakes.

(a) *Its Stakes*

These are indicated by what might be called "the paradox of the relations of capacity and power." We know that the great promise or the great hope of the eighteenth century, or a part of the eighteenth century, lay in the simultaneous and proportional growth of individuals with respect to one another. And, moreover, we can see that throughout the entire history of Western societies (it is perhaps here that the root of their singular historical destiny is located—such a peculiar destiny, so different from the others in its trajectory and so universalizing, so dominant with respect to the others), the acquisition of capabilities and the struggle for freedom have constituted permanent elements. Now the relations between the growth of capabilities and the growth of autonomy are not as simple as the eighteenth century may have believed. And we have been able to see what forms of power relation were conveyed by various technologies (whether we are speaking of productions with economic aims, or institutions whose goal is social regulation, or of techniques of communication): disciplines, both collective and individual, procedures of normalization exercised in the name of the power of the state, demands of society or of population zones, are examples. What is at stake, then, is this: How can the growth of capabilities be disconnected from the intensification of power relations?

(b) *Homogeneity*

This leads to the study of what could be called "practical systems." Here we are taking as a homogeneous domain of reference not the representations that men give of themselves, not the conditions that determine them without their knowledge, but rather what they do and the way they do it. That is, the forms of rationality that organize their ways of doing things (this might be called the technological aspect) and the freedom with which they act within these practical systems, reacting to what others do, modifying the rules of the game, up to a certain point (this might be called the strategic side of these practices). The homogeneity of these historico-critical analyses is thus ensured by this realm of practices, with their technological side and their strategic side.

(c) *Systematicity*

These practical systems stem from three broad areas: relations of control over things, relations of action upon others, relations with oneself. This does not mean that each of these three areas is completely foreign to the others. It is well known that control over things is mediated by relations with others; and relations with others in turn always entail relations with oneself, and vice versa. But we have three axes whose specificity and whose interconnections have to be analyzed: the axis of knowledge, the axis of power, the axis of ethics. In other terms, the historical ontology of ourselves has to answer an open series of questions; it has to make an indefinite number of inquiries which may be multiplied and specified as much as we like, but which will all address the questions systematized as follows: How are we constituted as subjects of our own knowledge? How are we constituted as subjects who exercise or submit to power relations? How are we constituted as moral subjects of our own actions?

(d) *Generality*

Finally, these historico-critical investigations are quite specific in the sense that they always bear upon a material, an epoch, a body of determined practices and discourses. And yet, at least at the level of the Western societies from which we derive, they have their generality, in the sense that they have continued to recur up to our time: for example, the problem of the relationship between sanity and insanity, or sickness and health, or crime and the law; the problem of the role of sexual relations; and so on.

But by evoking this generality, I do not mean to suggest that it has to be retraced in its metahistorical continuity over time, nor that its variations have to be pursued. What must be grasped is the extent to which what we know of it, the forms of power that are exercised in it, and the experience that we have in it of ourselves constitute nothing but determined historical figures, through a certain form of problematization that defines objects, rules of action, modes of relation to oneself. The study of [modes of] problematization (that is, of what is neither an anthropological constant nor a chronological variation) is thus the way to analyze questions of general import in their historically unique form.

A brief summary, to conclude and to come back to Kant.

I do not know whether we will ever reach mature adulthood. Many things in our experience convince us that the historical event of the Enlightenment did not make us mature adults, and we have not reached that stage yet. However, it seems to me that a meaning can be attributed to that critical interrogation on the present and on ourselves which Kant formulated by reflecting on the Enlightenment. It seems to me that Kant's reflection is even a way of philosophizing that has not been without its importance or effectiveness during the last two centuries. The critical ontology of ourselves has to be considered not, certainly, as a theory, a doctrine, nor even as a permanent body of knowledge that is accumulating; it has to be conceived as an attitude, an ethos, a philosophical life in which the critique of what we are is at one and the same time the historical analysis of the limits that are imposed on us and an experiment with the possibility of going beyond them.

This philosophical attitude has to be translated into the labor of diverse inquiries. These inquiries have their methodological coherence in the at once archaeological and genealogical study of practices envisaged simultaneously as a technological type of rationality and as strategic games of liberties; they have their theoretical coherence in the definition of the historically unique forms in which the generalities of our relations to things, to others, to ourselves, have been problematized. They have their practical coherence in the care brought to the process of putting historico-critical reflection to the test of concrete practices. I do not know whether it must be said today that the critical task still entails faith in Enlightenment; I continue to think that this task requires work on our limits, that is, a patient labor giving form to our impatience for liberty.

Notes

1 Giambattista Vico, *The New Science of Giambattista Vico*, 3rd ed., (1744), abridged trans. T. G. Bergin and M. H. Fisch (Ithaca/London: Cornell University Press, 1970), pp. 370, 372.

2 Charles Baudelaire, *The Painter of Modern Life and Other Essays*, trans. Jonathan Mayne (London: Phaidon, 1964), p. 13.

3 Charles Baudelaire, "On the Heroism of Modern Life," in *The Mirror of Art: Critical Studies by Charles Baudelaire*, trans. Jonathan Mayne (London: Phaidon, 1955), p. 127.

4 Baudelaire, *Painter*, pp. 12, 11.

5 Ibid., p. 12.

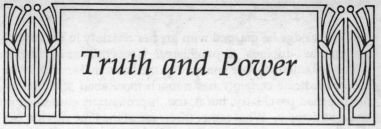

Truth and Power

(FROM *Power/Knowledge*)

Q. Could you briefly outline the route which led you from your work on madness in the classical age to the study of criminality and delinquency?

M.F. When I was studying during the early 1950s, one of the great problems that arose was that of the political status of science and the ideological functions which it could serve. It wasn't exactly the Lysenko business which dominated everything, but I believe that around that sordid affair—which had long remained buried and carefully hidden—a whole number of interesting questions were provoked. These can all be summed up in two words: power and knowledge. I believe I wrote *Madness and Civilization* to some extent within the horizon of these questions. For me, it was a matter of saying this: if, concerning a science like theoretical physics or organic chemistry, one poses the problem of its relations with the political and economic structures of society, isn't one posing an excessively complicated question? Doesn't this set the threshold of possible explanations impossibly high? But on the other hand, if one takes a form of knowledge (*savoir*) like psychiatry, won't the question be much easier to resolve, since the epistemological profile of psychiatry is a low one and psychiatric practice is linked with a whole range of institutions, economic requirements, and political issues of social regulation? Couldn't the interweaving of effects of power

This interview with Michel Foucault was conducted by Alessandro Fontana and Pasquale Pasquino. Foucault's response to the last question was given in writing.

and knowledge be grasped with greater certainty in the case of a science as "dubious" as psychiatry? It was this same question which I wanted to pose concerning medicine in *The Birth of the Clinic*: medicine certainly has a much more solid scientific armature than psychiatry, but it, too, is profoundly enmeshed in social structures. What rather threw me at the time was the fact that the question I was posing totally failed to interest those to whom I addressed it. They regarded it as a problem which was politically unimportant and epistemologically vulgar.

I think there were three reasons for this. The first is that for Marxist intellectuals in France (and there they were playing the role prescribed for them by the PCF [*Parti communiste français*]), the problem consisted in gaining for themselves the recognition of the university institutions and establishment. Consequently they found it necessary to pose the same theoretical questions as the academic establishment, to deal with the same problems and topics: "We may be Marxists, but for all that we are not strangers to your preoccupations; rather, we are the only ones able to provide new solutions for your old concerns." Marxism sought to win acceptance as a renewal of the liberal university tradition—just as, more broadly, during the same period the Communists presented themselves as the only people capable of taking over and reinvigorating the nationalist tradition. Hence, in the field we are concerned with here, it followed that they wanted to take up the "noblest," most academic problems in the history of the sciences: mathematics and physics, in short the themes valorized by Duhem, Husserl, and Koyré. Medicine and psychiatry didn't seem to them to be very noble or serious matters, nor to stand on the same level as the great forms of classical rationalism.

The second reason is that post-Stalinist Stalinism, by excluding from Marxist discourse everything that wasn't a frightened repetition of the already said, would not permit the broaching of uncharted domains. There were no ready-made concepts, no approved terms of vocabulary available for questions like the power effects of psychiatry or the political function of medicine, whereas, on the contrary, innumerable exchanges between Marxists and academics, from Marx via Engels and Lenin down to the present, had nourished a whole tradition of discourse on "science," in the nineteenth-century sense of that term. The price Marxists paid for their fidelity to the old positivism was a radical deafness to a whole series of questions posed by science.

Finally, there is perhaps a third reason, but I can't be absolutely sure that it played a part. I wonder, nevertheless, whether among intellectuals in or close to the PCF there wasn't a refusal to pose the problem of internment, of the political use of psychiatry, and, in a more general sense, of the disciplinary grid of society. No doubt little was then known in 1955–60 of the real extent of the Gulag, but I believe that many sensed it; in any case, many had a feeling that it was better not to talk about those things: it was a danger zone, marked by warning signs. Of course it's difficult in retrospect to judge people's degree of awareness. But in any case, you well know how easily the Party leadership—which knew everything of course—could circulate instructions preventing people from speaking about this or that, or precluding this or that line of research. At any rate, if the question of Pavlovian psychiatry did get discussed among a few doctors close to the PCF, psychiatric politics and psychiatry as politics were hardly considered to be respectable topics.

What I myself tried to do in this domain was met with a great silence among the French intellectual left. And it was only around 1968, and in spite of the Marxist tradition and the PCF, that all these questions came to assume their political significance, with a sharpness that I had never envisaged, showing how timid and hesitant those early books of mine had still been. Without the political opening created during those years, I would surely never have had the courage to take up these problems again and pursue my research in the direction of penal theory, prisons, and disciplines.

Q. So there is a certain "discontinuity" in your theoretical trajectory. Incidentally, what do you think today about this concept of discontinuity, on the basis of which you have been all too rapidly and readily labeled a "structuralist" historian?

M.F. This business about discontinuity has always rather bewildered me. In the new edition of the *Petit Larousse* it says: "Foucault: a philosopher who founds his theory of history on discontinuity." That leaves me flabbergasted. No doubt I didn't make myself sufficiently clear in *The Order of Things*, though I said a good deal there about this question. It seemed to me that in certain empirical forms of knowledge, like biology, political economy, psychiatry, medicine, etc., the rhythm of transformation doesn't follow the smooth, continuist schemas of development which are normally accepted. The great biological image of a progressive maturation of science still underpins a good many historical analyses; it does not seem to me to be pertinent to history. In a science like medicine, for example, up to the end of the eighteenth century one has a certain type of discourse whose gradual transformation, within a period of twenty-five or thirty years, broke not only with the "true" propositions which it had hitherto been possible to formulate, but also, more profoundly, with the ways of speaking and seeing, the whole ensemble of practices which served as supports for medical knowledge. These are not simply new discove... ...s; there is a whole new "regime" in discourse and forms of knowledge. And all this happens in the space of a few years. This is something which is undeniable, once one has looked at the texts with sufficient attention. My problem was not at all to say, "*Voilà*, long live discontinuity, we are in the discontinuous and a good thing too," but to pose the question, "How is it that at certain moments and in certain orders of knowledge, there are these sudden take-offs, these hastenings of evolution, these transformations which fail to correspond to the calm, continuist image that is normally accredited?" But the important thing here is not that such changes can be rapid and extensive, or rather it is that this extent and rapidity are only the sign of something else: a modification in the rules of formation of statements which are accepted as scientifically true. Thus it is not a change of content (refutation of old errors, recovery of old truths), nor is it a change of theoretical form (renewal of paradigm, modification of systematic ensembles). It is a question of what *governs* statements, and the way in which they *govern* each other so as to constitute a set of propositions which are scientifically acceptable, and hence capable of being verified or falsified by scientific procedures. In short, there is a problem of the regime, the politics of the scientific statement. At this level it's not so much a matter of knowing what external power imposes itself on science, as of what effects of power circulate among scientific statements, what constitutes, as it were, their internal regime of power, and how and why at certain moments that regime undergoes a global modification.

It was these different regimes that I tried to identify and describe in *The Order of Things*, all the while making it clear that I wasn't trying for the moment to explain them, and that it would be necessary to try and do this in a subsequent work. But what was lacking here was this problem of the "discursive regime," of the effects of power peculiar to the play of statements. I confused this too much with systematicity, theoretical form, or something like a paradigm. This same central problem of power, which at that time I had not yet properly isolated, emerges in two very different aspects at the point of junction of *Madness and Civilization* and *The Order of Things*.

Q. We need, then, to locate the notion of discontinuity in its proper context. And perhaps there is another concept which is both more difficult and more central to your thought—the concept of an event. For, in relation to the event, a whole generation was long trapped in an *impasse*, in that following the works of ethnologists, some of them great ethnologists, a dichotomy was established between structures (the *thinkable*) and the event considered as the site of the irrational, the unthinkable, that which doesn't and cannot enter into the mechanism and play of analysis, at least in the form which this took in structuralism. In a recent discussion published in the journal *L'Homme*, three eminent anthropologists posed this question once again about the concept of event, and said: the event is what always escapes our rational grasp, the domain of "absolute contingency"; we are thinkers who analyze structures, history is no concern of ours, what could we be expected to have to say about it, and so forth. This opposition, then, between event and structure is the site and the product of a certain anthropology. I would say this has had devastating effects among historians who have finally reached the point of trying to dismiss the event and the *évènementiel* as an inferior order of history dealing with trivial facts, chance occurrences, and so on. Whereas it is a fact that there are nodal problems in history which are neither a matter of trivial circumstances nor of those beautiful structures that are so orderly, intelligible, and transparent to analysis. For instance, the "great internment" which you described in *Madness and Civilization* perhaps represents one of these nodes which elude the dichotomy of structure and event. Could you elaborate from our present standpoint on this renewal and reformulation of the concept of event?

M.F. One can agree that structuralism formed the most systematic effort to evacuate the concept of the event, not only from ethnology but from a whole series of other sciences and in the extreme case from history. In that sense, I don't see who could be more of an anti-structuralist than myself. But the important thing is to avoid trying to do for the event what was previously done with the concept of structure. It's not a matter of locating everything on one level, that of the event, but of realizing that there is actually a whole order of levels of different types of events, differing in amplitude, chronological breadth, and capacity to produce effects.

The problem is at once to distinguish among events, to differentiate the networks and levels to which they belong, and to reconstitute the lines along which they are connected and engender one another. From this follows a refusal of analyses couched in terms of the symbolic field or the domain of signifying structures, and a recourse to analyses in terms of the genealogy of relations of force, strategic developments, and tactics. Here I believe one's point of reference should not be to the great model of language (*langue*) and signs, but to that of war and battle. The history which bears and determines us has the form of a war rather than that of a language: relations of power, not relations of meaning. History has no "meaning," though this is not to say that it is absurd or incoherent. On the contrary, it is intelligible and should be susceptible to analysis down to the smallest detail—but this in accordance with the intelligibility of struggles, of strategies and tactics. Neither the dialectic, as logic of contradictions, nor semiotics, as the structure of communication, can account for the intrinsic intelligibility of conflicts. "Dialectic" is a way of evading the always open and hazardous reality of conflict by reducing it to a Hegelian skeleton, and "semiology" is a way of avoiding its violent, bloody, and lethal character by reducing it to the calm Platonic form of language and dialogue.

Q. In the context of this problem of discursivity, I think one can be confident in saying that you were the first person to pose the question of power regarding discourse, and that at a time when analyses in terms of the concept or object of the "text," along with the accompanying methodology of semiology, structuralism, etc., were the prevailing fashion. Posing for discourse the question of power means basically to ask whom does discourse serve? It isn't so much a matter of analyzing discourse into its unsaid, its implicit meaning, because (as you have often repeated) discourses are transparent, they need no interpretation, no one to assign them a meaning. If one reads "texts" in a certain way, one perceives that they speak clearly to us and require no further supplementary sense or interpretation. This question of power that you have addressed to discourse naturally has particular effects and implications in relation to methodology and contemporary historical researches. Could you briefly situate within your work this question you have posed—if indeed it's true that you have posed it?

M.F. I don't think I was the first to pose the question. On the contrary, I'm struck by the difficulty I had in formulating it. When I think back now, I ask myself what else it was that I was talking about, in *Madness and Civilization* or *The Birth of the Clinic*, but power? Yet I'm perfectly aware that I scarcely ever used the word and never had such a field of analyses at my disposal. I can say that this was an incapacity linked undoubtedly with the political situation we found ourselves in. It is hard to see where, either on the right or the left, this problem of power could then have been posed. On the right, it was posed only in terms of constitution, sovereignty, etc., that is, in juridical terms; on the Marxist side, it was posed only in terms of the state apparatus. The way power was exercised—concretely and in detail—with its specificity, its techniques and tactics, was something that no one attempted to ascertain; they contented themselves with denouncing it in a polemical and global fashion as it existed among the "others," in the adversary camp. Where Soviet socialist power was in question, its opponents called it totalitarianism; power in Western capitalism was denounced by the Marxists as class domination; but the mechanics of power in themselves were never analyzed. This task could only begin after 1968, that is to say, on the basis of daily struggles at the grass-roots level, among those whose fight was located in the fine meshes of the web of power. This was where the concrete nature of power became visible, along with the prospect that these analyses of power would prove fruitful in accounting for all that had hitherto remained outside the field of political analysis. To put it very simply, psychiatric internment, the mental normalization of individuals, and penal institutions have no doubt a fairly limited importance if one is only looking for their economic significance. On the other hand, they are undoubtedly essential to the general functioning of the wheels of power. So long as the posing of the question of power was kept subordinate to the economic instance and the system of interests which this served, there was a tendency to regard these problems as of small importance.

Q. So a certain kind of Marxism and a certain kind of phenomenology constituted an objective obstacle to the formulation of this problematic?

M.F. Yes, if you like, to the extent that it's true that, in our student days, people of my generation were brought up on these two forms of analysis—one in terms of the constituent subject, the other in terms of the economic, in the last instance, ideology and the play of superstructures and infrastructures.

Q. Still, within this methodological context, how would you situate the genealogical approach? As a questioning of the conditions of possibility, modalities, and constitution of the "objects" and domains you have successively analyzed, what makes it necessary?

M.F. I wanted to see how these problems of constitution could be resolved within a historical framework, instead of referring them back to a constituent object (madness, criminality, or whatever). But this historical contextualization needed to be something more than the simple relativization of the phenomenological subject. I don't believe the problem can be solved by historicizing the subject as posited by the phenomenologists, fabricating a subject that evolves through the course of history. One has to dispense with the constituent subject, to get rid of the subject itself, that's to say, to arrive at an analysis which can account for the constitution of the subject within a historical framework. And this is what I would call genealogy, that is, a form of history which can account for the constitution of knowledges, discourses, domains of objects, etc., without having to make reference to a subject which is either transcendental in relation to the field of events or runs in its empty sameness throughout the course of history.

Q. Marxist phenomenology and a certain kind of Marxism have clearly acted as a screen and an obstacle; there are two further concepts which continue today to act as a screen and an obstacle: ideology, on the one hand, and repression, on the other.

All history comes to be thought of within these categories which serve to assign a meaning to such diverse phenomena as normalization, sexuality, and power. And regardless of whether these two concepts are explicitly utilized, in the end one always comes back, on the one hand to ideology—where it is easy to make the reference back to Marx—and on the other to repression, which is a concept often and readily employed by Freud throughout the course of his career. Hence I would like to put forward the following suggestion. Behind these concepts and among those who (properly or improperly) employ them, there is a kind of nostalgia; behind the concept of ideology, the nostalgia for a quasi-transparent form of knowledge, free from all error and illusion, and behind the concept of repression, the longing for a form of power innocent of all coercion, discipline, and normalization. On the one hand, a power without a bludgeon and, on the other hand, knowledge without deception. You have called these two concepts, ideology and repression, negative, "psychological," insufficiently analytical. This is particularly the case in *Discipline and Punish*, where, even if there isn't an extended discussion of these concepts, there is nevertheless a kind of analysis that allows one to go beyond the traditional forms of explanation and intelligibility which, in the last (and not only the last) instance, rest on the concepts of ideology and repression. Could you perhaps use this occasion to specify more explicitly your thoughts on these matters? With *Discipline and Punish*, a kind of positive history seems to be emerging, which is free of all the negativity and psychologism implicit in those two universal skeleton-keys.

M.F. The notion of ideology appears to me to be difficult to make use of, for three reasons. The first is that, like it or not, it always stands in virtual opposition to something else which is supposed to count as truth. Now I believe that the problem does not consist in drawing the line between that in a discourse which falls under the category of scientificity or truth, and that which comes under some other category, but in seeing historically how effects of truth are produced within discourses which in themselves are neither true nor false. The second drawback is that the concept of ideology refers, I think necessarily, to something of the order of a subject. Third, ideology stands in a secondary position relative to something which functions as its infrastructure, as its material, economic determinant, etc. For these three reasons, I think that this is a notion that cannot be used without circumspection.

The notion of repression is a more insidious one, or at all events I myself have had much more trouble in freeing myself of it, insofar as it does indeed appear to correspond so well with a whole range of phenomena which belong among the effects of power. When I wrote *Madness and Civilization*, I made at least an implicit use of this notion of repression. I think, indeed, that I was positing the existence of a sort of living, voluble, and anxious madness which the mechanisms of power and psychiatry were supposed to have come to repress and reduce to silence. But it seems to me now that the notion of repression is quite inadequate for capturing what is precisely the productive aspect of power. In defining the effects of power as repression, one adopts a purely juridical conception of such power; one identifies power with a law which says no; power is taken above all as carrying the force of a prohibition. Now I believe that this is a wholly negative, narrow, skeletal conception of power, one which has been curiously widespread. If power were never anything but repressive, if it never did anything but to say no, do you really think one would be brought to obey it? What makes power hold good, what makes it accepted, is simply the fact that it doesn't only weigh on us as a force that says no, but that it traverses and produces things, it induces pleasure, forms knowledge, produces discourse. It needs to be considered as a productive network which runs through the whole social body, much more than as a negative instance whose function is repression. In *Discipline and Punish*, what I wanted to show was how, from the seventeenth and eighteenth centuries onward, there was a veritable technological take-off in the productivity of power. Not only did the monarchies of the classical period develop great state apparatuses (the army, the police and fiscal administration), but above all there was established in this period what one might call a new "economy" of power, that is to say, procedures which allowed the effects of power to circulate in a manner at once continuous, uninterrupted, adapted, and "individualized" throughout the entire social body. These new techniques are both much more efficient and much less wasteful (less costly economically, less risky in their results, less open to loopholes and resistances) than the techniques previously employed, which were based on a mixture of more or less forced tolerances (from recognized privileges to endemic criminality) and costly ostentation (spectacular and discontinuous interventions of power, the most violent form of which was the "exemplary," because exceptional, punishment).

Q. Repression is a concept used above all in relation to sexuality. It was held that bourgeois society represses sexuality, stifles sexual desire, and so forth. And when one considers, for example, the campaign launched against masturbation in the eighteenth century, or the medical discourse on homosexuality in the second half of the nineteenth century, or discourse on sexuality in general, one does seem to be faced with a discourse of repression. In reality, however, this discourse serves to make possible a whole series of interventions, tactical and positive interventions of surveillance, circulation, control, and so forth, which seem to have been intimately linked with techniques that give the appearance of repression, or are at least liable to be interpreted as such. I believe the crusade against masturbation is a typical example of this.

M.F. Certainly. It is customary to say that bourgeois society repressed infantile sexuality to the point where it refused even to speak of it or acknowledge its existence. It was necessary to wait until Freud for the discovery at last to be made that children have a sexuality. Now if you read all the books on pedagogy and child medicine—all the manuals for parents that were published in the eighteenth century—you find that children's sex is spoken of constantly and in every possible context. One might argue that the purpose of these discourses was precisely to prevent children from having a sexuality. But their *effect* was to din it into parents' heads that their children's sex constituted a fundamental problem in terms of their parental educational responsibilities, and to din it into children's heads that their relationship with their own bodies and their own sex was to be a fundamental problem as far as *they* were concerned; and this had the consequence of sexually exciting the bodies of children while at the same time fixing the parental gaze and vigilance on the peril of infantile sexuality. The result was a sexualizing of the infantile body, a sexualizing of the bodily relationship between parent and child, a sexualizing of the familial domain. "Sexuality" is far more of a positive product of power than power was ever repression of sexuality. I believe that it is precisely these positive mechanisms that need to be investigated, and here one must free oneself of the juridical schematism of all previous characterizations of the nature of power. Hence a historical problem arises, namely, that of discovering why the West has insisted for so long on seeing the power it exercises as juridical and negative rather than as technical and positive.

Q. Perhaps this is because it has always been thought that power is mediated through the forms prescribed in the great juridical and philosophical theories, and that there is a fundamental, immutable gulf between those who exercise power and those who undergo it.

M.F. I wonder if this isn't bound up with the institution of monarchy. This developed during the Middle Ages against the backdrop of the previously endemic struggles between feudal power agencies. The monarchy presented itself as a referee, a power capable of putting an end to war, violence, and pillage and saying no to these struggles and private feuds. It made itself acceptable by allocating itself a juridical and negative function, albeit one whose limits it naturally began at once to overstep. Sovereign, law, and prohibition formed a system of representation of power which was extended during the subsequent era by the theories of right: political theory has never ceased to be obsessed with the person of the sovereign. Such theories still continue today to busy themselves with the problem of sovereignty. What we need, however, is a political philosophy that isn't erected around the problem of sovereignty, nor therefore around the problems of law and prohibition. We need to cut off the king's head: in political theory that has still to be done.

Q. The king's head still hasn't been cut off, yet already people are trying to replace it by discipline, that vast system instituted in the seventeenth century, comprising the functions of surveillance, normalization and control, and, a little later, those of punishment, correction, education, and so on. One wonders where this system comes from, why it emerges, and what its use is. And today there is rather a tendency to attribute a subject to it, a great, molar, totalitarian subject, namely, the modern state, constituted in the sixteenth and seventeenth centuries and bringing with it (according to the classical theories) the professional army, the police, and the administrative bureaucracy.

M.F. To pose the problem in terms of the state means to continue posing it in terms of sovereign and sovereignty, that is to say, in terms of law. If one describes all these phenomena of power as dependent on the state apparatus, this means grasping them as essentially repressive: the army as a power of death, police and justice as punitive instances, etc. I don't want to say that the state isn't important; what I want to say is that relations of power, and hence the analysis that must be made of them, necessarily extend beyond the limits of the state. In two senses: first of all because the state, for all the omnipotence of its apparatuses, is far from being able to occupy the whole field of actual power relations, and further because the state can only operate on the basis of other, already existing power relations. The state is superstructural in relation to a whole series of power networks that invest the body, sexuality, the family, kinship, knowledge, technology, and so forth. True, these networks stand in a conditioning-conditioned relationship to a kind of "metapower" which is structured essentially around a certain number of great prohibition functions; but this metapower with its prohibitions can only take hold and secure its footing where it is rooted in a whole series of multiple and indefinite power relations that supply the necessary basis for the great negative forms of power. That is just what I was trying to make apparent in my book.

Q. Doesn't this open up the possibility of overcoming the dualism of political struggles that eternally feed on the opposition between the state, on the one hand, and revolution, on the other? Doesn't it indicate a wider field of conflicts than that of those where the adversary is the state?

M.F. I would say that the state consists in the codification of a whole number of power relations which render its functioning possible, and that revolution is a different type of codification of the same relations. This implies that there are many different kinds of revolution, roughly speaking, as many kinds as there are possible subversive recodifications of power relations, and further that one can perfectly well conceive of revolutions which leave essentially untouched the power relations which form the basis for the functioning of the state.

Q. You have said about power as an object of research that one has to invert Clausewitz's formula so as to arrive at the idea that politics is the continuation of war by other means. Does the military model seem to you, on the basis of your most recent researches, to be the best one for describing power; is war here simply a metaphorical model, or is it the literal, regular, everyday mode of operation of power?

M.F. This is the problem I now find myself confronting. As soon as one endeavors to detach power with its techniques and procedures from the form of law within which it has been theoretically confined up until now, one is driven to ask this basic question: Isn't power simply a form of warlike domination? Shouldn't one therefore conceive all problems of power in terms of relations of war? Isn't power a sort of generalized war which assumes at particular moments the forms of peace and the state? Peace would then be a form of war, and the state a means of waging it.

A whole range of problems emerges here. Who wages war against whom? Is it between two classes, or more? Is it a war of all against all? What is the role of the army and military institutions in this civil society where permanent war is waged? What is the relevance of concepts of tactics and strategy for analyzing structures and political processes? What is the essence and mode of transformation of power relations? All these questions need to be explored. In any case it's astonishing to see how easily and self-evidently people talk of warlike relations of power or of class struggle without ever making it clear whether some form of war is meant, and if so what form.

Q. We have already talked about this disciplinary power whose effects, rules, and mode of constitution you describe in *Discipline and Punish*. One might ask here: Why surveillance? What is the use of surveillance? Now there is a phenomenon that emerges during the eighteenth century, namely, the discovery of population as an object of scientific investigation; people begin to inquire into birth rates, death rates, and changes in population and to say for the first time that it is impossible to govern a state without knowing its population. Moheau, for example, who was one of the first to organize this kind of research on an administrative basis, seems to see its goal as lying in the problems of political control of a population. Does this disciplinary power then act alone and of itself, or doesn't it, rather, draw support from something more general, namely, this fixed conception of a population that reproduces itself in the proper way, composed of people who marry in the proper way and behave in the proper way, according to precisely determined norms? One would then have, on the one hand, a sort of global, molar body, the body of the population, together with a whole series of discourses concerning it, and then, on the other hand and down below, the small bodies, the docile, individual bodies, the microbodies of discipline. Even if you are only perhaps at the beginning of your researches here, could you say how you see the nature of the relationships (if any) which are engendered between these different bodies: the molar body of the population and the microbodies of individuals?

M.F. Your question is exactly on target. I find it difficult to reply because I am working on this problem right now. I believe one must keep in view the fact that along with all the fundamental technical inventions and discoveries of the seventeenth and eighteenth centuries, a new technology of the exercise of power also emerged, which was probably even more important than the constitutional reforms and new forms of government established at the end of the eighteenth century. In the camp of the left, one often hears people saying that power is that which abstracts, which negates the body, represses, suppresses, and so forth. I would say instead that what I find most striking about these new technologies of power introduced since the seventeenth and eighteenth centuries is their concrete and precise character, their grasp of a multiple and differentiated reality. In feudal societies, power functioned essentially through signs and levies. Signs of loyalty to the feudal lords, rituals, ceremonies, and so forth, and levies in the form of taxes, pillage, hunting, war, etc. In the seventeenth and eighteenth centuries, a form of power comes into being that begins to exercise itself through social production and social service. It becomes a matter of obtaining productive service from individuals in their concrete lives. And, in consequence, a real and effective "incorporation" of power was necessary, in the sense that power had to be able to gain access to the bodies of individuals, to their acts, attitudes, and modes of everyday behavior. Hence the significance of methods like school discipline, which succeeded in making children's bodies the object of highly complex systems of manipulation and conditioning. But, at the same time, these new techniques of power needed to grapple with the phenomena of population, in short, to undertake the administration, control, and direction of the accumulation of men (the economic system that promotes the accumulation of capital and the system of power that ordains the accumulation of men are, from the seventeenth century on, correlated and inseparable phenomena): hence there arise the problems of demography, public health, hygiene, housing conditions, longevity, and fertility. And I believe that the political significance of the problem of sex is due to the fact that sex is located at the point of intersection of the discipline of the body and the control of the population.

Q. Finally, a question you have been asked before: The work you do, these preoccupations of yours, the results you arrive at, what use can one finally make of all this in everyday political struggles? You have spoken previously of local struggles as the specific site of confrontation with power, outside and beyond all such global, general instances as parties or classes. What does this imply about the role of intellectuals? If one isn't an "organic" intellectual acting as the spokesman for a global organization, if one doesn't purport to function as the bringer, the master of truth, what position is the intellectual to assume?

M.F. For a long period, the "left" intellectual spoke and was acknowledged the right of speaking in the capacity of master of truth and justice. He was heard, or purported to make himself heard, as the spokesman of the universal. To be an intellectual meant something like being the consciousness/conscience of us all. I think we have here an idea transposed from Marxism, from a faded Marxism indeed. Just as the proletariat, by the necessity of its historical situation, is the bearer of the universal (but its immediate, unreflected bearer, barely conscious of itself as such), so the intellectual, through his moral, theoretical, and political choice, aspires to be the bearer of this universality in its conscious, elaborated form. The intellectual is thus taken as the clear, individual figure of a universality whose obscure, collective form is embodied in the proletariat.

Some years have now passed since the intellectual was called upon to play this role. A new mode of the "connection between theory and practice" has been established. Intellectuals have become used to working, not in the modality of the "universal," the "exemplary," the "just-and-true-for-all," but within specific sectors, at the precise points where their own conditions of life or work situate them (housing, the hospital, the asylum, the laboratory, the university, family, and sexual relations). This has undoubtedly given them a much more immediate and concrete awareness of struggles. And they have met here with problems which are specific, "nonuniversal," and often different from those of the proletariat or the masses. And yet I believe intellectuals have actually been drawn closer to the proletariat and the masses, for two reasons. Firstly, because it has been a question of real, material, everyday struggles, and secondly because they have often been confronted, albeit in a different form, by the same adversary as the proletariat, namely, the multinational corporations, the judicial and police apparatuses, the property speculators, etc. This is what I would call the "specific" intellectual as opposed to the "universal" intellectual.

This new configuration has a further political significance. It makes it possible, if not to integrate, at least to rearticulate categories which were previously kept separate. The intellectual *par excellence* used to be the writer: as a universal consciousness, a free subject, he was counterposed to those intellectuals who were merely *competent instances* in the service of the state or capital—technicians, magistrates, teachers. Since the time when each individual's specific activity began to serve as the basis for politicization, the threshold of *writing*, as the sacralizing mark of the intellectual, has disappeared. And it has become possible to develop lateral connections across different forms of knowledge and from one focus of politicization to another. Magistrates and psychiatrists, doctors and social workers, laboratory technicians and sociologists have become able to participate, both within their own fields and through mutual exchange and support, in a global process of politicization of intellectuals. This process explains how, even as the writer tends to disappear as a figurehead, the university and the academic emerge, if not as principal elements, at least as "exchangers," privileged points of intersection. If the universities and education have become politically ultrasensitive areas, this is no doubt the reason why. And what is called the crisis of the universities should not be interpreted as a loss of power, but on the contrary as a multiplication and reinforcement of their power effects as centers in a polymorphous ensemble of intellectuals who virtually all pass through and relate themselves to the academic system. The whole relentless theorization of writing which we saw in the 1960s was doubtless only a swansong. Through it, the writer was fighting for the preservation of his political privilege; but the fact that it was precisely a matter of theory, that he needed scientific credentials, founded in linguistics, semiology, psychoanalysis, that this theory took its references from the direction of Saussure or Chomsky, etc., and that it gave rise to such mediocre literary products, all this proves that the activity of the writer was no longer at the focus of things.

It seems to me that this figure of the "specific" intellectual has emerged since the Second World War. Perhaps it was the atomic scientist (in a word, or rather a name: Oppenheimer) who acted as the point of transition between the universal and the specific intellectual. It's because he had a direct and localized relation to scientific knowledge and institutions that the atomic scientist could make his intervention; but, since the nuclear threat affected the whole human race and the fate of the world, his discourse could at the same time be the discourse of the universal. Under the rubric of this protest, which concerned the entire world, the atomic expert brought into play his specific position in the order of knowledge. And for the first time, I think, the intellectual was hounded by political powers, no longer on account of a general discourse which he conducted, but because of the knowledge at his disposal: it was at this level that he constituted a political threat. I am speaking here only of Western intellectuals. What happened in the Soviet Union is analogous with this on a number of points, but different on many others. There is certainly a whole study that needs to be made of scientific dissidence in the West and the socialist countries since 1945.

It is possible to suppose that the "universal" intellectual, as he functioned in the nineteenth and early twentieth centuries, was in fact derived from a quite specific historical figure: the man of justice, the man of law, who counterposes to power, despotism, and the abuses and arrogance of wealth the universality of justice and the equity of an ideal law. The great political struggles of the eighteenth century were fought over law, right, the constitution, the just in reason and law, that which can and must apply universally. What we call today "the intellectual" (I mean the intellectual in the political, not the sociological sense of the word; in other words, the person who utilizes his knowledge, his competence, and his relation to truth in the field of political struggles) was, I think, an offspring of the jurist, or at any rate of the man who invoked the universality of a just law, if necessary against the legal professions themselves (Voltaire, in France, is the prototype of such intellectuals). The "universal" intellectual derives from the jurist or notable, and finds his fullest manifestation in the writer, the bearer of values and significations in which all can recognize themselves. The "specific" intellectual derives from quite another figure, not the jurist or notable, but the savant or expert. I said just now that it's with the atomic scientists that this latter figure comes to the forefront. In fact, it was preparing in the wings for some time before, and was even present on at least a corner of the stage from about the end of the nineteenth century. No doubt it's with Darwin or, rather, with the post-Darwinian evolutionists that this figure begins to appear clearly. The stormy relationship between evolutionism and the socialists, as well as the highly ambiguous effects of evolutionism (on sociology, criminology, psychiatry, and eugenics, for example), marks the important moment when the savant begins to intervene in contemporary political struggles in the name of a "local" scientific truth—however important the latter may be. Historically, Darwin represents this point of inflection in the history of the Western intellectual. (Zola is very significant from this point of view: he is the type of the "universal" intellectual, bearer of law and militant of equity, but he ballasts his discourse with a whole invocation of nosology and evolutionism, which he believes to be scientific, grasps very poorly in any case, and whose political effects on his own discourse are very equivocal.) If one were to study this closely, one would have to follow how the physicists, at the turn of the century, reentered the field of political debate. The debates between the theorists of socialism and the theorists of relativity are of capital importance in this history.

At all events, biology and physics were to a privileged degree the zones of formation of this new personage, the specific intellectual. The extension of technico-scientific structures in the economic and strategic domain was what gave him his real importance. The figure in which the functions and prestige of this new intellectual are concentrated is no longer that of the "writer of genius," but that of the "absolute savant"; no longer he who bears the values of all, opposes the unjust sovereign or his ministers, and makes his cry resound even beyond the grave. It is, rather, he who, along with a handful of others, has at his disposal, whether in the service of the state or against it, powers which can either benefit or irrevocably destroy life. He is no longer the rhapsodist of the eternal, but the strategist of life and death. Meanwhile we are at present experiencing the disappearance of the figure of the "great writer."

Now let's come back to more precise details. We accept, alongside the development of technico-scientific structures in contemporary society, the importance gained by the specific intellectual in recent decades, as well as the acceleration of this process since around 1960. Now the specific intellectual encounters certain obstacles and faces certain dangers. The danger of remaining at the level of conjunctural struggles, pressing demands restricted to particular sectors. The risk of letting himself be manipulated by the political parties or trade union apparatuses which control these local struggles. Above all, the risk of being unable to develop these struggles for lack of a global strategy or outside support; the risk, too, of not being followed, or only by very limited groups. In France we can see at the moment an example of this. The struggle around the prisons, the penal system, and the police-judicial system, because it has developed "in solitary," among social workers and ex-prisoners, has tended increasingly to separate itself from the forces which would have enabled it to grow. It has allowed itself to be penetrated by a whole naive, archaic ideology which makes the criminal at once into the innocent victim and the pure rebel—society's scape-goat—and the young wolf of future revolutions. This return to anarchist themes of the late nineteenth century was possible only because of a failure of integration of current strategies. And the result has been a deep split between this campaign with its monotonous, lyrical little chant, heard only among a few small groups, and the masses who have good reason not to accept it as valid political currency, but who also—thanks to the studiously cultivated fear of criminals—tolerate the maintenance, or rather the reinforcement, of the judicial and police appara-tuses.

It seems to me that we are now at a point where the function of the specific intellectual needs to be reconsidered. Recon-sidered but not abandoned, despite the nostalgia of some for the great "universal" intellectuals and the desire for a new phi-losophy, a new world-view. Suffice it to consider the important results which have been achieved in psychiatry: they prove that these local, specific struggles haven't been a mistake and haven't led to a dead end. One may even say that the role of the specific intellectual must become more and more important in propor-tion to the political responsibilities which he is obliged willy-nilly to accept, as a nuclear scientist, computer expert, phar-macologist, etc. It would be a dangerous error to discount him politically in his specific relation to a local form of power, either on the grounds that this is a specialist matter which doesn't concern the masses (which is doubly wrong: they are already aware of it, and in any case implicated in it), or that the specific intellectual serves the interests of state or capital (which is true, but at the same time shows the strategic position he occupies), or, again, on the grounds that he propagates a scientific ideology (which isn't always true, and is anyway certainly a secondary matter compared with the fundamental point: the effects proper to true discourses).

The important thing here, I believe, is that truth isn't outside power, or lacking in power: contrary to a myth whose history and functions would repay further study, truth isn't the reward of free spirits, the child of protracted solitude, nor the privilege of those who have succeeded in liberating themselves. Truth is a thing of this world: it is produced only by virtue of multiple forms of constraint. And it induces regular effects of power. Each society has its regime of truth, its "general politics" of truth: that is, the types of discourse which it accepts and makes function as true; the mechanisms and instances which enable one to distinguish true and false statements, the means by which each is sanctioned; the techniques and procedures accorded value in the acquisition of truth; the status of those who are charged with saying what counts as true.

In societies like ours, the "political economy" of truth is characterized by five important traits. "Truth" is centered on the form of scientific discourse and the institutions which produce it; it is subject to constant economic and political incitement (the demand for truth, as much for economic production as for political power); it is the object, under diverse forms, of immense diffusion and consumption (circulating through apparatuses of education and information whose extent is relatively broad in the social body, notwithstanding certain strict limitations); it is produced and transmitted under the control, dominant if not exclusive, of a few great political and economic apparatuses (university, army, writing, media); lastly, it is the issue of a whole political debate and social confrontation ("ideological" struggles).

It seems to me that what must now be taken into account in the intellectual is not the "bearer of universal values." Rather, it's the person occupying a specific position—but whose specificity is linked, in a society like ours, to the general functioning of an apparatus of truth. In other words, the intellectual has a threefold specificity: that of his class position (whether as petty-bourgeois in the service of capitalism or "organic" intellectual of the proletariat); that of his conditions of life and work, linked to his condition as an intellectual (his field of research, his place in a laboratory, the political and economic demands to which he submits or against which he rebels, in the university, the hospital, etc.); lastly, the specificity of the politics of truth in our societies. And it's with this last factor that his position can take on a general significance and that his local, specific struggle can have effects and implications which are not simply professional or sectoral. The intellectual can operate and struggle at the general level of that regime of truth which is so essential to the structure and functioning of our society. There is a battle "for truth," or at least "around truth"—it being understood once again that by truth I do not mean "the ensemble of truths which are to be discovered and accepted," but rather "the ensemble of rules according to which the true and the false are separated and specific effects of power attached to the true," it being understood also that it's a matter not of a battle "on behalf" of the truth, but of a battle about the status of truth and the economic and political role it plays. It is necessary to think of the political problems of intellectuals not in terms of "science" and "ideology," but in terms of "truth" and "power." And thus the question of the professionalization of intellectuals and the division between intellectual and manual labor can be envisaged in a new way.

All this must seem very confused and uncertain. Uncertain indeed, and what I am saying here is above all to be taken as a hypothesis. In order for it to be a little less confused, however, I would like to put forward a few "propositions"—not firm assertions, but simply suggestions to be further tested and evaluated.

"Truth" is to be understood as a system of ordered procedures for the production, regulation, distribution, circulation, and operation of statements.

"Truth" is linked in a circular relation with systems of power which produce and sustain it, and to effects of power which it induces and which extends it. A "regime" of truth.

This regime is not merely ideological or superstructural; it was a condition of the formation and development of capitalism. And it's this same regime which, subject to certain modifications, operates in the socialist countries (I leave open here the question of China, about which I know little).

The essential political problem for the intellectual is not to criticize the ideological contents supposedly linked to science, or to ensure that his own scientific practice is accompanied by a correct ideology, but that of ascertaining the possibility of constituting a new politics of truth. The problem is not changing people's consciousnesses—or what's in their heads—but the political, economic, institutional regime of the production of truth.

It's not a matter of emancipating truth from every system

of power (which would be a chimera, for truth is already power), but of detaching the power of truth from the forms of hegemony, social, economic, and cultural, within which it operates at the present time.

The political question, to sum up, is not error, illusion, alienated consciousness, or ideology; it is truth itself. Hence the importance of Nietzsche.

Nietzsche, Genealogy, History

1. Genealogy is gray, meticulous, and patiently documentary. It operates on a field of entangled and confused parchments, on documents that have been scratched over and recopied many times.

On this basis, it is obvious that Paul Ree[1] was wrong to follow the English tendency in describing the history of morality in terms of a linear development—in reducing its entire history and genesis to an exclusive concern for utility. He assumed that words had kept their meaning, that desires still pointed in a single direction, and that ideas retained their logic; and he ignored the fact that the world of speech and desires has known invasions, struggles, plundering, disguises, ploys. From these elements, however, genealogy retrieves an indispensable restraint: it must record the singularity of events outside of any monotonous finality; it must seek them in the most unpromising places, in what we tend to feel is without history—in sentiments, love, conscience, instincts; it must be sensitive to their recurrence, not in order to trace the gradual curve of their evolution, but to isolate the different scenes where they engaged in different roles. Finally, genealogy must define even those instances when they are absent, the moment when they remained unrealized (Plato, at Syracuse, did not become Mohammed).

Genealogy, consequently, requires patience and a knowledge of details, and it depends on a vast accumulation of source

This essay first appeared in *Hommage à Jean Hyppolite* (Paris: Presses Universitaires de France, 1971), pp. 145–72. Along with "Réponse au cercle d'épistémologie," which became the introductory chapter of *The Archaeology of Knowledge*, this essay represents Foucault's attempt to explain his relationship to those sources which are fundamental to his development. Its importance, in terms of understanding Foucault's objectives, cannot be exaggerated. It is reproduced here by permission of Presses Universitaires de France.

material. Its "cyclopean monuments"[2] are constructed from "discreet and apparently insignificant truths and according to a rigorous method"; they cannot be the product of "large and well-meaning errors."[3] In short, genealogy demands relentless erudition. Genealogy does not oppose itself to history as the lofty and profound gaze of the philosopher might compare to the molelike perspective of the scholar; on the contrary, it rejects the metahistorical deployment of ideal significations and indefinite teleologies. It opposes itself to the search for "origins."

2. In Nietzsche, we find two uses of the word *Ursprung*. The first is unstressed, and it is found alternately with other terms such as *Entstehung, Herkunft, Abkunft, Geburt*. In *The Genealogy of Morals*, for example, *Entstehung* or *Ursprung* serves equally well to denote the origin of duty or guilty conscience;[4] and in the discussion of logic and knowledge in *The Gay Science*, their origin is indiscriminately referred to as *Ursprung, Entstehung*, or *Herkunft*.[5]

The other use of the word is stressed. On occasion, Nietzsche places the term in opposition to another: in the first paragraph of *Human, All Too Human* the miraculous origin (*Wunderursprung*) sought by metaphysics is set against the analyses of historical philosophy, which poses questions *über Herkunft und Anfang*. *Ursprung* is also used in an ironic and deceptive manner. In what, for instance, do we find the original basis (*Ursprung*) of morality, a foundation sought after since Plato? "In detestable, narrow-minded conclusions. *Pudenda origo*."[6] Or in a related context, where should we seek the origin of religion (*Ursprung*), which Schopenhauer located in a particular metaphysical sentiment of the hereafter? It belongs, very simply, to an invention (*Erfindung*), a sleight-of-hand, an artifice (*Kunststück*), a secret formula, in the rituals of black magic, in the work of the *Schwarzkünstler*.[7]

One of the most significant texts with respect to the use of all these terms and to the variations in the use of *Ursprung* is the preface to the *Genealogy*. At the beginning of the text, its objective is defined as an examination of the origin of moral preconceptions and the term used is *Herkunft*. Then, Nietzsche proceeds by retracing his personal involvement with this question: he recalls the period when he "calligraphied" philosophy, when he questioned if God must be held responsible for the origin of evil. He now finds this question amusing and properly characterizes it as a search for *Ursprung* (he will shortly use the same term to summarize Paul Ree's activity).[8] Further on, he evokes the analyses that are characteristically Nietzschean and that begin with *Human, All Too Human*. Here, he speaks of *Herkunfthypothesen*. This use of the word *Herkunft* cannot be arbitrary, since it serves to designate a number of texts, beginning with *Human, All Too Human*, which deal with the origin of morality, asceticism, justice, and punishment. And yet the word used in all these works had been *Ursprung*.[9] It would seem that at this point in the *Genealogy* Nietzsche wished to validate an opposition between *Herkunft* and *Ursprung* that did not exist ten years earlier. But immediately following the use of the two terms in a specific sense, Nietzsche reverts, in the final paragraphs of the preface, to a usage that is neutral and equivalent.[10]

Why does Nietzsche challenge the pursuit of the origin (*Ursprung*), at least on those occasions when he is truly a genealogist? First, because it is an attempt to capture the exact essence of things, their purest possibilities, and their carefully protected identities; because this search assumes the existence of immobile forms that precede the external world of accident and succession. This search is directed to "that which was already there," the image of a primordial truth fully adequate to its nature, and it necessitates the removal of every mask to ultimately disclose an original identity. However, if the genealogist refuses to extend his faith in metaphysics, if he listens to history, he finds that there is "something altogether different" behind things: not a timeless and essential secret, but the secret that they have no essence or that their essence was fabricated in a piecemeal fashion from alien forms. Examining the history of reason, he learns that it was born in an altogether "reasonable" fashion—from chance;[11] devotion to truth and the precision of scientific methods arose from the passion of scholars, their reciprocal hatred, their fanatical and unending discussions, and their spirit of competition—the personal conflicts that slowly forged the weapons of reason.[12] Further, genealogical analysis shows that the concept of liberty is an "invention of the ruling classes"[13] and not fundamental to man's nature or at the root of his attachment to being and truth. What is found at the historical beginning of things is not the inviolable identity of their origin; it is the dissension of other things. It is disparity.[14]

History also teaches how to laugh at the solemnities of the origin. The lofty origin is no more than "a metaphysical extension which arises from the belief that things are most precious and essential at the moment of birth." [15] We tend to think that this is the moment of their greatest perfection, when they emerged dazzling from the hands of a creator or in the shadowless light of a first morning. The origin always precedes the Fall. It comes before the body, before the world and time; it is associated with the gods, and its story is always sung as a theogony. But historical beginnings are lowly: not in the sense of modest or discreet like the steps of a dove, but derisive and ironic, capable of undoing every infatuation. "We wished to awaken the feeling of man's sovereignty by showing his divine birth: this path is now forbidden, since a monkey stands at the entrance." [16] Man originated with a grimace over his future development; and Zarathustra himself is plagued by a monkey who jumps along behind him, pulling on his coattails.

The final postulate of the origin is linked to the first two in being the site of truth. From the vantage point of an absolute distance, free from the restraints of positive knowledge, the origin makes possible a field of knowledge whose function is to recover it, but always in a false recognition due to the excesses of its own speech. The origin lies at a place of inevitable loss, the point where the truth of things corresponded to a truthful discourse, the site of a fleeting articulation that discourse has obscured and finally lost. It is a new cruelty of history that compels a reversal of this relationship and the abandonment of "adolescent" quests: behind the always recent, avaricious, and measured truth, it posits the ancient proliferation of errors. It is now impossible to believe that "in the rending of the veil, truth remains truthful; we have lived long enough not to be taken in." [17] Truth is undoubtedly the sort of error that cannot be refuted because it was hardened into an unalterable form in the long baking process of history.[18] Moreover, the very question of truth, the right it appropriates to refute error and oppose itself to appearance, the manner in which it developed (initially made available to the wise, then withdrawn by men of piety to an unattainable world where it was given the double role of consolation and imperative, finally rejected as a useless notion, superfluous and contradicted on all sides)—does this not form a history, the history of an error we call truth? Truth, and its original reign, has had a history within history from which we are barely emerging "in the time of the shortest shadow," when light no longer seems to flow from the depths of the sky or to arise from the first moments of the day.[19]

A genealogy of values, morality, asceticism, and knowledge will never confuse itself with a quest for their "origins," will never neglect as inaccessible the vicissitudes of history. On the contrary, it will cultivate the details and accidents that accompany every beginning; it will be scrupulously attentive to their petty malice; it will await their emergence, once unmasked, as the face of the other. Wherever it is made to go, it will not be reticent—in "excavating the depths," in allowing time for these elements to escape from a labyrinth where no truth had ever detained them. The genealogist needs history to dispel the chimeras of the origin, somewhat in the manner of the pious philosopher who needs a doctor to exorcise the shadow of his soul. He must be able to recognize the events of history, its jolts, its surprises, its unsteady victories and unpalatable defeats—the basis of all beginnings, atavisms, and heredities. Similarly, he must be able to diagnose the illnesses of the body, its conditions of weakness and strength, its breakdowns and resistances, to be in a position to judge philosophical discourse. History is the concrete body of a development, with its moments of intensity, its lapses, its extended periods of feverish agitation, its fainting spells; and only a metaphysician would seek its soul in the distant ideality of the origin.

3. *Entstehung* and *Herkunft* are more exact than *Ursprung* in recording the true objective of genealogy; and, while they are ordinarily translated as "origin," we must attempt to reestablish their proper use.

Herkunft is the equivalent of stock or *descent*; it is the ancient affiliation to a group, sustained by the bonds of blood, tradition,

or social class. The analysis of *Herkunft* often involves a consideration of race or social type.[20] But the traits it attempts to
identify are not the exclusive generic characteristics of an individual, a sentiment, or an idea, which permit us to qualify them
as "Greek" or "English"; rather, it seeks the subtle, singular,
and subindividual marks that might possibly intersect in them
to form a network that is difficult to unravel. Far from being a
category of resemblance, this origin allows the sorting out of
different traits: the Germans imagined that they had finally accounted for their complexity by saying they possessed a double
soul; they were fooled by a simple computation, or rather, they
were simply trying to master the racial disorder from which they
had formed themselves.[21] Where the soul pretends unification
or the self fabricates a coherent identity, the genealogist sets out
to study the beginning—numberless beginnings, whose faint
traces and hints of color are readily seen by a historical eye. The
analysis of descent permits the dissociation of the self, its recognition and displacement as an empty synthesis, in liberating
a profusion of lost events.

An examination of descent also permits the discovery, under the unique aspect of a trait or a concept, of the myriad events
through which—thanks to which, against which—they were
formed. Genealogy does not pretend to go back in time to restore an unbroken continuity that operates beyond the dispersion of forgotten things; its duty is not to demonstrate that the
past actively exists in the present, that it continues secretly to
animate the present, having imposed a predetermined form on
all its vicissitudes. Genealogy does not resemble the evolution
of a species and does not map the destiny of a people. On the
contrary, to follow the complex course of descent is to maintain
passing events in their proper dispersion; it is to identify the
accidents, the minute deviations—or conversely, the complete
reversals—the errors, the false appraisals, and the faulty calculations that gave birth to those things that continue to exist
and have value for us; it is to discover that truth or being does
not lie at the root of what we know and what we are, but the
exteriority of accidents.[22] This is undoubtedly why every origin
of morality from the moment it stops being pious—and *Herkunft*
can never be—has value as a critique.[23]

Deriving from such a source is a dangerous legacy. In numerous instances, Nietzsche associates the terms *Herkunft* and *Erbschaft*. Nevertheless, we should not be deceived into thinking that this heritage is an acquisition, a possession that grows and solidifies; rather, it is an unstable assemblage of faults, fissures, and heterogeneous layers that threaten the fragile inheritor from within or from underneath: "injustice or instability in the minds of certain men, their disorder and lack of decorum, are the final consequences of their ancestors' numberless logical inaccuracies, hasty conclusions, and superficiality." [24] The search for descent is not the erecting of foundations: on the contrary, it disturbs what was previously considered immobile; it fragments what was thought unified; it shows the heterogeneity of what was imagined consistent with itself. What convictions and, far more decisively, what knowledge can resist it? If a genealogical analysis of a scholar were made—of one who collects facts and carefully accounts for them—his *Herkunft* would quickly divulge the official papers of the scribe and the pleadings of the lawyer—their father[25]—in their apparently disinterested attention, in the "pure" devotion to objectivity.

Finally, descent attaches itself to the body.[26] It inscribes itself in the nervous system, in temperament, in the digestive apparatus; it appears in faulty respiration, in improper diets, in the debilitated and prostrate bodies of those whose ancestors committed errors. Fathers have only to mistake effects for causes, believe in the reality of an "afterlife," or maintain the value of eternal truths, and the bodies of their children will suffer. Cowardice and hypocrisy, for their part, are the simple offshoots of error: not in a Socratic sense, not that evil is the result of a mistake, not because of a turning away from an original truth, but because the body maintains, in life as in death, through its strength or weakness, the sanction of every truth and error, as it sustains, in an inverse manner, the origin—descent. Why did men invent the contemplative life? Why give a supreme value to this form of existence? Why maintain the absolute truth of those fictions which sustain it? "During barbarous ages . . . if the strength of an individual declined, if he felt himself tired or sick, melancholy or satiated and, as a consequence, without desire or appetite for a short time, he became relatively a better man, that is, less dangerous. His pessimistic ideas only take form as words or reflections. In this frame of mind, he either became a thinker and prophet or used his imagination to feed his superstitions." [27] The body—and everything that touches it: diet, climate, and soil—is the domain of the *Herkunft*. The body manifests the stigmata of past experience and also gives rise to desires, failings, and errors. These elements may join in a body where they achieve a sudden expression, but as often, their encounter is an engagement in which they efface each other, where the body becomes the pretext of their insurmountable conflict.

The body is the inscribed surface of events (traced by language and dissolved by ideas), the locus of a dissociated self (adopting the illusion of a substantial unity), and a volume in perpetual disintegration. Genealogy, as an analysis of descent, is thus situated within the articulation of the body and history. Its task is to expose a body totally imprinted by history and the process of history's destruction of the body.

4. *Entstehung* designates *emergence*, the moment of arising. It stands as the principle and the singular law of an apparition. As it is wrong to search for descent in an uninterrupted continuity, we should avoid thinking of emergence as the final term of a historical development; the eye was not always intended for contemplation, and punishment has had other purposes than setting an example. These developments may appear as a culmination, but they are merely the current episodes in a series of subjugations: the eye initially responded to the requirements of hunting and warfare; and punishment has been subjected, throughout its history, to a variety of needs—revenge, excluding an aggressor, compensating a victim, creating fear. In placing present needs at the origin, the metaphysician would convince us of an obscure purpose that seeks its realization at the moment it arises. Genealogy, however, seeks to reestablish the various systems of subjection: not the anticipatory power of meaning, but the hazardous play of dominations.

Emergence is always produced through a particular stage of forces. The analysis of the *Entstehung* must delineate this interaction, the struggle these forces wage against each other or against adverse circumstances, and the attempt to avoid degeneration and regain strength by dividing these forces against themselves. It is in this sense that the emergence of a species (animal or human) and its solidification are secured "in an extended battle against conditions which are essentially and constantly unfavorable." In fact, "the species must realize itself as a species, as something—characterized by the durability, uniformity, and simplicity of its form—which can prevail in the perpetual struggle against outsiders or the uprising of those it oppresses from within." On the other hand, individual differences emerge at another stage of the relationship of forces, when the species has become victorious and when it is no longer threatened from outside. In this condition, we find a struggle "of egoisms turned against each other, each bursting forth in a splintering of forces and a general striving for the sun and for the light." [28] There are also times when force contends against itself, and not only in the intoxication of an abundance, which allows it to divide itself, but at the moment when it weakens. Force reacts against its growing lassitude and gains strength; it imposes limits, inflicts torments and mortifications; it masks these actions as a higher morality and, in exchange, regains its strength. In this manner, the ascetic ideal was born, "in the instinct of a decadent life which . . . struggles for its own existence." [29] This also describes the movement in which the Reformation arose, precisely where the church was least corrupt;[30] German Catholicism, in the sixteenth century, retained enough strength to turn against itself, to mortify its own body and history, and to spiritualize itself into a pure religion of conscience.

Emergence is thus the entry of forces; it is their eruption, the leap from the wings to center stage, each in its youthful strength. What Nietzsche calls the *Entstehungsherd* [31] of the concept of goodness is not specifically the energy of the strong or the reaction of the weak, but precisely this scene where they are displayed superimposed or face-to-face. It is nothing but the space that divides them, the void through which they exchange their threatening gestures and speeches. As descent qualifies the strength or weakness of an instinct and its inscription on a body, emergence designates a place of confrontation, but not as a closed field offering the spectacle of a struggle among equals.

Rather, as Nietzsche demonstrates in his analysis of good and evil, it is a "non-place," a pure distance, which indicates that the adversaries do not belong to a common space. Consequently, no one is responsible for an emergence; no one can glory in it, since it always occurs in the interstice.

In a sense, only a single drama is ever staged in this "non-place," the endlessly repeated play of dominations. The domination of certain men over others leads to the differentiation of values;[32] class domination generates the idea of liberty;[33] and the forceful appropriation of things necessary to survival and the imposition of a duration not intrinsic to them account for the origin of logic.[34] This relationship of domination is no more a "relationship" than the place where it occurs is a place; and, precisely for this reason, it is fixed, throughout its history, in rituals, in meticulous procedures that impose rights and obligations. It establishes marks of its power and engraves memories on things and even within bodies. It makes itself accountable for debts and gives rise to the universe of rules, which is by no means designed to temper violence, but rather to satisfy it. Following traditional beliefs, it would be false to think that total war exhausts itself in its own contradictions and ends by renouncing violence and submitting to civil laws. On the contrary, the law is a calculated and relentless pleasure, delight in the promised blood, which permits the perpetual instigation of new dominations and the staging of meticulously repeated scenes of violence. The desire for peace, the serenity of compromise, and the tacit acceptance of the law, far from representing a major moral conversion or a utilitarian calculation that gave rise to the law, are but its result and, in point of fact, its perversion: "guilt, conscience, and duty had their threshold of emergence in the right to secure obligations; and their inception, like that of any major event on earth, was saturated in blood." [35] Humanity does not gradually progress from combat to combat until it arrives at universal reciprocity, where the rule of law finally replaces warfare; humanity installs each of its violences in a system of rules and thus proceeds from domination to domination.

The nature of these rules allows violence to be inflicted on violence and the resurgence of new forces that are sufficiently strong to dominate those in power. Rules are empty in themselves, violent and unfinalized; they are impersonal and can be bent to any purpose. The successes of history belong to those who are capable of seizing these rules, to replace those who had used them, to disguise themselves so as to pervert them, invert their meaning, and redirect them against those who had initially imposed them; controlling this complex mechanism, they will make it function so as to overcome the rulers through their own rules.

The isolation of different points of emergence does not conform to the successive configurations of an identical meaning; rather, they result from substitutions, displacements, disguised conquests, and systematic reversals. If interpretation were the slow exposure of the meaning hidden in an origin, then only metaphysics could interpret the development of humanity. But if interpretation is the violent or surreptitious appropriation of a system of rules, which in itself has no essential meaning, in order to impose a direction, to bend it to a new will, to force its participation in a different game, and to subject it to secondary rules, then the development of humanity is a series of interpretations. The role of genealogy is to record its history: the history of morals, ideals, and metaphysical concepts, the history of the concept of liberty or of the ascetic life; as they stand for the emergence of different interpretations, they must be made to appear as events on the stage of historical process.

5. How can we define the relationship between genealogy, seen as the examination of *Herkunft* and *Entstehung*, and history in the traditional sense? We could, of course, examine Nietzsche's celebrated apostrophes against history, but we will put these aside for the moment and consider those instances when he conceives of genealogy as *wirkliche Historie*, or its more frequent characterization as historical "spirit" or "sense." [36] In fact, Nietzsche's criticism, beginning with the second of the *Untimely Meditations*, always questioned the form of history that reintroduces (and always assumes) a suprahistorical perspective: a history whose function is to compose the finally reduced diversity of time into a totality fully closed upon itself; a history that always encourages subjective recognitions and attributes a form of reconciliation to all the displacements of the past; a history

whose perspective on all that precedes it implies the end of time, a completed development. The historian's history finds its support outside of time and pretends to base its judgments on an apocalyptic objectivity. This is only possible, however, because of its belief in eternal truth, the immortality of the soul, and the nature of consciousness as always identical to itself. Once the historical sense is mastered by a suprahistorical perspective, metaphysics can bend it to its own purpose, and, by aligning it to the demands of objective science, it can impose its own "Egyptianism." On the other hand, the historical sense can evade metaphysics and become a privileged instrument of genealogy if it refuses the certainty of absolutes. Given this, it corresponds to the acuity of a glance that distinguishes, separates, and disperses; that is capable of liberating divergence and marginal elements—the kind of dissociating view that is capable of decomposing itself, capable of shattering the unity of man's being through which it was thought that he could extend his sovereignty to the events of his past.

Historical meaning becomes a dimension of *wirkliche Historie* to the extent that it places within a process of development everything considered immortal in man. We believe that feelings are immutable, but every sentiment, particularly the noblest and most disinterested, has a history. We believe in the dull constancy of instinctual life and imagine that it continues to exert its force indiscriminately in the present as it did in the past. But a knowledge of history easily disintegrates this unity, depicts its wavering course, locates its moments of strength and weakness, and defines its oscillating reign. It easily seizes the slow elaboration of instincts and those movements where, in turning upon themselves, they relentlessly set about their self-destruction.[37] We believe, in any event, that the body obeys the exclusive laws of physiology and that it escapes the influence of history, but this too is false. The body is molded by a great many distinct regimes; it is broken down by the rhythms of work, rest, and holidays; it is poisoned by food or values, through eating habits or moral laws; it constructs resistances.[38] "Effective" history differs from traditional history in being without constants. Nothing in man—not even his body—is sufficiently stable to serve as the basis for self-recognition or for understanding other men. The traditional devices for constructing a comprehensive view of history and for retracing the past as a patient and continuous development must be systematically dismantled. Necessarily, we must dismiss those tendencies that encourage the consoling play of recognitions. Knowledge, even under the banner of history, does not depend on "rediscovery," and it emphatically excludes the "rediscovery of ourselves." History becomes "effective" to the degree that it introduces discontinuity into our very being—as it divides our emotions, dramatizes our instincts, multiplies our body and sets it against itself. "Effective" history deprives the self of the reassuring stability of life and nature, and it will not permit itself to be transported by a voiceless obstinacy toward a millennial ending. It will uproot its traditional foundations and relentlessly disrupt its pretended continuity. This is because knowledge is not made for understanding; it is made for cutting.

From these observations, we can grasp the particular traits of historical meaning as Nietzsche understood it—the sense which opposes *wirkliche Historie* to traditional history. The former transposes the relationship ordinarily established between the eruption of an event and necessary continuity. An entire historical tradition (theological or rationalistic) aims at dissolving the singular event into an ideal continuity—as a teleological movement or a natural process. "Effective" history, however, deals with events in terms of their most unique characteristics, their most acute manifestations. An event, consequently, is not a decision, a treaty, a reign, or a battle, but the reversal of a relationship of forces, the usurpation of power, the appropriation of a vocabulary turned against those who had once used it, a feeble domination that poisons itself as it grows lax, the entry of a masked "other." The forces operating in history are not controlled by destiny or regulative mechanisms, but respond to haphazard conflicts.[39] They do not manifest the successive forms of a primordial intention and their attraction is not that of a conclusion, for they always appear through the singular randomness of events. The inverse of the Christian world, spun entirely by a divine spider, and different from the world of the Greeks, divided between the realm of will and the great cosmic folly, the world of effective history knows only one kingdom, without providence or final cause, where there is only "the iron hand of necessity shaking the dice-box of chance." [40] Chance is not simply the drawing of lots, but raising the stakes in every attempt to master chance through the will to power, and giving rise to the risk of an even greater chance. [41] The world we know is not this ultimately simple configuration where events are reduced to accentuate their essential traits, their final meaning, or their initial and final value. On the contrary, it is a profusion of entangled events. If it appears as a "marvelous motley, profound and totally meaningful," this is because it began and continues its secret existence through a "host of errors and phantasms." [42] We want historians to confirm our belief that the present rests upon profound intentions and immutable necessities. But the true historical sense confirms our existence among countless lost events, without a landmark or a point of reference.

Effective history can also invert the relationship that traditional history, in its dependence on metaphysics, establishes between proximity and distance. The latter is given to a contemplation of distances and heights: the noblest periods, the highest forms, the most abstract ideas, the purest individualities. It accomplishes this by getting as near as possible, placing itself at the foot of its mountain peaks, at the risk of adopting the famous perspective of frogs. Effective history, on the other hand, shortens its vision to those things nearest to it—the body, the nervous system, nutrition, digestion, and energies; it unearths the periods of decadence, and if it chances upon lofty epochs, it is with the suspicion—not vindictive but joyous—of finding a barbarous and shameful confusion. It has no fear of looking down, so long as it is understood that it looks from above and descends to seize the various perspectives, to disclose dispersions and differences, to leave things undisturbed in their own dimension and intensity. It reverses the surreptitious practice of historians, their pretension to examine things furthest from themselves, the groveling manner in which they approach this promising distance (like the metaphysicians who proclaim the existence of an afterlife, situated at a distance from this world, as a promise of their reward). Effective history studies what is closest, but in an abrupt dispossession, so as to seize it at a distance (an approach similar to that of a doctor who looks closely, who plunges to make a diagnosis and to state its difference). Historical sense has more in common with medicine than philosophy; and it should not surprise us that Nietzsche occasionally employs the phrase "historically and physiologically," [43] since among the philosopher's idiosyncracies is a complete denial of the body. This includes, as well, "the absence of historical sense, a hatred for the idea of development, Egyptianism," the obstinate "placing of conclusions at the beginning," of "making last things first." [44] History has a more important task than to be a handmaiden to philosophy, to recount the necessary birth of truth and values; it should become a differential knowledge of energies and failings, heights and degenerations, poisons and antidotes. Its task is to become a curative science. [45]

The final trait of effective history is its affirmation of knowledge as perspective. Historians take unusual pains to erase the elements in their work which reveal their grounding in a particular time and place, their preferences in a controversy—the unavoidable obstacles of their passion. Nietzsche's version of historical sense is explicit in its perspective and acknowledges its system of injustice. Its perception is slanted, being a deliberate appraisal, affirmation, or negation; it reaches the lingering and poisonous traces in order to prescribe the best antidote. It is not given to a discreet effacement before the objects it observes and does not submit itself to their processes; nor does it seek laws, since it gives equal weight to its own sight and to its objects. Through this historical sense, knowledge is allowed to create its own genealogy in the act of cognition; and *wirkliche Historie* composes a genealogy of history as the vertical projection of its position.

6. In this context, Nietzsche links historical sense to the historian's history. They share a beginning that is similarly impure and confused, share the same sign in which the symptoms of sickness can be recognized as well as the seed of an exquisite flower. [46] They arose simultaneously to follow their separate ways, but our task is to trace their common genealogy.

The descent (*Herkunft*) of the historian is unequivocal: he is of humble birth. A characteristic of history is to be without choice: it encourages thorough understanding and excludes qualitative judgments—a sensitivity to all things without distinction, a comprehensive view excluding differences. Nothing must escape it and, more importantly, nothing must be excluded. Historians argue that this proves their tact and discretion. After all, what right have they to impose their tastes and preferences when they seek to determine what actually occurred in the past? Their mistake is to exhibit a total lack of taste, the kind of crudeness that becomes smug in the presence of the loftiest elements and finds satisfaction in reducing them to size. The historian is insensitive to the most disgusting things; or rather, he especially enjoys those things that should be repugnant to him. His apparent serenity follows from his concerted avoidance of the exceptional and his reduction of all things to the lowest common denominator. Nothing is allowed to stand above him; and underlying his desire for total knowledge is his search for the secrets that belittle everything: "base curiosity." What is the source of history? It comes from the plebs. To whom is it addressed? To the plebs. And its discourse strongly resembles the demagogue's refrain: "No one is greater than you and anyone who presumes to get the better of you—you who are good—is evil." The historian, who functions as his double, can be heard to echo: "No past is greater than your present, and, through my meticulous erudition, I will rid you of your infatuations and transform the grandeur of history into pettiness, evil, and misfortune." The historian's ancestry goes back to Socrates.

This demagoguery, of course, must be masked. It must hide its singular malice under the cloak of universals. As the demagogue is obliged to invoke truth, laws of essences, and eternal necessity, the historian must invoke objectivity, the accuracy of facts, and the permanence of the past. The demagogue denies the body to secure the sovereignty of a timeless idea, and the historian effaces his proper individuality so that others may enter the stage and reclaim their own speech. He is divided against himself: forced to silence his preferences and overcome his distaste, to blur his own perspective and replace it with the fiction of a universal geometry, to mimic death in order to enter the kingdom of the dead, to adopt a faceless anonymity. In this world where he has conquered his individual will, he becomes a guide to the inevitable law of a superior will. Having curbed the demands of his individual will in his knowledge, he will disclose the form of an eternal will in his object of study. The objectivity of historians inverts the relationships of will and knowledge and it is, in the same stroke, a necessary belief in providence, in final causes and teleology—the beliefs that place the historian in the family of ascetics. "I can't stand these lustful eunuchs of history, all the seductions of an ascetic ideal; I can't stand these blanched tombs producing life or those tired and indifferent beings who dress up in the part of wisdom and adopt an objective point of view." [47]

The *Entstehung* of history is found in nineteenth-century Europe: the land of interminglings and bastardy, the period of the "man-of-mixture." We have become barbarians with respect to those rare moments of high civilization: cities in ruin and enigmatic monuments are spread out before us; we stop before gaping walls; we ask what gods inhabited these empty temples. Great epochs lacked this curiosity, lacked our excessive deference; they ignored their predecessors: the classical period ignored Shakespeare. The decadence of Europe presents an immense spectacle (while stronger periods refrained from such exhibitions), and the nature of this scene is to represent a theater; lacking monuments of our own making, which properly belong to us, we live among crowded scenes. But there is more. Europeans no longer know themselves; they ignore their mixed ancestries and seek a proper role. They lack individuality. We can begin to understand the spontaneous historical bent of the nineteenth century: the anemia of its forces and those mixtures that effaced all its individual traits produced the same results as the mortifications of asceticism; its inability to create, its absence of artistic works, and its need to rely on past achievements forced it to adopt the base curiosity of plebs.

If this fully represents the genealogy of history, how could it become, in its own right, a genealogical analysis? Why did it not continue as a form of demogogic or religious knowledge? How could it change roles on the same stage? Only by being seized, dominated, and turned against its birth. And it is this movement which properly describes the specific nature of the *Entstehung*: it is not the unavoidable conclusion of a long preparation, but a scene where forces are risked in the chance of confrontations, where they emerge triumphant, where they can also be confiscated. The locus of emergence for metaphysics was surely Athenian demogoguery, the vulgar spite of Socrates and his belief in immortality, and Plato could have seized this Socratic philosophy to turn it against itself. Undoubtedly, he was often tempted to do so, but his defeat lies in its consecration. The problem was similar in the nineteenth century: to avoid doing for the popular asceticism of historians what Plato did for Socrates. This historical trait should not be founded on a philosophy of history, but dismantled, beginning with the things it produced; it is necessary to master history so as to turn it to genealogical uses, that is, strictly anti-Platonic purposes. Only then will the historical sense free itself from the demands of a suprahistorical history.

7. The historical sense gives rise to three uses that oppose and correspond to the three Platonic modalities of history. The first is parodic, directed against reality, and opposes the theme of history as reminiscence or recognition; the second is dissociative, directed against identity, and opposes history given as continuity or representative of a tradition; the third is sacrificial, directed against truth, and opposes history as knowledge. They imply a use of history that severs its connection to memory, its metaphysical and anthropological model, and constructs a countermemory—a transformation of history into a totally different form of time.

First, the parodic and farcical use. The historian offers this confused and anonymous European, who no longer knows himself or what name he should adopt, the possibility of alternative identities, more individualized and substantial than his own. But the man with historical sense will see that this substitution is simply a disguise. Historians supplied the Revolution with Roman prototypes, romanticism with knight's armor, and the Wagnerian era was given the sword of a German hero—ephemeral props that point to our own unreality. No one kept them from venerating these religions, from going to Bayreuth to commemorate a new afterlife; they were free, as well, to be transformed into street vendors of empty identities. The new historian, the genealogist, will know what to make of this masquerade. He will not be too serious to enjoy it; on the contrary, he will push the masquerade to its limit and prepare the great carnival of time where masks are constantly reappearing. No longer the identification of our faint individuality with the solid identities of the past, but our "unrealization" through the excessive choice of identities—Frederick of Hohenstaufen, Caesar, Jesus, Dionysus, and possibly Zarathustra. Taking up these masks, revitalizing the buffoonery of history, we adopt an identity whose unreality surpasses that of God, who started the charade. "Perhaps, we can discover a realm where originality is again possible as parodists of history and buffoons of God." [48] In this, we recognize the parodic double of what the second of the *Untimely Meditations* called "monumental history": a history given to reestablishing the high points of historical development and their maintenance in a perpetual presence, given to the recovery of works, actions, and creations through the monogram of their personal essence. But in 1874, Nietzsche accused this history, one totally devoted to veneration, of barring access to the actual intensities and creations of life. The parody of his last texts serves to emphasize that "monumental history" is itself a parody. Genealogy is history in the form of a concerted carnival.

The second use of history is the systematic dissociation of identity. This is necessary because this rather weak identity, which we attempt to support and to unify under a mask, is in itself only a parody: it is plural; countless spirits dispute its possession; numerous systems intersect and compete. The study of history makes one "happy, unlike the metaphysicians, to possess in oneself not an immortal soul but many mortal ones." [49] And in each of these souls, history will not discover a forgotten identity, eager to be reborn, but a complex system of distinct and multiple elements, unable to be mastered by the powers of synthesis: "it is a sign of superior culture to maintain, in a fully conscious way, certain phases of its evolution which lesser men pass through without thought. The initial result is that we can understand those who resemble us as completely determined systems and as representative of diverse cultures, that is to say, as necessary and capable of modification. And in return, we are able to separate the phases of our own evolution and consider them individually." [50] The purpose of history, guided by genealogy, is not to discover the roots of our identity, but to commit itself to its dissipation. It does not seek to define our unique threshold of emergence, the homeland to which metaphysicians promise a return; it seeks to make visible all of those discontinuities that cross us. "Antiquarian history," according to the *Untimely Meditations*, pursues opposite goals. It seeks the continuities of soil, language, and urban life in which our present is rooted, and, "by cultivating in a delicate manner that which existed for all time, it tries to conserve for posterity the conditions under which we were born." [51] This type of history was objected to in the *Meditations* because it tended to block creativity in support of the laws of fidelity. Somewhat later—and already in *Human, All Too Human*—Nietzsche reconsiders the task of the antiquarian, but with an altogether different emphasis. If genealogy in its own right gives rise to questions concerning our native land, native language, or the laws that govern us, its intention is to reveal the heterogeneous systems which, masked by the self, inhibit the formation of any form of identity.

The third use of history is the sacrifice of the subject of knowledge. In appearance, or rather, according to the mask it bears, historical consciousness is neutral, devoid of passions, and committed solely to truth. But if it examines itself and if, more generally, it interrogates the various forms of scientific consciousness in its history, it finds that all these forms and transformations are aspects of the will to knowledge: instinct, passion, the inquisitor's devotion, cruel subtlety, and malice. It discovers the violence of a position that sides against those who are happy in their ignorance, against the effective illusions by which humanity protects itself, a position that encourages the dangers of research and delights in disturbing discoveries. [52] The historical analysis of this rancorous will to knowledge [53] reveals that all knowledge rests upon injustice (that there is no right, not even in the act of knowing, to truth or a foundation for truth) and that the instinct for knowledge is malicious (something murderous, opposed to the happiness of mankind). Even in the greatly expanded form it assumes today, the will to knowledge does not achieve a universal truth; man is not given an exact and serene mastery of nature. On the contrary, it ceaselessly multiplies the risks, creates dangers in every area; it breaks down illusory defenses; it dissolves the unity of the subject; it releases those elements of itself that are devoted to its subversion and destruction. Knowledge does not slowly detach itself from its empirical roots, the initial needs from which it arose, to become pure speculation subject only to the demands of reason; its development is not tied to the constitution and affirmation of a free subject; rather, it creates a progressive enslavement to its instinctive violence. Where religions once demanded the sacrifice of bodies, knowledge now calls for experimentation on ourselves,[54] calls us to the sacrifice of the subject of knowledge. "The desire for knowledge has been transformed among us into a passion which fears no sacrifice, which fears nothing but its own extinction. It may be that mankind will eventually perish from this passion for knowledge. If not through passion, then through weakness. We must be prepared to state our choice: do we wish humanity to end in fire and light or to end on the sands?"[55] We should now replace the two great problems of nineteenth-century philosophy, passed on by Fichte and Hegel (the reciprocal basis of truth and liberty and the possibility of absolute knowledge), with the theme that "to perish through absolute knowledge may well form a part of the basis of being."[56] This does not mean, in terms of a critical procedure, that the will to truth is limited by the intrinsic finitude of cognition, but that it loses all sense of limitations and all claim to truth in its unavoidable sacrifice of the subject of knowledge. "It may be that there remains one prodigious idea which might be made to prevail over every other aspiration, which might overcome the most victorious: the idea of humanity sacrificing itself. It seems indisputable that if this new constellation appeared on the horizon, only the desire for truth, with its enormous prerogatives, could direct and sustain such a sacrifice. For to knowledge, no sacrifice is too great. Of course, this problem has never been posed."[57]

The *Untimely Meditations* discussed the critical use of history: its just treatment of the past, its decisive cutting of the roots, its rejection of traditional attitudes of reverence, its liberation of man by presenting him with other origins than those in which he prefers to see himself. Nietzsche, however, reproached critical history for detaching us from every real source and for sacrificing the very movement of life to the exclusive concern for truth. Somewhat later, as we have seen, Nietzsche reconsiders this line of thought he had at first refused, but directs it to altogether different ends. It is no longer a question of judging the past in the name of a truth that only we can possess in the present, but of risking the destruction of the subject who seeks knowledge in the endless deployment of the will to knowledge.

In a sense, genealogy returns to the three modalities of history that Nietzsche recognized in 1874. It returns to them in spite of the objections that Nietzsche raised in the name of the affirmative and creative powers of life. But they are metamorphosed: the veneration of monuments becomes parody; the respect for ancient continuities becomes systematic dissociation; the critique of the injustices of the past by a truth held by men in the present becomes the destruction of the man who maintains knowledge by the injustice proper to the will to knowledge.

Notes

1 *Ed.*: See F. W. Nietzsche's Preface to *On the Genealogy of Morals* (1887), in *Basic Writings of Nietzsche*, ed. and trans. Walter Kaufmann (New York: Modern Library, 1968), sec. 4, 7.

2 F. W. Nietzsche, *The Gay Science* (1882), trans. Walter Kaufmann (New York: Random House, 1974), no. 7.

3 F. W. Nietzsche, *Human, All Too Human* (1878; New York: Gordon Press, 1974), no. 3.

4 Nietzsche, *Genealogy*, II, sec. 6, 8.

5 Nietzsche, *Gay Science*, nos. 110, 111, 300

6 F. W. Nietzsche, *The Dawn of Day* (1881; New York: Gordon Press, 1974), no. 102. (*Ed.*: *Pudenda origo* is "shameful origin.")

7 Nietzsche, *Gay Science*, nos. 151, 353; also *Dawn*, no. 62; *Genealogy*, I, sec. 14; F. W. Nietzsche, "The Four Great Errors," in *Twilight of the Idols* (1888) in *The Portable Nietzsche*, ed. and trans. Walter Kaufmann (New York: Viking Press, 1954), sec. 7. (*Ed.*: *Schwarzkünstler* is a black magician.)

8 Paul Ree's text was entitled *Ursprung der Moralischen Empfindungen*.

[9] In *Human, All Too Human*, aphorism 92 was entitled *Ursprung der Gerechtigkeit*.

[10] In the main body of the *Genealogy*, *Ursprung* and *Herkunpt* are used interchangeably in numerous instances (I, sec. 2; II, sec. 8, 11, 12, 16, 17).

[11] Nietzsche, *Dawn*, no. 123.

[12] Nietzsche, *Human, All Too Human*, no. 34.

[13] F. W. Nietzsche, *The Wanderer and His Shadow* (1880), in *Complete Works* (New York: Gordon Press, 1974), no. 9.

[14] *Ed.*: A wide range of key terms, found in Foucault's *The Archaeology of Knowledge*, are related to this theme of "disparity": the concepts of series, discontinuity, division, and difference. If the *same* is found in the realm and movement of the dialectics, the *disparate* presents itself as an "event" in the world of chance.

[15] Nietzsche, *Wanderer*, no. 3.

[16] Nietzsche, *Dawn*, no. 49.

[17] F. W. Nietzsche, *Nietzsche contra Wagner* (1888), in *Portable Nietzsche*.

[18] Nietzsche, *Gay Science*, nos. 110, 265.

[19] Nietzsche, "How the True World Finally Became a Fable," *Twilight of Idols*.

[20] For example, on race, see Nietzsche's *Gay Science*, no. 135; *Beyond Good and Evil* (1886), in *Basic Writings*, nos. 200, 242, 244; *Genealogy*, I, sec. 5; on social type see *Gay Science*, nos. 348–9; *Beyond Good and Evil*, no. 260.

[21] Nietzsche, *Beyond Good and Evil*, no. 244.

[22] Nietzsche, *Genealogy*, III, sec. 17. The *abkunft* of feelings of depression.

[23] Nietzsche, " 'Reason' in Philosophy," *Twilight of Idols*.

[24] Nietzsche, *Dawn*, no. 247.

[25] Nietzsche, *Gay Science*, nos. 348–9.

[26] Ibid.

[27] Nietzsche, *Dawn*, no. 42.

[28] Nietzsche, *Beyond Good and Evil*, no. 262.

[29] Nietzsche, *Genealogy*, III, no. 13.

[30] Nietzsche, *Gay Science*, no. 148. It is also to an anemia of the will that one must attribute the *Entstehung* of Buddhism and Christianity.

[31] Nietzsche, *Genealogy*, I, sec. 2.

[32] Nietzsche, *Beyond Good and Evil*, no. 260; see also *Genealogy*, II, sec. 12.

[33] Nietzsche, *Wanderer*, no. 9.

[34] Nietzsche, *Gay Science*, no. 111.

[35] Nietzsche, *Genealogy*, II, no. 6.

[36] Nietzsche, *Genealogy*, Preface, sec. 7, and I, sec. 2; *Beyond Good and Evil*, no. 224.

[37] Nietzsche, *Gay Science*, no. 7.

[38] Ibid.

[39] Nietzsche, *Genealogy*, II, sec. 12.

[40] Nietzsche, *Dawn*, no. 130.

[41] Nietzsche, *Genealogy*, II, sec. 12.

[42] Nietzsche, *Human, All Too Human*, no. 16.

[43] Nietzsche, *Twilight of Idols*, no. 44.

[44] Nietzsche, " 'Reason' in Philosophy," *Twilight of Idols*, nos. 1, 4.

[45] Nietzsche, *Wanderer*, no. 188. (*Ed.*: This conception underlies the task of Foucault's *Madness and Civilization* and *The Birth of the Clinic* even though it is not found as a conscious formulation until *The Archaeology of Knowledge*.)

[46] Nietzsche, *Gay Science*, no. 337.

[47] Nietzsche, *Genealogy*, III, sec. 26.

[48] Nietzsche, *Beyond Good and Evil*, no. 223.

[49] Nietzsche, *Wanderer* (Opinions and Mixed Statements), no. 17.

[50] Nietzsche, *Human, All Too Human*, no. 274.

[51] F. W. Nietzsche, *Untimely Meditations* (1873–4), in *Complete Works*, II, no. 3.

[52] Cf. Nietzsche's *Dawn*, nos. 429, 432; *Gay Science*, no. 333; *Beyond Good and Evil*, nos. 229–30.

[53] *Ed.*: The French phrase *vouloir-savoir* means both the will to knowledge and knowledge as revenge.

[54] Nietzsche, *Dawn*, no. 501.

[55] Ibid.

[56] Nietzsche, *Beyond Good and Evil*, no. 39.

[57] Nietzsche, *Dawn*, no. 45.

What Is an Author?

The coming into being of the notion of "author" constitutes the privileged moment of *individualization* in the history of ideas, knowledge, literature, philosophy, and the sciences. Even today, when we reconstruct the history of a concept, literary genre, or school of philosophy, such categories seem relatively weak, secondary, and superimposed scansions in comparison with the solid and fundamental unit of the author and the work.

I shall not offer here a sociohistorical analysis of the author's persona. Certainly it would be worth examining how the author became individualized in a culture like ours, what status he has been given, at what moment studies of authenticity and attribution began, in what kind of system of valorization the author was involved, at what point we began to recount the lives of authors rather than of heroes, and how this fundamental category of "the-man-and-his-work criticism" began. For the moment, however, I want to deal solely with the relationship between text and author and with the manner in which the text points to this "figure" that, at least in appearance, is outside it and antecedes it.

Beckett nicely formulates the theme with which I would like to begin: " 'What does it matter who is speaking,' someone said, 'what does it matter who is speaking.' " In this indifference appears one of the fundamental ethical principles of contemporary writing (*écriture*). I say "ethical" because this indifference is not really a trait characterizing the manner in which one speaks and writes, but rather a kind of immanent rule, taken up over and over again, never fully applied, not designating writing as something completed, but dominating it as a practice. Since it is too familiar to require a lengthy analysis, this immanent rule can be adequately illustrated here by tracing two of its major themes.

First of all, we can say that today's writing has freed itself from the dimension of expression. Referring only to itself, but without being restricted to the confines of its interiority, writing is identified with its own unfolded exteriority. This means that it is an interplay of signs arranged less according to its signified content than according to the very nature of the signifier. Writing unfolds like a game (*jeu*) that invariably goes beyond its own rules and transgresses its limits. In writing, the point is not to manifest or exalt the act of writing, nor is it to pin a subject within language; it is, rather, a question of creating a space into which the writing subject constantly disappears.

The second theme, writing's relationship with death, is even more familiar. This link subverts an old tradition exemplified by the Greek epic, which was intended to perpetuate the immortality of the hero: if he was willing to die young, it was so that his life, consecrated and magnified by death, might pass into immortality; the narrative then redeemed this accepted death. In another way, the motivation, as well as the theme and the pretext of Arabian narratives—such as *The Thousand and One Nights*—was also the eluding of death: one spoke, telling stories into the early morning, in order to forestall death, to postpone the day of reckoning that would silence the narrator. Scheherazade's narrative is an effort, renewed each night, to keep death outside the circle of life.

Our culture has metamorphosed this idea of narrative, or writing, as something designed to ward off death. Writing has become linked to sacrifice, even to the sacrifice of life: it is now a voluntary effacement which does not need to be represented in books, since it is brought about in the writer's very existence. The work, which once had the duty of providing immortality, now possesses the right to kill, to be its author's murderer, as in the cases of Flaubert, Proust, and Kafka. That is not all, however: this relationship between writing and death is also manifested in the effacement of the writing subject's individual characteristics. Using all the contrivances that he sets up between himself and what he writes, the writing subject cancels out the signs of his particular individuality. As a result, the mark of the writer is reduced to nothing more than the singularity of his absence; he must assume the role of the dead man in the game of writing.

None of this is recent; criticism and philosophy took note of the disappearance—or death—of the author some time ago. But the consequences of their discovery of it have not been sufficiently examined, nor has its import been accurately measured. A certain number of notions that are intended to replace the privileged position of the author actually seem to preserve that privilege and suppress the real meaning of his disappearance. I shall examine two of these notions, both of great importance today.

The first is the idea of the work. It is a very familiar thesis that the task of criticism is not to bring out the work's relationships with the author, nor to reconstruct through the text a thought or experience, but rather to analyze the work through its structure, its architecture, its intrinsic form, and the play of its internal relationships. At this point, however, a problem arises: What is a work? What is this curious unity which we designate as a work? Of what elements is it composed? Is it not what an author has written? Difficulties appear immediately. If an individual were not an author, could we say that what he wrote, said, left behind in his papers, or what has been collected of his remarks, could be called a "work"? When Sade was not considered an author, what was the status of his papers? Were they simply rolls of paper onto which he ceaselessly uncoiled his fantasies during his imprisonment?

Even when an individual has been accepted as an author, we must still ask whether everything that he wrote, said, or left behind is part of his work. The problem is both theoretical and technical. When undertaking the publication of Nietzsche's works, for example, where should one stop? Surely everything must be published, but what is "everything"? Everything that Nietzsche himself published, certainly. And what about the rough drafts for his works? Obviously. The plans for his aphorisms? Yes. The deleted passages and the notes at the bottom of the page? Yes. What if, within a workbook filled with aphorisms, one finds a reference, the notation of a meeting or of an address, or a laundry list: Is it a work, or not? Why not? And so on, ad infinitum. How can one define a work amid the millions of traces left by someone after his death? A theory of the work does not exist, and the empirical task of those who naively undertake the editing of works often suffers in the absence of such a theory.

We could go even further: Does *The Thousand and One Nights* constitute a work? What about Clement of Alexandria's *Miscellanies* or Diogenes Laertius's *Lives*? A multitude of questions arises with regard to this notion of the work. Consequently, it is not enough to declare that we should do without the writer (the author) and study the work itself. The word *work* and the unity that it designates are probably as problematic as the status of the author's individuality.

Another notion which has hindered us from taking full measure of the author's disappearance, blurring and concealing the moment of this effacement and subtly preserving the author's existence, is the notion of writing (*écriture*). When rigorously applied, this notion should allow us not only to circumvent references to the author, but also to situate his recent absence. The notion of writing, as currently employed, is concerned with neither the act of writing nor the indication—be it symptom or sign—of a meaning which someone might have wanted to express. We try, with great effort, to imagine the general condition of each text, the condition of both the space in which it is dispersed and the time in which it unfolds.

In current usage, however, the notion of writing seems to transpose the empirical characteristics of the author into a transcendental anonymity. We are content to efface the more visible marks of the author's empiricity by playing off, one against the other, two ways of characterizing writing, namely, the critical and the religious approaches. Giving writing a primal status seems to be a way of retranslating, in transcendental terms, both the theological affirmation of its sacred character and the critical affirmation of its creative character. To admit that writing is, because of the very history that it made possible, subject to the test of oblivion and repression, seems to represent, in transcendental terms, the religious principle of the hidden meaning (which requires interpretation) and the critical principle of implicit significations, silent determinations, and obscured contents (which gives rise to commentary). To imagine writing as absence seems to be a simple repetition, in transcendental terms, of both the religious principle of inalterable and yet never fulfilled tradition, and the aesthetic principle of the work's survival, its perpetuation beyond the author's death, and its enigmatic *excess* in relation to him.

This usage of the notion of writing runs the risk of maintaining the author's privileges under the protection of writing's *a priori* status: it keeps alive, in the gray light of neutralization, the interplay of those representations that formed a particular image of the author. The author's disappearance, which, since Mallarmé, has been a constantly recurring event, is subject to a series of transcendental barriers. There seems to be an important dividing line between those who believe that they can still locate today's discontinuities (*ruptures*) in the historico-transcendental tradition of the nineteenth century, and those who try to free themselves once and for all from that tradition.

It is not enough, however, to repeat the empty affirmation that the author has disappeared. For the same reason, it is not enough to keep repeating (after Nietzsche) that God and man have died a common death. Instead, we must locate the space left empty by the author's disappearance, follow the distribution of gaps and breaches, and watch for the openings that this disappearance uncovers.

First, we need to clarify briefly the problems arising from the use of the author's name. What is an author's name? How does it function? Far from offering a solution, I shall only indicate some of the difficulties that it presents.

The author's name is a proper name, and therefore it raises the problems common to all proper names. (Here I refer to Searle's analyses, among others.[1]) Obviously, one cannot turn a proper name into a pure and simple reference. It has other than indicative functions: more than an indication, a gesture, a finger pointed at someone, it is the equivalent of a description. When one says "Aristotle," one employs a word that is the equivalent of one, or a series, of definite descriptions, such as "the author of the *Analytics*," "the founder of ontology," and so forth. One cannot stop there, however, because a proper name does not have just one signification. When we discover that Rimbaud did not write *La Chasse spirituelle*, we cannot pretend that the meaning of this proper name, or that of the author, has been altered. The proper name and the author's name are situated between the two poles of description and designation: they must have a certain link with what they name, but one that is neither entirely in the mode of designation nor in that of description; it must be a *specific* link. However—and it is here that the particular difficulties of the author's name arise—the links between the proper name and the individual named and between the author's name and what it names are not isomorphic and do not function in the same way. There are several differences.

If, for example, Pierre Dupont does not have blue eyes, or was not born in Paris, or is not a doctor, the name Pierre Dupont will still always refer to the same person; such things do not modify the link of designation. The problems raised by the author's name are much more complex, however. If I discover that Shakespeare was not born in the house that we visit today, this is a modification which, obviously, will not alter the functioning of the author's name. But if we proved that Shakespeare did not write those sonnets which pass for his, that would constitute a significant change and affect the manner in which the author's name functions. If we proved that Shakespeare wrote Bacon's *Organon* by showing that the same author wrote both the works of Bacon and those of Shakespeare, that would be a third type of change which would entirely modify the functioning of the author's name. The author's name is not, therefore, just a proper name like the rest.

Many other facts point out the paradoxical singularity of the author's name. To say that Pierre Dupont does not exist is not at all the same as saying that Homer or Hermes Trismegistus did not exist. In the first case, it means that no one has the name Pierre Dupont; in the second, it means that several people were mixed together under one name, or that the true author had none of the traits traditionally ascribed to the personae of Homer or Hermes. To say that X's real name is actually Jacques Durand instead of Pierre Dupont is not the same as saying that

Stendhal's name was Henri Beyle. One could also question the meaning and functioning of propositions like "Bourbaki is so-and-so, so-and-so, etc." and "Victor Eremita, Climacus, Anti-climacus, Frater Taciturnus, Constantine Constantius, all of these are Kierkegaard."

These differences may result from the fact that an author's name is not simply an element in a discourse (capable of being either subject or object, of being replaced by a pronoun, and the like); it performs a certain role with regard to narrative discourse, assuring a classificatory function. Such a name permits one to group together a certain number of texts, define them, differentiate them from and contrast them to others. In addition, it establishes a relationship among the texts. Hermes Trismegistus did not exist, nor did Hippocrates—in the sense that Balzac existed—but the fact that several texts have been placed under the same name indicates that there has been established among them a relationship of homogeneity, filiation, authentication of some texts by the use of others, reciprocal explication, or con-comitant utilization. The author's name serves to characterize a certain mode of being of discourse: the fact that the discourse has an author's name, that one can say "this was written by so-and-so" or "so-and-so is its author," shows that this discourse is not ordinary everyday speech that merely comes and goes, not something that is immediately consumable. On the contrary, it is a speech that must be received in a certain mode and that, in a given culture, must receive a certain status.

It would seem that the author's name, unlike other proper names, does not pass from the interior of a discourse to the real and exterior individual who produced it; instead, the name seems always to be present, marking off the edges of the text, revealing, or at least characterizing, its mode of being. The author's name manifests the appearance of a certain discursive set and indicates the status of this discourse within a society and a culture. It has no legal status, nor is it located in the fiction of the work; rather, it is located in the break that founds a certain discursive construct and its very particular mode of being. As a result, we could say that in a civilization like our own there are a certain number of discourses that are endowed with the "author func-tion," while others are deprived of it. A private letter may well have a signer—it does not have an author; a contract may well have a guarantor—it does not have an author. An anonymous text posted on a wall probably has a writer—but not an author. The author function is therefore characteristic of the mode of existence, circulation, and functioning of certain discourses within a society.

Let us analyze this "author function" as we have just described it. In our culture, how does one characterize a discourse containing the author function? In what way is this discourse different from other discourses? If we limit our remarks to the author of a book or a text, we can isolate four different characteristics.

First of all, discourses are objects of appropriation. The form of ownership from which they spring is of a rather particular type, one that has been codified for many years. We should note that, historically, this type of ownership has always been subsequent to what one might call penal appropriation. Texts, books, and discourses really began to have authors (other than mythical, "sacralized" and "sacralizing" figures) to the extent that authors became subject to punishment, that is, to the extent that discourses could be transgressive. In our culture (and doubtless in many others), discourse was not originally a product, a thing, a kind of goods; it was essentially an act—an act placed in the bipolar field of the sacred and the profane, the licit and the illicit, the religious and the blasphemous. Historically, it was a gesture fraught with risks before becoming goods caught up in a circuit of ownership.

Once a system of ownership for texts came into being, once strict rules concerning author's rights, author-publisher relations, rights of reproduction, and related matters were enacted—at the end of the eighteenth and the beginning of the nineteenth century—the possibility of transgression attached to the act of writing took on, more and more, the form of an imperative peculiar to literature. It is as if the author, beginning with the moment at which he was placed in the system of property that characterizes our society, compensated for the status that he thus acquired by rediscovering the old bipolar field of discourse, systematically practicing transgression and thereby restoring danger to a writing which was now guaranteed the benefits of ownership.

The author function does not affect all discourses in a universal and constant way, however. This is its second characteristic. In our civilization, it has not always been the same types of texts which have required attribution to an author. There was a time when the texts that we today call "literary" (narratives, stories, epics, tragedies, comedies) were accepted, put into circulation, and valorized without any question about the identity of their author; their anonymity caused no difficulties since their ancientness, whether real or imagined, was regarded as a sufficient guarantee of their status. On the other hand, those texts that we now would call scientific—those dealing with cosmology and the heavens, medicine and illnesses, natural sciences and geography—were accepted in the Middle Ages, and accepted as "true," only when marked with the name of their author. "Hippocrates said," "Pliny recounts," were not really formulas of an argument based on authority; they were the markers inserted in discourses that were supported to be received as statements of demonstrated truth.

A reversal occurred in the seventeenth or eighteenth century. Scientific discourses began to be received for themselves, in the anonymity of an established or always redemonstrable truth; their membership in a systematic ensemble, and not the reference to the individual who produced them, stood as their guarantee. The author function faded away, and the inventor's name served only to christen a theorem, proposition, particular effect, property, body, group of elements, or pathological syndrome. By the same token, literary discourses came to be accepted only when endowed with the author function. We now ask of each poetic or fictional text: From where does it come, who wrote it, when, under what circumstances, or beginning with what design? The meaning ascribed to it and the status or value accorded it depend on the manner in which we answer these questions. And if a text should be discovered in a state of anonymity—whether as a consequence of an accident or the author's explicit wish—the game becomes one of rediscovering the author. Since literary anonymity is not tolerable, we can accept it only in the guise of an enigma. As a result, the author function today plays an important role in our view of literary works. (These are obviously generalizations that would have to be refined insofar as recent critical practice is concerned.)

The third characteristic of this author function is that it does not develop spontaneously as the attribution of a discourse to an individual. It is, rather, the result of a complex operation which constructs a certain rational being that we call "author." Critics doubtless try to give this intelligible being a realistic status, by discerning, in the individual, a "deep" motive, a "creative" power, or a "design," the milieu in which writing originates. Nevertheless, these aspects of an individual which we designate as making him an author are only a projection, in more or less psychologizing terms, of the operations that we force texts to undergo, the connections that we make, the traits that we establish as pertinent, the continuities that we recognize, or the exclusions that we practice. All these operations vary according to periods and types of discourse. We do not construct a "philosophical author" as we do a "poet," just as, in the eighteenth century, one did not construct a novelist as we do today. Still, we can find through the ages certain constants in the rules of author construction.

It seems, for example, that the manner in which literary criticism once defined the author—or, rather, constructed the figure of the author beginning with existing texts and discourses—is directly derived from the manner in which Christian tradition authenticated (or rejected) the texts at its disposal. In order to "rediscover" an author in a work, modern criticism uses methods similar to those that Christian exegesis employed when trying to prove the value of a text by its author's saintliness. In *De viris illustribus*, Saint Jerome explains that homonymy is not sufficient to identify legitimately authors of more than one work: different individuals could have had the same name, or one man could have, illegitimately, borrowed another's patronymic. The name as an individual trademark is not enough when one works within a textual tradition.

How, then, can one attribute several discourses to one and the same author? How can one use the author function to determine if one is dealing with one or several individuals? Saint

Jerome proposes four criteria: (1) if among several books attributed to an author one is inferior to the others, it must be withdrawn from the list of the author's works (the author is therefore defined as a constant level of value); (2) the same should be done if certain texts contradict the doctrine expounded in the author's other works (the author is thus defined as a field of conceptual or theoretical coherence); (3) one must also exclude works that are written in a different style, containing words and expressions not ordinarily found in the writer's production (the author is here conceived as a stylistic unity); (4) finally, passages quoting statements that were made or mentioning events that occurred after the author's death must be regarded as interpolated texts (the author is here seen as a historical figure at the crossroads of a certain number of events).

Modern literary criticism, even when—as is now customary—it is not concerned with questions of authentication, still defines the author the same way: the author provides the basis for explaining not only the presence of certain events in a work, but also their transformations, distortions, and diverse modifications (through his biography, the determination of his individual perspective, the analysis of his social position, and the revelation of his basic design). The author is also the principle of a certain unity of writing—all differences having to be resolved, at least in part, by the principles of evolution, maturation, or influence. The author also serves to neutralize the contradictions that may emerge in a series of texts: there must be—at a certain level of his thought or desire, of his consciousness or unconscious—a point where contradictions are resolved, where incompatible elements are at last tied together or organized around a fundamental or originating contradiction. Finally, the author is a particular source of expression that, in more or less completed forms, is manifested equally well, and with similar validity, in works, sketches, letters, fragments, and so on. Clearly, Saint Jerome's four criteria of authenticity (criteria which seem totally insufficient for today's exegetes) do define the four modalities according to which modern criticism brings the author function into play.

But the author function is not a pure and simple reconstruction made secondhand from a text given as passive material.

The text always contains a certain number of signs referring to the author. These signs, well known to grammarians, are personal pronouns, adverbs of time and place, and verb conjugation. Such elements do not play the same role in discourses provided with the author function as in those lacking it. In the latter, such "shifters" refer to the real speaker and to the spatio-temporal coordinates of his discourse (although certain modifications can occur, as in the operation of relating discourses in the first person). In the former, however, their role is more complex and variable. Everyone knows that, in a novel narrated in the first person, neither the first-person pronoun nor the present indicative refers exactly either to the writer or to the moment in which he writes, but rather to an alter ego whose distance from the author varies, often changing in the course of the work. It would be just as wrong to equate the author with the real writer as to equate him with the fictitious speaker; the author function is carried out and operates in the scission itself, in this division and this distance.

One might object that this is a characteristic peculiar to novelistic or poetic discourse, a "game" in which only "quasi-discourses" participate. In fact, however, all discourses endowed with the author function do possess this plurality of self. The self that speaks in the preface to a treatise on mathematics—and that indicates the circumstances of the treatise's composition—is identical neither in its position nor in its functioning to the self that speaks in the course of a demonstration, and that appears in the form of "I conclude" or "I suppose." In the first case, the "I" refers to an individual without an equivalent who, in a determined place and time, completed a certain task; in the second, the "I" indicates an instance and a level of demonstration which any individual could perform provided that he accepted the same system of symbols, play of axioms, and set of previous demonstrations. We could also, in the same treatise, locate a third self, one that speaks to tell the work's meaning, the obstacles encountered, the results obtained, and the remaining problems; this self is situated in the field of already existing or yet-to-appear mathematical discourses. The author function is not assumed by the first of these selves at the expense of the other two, which would then be nothing more than a fictitious splitting in two of the first one. On the contrary, in these discourses the author function operates so as to effect the dispersion of these three simultaneous selves.

No doubt analysis could discover still more characteristic traits of the author function. I will limit myself to these four, however, because they seem both the most visible and the most important. They can be summarized as follows: (1) the author function is linked to the juridical and institutional system that encompasses, determines, and articulates the universe of discourses; (2) it does not affect all discourses in the same way at all times and in all types of civilization; (3) it is not defined by the spontaneous attribution of a discourse to its producer, but rather by a series of specific and complex operations; (4) it does not refer purely and simply to a real individual, since it can give rise simultaneously to several selves, to several subjects—positions that can be occupied by different classes of individuals.

Up to this point I have unjustifiably limited my subject. Certainly the author function in painting, music, and other arts should have been discussed, but even supposing that we remain within the world of discourse, as I want to do, I seem to have given the term "author" much too narrow a meaning. I have discussed the author only in the limited sense of a person to whom the production of a text, a book, or a work can be legitimately attributed. It is easy to see that in the sphere of discourse one can be the author of much more than a book—one can be the author of a theory, tradition, or discipline in which other books and authors will in their turn find a place. These authors are in a position which we shall call "transdiscursive." This is a recurring phenomenon—certainly as old as our civilization. Homer, Aristotle, and the Church Fathers, as well as the first mathematicians and the originators of the Hippocratic tradition, all played this role.

Furthermore, in the course of the nineteenth century, there appeared in Europe another, more uncommon, kind of author, whom one should confuse with neither the "great" literary authors, nor the authors of religious texts, nor the founders of science. In a somewhat arbitrary way we shall call those who belong in this last group "founders of discursivity." They are unique in that they are not just the authors of their own works. They have produced something else: the possibilities and the rules for the formation of other texts. In this sense, they are very different, for example, from a novelist, who is, in fact, nothing more than the author of his own text. Freud is not just the author of *The Interpretation of Dreams* or *Jokes and Their Relation to the Unconscious*; Marx is not just the author of the *Communist Manifesto* or *Das Kapital*: they both have established an endless possibility of discourse.

Obviously, it is easy to object. One might say that it is not true that the author of a novel is only the author of his own text; in a sense, he also, provided that he acquires some "importance," governs and commands more than that. To take a very simple example, one could say that Ann Radcliffe not only wrote *The Castles of Athlin and Dunbayne* and several other novels, but also made possible the appearance of the Gothic horror novel at the beginning of the nineteenth century; in that respect, her author function exceeds her own work. But I think there is an answer to this objection. These founders of discursivity (I use Marx and Freud as examples, because I believe them to be both the first and the most important cases) make possible something altogether different from what a novelist makes possible. Ann Radcliffe's texts opened the way for a certain number of resemblances and analogies which have their model or principle in her work. The latter contains characteristic signs, figures, relationships, and structures which could be reused by others. In other words, to say that Ann Radcliffe founded the Gothic horror novel means that in the nineteenth-century Gothic novel one will find, as in Ann Radcliffe's works, the theme of the heroine caught in the trap of her own innocence, the hidden castle, the character of the black, cursed hero devoted to making the world expiate the evil done to him, and all the rest of it.

On the other hand, when I speak of Marx or Freud as founders of discursivity, I mean that they made possible not only a certain number of analogies, but also (and equally important) a certain number of differences. They have created a possibility for something other than their discourse, yet something belonging to what they founded. To say that Freud founded psychoanalysis does not (simply) mean that we find the concept of the libido or the technique of dream analysis in the works of Karl Abraham or Melanie Klein; it means that Freud made possible a certain number of divergences—with respect to his own texts, concepts, and hypotheses—that all arise from the psychoanalytic discourse itself.

This would seem to present a new difficulty, however: is the above not true, after all, of any founder of a science, or of any author who has introduced some important transformation into a science? After all, Galileo made possible not only those discourses that repeated the laws that he had formulated, but also statements very different from what he himself had said. If Cuvier is the founder of biology or Saussure the founder of linguistics, it is not because they were imitated, nor because people have since taken up again the concept of organism or sign; it is because Cuvier made possible, to a certain extent, a theory of evolution diametrically opposed to his own fixism; it is because Saussure made possible a generative grammar radically different from his structural analyses. Superficially, then, the initiation of discursive practices appears similar to the founding of any scientific endeavor.

Still, there is a difference, and a notable one. In the case of a science, the act that founds it is on an equal footing with its future transformations; this act becomes in some respects part of the set of modifications that it makes possible. Of course, this belonging can take several forms. In the future development of a science, the founding act may appear as little more than a particular instance of a more general phenomenon which unveils itself in the process. It can also turn out to be marred by intuition and empirical bias; one must then reformulate it, making it the object of a certain number of supplementary theoretical operations which establish it more rigorously, etc. Finally, it can seem to be a hasty generalization which must be limited, and whose restricted domain of validity must be retraced. In other words, the founding act of a science can always be reintroduced within the machinery of those transformations that derive from it.

In contrast, the initiation of a discursive practice is heterogeneous to its subsequent transformations. To expand a type of discursivity, such as psychoanalysis as founded by Freud, is not to give it a formal generality that it would not have permitted at the outset, but rather to open it up to a certain number of possible applications. To limit psychoanalysis as a type of discursivity is, in reality, to try to isolate in the founding act an eventually restricted number of propositions or statements to which, alone, one grants a founding value, and in relation to which certain concepts or theories accepted by Freud might be considered as derived, secondary, and accessory. In addition, one does not declare certain propositions in the work of these founders to be false: instead, when trying to seize the act of founding, one sets aside those statements that are not pertinent, either because they are deemed inessential, or because they are considered "prehistoric" and derived from another type of discursivity. In other words, unlike the founding of a science, the initiation of a discursive practice does not participate in its later transformations.

As a result, one defines a proposition's theoretical validity in relation to the work of the founders—while, in the case of Galileo and Newton, it is in relation to what physics or cosmology *is* (in its intrinsic structure and "normativity") that one affirms the validity of any proposition that those men may have put forth. To phrase it very schematically: the work of initiators of discursivity is not situated in the space that science defines; rather, it is the science or the discursivity which refers back to their work as primary coordinates.

In this way we can understand the inevitable necessity, within these fields of discursivity, for a "return to the origin." This return, which is part of the discursive field itself, never stops modifying it. The return is not a historical supplement which would be added to the discursivity, or merely an ornament; on the contrary, it constitutes an effective and necessary task of transforming the discursive practice itself. Reexamination of Galileo's text may well change our knowledge of the history of mechanics, but it will never be able to change mechanics itself. On the other hand, reexamining Freud's texts modifies psychoanalysis itself, just as a reexamination of Marx's would modify Marxism.

What I have just outlined regarding the initiation of discursive practices is, of course, very schematic; this is true, in particular, of the opposition that I have tried to draw between discursive initiation and scientific founding. It is not always easy to distinguish between the two; moreover, nothing proves that they are two mutually exclusive procedures. I have attempted the distinction for only one reason: to show that the author function, which is complex enough when one tries to situate it at the level of a book or a series of texts that carry a given signature, involves still more determining factors when one tries to analyze it in larger units, such as groups of works or entire disciplines.

To conclude, I would like to review the reasons why I attach a certain importance to what I have said.

First, there are theoretical reasons. On the one hand, an analysis in the direction that I have outlined might provide for an approach to a typology of discourse. It seems to me, at least at first glance, that such a typology cannot be constructed solely from the grammatical features, formal structures, and objects of discourse: more likely there exist properties or relationships peculiar to discourse (not reducible to the rules of grammar and logic), and one must use these to distinguish the major categories of discourse. The relationship (or nonrelationship) with an author, and the different forms this relationship takes, constitute—in a quite visible manner—one of these discursive properties.

On the other hand, I believe that one could find here an introduction to the historical analysis of discourse. Perhaps it is time to study discourses not only in terms of their expressive value or formal transformations, but according to their modes of existence. The modes of circulation, valorization, attribution, and appropriation of discourses vary with each culture and are modified within each. The manner in which they are articulated according to social relationships can be more readily understood, I believe, in the activity of the author function and in its modifications than in the themes or concepts that discourses set in motion.

It would seem that one could also, beginning with analyses of this type, reexamine the privileges of the subject. I realize that in undertaking the internal and architectonic analysis of a work (be it a literary text, philosophical system, or scientific work), in setting aside biographical and psychological references, one has already called back into question the absolute character and founding role of the subject. Still, perhaps one must return to this question, not in order to reestablish the theme of an originating subject, but to grasp the subject's points of insertion, modes of functioning, and system of dependencies. Doing so means overturning the traditional problem, no longer raising the questions: How can a free subject penetrate the substance of things and give it meaning? How can it activate the rules of a language from within and thus give rise to the designs which are properly its own? Instead, these questions will be raised: How, under what conditions, and in what forms can something like a subject appear in the order of discourse? What place can it occupy in each type of discourse, what functions can it assume, and by obeying what rules? In short, it is a matter of depriving the subject (or its substitute) of its role as originator, and of analyzing the subject as a variable and complex function of discourse.

Second, there are reasons dealing with the "ideological" status of the author. The question then becomes: How can one reduce the great peril, the great danger with which fiction threatens our world? The answer is: one can reduce it with the author. The author allows a limitation of the cancerous and dangerous proliferation of significations within a world where one is thrifty not only with one's resources and riches, but also with one's discourses and their significations. The author is the principle of thrift in the proliferation of meaning. As a result, we must entirely reverse the traditional idea of the author. We are accustomed, as we have seen earlier, to saying that the author is the genial creator of a work in which he deposits, with infinite wealth and generosity, an inexhaustible world of significations. We are used to thinking that the author is so different from all other men, and so transcendent with regard to all languages that, as soon as he speaks, meaning begins to proliferate, to proliferate indefinitely.

The truth is quite the contrary: the author is not an indefinite source of significations which fill a work; the author does not precede the works; he is a certain functional principle by which, in our culture, one limits, excludes, and chooses; in short, by which one impedes the free circulation, the free manipulation, the free composition, decomposition, and recomposition of fiction. In fact, if we are accustomed to presenting the author as a genius, as a perpetual surging of invention, it is because, in reality, we make him function in exactly the opposite fashion. One can say that the author is an ideological product, since we represent him as the opposite of his historically real function. (When a historically given function is represented in a figure that inverts it, one has an ideological production.) The author is therefore the ideological figure by which one marks the manner in which we fear the proliferation of meaning.

In saying this, I seem to call for a form of culture in which fiction would not be limited by the figure of the author. It would be pure romanticism, however, to imagine a culture in which the fictive would operate in an absolutely free state, in which fiction would be put at the disposal of everyone and would develop without passing through something like a necessary or constraining figure. Although, since the eighteenth century, the author has played the role of the regulator of the fictive, a role quite characteristic of our era of industrial and bourgeois society, of individualism and private property, still, given the historical modifications that are taking place, it does not seem necessary that the author function remain constant in form, complexity, and even in existence. I think that, as our society changes, at the very moment when it is in the process of changing, the author function will disappear, and in such a manner that fiction and its polysemous texts will once again function according to another mode, but still with a system of constraint—one which will no longer be the author, but which will have to be determined or, perhaps, experienced.

All discourses, whatever their status, form, value, and whatever the treatment to which they will be subjected, would then develop in the anonymity of a murmur. We would no longer hear the questions that have been rehashed for so long: Who really spoke? Is it really he and not someone else? With what authenticity or originality? And what part of his deepest self did he express in his discourse? Instead, there would be other questions, like these: What are the modes of existence of this discourse? Where has it been used, how can it circulate, and who can appropriate it for himself? What are the places in it where there is room for possible subjects? Who can assume these various subject functions? And behind all these questions, we would hear hardly anything but the stirring of an indifference: What difference does it make who is speaking?

Notes

[1] *Ed.*: John Searle, *Speech Acts: An Essay in the Philosophy of Language* (Cambridge, Eng.: Cambridge University Press, 1969), pp. 162–74.

Part

II

*Practices
and Knowledge*

MADNESS AND CIVILIZATION

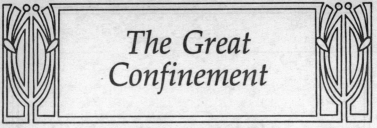

The Great Confinement

(FROM *Madness and Civilization*)

Compelle Intrare

It is common knowledge that the seventeenth century created enormous houses of confinement; it is less commonly known that more than one out of every hundred inhabitants of the city of Paris found themselves confined there, within several months. It is common knowledge that absolute power made use of *lettres de cachet* and arbitrary measures of imprisonment; what is less familiar is the judicial conscience that could inspire such practices. Since Pinel, Tuke, Wagnitz, we know that madmen were subjected to the regime of this confinement for a century and a half, and that they would one day be discovered in the wards of the Hôpital Général, in the cells of prisons; they would be found mingled with the population of the workhouses or *Zuchthäusern*. But it has rarely been made clear what their status was there, what the meaning was of this proximity which seemed to assign the same homeland to the poor, to the unemployed, to prisoners, and to the insane. It is within the walls of confinement that Pinel and nineteenth-century psychiatry would come upon madmen; it is there—let us remember—that they would leave them, not without boasting of having "delivered" them. From the middle of the seventeenth century, madness was linked with this country of confinement, and with the act which designated confinement as its natural abode.

A date can serve as a landmark: 1656, the decree that founded, in Paris, the Hôpital Général. At first glance, this is merely a reform—little more than an administrative reorganization. Several already existing establishments are grouped under a single administration: La Salpêtrière, rebuilt under the preceding reign to house an arsenal; Bicêtre, which Louis XIII had wanted to give to the Commandery of Saint Louis as a rest home for military invalids; "the House and the Hospital of La Pitié, the larger as well as the smaller, those of Le Refuge, situated in the Faubourg Saint-Victor, the House and Hospital of Scipion, the House of La Savonnerie, with all the lands, places, gardens, houses, and buildings thereto appertaining." [1] All were now assigned to the poor of Paris "of both sexes, of all ages and from all localities, of whatever breeding and birth, in whatever state they may be, able-bodied or invalid, sick or convalescent, curable or incurable." These establishments had to accept, lodge, and feed those who presented themselves or those sent by royal or judicial authority; it was also necessary to assure the subsistence, the appearance, and the general order of those who could not find room, but who might or who deserved to be there. This responsibility was entrusted to directors appointed for life, who exercised their powers, not only in the buildings of the Hôpital but throughout the city of Paris, over all those who came under their jurisdiction: "They have all power of authority, of direction, of administration, of commerce, of police, of jurisdiction, of correction and punishment over all the poor of Paris, both within and without the Hôpital Général." The directors also appointed a doctor at a salary of one thousand livres a year; he was to reside at La Pitié, but had to visit each of the houses of the Hôpital twice a week.

From the very start, one thing is clear: the Hôpital Général is not a medical establishment. It is, rather, a sort of semijudicial structure, an administrative entity which, along with the already constituted powers, and outside of the courts, decides, judges, and executes. "The directors having for these purposes stakes, irons, prisons, and dungeons in the said Hôpital Général and the places thereto appertaining so much as they deem necessary, no appeal will be accepted from the regulations they establish within the said hospital; and as for such regulations as intervene from without, they will be executed according to their form and tenor, notwithstanding opposition or whatsoever appeal made or to be made, and without prejudice to these, and for which, notwithstanding all defense or suits for justice, no distinction will be made." [2] A quasi-absolute sovereignty, jurisdiction without appeal, a writ of execution against which nothing can prevail—the Hôpital Général is a strange power that the king establishes between the police and the courts, at the limits of the law: a third order of repression. The insane whom Pinel would find at Bicêtre and at La Salpêtrière belonged to this world.

In its functioning, or in its purpose, the Hôpital Général had nothing to do with any medical concept. It was an instance of order, of the monarchical and bourgeois order being organized in France during this period. It was directly linked with the royal power which placed it under the authority of the civil government alone; the Grand Almonry of the Realm, which previously formed an ecclesiastical and spiritual mediation in the politics of assistance, was abruptly elided. The king decreed: "We choose to be guardian and protector of the said Hôpital Général as being of our royal founding and especially as it does not depend in any manner whatsoever upon our Grand Almonry, nor upon any of our high officers, but is to be totally exempt from the direction, visitation, and jurisdiction of the officers of the General Reform and others of the Grand Almonry, and from all others to whom we forbid all knowledge and jurisdiction in any fashion or manner whatsoever." The origin of the project had been parliamentary, and the first two administrative heads appointed were the first president of the parliament and the procurator general. But they were soon supplemented by the archbishop of Paris, the president of the Court of Assistance, the president of the Court of Exchequer, the chief of police, and the provost of merchants. Henceforth the "Grand Bureau" had no more than a deliberative role. The actual administration and the real responsibilities were entrusted to agents recruited by co-optation. These were the true governors, the delegates of royal power and bourgeois fortune to the world of poverty. The Revolution was able to give them this testimony: "Chosen from the best families of the bourgeoisie, . . . they brought to their administration disinterested views and pure intentions." [3]

This structure proper to the monarchical and bourgeois order of France, contemporary with its organization in absolutist forms, soon extended its network over the whole of France. An edict of the king, dated June 16, 1676, prescribed the establishment of an *"hôpital général* in each city of his kingdom." Occasionally the measure had been anticipated by the local authorities; the bourgeoisie of Lyons had already organized in 1612 a charity establishment that functioned in an analogous manner. The archbishop of Tours was proud to declare on July 10, 1676, that his "archepiscopal city has happily foreseen the pious intentions of the King and erected an *hôpital général* called La Charité even before the one in Paris, whose order has served as a model for all those subsequently established, within or outside the kingdom." The Charité of Tours, in fact, had been founded in 1656, and the king had endowed it with an income of four thousand livres. Over the entire face of France, *hôpitaux généraux* were opened; on the eve of the Revolution, they were to be found in thirty-two provincial cities.

Even if it had been deliberately excluded from the organization of the *hôpitaux généraux*—by complicity, doubtless, between royal power and bourgeoisie—the Church nonetheless did not remain a stranger to the movement. It reformed its own hospital institutions, redistributed the wealth of its foundations, even created congregations whose purposes were rather analogous to those of the Hôpital Général. Vincent de Paul reorganized Saint-Lazare, the most important of the former lazar houses of Paris; on January 7, 1632, he signed a contract in the name of the Congregationists of the Mission with the "Priory" of Saint-Lazare, which was now to receive "persons detained by order of His Majesty." The Order of Good Sons opened hospitals of this nature in the north of France. The Brothers of Saint John of God, called into France in 1602, founded first the Charité of Paris in the Faubourg Saint-Germain, then Charenton, into which they moved on May 10, 1645. Not far from Paris, they also operated the Charité of Senlis, which opened on October 27, 1670. Some years before, the duchess of Bouillon had donated them the buildings and benefices of La Maladrerie, founded in the fourteenth century by Thibaut de Champagne, at Château-Thierry. They administered also the Charités of Saint-Yon, Pontorson, Cadillac, and Romans. In 1699, the Lazarists founded in Marseilles the establishment that was to become the Hôpital Saint-Pierre. Then, in the eighteenth century, came Armentières (1712), Maréville (1714), the Good Savior of Caen (1735); Saint-Meins of Rennes opened shortly before the Revolution (1780).

The phenomenon has European dimensions. The constitution of an absolute monarchy and the intense Catholic renaissance during the Counter-Reformation produced in France a very particular character of simultaneous competition and complicity between the government and the Church. Elsewhere it assumed quite different forms; but its localization in time was just as precise. The great hospitals, houses of confinement, establishments of religion and public order, of assistance and punishment, of governmental charity and welfare measures, are a phenomenon of the classical period: as universal as itself and almost contemporary with its birth. In German-speaking countries, it was marked by the creation of houses of correction, the *Zuchthäusern*; the first antedates the French houses of confinement (except for the Charité of Lyons); it opened in Hamburg around 1620. The others were founded in the second half of the century: Basel (1667), Breslau (1668), Frankfort (1684), Spandau (1684), Königsberg (1691). They continued to multiply in the eighteenth century; Leipzig first in 1701, then Halle and Cassel in 1717 and 1720, later Brieg and Osnabrück (1756), and finally Torgau in 1771. . . .

Confinement, that massive phenomenon, the signs of which are found all across eighteenth-century Europe, is a "police" matter. Police, in the precise sense that the classical epoch gave to it—that is, the totality of measures which make work possible and necessary for all those who could not live without it; the question Voltaire would soon formulate, Colbert's contemporaries had already asked: "Since you have established yourselves as a people, have you not yet discovered the secret of forcing all the rich to make all the poor work? Are you still ignorant of the first principles of the police?"

Before having the medical meaning we give it, or that at least we like to suppose it has, confinement was required by something quite different from any concern with curing the sick. What made it necessary was an imperative of labor. Our philanthropy prefers to recognize the signs of a benevolence toward sickness where there is only a condemnation of idleness.

Let us return to the first moments of the "Confinement,"

and to that royal edict of April 27, 1656, that led to the creation of the Hôpital Général. From the beginning, the institution set itself the task of preventing "mendicancy and idleness as the source of all disorders." In fact, this was the last of the great measures that had been taken since the Renaissance to put an end to unemployment or at least to begging.[4] In 1532, the parliament of Paris decided to arrest beggars and force them to work in the sewers of the city, chained in pairs. The situation soon reached critical proportions: on March 23, 1534, the order was given "to poor scholars and indigents" to leave the city, while it was forbidden "henceforth to sing hymns before images in the streets." The wars of religion multiplied this suspect crowd, which included peasants driven from their farms, disbanded soldiers or deserters, unemployed workers, impoverished students, and the sick. When Henri IV began the siege of Paris, the city, which had less than 100,000 inhabitants, contained more than 30,000 beggars. An economic revival began early in the seventeenth century; it was decided to reabsorb by force the unemployed who had not regained a place in society; a decree of the parliament dated 1606 ordered the beggars of Paris to be whipped in the public square, branded on the shoulder, shorn, and then driven from the city; to keep them from returning, an ordinance of 1607 established companies of archers at all the city gates to forbid entry to indigents. When the effects of the economic renaissance disappeared with the Thirty Years' War, the problems of mendicancy and idleness reappeared; until the middle of the century, the regular increase of taxes hindered manufactures and augmented unemployment. This was the period of uprisings in Paris (1621), in Lyons (1652), in Rouen (1639). At the same time, the world of labor was disorganized by the appearance of new economic structures; as the large manufactories developed, the guilds lost their powers and their rights, the "General Regulations" prohibited all assemblies of workers, all leagues, all "associations." In many professions, however, the guilds were reconstituted. They were prosecuted, but it seems that the parliaments showed a certain apathy; the parliament of Normandy disclaimed all competence to judge the rioters of Rouen. This is doubtless why the Church intervened and accused the workers' secret gatherings of sorcery. A decree of the Sorbonne, in 1655, proclaimed "guilty of sacrilege and mortal sin" all those who were found in such bad company.

In this silent conflict that opposed the severity of the Church to the indulgence of the parliaments, the creation of the Hôpital was certainly, at least in the beginning, a victory for the parliament. It was, in any case, a new solution. For the first time, purely negative measures of exclusion were replaced by a measure of confinement; the unemployed person was no longer driven away or punished; he was taken in charge, at the expense of the nation but at the cost of his individual liberty. Between him and society, an implicit system of obligation was established: he had the right to be fed, but he must accept the physical and moral constraint of confinement.

It is this entire, rather undifferentiated mass at which the edict of 1657 is aimed: a population without resources, without social moorings, a class rejected or rendered mobile by new economic developments. Less than two weeks after it was signed, the edict was read and proclaimed in the streets. Paragraph 9: "We expressly prohibit and forbid all persons of either sex, of any locality and of any age, of whatever breeding and birth, and in whatever condition they may be, able-bodied or invalid, sick or convalescent, curable or incurable, to beg in the city and suburbs of Paris, neither in the churches, nor at the doors of such, nor at the doors of houses nor in the streets, nor anywhere else in public, nor in secret, by day or night . . . under pain of being whipped for the first offense, and for the second condemned to the galleys if men and boys, banished if women and girls." The year after—Sunday, May 13, 1657—a high mass in honor of the Holy Ghost was sung at the Church of Saint-Louis de la Pitié, and on the morning of Monday the fourteenth, the militia, which was to become, in the mythology of popular terror, "the archers of the Hôpital," began to hunt down beggars and herd them into the different buildings of the Hôpital. Four years later, La Salpêtrière housed 1,460 women and small children; at La Pitié there were 98 boys, 897 girls between seven and seventeen, and 95 women; at Bicêtre, 1,615 adult men; at La Savonnerie, 305 boys between eight and thirteen; finally, Scipion lodged 530 pregnant women, nursing women, and very young children. Initially, married people, even in need, were not admitted; the administration was instructed to feed them at home; but soon, thanks to a grant from Mazarin, it was possible to lodge them at La Salpêtrière. In all, between five and six thousand persons.

Throughout Europe, confinement had the same meaning, at least if we consider its origin. It constituted one of the answers the seventeenth century gave to an economic crisis that affected the entire Western world: reduction of wages, unemployment, scarcity of coin—the coincidence of these phenomena probably being due to a crisis in the Spanish economy. Even England, of all the countries of Western Europe the least dependent on the system, had to solve the same problems. Despite all the measures taken to avoid unemployment and the reduction of wages, poverty continued to spread in the nation. In 1622 appeared a pamphlet, *Grievous Groan for the Poor*, attributed to Thomas Dekker, which, emphasizing the danger, condemns the general negligence: "Though the number of the poor do daily increase, all things yet worketh for the worst in their behalf; . . . many of these parishes turneth forth their poor, yea, and their lusty labourers that will not work . . . to beg, filch, and steal for their maintenance, so that the country is pitifully pestered with them." It was feared that they would overrun the country, and since they could not, as on the Continent, cross the border into another nation, it was proposed that they be "banished and conveyed to the New-found Land, the East and West Indies." In 1630, the king established a commission to assure the rigorous observance of the Poor Laws. That same year, it published a series of "orders and directions"; it recommended prosecuting beggars and vagabonds, as well as "all those who live in idleness and will not work for reasonable wages or who spend what they have in taverns." They must be punished according to law and placed in houses of correction; as for those with wives and children, investigation must be made as to whether they were married and their children baptized, "for these people live like savages without being married, nor buried, nor baptized; and it is this licentious liberty which causes so many to rejoice in vagabondage." Despite the recovery that began in England in the middle of the century, the problem was still unsolved in Cromwell's time, for the lord mayor complains of "this vermin that troops about the city, disturbing public order, assaulting carriages, demanding alms with loud cries at the doors of churches and private houses."

For a long time, the house of correction or the premises of the Hôpital Général would serve to contain the unemployed, the idle, and vagabonds. Each time a crisis occurred and the number of the poor sharply increased, the houses of confinement regained, at least for a time, their initial economic significance. In the middle of the eighteenth century, there was another great crisis: 12,000 begging workers at Rouen and as many at Tours; at Lyons the manufactories closed. The count d'Argenson, "who commands the department of Paris and the marshalseas," gave orders "to arrest all the beggars of the kingdom; the marshalseas will perform this task in the countryside, while the same thing is done in Paris, whither they are sure not to return, being entrapped on all sides."

But outside of the periods of crisis, confinement acquired another meaning. Its repressive function was combined with a new use. It was no longer merely a question of confining those out of work, but of giving work to those who had been confined and thus making them contribute to the prosperity of all. The alternation is clear: cheap manpower in the periods of full employment and high salaries; and in periods of unemployment, reabsorption of the idle and social protection against agitation and uprisings. Let us not forget that the first houses of confinement appear in England in the most industrialized parts of the country: Worcester, Norwich, Bristol; that the first *hôpital général* was opened in Lyons, forty years before that of Paris; that Hamburg was the first German city to have its *Zuchthaus*, in 1620. Its regulations, published in 1622, were quite precise. The internees must all work. Exact record was kept of the value of their work, and they were paid a fourth of it. For work was not only an occupation; it must be productive. The eight directors of the house established a general plan. The *Werkmeister* assigned a task to each, and ascertained at the end of the week that it had been accomplished. The rule of work would remain in effect until the end of the eighteenth century, since John Howard could still attest that they were "knitting and spinning;

weaving stockings, linen, hair, and wool—and rasping logwood and hartshorn. The quota of a robust man who shreds such wood is forty-five pounds a day. Some men and horses labour at a fulling-mill. A blacksmith works there without cease." Each house of confinement in Germany had its specialty: spinning was paramount in Bremen, Brunswick, Munich, Breslau, Berlin; weaving in Hanover. The men shredded wood in Bremen and Hamburg. In Nuremberg they polished optical glass; at Mainz the principal labor was the milling of flour.

The first houses of correction were opened in England during a full economic recession. The act of 1610 recommended only joining certain mills and weaving and carding shops to all houses of correction in order to occupy the pensioners. But what had been a moral requirement became an economic tactic when commerce and industry recovered after 1651, the economic situation having been reestablished by the Navigation Act and the lowering of the discount rate. All able-bodied manpower was to be used to the best advantage, that is, as cheaply as possible. When John Carey established his workhouse project in Bristol, he ranked the need for work first: "The poor of both sexes . . . may be employed in beating hemp, dressing and spinning flax, or in carding wool and cotton." At Worcester, they manufactured clothes and stuffs; a workshop for children was established. All of which did not always proceed without difficulties. It was suggested that the workhouses might enter the local industries and markets, on the principle perhaps that such cheap production would have a regulatory effect on the sale price. But the manufactories protested. Daniel Defoe noticed that by the effect of the too easy competition of the workhouses, poverty was created in one area on the pretext of suppressing it in another; "it is giving to one what you take away from another; putting a vagabond in an honest man's employment, and putting diligence on the tenters to find out some other work to maintain his family." Faced with this danger of competition, the authorities let the work gradually disappear. The pensioners could no longer earn even enough to pay for their upkeep; at times it was necessary to put them in prison so that they might at least have free bread. As for the bridewells, as Howard attested, there were few "in which any work is done, or can be done. The prisoners have neither tools, nor materials of any kind: but spend their time in sloth, profaneness and debauchery."

When the Hôpital Général was created in Paris, it was intended above all to suppress beggary, rather than to provide an occupation for the internees. It seems, however, that Colbert, like his English contemporaries, regarded assistance through work as both a remedy to unemployment and a stimulus to the development of manufactories. In any case, in the provinces the directors were to see that the houses of charity had a certain economic significance. "All the poor who are capable of working must, upon work days, do what is necessary to avoid idleness, which is the mother of all evils, as well as to accustom them to honest toil and also to earning some part of their sustenance."

Sometimes there were even arrangements which permitted private entrepreneurs to utilize the manpower of the asylums for their own profit. It was stipulated, for example, according to an argeement made in 1708, that an entrepreneur should furnish the Charité of Tulle with wool, soap, and coal, and in return the establishment would redeliver the wool carded and spun. The profit was divided between the entrepreneur and the hospital. Even in Paris, several attempts were made to transform the buildings of the Hôpital Général into factories. If we can believe the author of an anonymous *mémoire* that appeared in 1790, at La Pitié "all the varieties of manufacture that could be offered to the capital" were attempted; finally, "in a kind of despair, a manufacture was undertaken of a sort of lacing found to be the least costly." Elsewhere, such efforts were scarcely more fruitful. Numerous efforts were made at Bicêtre: manufacture of thread and rope, mirror polishing, and especially the famous "great well." An attempt was even made, in 1781, to substitute teams of prisoners for the horses that brought up the water, in relay from five in the morning to eight at night: "What reason could have determined this strange occupation? Was it that of economy or simply the necessity of busying the prisoners? If the latter, would it not have been better to occupy them with work more useful both for them and for the hospital? If for reasons of economy, we are a long way from finding any." [5] During the entire eighteenth century, the economic significance Colbert wanted to give the Hôpital Général continued to recede;

that center of forced labor would become a place of privileged idleness. "What is the source of the disorders at Bicêtre?" the men of the Revolution were again to ask. And they would supply the answer that had already been given in the seventeenth century: "It is idleness. What is the means of remedying it? Work."

The classical age used confinement in an equivocal manner, making it play a double role: to reabsorb unemployment, or at least eliminate its most visible social effects, and to control costs when they seemed likely to become too high; to act alternately on the manpower market and on the cost of production. As it turned out, it does not seem that the houses of confinement were able to play effectively the double role that was expected of them. If they absorbed the unemployed, it was mostly to mask their poverty, and to avoid the social or political disadvantages of agitation; but at the very moment the unemployed were herded into forced-labor shops, unemployment increased in neighboring regions or in similar areas. As for the effect on production costs, it could only be artificial, the market price of such products being disproportionate to the cost of manufacture, calculated according to the expenses occasioned by confinement itself.

. . . It was in a certain experience of labor that the indissociably economic and moral demand for confinement was formulated. Between labor and idleness in the classical world ran a line of demarcation that replaced the exclusion of leprosy. The asylum was substituted for the lazar house, in the geography of haunted places as in the landscape of the moral universe. The old rites of excommunication were revived, but in the world of production and commerce. It was in these places of doomed and despised idleness, in this space invented by a society which had derived an ethical transcendence from the law of work, that madness would appear and soon expand until it had annexed them. A day was to come when it could possess these sterile reaches of idleness by a sort of very old and very dim right of inheritance. The nineteenth century would consent, would even insist that to the mad and to them alone be transferred these lands on which, a hundred and fifty years before, men had sought to pen the poor, the vagabond, the unemployed.

It is not immaterial that madmen were included in the proscription of idleness. From its origin, they would have their place beside the poor, deserving or not, and the idle, voluntary or not. Like them, they would be subject to the rules of forced labor. More than once, in fact, they figured in their singular fashion within this uniform constraint. In the workshops in which they were interned, they distinguished themselves by their inability to work and to follow the rhythms of collective life. The necessity, discovered in the eighteenth century, to provide a special regime for the insane and the great crisis of confinement that shortly preceded the Revolution are linked to the experience of madness available in the universal necessity of labor. Men did not wait until the seventeenth century to "shut up" the mad, but it was in this period that they began to "confine" or "intern" them, along with an entire population with whom their kinship was recognized. Until the Renaissance, the sensibility to madness was linked to the presence of imaginary transcendences. In the classical age, for the first time, madness was perceived through a condemnation of idleness and in a social immanence guaranteed by the community of labor. This community acquired an ethical power of segregation, which permitted it to eject, as into another world, all forms of social uselessness. It was in this *other world*, encircled by the sacred powers of labor, that madness would assume the status we now attribute to it. If there is, in classical madness, something which refers elsewhere, and to *other things*, it is no longer because the madman comes from the world of the irrational and bears its stigmata; rather, it is because he crosses the frontiers of bourgeois order of his own accord, and alienates himself outside the sacred limits of its ethic.

In fact, the relation between the practice of confinement and the insistence on work is not defined by economic conditions; far from it. A moral perception sustains and animates it. When the Board of Trade published its report on the poor in which it proposed the means "to render them useful to the public," it was made quite clear that the origin of poverty was neither scarcity of commodities nor unemployment, but "the weakening of discipline and the relaxation of morals." The edict of 1657, too, was full of moral denunciations and strange threats. "The libertinage of beggars has risen to excess because of an unfortunate tolerance of crimes of all sorts, which attract the curse of God upon the State when they remain unpunished." This "libertinage" is not the kind that can be defined in relation to the great law of work, but a moral libertinage: "Experience having taught those persons who are employed in charitable occupations that many among them of either sex live together without marriage, that many of their children are unbaptized, and that almost all of them live in ignorance of religion, disdaining the sacraments, and continually practicing all sorts of vice." Hence the Hôpital does not have the appearance of a mere refuge for those whom age, infirmity, or sickness keep from working; it will have not only the aspect of a forced labor camp, but also that of a moral institution responsible for punishing, for correcting a certain moral "abeyance" which does not merit the tribunal of men, but cannot be corrected by the severity of penance alone. The Hôpital Général has an ethical status. It is this moral charge which invests its directors, and they are granted every judicial apparatus and means of repression: "They have power of authority, of direction, of administration, of commerce, of police, of jurisdiction, of correction and punishment"; and to accomplish this task "stakes, irons, prisons, and dungeons"[6] are put at their disposal.

And it is in this context that the obligation to work assumes its meaning as both ethical exercise and moral guarantee. It will serve as *askesis*, as punishment, as symptom of a certain disposition of the heart. The prisoner who could and who would work would be released, not so much because he was again useful to society, but because he had again subscribed to the great ethical pact of human existence. In April 1684, a decree created within the Hôpital a section for boys and girls under twenty-five; it specified that work must occupy the greater part of the day, and must be accompanied by "the reading of pious books." But the ruling defines the purely repressive nature of this work, beyond any concern for production: "They will be made to work as long and as hard as their strengths and situations will permit." It is then, but only then, that they can be taught an occupation "fitting their sex and inclination," insofar as the measure of their zeal in the first activities makes it possible to "judge that they desire to reform." Finally, every fault "will be punished by reduction of gruel, by increase of work, by imprisonment and other punishments customary in the said hospitals, as the directors shall see fit." It is enough to read the "general regulations for daily life in the House of Saint-Louis de la Salpêtrière" to understand that the very requirement of labor was instituted as an exercise in moral reform and constraint, which reveals, if not the ultimate meaning, at least the essential justification of confinement.

An important phenomenon, this invention of a site of constraint, where morality castigates by means of administrative enforcement. For the first time, institutions of morality are established in which an astonishing synthesis of moral obligation and civil law is effected. The law of nations will no longer countenance the disorder of hearts. To be sure, this is not the first time in European culture that moral error, even in its most private form, has assumed the aspect of a transgression against the written or unwritten laws of the community. But in this great confinement of the classical age, the essential thing—and the new event—is that men were confined in cities of pure morality, where the law that should reign in all hearts was to be applied without compromise, without concession, in the rigorous forms of physical constraint. Morality permitted itself to be administered like trade or economy.

Thus we see inscribed in the institutions of absolute monarchy—in the very ones that long remained the symbol of its arbitrary power—the great bourgeois, and soon republican, idea that virtue, too, is an affair of state, that decrees can be published to make it flourish, that an authority can be established to make sure it is respected. The walls of confinement actually enclose the negative of that moral city of which the bourgeois conscience began to dream in the seventeenth century; a moral city for those who sought, from the start, to avoid it; a city where right reigns only by virtue of a force without appeal—a sort of sovereignty of good, in which intimidation alone prevails and the only recompense of virtue (to this degree its own reward) is to escape punishment. In the shadows of the bourgeois city is born this strange republic of the good which is imposed by force on all those suspected of belonging to evil. This is the underside of the bourgeoisie's great dream and great preoccupation in the classical age: the laws of the state and the laws of the heart at last identical. "Let our politicians leave off their calculations . . . let them learn once and for all that everything can be had for money, except morals and citizens." [7]

All [the] prisons of moral order might have borne the motto which Howard could still read on the one in Mainz: "If wild beasts can be broken to the yoke, it must not be despaired of correcting the man who has strayed." For the Catholic Church, as in the Protestant countries, confinement represents, in the form of an authoritarian model, the myth of social happiness: a police whose order will be entirely transparent to the principles of religion, and a religion whose requirements will be satisfied, without restrictions, by the regulations of the police and the constraints with which it can be armed. There is, in these institutions, an attempt of a kind to demonstrate that order may be adequate to virtue. In this sense, "confinement" conceals both a metaphysics of government and a politics of religion; it is situated, as an effort of tyrannical synthesis, in the vast space separating the garden of God and the cities which men, driven from paradise, have built with their own hands. The house of confinement in the classical age constitutes the densest symbol of that "police" which conceived of itself as the civil equivalent of religion for the edification of a perfect city. . . .

Notes

[1] Edict of 1656, Article IV. Later the Saint-Esprit and the Enfants-Trouvés would be added, and the Savonnerie withdrawn.

[2] Ibid., Article XII.

[3] La Rochefoucauld-Liancourt's report in the name of the Committee on Mendicity to the Constituent Assembly, *Procès verbaux de l'Assemblée nationale*, Vol. XXI.

[4] From a spiritual point of view, poverty at the end of the sixteenth and the beginning of the seventeenth century was experienced as an apocalyptic threat. "One of the most evident signs that the coming of the

Son of God and the end of time are at hand is the extreme of both spiritual and temporal poverty to which the world is reduced. These are evil days . . . afflictions have multiplied because of the multitude of transgressions, pain being the inseparable shadow of evil" (Jean-Pierre Camus, *De la mendicité légitime des pauvres* [Douai, 1634], pp. 3–4).

[5] Musquinet de la Pagne, *Bicêtre réformé ou établissement d'une maison de discipline* (Paris, 1790), p. 22.

[6] Regulations of the Hôpital Général, Articles XII and XIII.

[7] Jean-Jacques Rousseau, *Discours sur les sciences et les arts*.

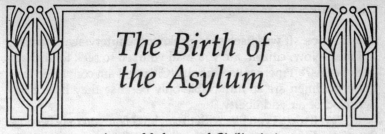

The Birth of the Asylum

(FROM *Madness and Civilization*)

We know the images. They are familiar in all histories of psychiatry, where their function is to illustrate that happy age when madness was finally recognized and treated according to a truth to which we had too long remained blind.

"The worthy Society of Friends . . . sought to assure those of its members who might have the misfortune to lose their reason without a sufficient fortune to resort to expensive establishments all the resources of medicine and all the comforts of life compatible with their state; a voluntary subscription furnished the funds, and for the last two years, an establishment that seems to unite many advantages with all possible economy has been founded near the city of York. If the soul momentarily quails at the sight of that dread disease which seems created to humiliate human reason, it subsequently experiences gentler emotions when it considers all that an ingenious benevolence has been able to invent for its care and cure.

"This house is situated a mile from York, in the midst of a fertile and smiling countryside; it is not at all the idea of a prison that it suggests, but rather that of a large farm; it is surrounded by a great, walled garden. No bars, no grilles on the windows." [1]

As for the liberation of the insane at Bicêtre, the story is famous: the decision to remove the chains from the prisoners in the dungeons; Couthon visiting the hospital to find out whether any suspects were being hidden; Pinel courageously going to meet him, while everyone trembled at the sight of the "invalid carried in men's arms." The confrontation of the wise, firm philanthropist and the paralytic monster. "Pinel immediately led him to the section for the deranged, where the sight of the cells made a painful impression on him. He asked to interrogate all the patients. From most, he received only insults and obscene

141

apostrophes. It was useless to prolong the interview. Turning to Pinel: 'Now, citizen, are you mad yourself to seek to unchain such beasts?' Pinel replied calmly: 'Citizen, I am convinced that these madmen are so intractable only because they have been deprived of air and liberty.'

" 'Well, do as you like with them, but I fear you may become the victim of your own presumption.' Whereupon, Couthon was taken to his carriage. His departure was a relief; everyone breathed again; the great philanthropist immediately set to work." [2]

These are images, at least insofar as each of the stories derives the essence of its power from imaginary forms: the patriarchal calm of Tuke's home, where the heart's passions and the mind's disorders slowly subside; the lucid firmness of Pinel, who masters in a word and a gesture the two animal frenzies that roar against him as they hunt him down; and the wisdom that could distinguish, between the raving madman and the bloodthirsty member of the Convention, which was the true danger: images that will carry far—to our own day—their weight of legend.

The legends of Pinel and Tuke transmit mythical values, which nineteenth-century psychiatry would accept as obvious in nature. But beneath the myths themselves, there was an operation, or rather a series of operations, which silently organized the world of the asylum, the methods of cure, and at the same time the concrete experience of madness.

Tuke's gesture, first of all. Because it is contemporary with Pinel's, because he is known to have been borne along by a whole current of "philanthropy," this gesture is regarded as an act of "liberation." The truth was quite different: "there has also been particular occasion to observe the great loss, which individuals of our society have sustained, by being put under the care of those who are not only strangers to our principles, but by whom they are frequently mixed with other patients, who may indulge themselves in ill language, and other exceptionable practices. This often seems to leave an unprofitable effect upon the patients' minds after they are restored to the use of their reason, alienating them from those religious attachments which they had before experienced; and sometimes, even corrupting them with vicious habits to which they had been strangers."³ The Retreat would serve as an instrument of segregation: a moral and religious segregation which sought to reconstruct around madness a milieu as much as possible like that of the Community of Quakers. And this for two reasons: first, the sight of evil is for every sensitive soul the cause of suffering, the origin of all those strong and untoward passions such as horror, hate, and disgust which engender or perpetuate madness: "It was thought, very justly, that the indiscriminate mixture, which must occur in large public establishments, of persons of opposite religious sentiments and practices; of the profligate and the virtuous; the profane and the serious; was calculated to check the progress of returning reason, and to fix, still deeper, the melancholy and misanthropic train of ideas."⁴ But the principal reason lies elsewhere: it is that religion can play the double role of nature and of rule, since it has assumed the depth of nature in ancestral habit, in education, in everyday exercise, and since it is at the same time a constant principle of coercion. It is both spontaneity and constraint, and to this degree it controls the only forces that can, in reason's eclipse, counterbalance the measureless violence of madness; its precepts, "where these have been strongly imbued in early life . . . become little less than principles of our nature; and their restraining power is frequently felt, even under the delirious excitement of insanity. To encourage the influence of religious principles over the mind of the insane is considered of great consequence, as a means of cure."⁵ In the dialectic of insanity, where reason hides without abolishing itself, religion constitutes the concrete form of what cannot go mad; it bears what is invincible in reason; it bears what subsists beneath madness as quasi-nature and around it as the constant solicitation of a milieu "where, during lucid intervals, or the state of convalescence, the patient might enjoy the society of those who [are] of similar habits and opinions." Religion safeguards the old secret of reason in the presence of madness, thus making closer, more immediate, the constraint that was already rampant in classical confinement. There, the religious and moral milieu was imposed from without, in such a way that madness was controlled, not cured. At the Retreat, religion was part of the movement which indicated in spite of everything the presence of reason in madness, and which led from insanity to health. Religious segregation has a very precise meaning: it does not attempt to preserve the sufferers from the profane presence of non-Quakers, but to place the insane individual within a moral element where he will be in debate with himself and his surroundings: to constitute for him a milieu where, far from being protected, he will be kept in a perpetual anxiety, ceaselessly threatened by Law and Transgression.

"The principle of fear, which is rarely decreased by insanity, is considered as of great importance in the management of the patients."[6] Fear appears as an essential presence in the asylum. Already an ancient figure, no doubt, if we think of the terrors of confinement. But these terrors surrounded madness from the outside, marking the boundary of reason and unreason, and enjoying a double power: over the violence of fury in order to contain it, and over reason itself to hold it at a distance; such fear was entirely on the surface. The fear instituted at the Retreat is of great depth; it passes between reason and madness like a mediation, like an evocation of a common nature they still share, and by which it could link them together. The terror that once reigned was the most visible sign of the alienation of madness in the classical period; fear was now endowed with a power of disalienation, which permitted it to restore a primitive complicity between the madman and the man of reason. It reestablished a solidarity between them. Now madness would never—could never—cause fear again; it would *be afraid* without recourse or return, thus entirely in the hands of the pedagogy of good sense, of truth, and of morality.

Samuel Tuke tells how he received at the Retreat a maniac, young and prodigiously strong, whose seizures caused panic in those around him and even among his guards. When he entered the Retreat he was loaded with chains; he wore handcuffs; his clothes were attached by ropes. He had no sooner arrived than all his shackles were removed, and he was permitted to dine with the keepers; his agitation immediately ceased; "his attention appeared to be arrested by his new situation." He was taken to his room; the keeper explained that the entire house was organized in terms of the greatest liberty and the greatest comfort for all, and that he would not be subject to any constraint so long as he did nothing against the rules of the house or the general principles of human morality. For his part, the keeper declared he had no desire to use the means of coercion at his disposal. "The maniac was sensible of the kindness of his treatment. *He promised to restrain himself.*" He sometimes still raged, shouted, and frightened his companions. The keeper reminded him of the threats and promises of the first day; if he did not control himself, it would be necessary to go back to the old ways. The patient's agitation would then increase for a while, and then rapidly decline. "He would listen with attention to the persuasions and arguments of his friendly visitor. After such conversations, the patient was generally better for some days or a week." At the end of four months, he left the Retreat, entirely cured. Here fear is addressed to the invalid directly, not by instruments but in speech; there is no question of limiting a liberty that rages beyond its bounds, but of marking out and glorifying a region of simple responsibility where any manifestation of madness will be linked to punishment. The obscure guilt that once linked transgression and unreason is thus shifted; the madman, as a human being originally endowed with reason, is no longer guilty of being mad; but the madman, as a madman, and in the interior of that disease of which he is no longer guilty, must feel morally responsible for everything within him that may disturb morality and society, and must hold no one but himself responsible for the punishment he receives. The assignation of guilt is no longer the mode of relation that obtains between the madman and the sane man in their generality; it becomes both the concrete form of coexistence of each madman with his keeper, and the form of awareness that the madman must have of his own madness.

We must therefore reevaluate the meanings assigned to Tuke's work: liberation of the insane, abolition of constraint, constitution of a human milieu—these are only justifications. The real operations were different. In fact, Tuke created an asylum where he substituted for the free terror of madness the stifling anguish of responsibility; fear no longer reigned on the other side of the prison gates, it now raged under the seals of conscience. Tuke now transferred the age-old terrors in which the insane had been trapped to the very heart of madness. The asylum no longer punished the madman's guilt, it is true; but it did more, it organized that guilt; it organized it for the madman as a consciousness of himself, and as a nonreciprocal relation to the keeper; it organized it for the man of reason as an awareness of the other, a therapeutic intervention in the madman's existence. In other words, by this guilt the madman became an object of punishment always vulnerable to himself and to the other; and, from the acknowledgment of his status as object, from the awareness of his guilt, the madman was to return to his awareness of himself as a free and responsible subject, and consequently to reason. This movement by which, objectifying himself for the other, the madman thus returned to his liberty, was to be found as much in Work as in Observation. . . .

Pinel advocates no religious segregation. Or rather, a segregation that functions in the opposite direction from that practiced by Tuke. The benefits of the renovated asylum were offered to all, or almost all, except the fanatics "who believe themselves inspired and seek to make converts." Bicêtre and La Salpêtrière, according to Pinel's intention, form a complementary figure to the Retreat.

Religion must not be the moral substratum of life in the asylum, but purely and simply a medical object: "Religious opinions in a hospital for the insane must be considered only in a strictly medical relation, that is, one must set aside all other considerations of public worship and political belief, and investigate only whether it is necessary to oppose the exaltation of ideas and feelings that may originate in this source, in order to effect the cure of certain alienated minds." [7] A source of strong emotions and terrifying images which it arouses through fears of the Beyond, Catholicism frequently provokes madness; it generates delirious beliefs, entertains hallucinations, leads men to despair and to melancholia. We must not be surprised if, "examining the registers of the insane asylum at Bicêtre, we find inscribed there many priests and monks, as well as country people maddened by a frightening picture of the future." Still less surprising is it to see the number of religious madnesses vary.

Under the Old Regime and during the Revolution, the strength of superstitious beliefs, or the violence of the struggles in which the Republic opposed the Catholic Church, multiplied melancholias of religious origin. With the return of peace, the Concordat having erased the struggles, these forms of delirium disappeared; in the Year X, fifty percent of the melancholics in Bicêtre were suffering from religious madness, thirty-three percent the following year, and only eighteen percent in the Year XII. The asylum must thus be freed from religion and from all its iconographic connections; "melancholics by devotion" must not be allowed their pious books; experience "teaches that this is the surest means of perpetuating insanity or even of making it incurable, and the more such permission is granted, the less we manage to calm anxiety and scruples." Nothing takes us further from Tuke and his dreams of a religious community that would at the same time be a privileged site of mental cures, than this notion of a neutralized asylum, purified of those images and passions to which Christianity gave birth and which made the mind wander toward illusion, toward terror, and soon toward delirium and hallucinations.

But Pinel's problem was to reduce the iconographic forms, not the moral content of religion. Once "filtered," religion possesses a disalienating power that dissipates the images, calms the passions, and restores man to what is most immediate and essential: it can bring him closer to his moral truth. And it is here that religion is often capable of effecting cures. Pinel relates several Voltairean stories. One, for example, of a woman of twenty-five, "of strong constitution, united in wedlock to a weak and delicate man"; she suffered "quite violent fits of hysteria, imagining she was possessed by a demon who followed her in different shapes, sometimes emitting bird noises, sometimes mournful sounds and piercing cries." Happily, the local curé was more concerned with natural religion than learned in the techniques of exorcism; he believed in curing through the benevolence of nature; this "enlightened man, of kindly and persuasive character, gained ascendancy over the patient's mind and managed to induce her to leave her bed, to resume her domestic tasks, and even to spade her garden. . . . This was followed by the most fortunate effects, and by a cure that lasted three years." Restored to the extreme simplicity of this moral content, religion could not help conniving with philosophy and with medicine, with all the forms of wisdom and science that can restore the reason in a disturbed mind. There are even instances of religion serving as a preliminary treatment, preparing for what will be done in the asylum: take the case of the young girl "of an ardent temperament, though very docile and pious," who was torn between "the inclinations of her heart and the severe principles of her conduct"; her confessor, after having vainly counseled her to attach herself to God, proposed examples of a firm and measured holiness, and "offered her the best remedy against high passions: patience and time." Taken to La Salpêtrière, she was treated, on Pinel's orders, "according to the same moral principles," and her illness proved "of very short duration." Thus the asylum assimilates not the social theme of a religion in which men feel themselves brothers in the same communion and the same community, but the moral power of consolation, of confidence, and a docile fidelity to nature. It must resume the moral enterprise of religion, exclusive of its fantastic text, exclusively on the level of virtue, labor, and social life.

The asylum is a religious domain without religion, a domain of pure morality, of ethical uniformity. Everything that might retain the signs of the old differences was eliminated. The last vestiges of rite were extinguished. Formerly the house of confinement had inherited, in the social sphere, the almost absolute limits of the lazar house; it was a foreign country. Now the asylum must represent the great continuity of social morality. The values of family and work, all the acknowledged virtues, now reign in the asylum. But their reign is a double one. First, they prevail in fact, at the heart of madness itself; beneath the violence and disorder of insanity, the solid nature of the essential virtues is not disrupted. There is a primitive morality which is ordinarily not affected even by the worst dementia; it is this morality which both appears and functions in the cure: "I can generally testify to the pure virtues and severe principles often manifested by the cure. Nowhere except in novels have I seen spouses more worthy of being cherished, parents more tender, lovers more passionate, or persons more attached to their duties than the majority of the insane fortunately brought to the period of convalescence." [8] This inalienable virtue is both the truth and the resolution of madness. Which is why, if it reigns, it *must* reign as well. The asylum reduces differences, represses vice, eliminates irregularities. It denounces everything that opposes the essential virtues of society: celibacy—"the number of girls fallen into idiocy is seven times greater than the number of married women for the Year XI and the Year XIII; for dementia, the proportion is two to four times greater; we can thus deduce that marriage constitutes for women a kind of preservative against the two sorts of insanity which are most inveterate and most often incurable"; debauchery, misconduct, and "extreme perversity of habits"—"vicious habits such as drunkenness, limitless promiscuity, an apathetic lack of concern can gradually degrade the reason and end in outright insanity"; laziness—"it is the most constant and unanimous result of experience that in all public asylums, as in prisons and hospitals, the surest and perhaps the sole guarantee of the maintenance of health and good habits and order is the law of rigorously executed mechanical work." The asylum sets itself the task of the homogeneous rule of morality, its rigorous extension to all those who tend to escape from it.

But it thereby generates an indifference; if the law does not reign universally, it is because there are men who do not recognize it, a class of society that lives in disorder, in negligence, and almost in illegality: "If on the one hand we see families prosper for a long series of years in the bosom of harmony and order and concord, how many others, especially in the lower classes, afflict the eye with a repulsive spectacle of debauchery, of dissensions, and shameful distress! That, according to my daily notes, is the most fertile source of the insanity we treat in the hospitals." [9]

In one and the same movement, the asylum becomes, in Pinel's hands, an instrument of moral uniformity and of social denunciation. The problem is to impose, in a universal form, a morality that will prevail from within upon those who are strangers to it and in whom insanity is already present before it has made itself manifest. In the first case, the asylum must act as an awakening and a reminder, invoking a forgotten nature; in the second, it must act by means of a social shift in order to snatch the individual from his condition. The operation as practiced at the Retreat was still simple: religious segregation for purposes of moral purification. The operation as practiced by Pinel was relatively complex: to effect moral syntheses, assuring an ethical continuity between the world of madness and the world of reason, but by practicing a social segregation that would guarantee bourgeois morality a universality of fact and permit it to be imposed as a law upon all forms of insanity.

In the classical period, indigence, laziness, vice, and madness mingled in an equal guilt within unreason; madmen were caught in the great confinement of poverty and unemployment, but all had been promoted, in the proximity of transgression, to the essence of a Fall. Now madness belonged to social failure, which appeared without distinction as its cause, model, and limit. Half a century later, mental disease would become degeneracy. Henceforth, the essential madness, and the really dangerous one, was that which rose from the lower depths of society.

Pinel's asylum would never be, as a retreat from the world, a space of nature and immediate truth like Tuke's, but a uniform domain of legislation, a site of moral syntheses where insanities born on the outer limits of society were eliminated. The entire life of the inmates, and the entire conduct of their keepers and doctors, were organized by Pinel so that these moral syntheses would function. And this by three principal means:

1. *Silence.* The fifth chained prisoner released by Pinel was a former ecclesiastic whose madness had caused him to be excommunicated; suffering from delusions of grandeur, he believed he was Christ; this was "the height of human arrogance in delirium." Sent to Bicêtre in 1782, he had been in chains for twelve years. For the pride of his bearing, the grandiloquence of his ideas, he was one of the most celebrated spectacles of the entire hospital, but as he knew that he was reliving Christ's Passion, "he endured with patience this long martyrdom and the continual sarcasms his mania exposed him to." Pinel chose him as one of the first twelve to be released, though his delirium was still acute. But Pinel did not treat him as he did the others;

without a word, he had his chains struck off, and "ordered expressly that everyone imitate his own reserve and not address a word to this poor madman. This prohibition, which was rigorously observed, produced upon this self-intoxicated creature an effect much more perceptible than irons and the dungeon; he felt humiliated in an abandon and an isolation so new to him amid his freedom. Finally, after long hesitations, they saw him come of his own accord to join the society of the other patients; henceforth, he returned to more sensible and true ideas." [10]

Deliverance here has a paradoxical meaning. The dungeon, the chains, the continual spectacle, the sarcasms were, to the sufferer in his delirium, the very element of his liberty. Acknowledged in that very fact and fascinated from without by so much complicity, he could not be dislodged from his immediate truth. But the chains that fell, the indifference and silence of all those around him, confined him in the limited use of an empty liberty; he was delivered in silence to a truth which was not acknowledged and which he would demonstrate in vain, since he was no longer a spectacle, and from which he could derive no exaltation, since he was not even humiliated. It was the man himself, not his projection in a delirium, who was now humiliated: for physical constraint yielded to a liberty that constantly touched the limits of solitude; the dialogue of delirium and insult gave way to a monologue in a language which exhausted itself in the silence of others; the entire show of presumption and outrage was replaced by indifference. Henceforth, more genuinely confined than he could have been in a dungeon and chains, a prisoner of nothing but himself, the sufferer was caught in a relation to himself that was of the order of transgression, and in a nonrelation to others that was of the order of shame. The others are made innocent, they are no longer persecutors; the guilt is shifted inside, showing the madman that he was fascinated by nothing but his own presumption; the enemy faces disappear; he no longer feels their presence as observation, but as denial of attention, as observation deflected; the others are now nothing but a limit that ceaselessly recedes as he advances. Delivered from his chains, he is now chained, by silence, to transgression and to shame. He feels himself punished, and he sees the sign of his innocence in that fact; free from all physical punishment, he must prove himself guilty. His torment was his glory; his deliverance must humiliate him.

Compared to the incessant dialogue of reason and madness during the Renaissance, classical internment had been a silencing. But it was not total: language was engaged in things rather than really suppressed. Confinement, prisons, dungeons, even tortures, engaged in a mute dialogue between reason and unreason—the dialogue of struggle. This dialogue itself was now disengaged; silence was absolute; there was no longer any common language between madness and reason; the language of delirium can be answered only by an absence of language, for delirium is not a fragment of dialogue with reason, it is not language at all; it refers, in an ultimately silent awareness, only to transgression. And it is only at this point that a common language becomes possible again, insofar as it will be one of acknowledged guilt. "Finally, after long hesitation, they saw him come of his own accord to join the society of the other patients." The absence of language, as a fundamental structure of asylum life, has its correlative in the exposure of confession. When Freud, in psychoanalysis, cautiously reinstitutes exchange, or rather begins once again to listen to this language, henceforth eroded into monologue, should we be astonished that the formulations he hears are always those of transgression? In this inveterate silence, transgression has taken over the very sources of speech.

2. *Recognition by Mirror.* At the Retreat, the madman was observed, and knew he was observed; but except for that direct observation which permitted only an indirect apprehension of itself, madness had no immediate grasp of its own character. With Pinel, on the contrary, observation operated only within the space defined by madness, without surface or exterior limits. Madness would see itself, would be seen by itself—pure spectacle and absolute subject.

"Three insane persons, each of whom believed himself to be a king, and each of whom took the title Louis XVI, quarreled one day over the prerogatives of royalty, and defended them somewhat too energetically. The keeper approached one of them, and drawing him aside, asked: 'Why do you argue with these men who are evidently mad? Doesn't everyone know that you should be recognized as Louis XVI?' Flattered by his homage, the madman immediately withdrew, glancing at the others with a disdainful hauteur. The same trick worked with the second patient. And thus in an instant there no longer remained any trace of an argument." [11] This is the first phase, that of exaltation. Madness is made to observe itself, but in others: it appears in them as a baseless pretense—in other words, as absurd. However, in this observation that condemns others, the madman assures his own justification and the certainty of being adequate to his delirium. The rift between presumption and reality allows itself to be recognized only in the object. It is entirely masked, on the contrary, in the subject, which becomes immediate truth and absolute judge: the exalted sovereignty that denounces the others' false sovereignty dispossesses them and thus confirms itself in the unfailing plenitude of presumption. Madness, as simple delirium, is projected onto others; as perfect unconsciousness, it is entirely accepted.

It is at this point that the mirror, as an accomplice, becomes an agent of demystification. Another inmate of Bicêtre, also believing himself a king, always expressed himself "in a tone of command and with supreme authority." One day when he was calmer, the keeper approached him and asked why, if he were a sovereign, he did not put an end to his detention, and why he remained mingled with madmen of all kinds. Resuming this speech the following days, "he made him see, little by little, the absurdity of his pretensions, showed him another madman who had also been long convinced that he possessed supreme power and had become an object of mockery. At first the maniac felt shaken, soon he cast doubts upon his title of sovereign, and finally he came to realize his chimerical vagaries. It was in two weeks that this unexpected moral revolution took place, and after several months of tests, this worthy father was restored to his family." [12] This, then, is the phase of abasement: presumptuously identified with the object of his delirium, the madman recognizes himself as in a mirror in this madness whose absurd pretensions he has denounced; his solid sovereignty as a subject dissolves in this object he has demystified by accepting it. He is now pitilessly observed by himself. And in the silence of those who represent reason, and who have done nothing but hold up the perilous mirror, he recognizes himself as objectively mad.

We have seen by what means—and by what mystifications—eighteenth-century therapeutics tried to persuade the madman of his madness in order to release him from it. Here the movement is of an entirely different nature; it is not a question of dissipating error by the impressive spectacle of a truth, even a pretended truth; but of treating madness in its arrogance rather than in its aberration. The classical mind condemned in madness a certain blindness to the truth; from Pinel on, madness would be regarded, rather, as an impulse from the depths which exceeds the juridical limits of the individual, ignores the moral limits fixed for him, and tends to an apotheosis of the self. For the nineteenth century, the initial model of madness would be to believe oneself to be God, while for the preceding centuries it had been to deny God. Thus madness, in the spectacle of itself as unreason humiliated, was able to find its salvation when, imprisoned in the absolute subjectivity of its delirium, it surprised the absurd and objective image of that delirium in the identical madman. Truth insinuated itself, as if by surprise (and not by violence, in the eighteenth-century mode), in this play of reciprocal observations where it never saw anything but itself. But the asylum, in this community of madmen, placed the mirrors in such a way that the madman, when all was said and done, inevitably surprised himself, despite himself, *as a madman*. Freed from the chains that made it a purely observed object, madness lost, paradoxically, the essence of its liberty, which was solitary exaltation; it became responsible for what it knew of its truth; it imprisoned itself in an infinitely self-referring observation; it was finally chained to the humiliation of being its own object. Awareness was now linked to the shame of being identical to that other, of being compromised in him, and of already despising oneself before being able to recognize or to know oneself.

3. *Perpetual Judgment.* By this play of mirrors, as by silence, madness is ceaselessly called upon to judge itself. But beyond

this, it is at every moment judged from without; judged not by moral or scientific conscience, but by a sort of invisible tribunal in permanent session. The asylum Pinel dreamed of and partly realized at Bicêtre, but especially at La Salpêtrière, is a juridical microcosm. To be efficacious, this judgment must be redoubtable in aspect; all the iconographic apanage of the judge and the executioner must be present in the mind of the madman, so that he understands what universe of judgment he now belongs to. The decor of justice, in all its terror and implacability, will thus be part of the treatment. One of the inmates at Bicêtre suffered from a religious delirium animated by a fear of hell; he believed that the only way he could escape eternal damnation was by rigorous abstinence. It was necessary to compensate this fear of a remote justice by the presence of a more immediate and still more redoubtable one: "Could the irresistible curse of his sinister ideas be counterbalanced other than by the impression of a strong and deep fear?" One evening, the director came to the patient's door "with matter likely to produce fear—an angry eye, a thundering tone of voice, a group of staff armed with strong chains that they shook noisily. They set some soup beside the madman and gave him precise orders to eat it during the night, or else suffer the most cruel treatment. They retired, and left the madman in the most distressed state of indecision between the punishment with which he was threatened and the frightening prospect of the torments in the life to come. After an inner combat of several hours, the former idea prevailed, and he decided to take some nourishment." [13]

The asylum as a juridical instance recognized no other. It judged immediately, and without appeal. It possessed its own instruments of punishment, and used them as it saw fit. The old confinement had generally been practiced outside of normal juridical forms, but it imitated the punishment of criminals, using the same prisons, the same dungeons, the same physical brutality. The justice that reigned in Pinel's asylum did not borrow its modes of repression from the other justice, but invented its own. Or rather, it used the therapeutic methods that had become known in the eighteenth century, but used them as chastisements. And this is not the least of the paradoxes of Pinel's "philanthropic" and "liberating" enterprise, this conversion of medicine into justice, of therapeutics into repression. In the medicine of the classical period, baths and showers were used as remedies as a result of the physicians' vagaries about the nature of the nervous system: the intention was to refresh the organism, to relax the desiccated fibers; it is true that they also added, among the happy consequences of the cold shower, the psychological effect of the unpleasant surprise which interrupted the course of ideas and changed the nature of sentiments; but we were still in the landscape of medical speculation. With Pinel, the use of the shower became frankly juridical; the shower was the habitual punishment of the ordinary police tribunal that sat permanently at the asylum: "Considered as a means of repression, it often suffices to subject to the general law of manual labor a madman who is susceptible to it, in order to conquer an obstinate refusal to take nourishment, and to subjugate insane persons carried away by a sort of turbulent and reasoned humor."

Everything was organized so that the madman would recognize himself in a world of judgment that enveloped him on all sides; he must know that he is watched, judged, and condemned; from transgression to punishment, the connection must be evident, as a guilt recognized by all: "We profit from the circumstance of the bath, remind him of the transgression, or of the omission of an important duty, and with the aid of a faucet suddenly release a shower of cold water upon his head, which often disconcerts the madman or drives out a predominant idea by a strong and unexpected impression; if the idea persists, the shower is repeated, but care is taken to avoid the hard tone and the shocking terms that would cause rebellion; on the contrary, the madman is made to understand that it is for his sake and reluctantly that we resort to such violent measures; sometimes we add a joke, taking care not to go too far with it." [14] This almost arithmetical obviousness of punishment, repeated as often as necessary, the recognition of transgression by its repression—all this must end in the internalization of the juridical instance, and the birth of remorse in the inmate's mind: it is only at this point that the judges agree to stop the punishment, certain that it will continue indefinitely in the inmate's conscience. One maniac had the habit of tearing her clothes and breaking any object that came into her hands; she was given showers, she was put into a straitjacket, she finally appeared "humiliated and dismayed"; but fearing that this shame might be transitory and this remorse too superficial, "the director, in order to impress a feeling of terror upon her, spoke to her with the most energetic firmness, but without anger, and announced to her that she would henceforth be treated with the greatest severity." The desired result was not long in coming: "Her repentance was announced by a torrent of tears which she shed for almost two hours." The cycle is complete twice over: the transgression is punished and its author recognizes her guilt.

There were, however, madmen who escaped from this movement and resisted the moral synthesis it brought about. These latter would be set apart in the heart of the asylum, forming a new confined population, which could not even relate to justice. When we speak of Pinel and his work of liberation, we too often omit this second reclusion. We have already seen that he denied the benefits of asylum reform to "fanatics who believe themselves inspired and seek to make converts, and who take a perfidious pleasure in inciting the other madmen to disobedience on the pretext that it is better to obey God than man." But confinement and the dungeon will be equally obligatory for "those who cannot be subjected to the general law of work and who, in malicious activity, enjoy tormenting the other inmates, provoking and ceaselessly inciting them to subjects of discord," and for women "who during their seizures have an irresistible propensity to steal anything they can lay their hands on." Disobedience by religious fanaticism, resistance to work, and theft, the three great transgressions against bourgeois society, the three major offenses against its essential values, are not excusable, even by madness; they deserve imprisonment pure and simple, exclusion in the most rigorous sense of the term, since they all manifest the same resistance to the moral and social uniformity that forms the *raison d'être* of Pinel's asylum.

Formerly, unreason was set outside of judgment, to be delivered, arbitrarily, to the powers of reason. Now it is judged, and not only upon entering the asylum, in order to be recognized, classified, and made innocent forever; it is caught, on the contrary, in a perpetual judgment, which never ceases to pursue it and to apply sanctions, to proclaim its transgressions, to require honorable amends, to exclude, finally, those whose transgressions risk compromising the social order. Madness escaped from the arbitrary only in order to enter a kind of endless trial for which the asylum furnished simultaneously police, magistrates, and torturers; a trial whereby any transgression in life, by a virtue proper to life in the asylum, becomes a social crime, observed, condemned, and punished; a trial which has no outcome but in a perpetual recommencement in the internalized form of remorse. The madmen "delivered" by Pinel and, after him, the madmen of modern confinement are under arraignment; if they have the privilege of no longer being associated or identified with convicts, they are condemned, at every moment, to be subject to an accusation whose text is never given, for it is their entire life in the asylum which constitutes it. The asylum of the age of positivism, which it is Pinel's glory to have founded, is not a free realm of observation, diagnosis, and therapeutics; it is a juridical space where one is accused, judged, and condemned, and from which one is never released except by the version of this trial in psychological depth—that is, by remorse. Madness will be punished in the asylum, even if it is innocent outside of it. For a long time to come, and until our own day at least, it is imprisoned in a moral world.

To silence, to recognition in the mirror, to perpetual judgment, we must add a fourth structure peculiar to the world of the asylum as it was constituted at the end of the eighteenth century: this is the apotheosis of the *medical personage*. Of them all, it is doubtless the most important, since it would authorize not only new contacts between doctor and patient, but a new relation between insanity and medical thought, and ultimately command the whole modern experience of madness. Hitherto, we find in the asylums only the same structures of confinement, but displaced and deformed. With the new status of the medical personage, the deepest meaning of confinement is abolished: mental disease, with the meanings we now give it, is made possible.

The work of Tuke and of Pinel, whose spirit and values are so different, meet in this transformation of the medical personage. The physician, as we have seen, played no part in the life of confinement. Now he becomes the essential figure of the asylum. He is in charge of entry. The ruling at the Retreat is precise: "On the admission of patients, the committee should, in general, require a certificate signed by a medical person. . . . It should also be stated whether the patient is afflicted with any complaint independent of insanity. It is also desirable that some account should be sent, how long the patient has been disordered; whether any, or what sort of medical means have been used." [15] From the end of the eighteenth century, the medical certificate becomes almost obligatory for the confinement of madmen. But within the asylum itself, the doctor takes a preponderant place, insofar as he converts it into a medical space. However, and this is the essential point, the doctor's intervention is not made by virtue of a medical skill or power that he possesses in himself and that would be justified by a body of objective knowledge. It is not as a scientist that *homo medicus* has authority in the asylum, but as a wise man. If the medical profession is required, it is as a juridical and moral guarantee, not in the name of science. A man of great probity, of utter virtue and scruple, who had had long experience in the asylum, would do as well. For the medical enterprise is only a part of an enormous moral task that must be accomplished at the asylum, and which alone can ensure the cure of the insane: "Must it not be an inviolable law in the administration of any establishment for the insane, whether public or private, to grant the maniac all the liberty that the safety of his person and of that of others permits, and to proportion his repression to the greater or lesser seriousness of danger of his deviations . . . , to gather all the facts that can serve to enlighten the physician in treatment, to study with care the particular varieties of behavior and temperament, and accordingly to use gentleness or firmness, conciliatory terms or the tone of authority and an inflexible severity?" [16] According to Samuel Tuke, the first doctor appointed at the Retreat was recommended by his "indefatigable perseverance"; doubtless he had no particular knowledge of mental illnesses when he entered the asylum, but "he entered on his office with the anxiety and ardor of a feeling mind, upon the exertion of whose skill, depended the dearest interest of many of his fellow-creatures." He tried the various remedies that his own common sense and the experience of his predecessors suggested. But he was soon disappointed, not because the results were bad, or the number of cures was minimal: "Yet the medical means were so imperfectly connected with the progress of recovery, that he could not avoid suspecting them, to be rather concomitants than causes." He then realized that there was little to be done using the medical methods known up to that time. The concern for humanity prevailed within him, and he decided to use no medicament that would be too disagreeable to the patient. But it must not be thought that the doctor's role had little importance at the Retreat: by the visits he paid regularly to the patients, by the authority he exercised in the house over all the staff, "the physician . . . sometimes possesses more influence over the patients' minds, than the other attendants."

It is thought that Tuke and Pinel opened the asylum to medical knowledge. They did not introduce science, but a personality, whose powers borrowed from science only their disguise, or at most their justification. These powers, by their nature, were of a moral and social order; they took root in the madman's minority status, in the insanity of his person, not of his mind. If the medical personage could isolate madness, it was not because he knew it, but because he mastered it; and what for positivism would be an image of objectivity was only the other side of this domination. "It is a very important object to win the confidence of these sufferers, and to arouse in them feelings of respect and obedience, which can only be the fruit of superior discernment, distinguished education, and dignity of tone and manner. Stupidity, ignorance, and the lack of principles, sustained by a tyrannical harshness, may incite fear, but always inspire distrust. The keeper of madmen who has obtained domination over them directs and rules their conduct as he pleases; he must be endowed with a firm character, and on occasion display an imposing strength. He must threaten little but carry out his threats, and if he is disobeyed, punishment must immediately ensue." [17] The physician could exercise his absolute authority in the world of the asylum only insofar as, from the beginning, he was Father and Judge, Family and Law—his medical practice being for a long time no more than a complement to the old rites of Order, Authority, and Punishment. And Pinel was well aware that the doctor cures when, exclusive of modern therapeutics, he brings into play these immemorial figures.

Pinel cites the case of a girl of seventeen who had been raised by her parents with "extreme indulgence"; she had fallen into a "giddy, mad delirium without any cause that could be determined"; at the hospital she was treated with great gentleness, but she always showed a certain "haughtiness" which could not be tolerated at the asylum; she spoke "of her parents with nothing but bitterness." It was decided to subject her to a regime of strict authority; "the keeper, in order to tame this inflexible character, seized the moment of the bath and expressed himself forcibly concerning certain unnatural persons who dared oppose their parents and disdain their authority. He warned the girl she would henceforth be treated with all the severity she deserved, for she herself was opposed to her cure and dissimulated with insurmountable obstinacy the basic cause of her illness." Through this new rigor and these threats, the sick girl felt "profoundly moved . . . she ended by acknowledging her wrongs and making a frank confession that she had suffered a loss of reason as the result of a forbidden romantic attachment, naming the person who had been its object." After this first confession, the cure became easy: "a most favorable alteration occurred . . . she was henceforth soothed and could not sufficiently express her gratitude toward the keeper who had brought an end to her continual agitation, and had restored tranquillity and calm to her heart." There is not a moment of the story that could not be transcribed in psychoanalytic terms. To such a degree was it true that the medical personage, according to Pinel, had to act not as the result of an objective definition of the disease or a specific classifying diagnosis, but by relying on that prestige which envelops the secrets of the Family, of Authority, of Punishment, and of Love; it is by bringing such powers into play, by wearing the mask of Father and of Judge, that the physician, by one of those abrupt shortcuts that leave aside mere medical competence, became the almost magic perpetrator of the cure, and assumed the aspect of a thaumaturge; it was enough that he observed and spoke, to cause secret faults to appear, insane presumptions to vanish, and madness at last to yield to reason. His presence and his words were gifted with that power of disalienation, which at one blow revealed the transgression and restored the order of morality.

It is a curious paradox to see medical practice enter the uncertain domain of the quasi-miraculous at the very moment when the knowledge of mental illness tries to assume a positive meaning. On the one hand, madness puts itself at a distance in an objective field where the threats of unreason disappear; but at this same moment, the madman tends to form with the doctor, in an unbroken unity, a "couple" whose complicity dates back to very old links. Life in the asylum as Tuke and Pinel constituted it permitted the birth of that delicate structure which would become the essential nucleus of madness—a structure that formed a kind of microcosm in which were symbolized the massive structures of bourgeois society and its values: Family-Child relations, centered on the theme of paternal authority; Transgression-Punishment relations, centered on the theme of immediate justice; Madness-Disorder relations, centered on the theme of social and moral order. It is from these that the physician derives his power to cure; and it is to the degree that the patient finds himself, by so many old links, already alienated in the doctor, within the doctor-patient couple, that the doctor has the almost miraculous power to cure him.

In the time of Pinel and Tuke, this power had nothing extraordinary about it; it was explained and demonstrated in the efficacy, simply, of moral behavior; it was no more mysterious than the power of the eighteenth-century doctor when he diluted fluids or relaxed fibers. But very soon the meaning of this moral practice escaped the physician, to the very extent that he enclosed his knowledge in the norms of positivism: from the beginning of the nineteenth century, the psychiatrist no longer quite knew what was the nature of the power he had inherited from the great reformers, and whose efficacy seemed so foreign to his idea of mental illness and to the practice of all other doctors.

This psychiatric practice, mysterious even to those who used it, is very important in the situation of the madman within the medical world. First, because medicine of the mind for the first time in the history of Western science was to assume almost complete autonomy: from the time of the Greeks, it had been no more than a chapter of medicine, and we have seen Willis study madness under the rubric "diseases of the head";[18] after Pinel and Tuke, psychiatry would become a medicine of a particular style: those most eager to discover the origin of madness in organic causes or in hereditary dispositions would not be able to avoid this style. They would be all the more unable to avoid it in that this particular style—bringing into play increasingly obscure moral powers—would originally be a sort of bad conscience; they would increasingly confine themselves in positivism, the more they felt their practice slipping out of it.

As positivism imposes itself on medicine and psychiatry, this practice becomes more and more obscure, the psychiatrist's power more and more miraculous, and the doctor-patient couple sinks deeper into a strange world. In the patient's eyes, the doctor becomes a thaumaturge; the authority he has borrowed from order, morality, and the family now seems to derive from himself; it is because he is a doctor that he is believed to possess these powers, and while Pinel, with Tuke, strongly asserted that his moral action was not necessarily linked to any scientific competence, it was thought, and by the patient first of all, that it was in the esotericism of his knowledge, in some almost daemonic secret of knowledge, that the doctor had found the power to unravel insanity; and increasingly the patient would accept this self-surrender to a doctor both divine and satanic, beyond human measure in any case; increasingly he would alienate himself in the physician, accepting entirely and in advance all his prestige, submitting from the very first to a will he experienced as magic, and to a science he regarded as prescience and divination, thus becoming the ideal and perfect correlative of those powers he projected onto the doctor, pure object without any resistance except his own inertia, quite ready to become precisely that hysteric in whom Charcot exalted the doctor's marvelous powers. If we wanted to analyze the profound structures of objectivity in the knowledge and practice of nineteenth-century psychiatry from Pinel to Freud,[19] we should have to show in fact that such objectivity was from the start a reification of a magical nature, which could only be accomplished with the complicity of the patient himself, and beginning from a transparent and clear moral practice, gradually forgotten as positivism imposed its myths of scientific objectivity; a practice forgotten in its origins and its meaning, but always used and always present. What we call psychiatric practice is a certain moral tactic contemporary with the end of the eighteenth century, preserved in the rites of asylum life, and overlaid by the myths of positivism.

But if the doctor soon became a thaumaturge for the patient, he could not be one in his own positivist doctor's eyes. That obscure power whose origin he no longer knew, in which he could not decipher the patient's complicity, and in which he would not consent to acknowledge the ancient powers which constituted it, nevertheless had to be given some status; and since nothing in positivist understanding could justify such a transfer of will or similar remote-control operations, the moment would soon come when madness itself would be held responsible for such anomalies. These cures without basis, which must be recognized as not being false cures, would soon become the true cures of false illnesses. Madness was not what one believed, nor what it believed itself to be; it was infinitely less than itself: a combination of persuasion and mystification. We can see here the genesis of Babinski's pithiatism. And by a strange reversal, thought leaped back almost two centuries to the era when between madness, false madness, and the simulation of madness, the limit was indistinct—identical symptoms confused to the point where transgression replaced unity; further still, medical thought finally effected an identification over which all Western thought since Greek medicine had hesitated: the identification of madness with madness—that is, of the medical concept with the critical concept of madness. At the end of the nineteenth century, and in the thought of Babinski's contemporaries, we find that prodigious postulate, which no medicine had yet dared formulate: that madness, after all, was only madness.

Thus while the victim of mental illness is entirely alienated in the real person of his doctor, the doctor dissipates the reality of the mental illness in the critical concept of madness. So that there remains, beyond the empty forms of positivist thought, only a single concrete reality: the doctor-patient couple in which all alienations are summarized, linked, and loosened. And it is to this degree that all nineteenth-century psychiatry really converges on Freud, the first man to accept in all its seriousness the reality of the physician-patient couple, the first to consent not to look away nor to investigate elsewhere, the first not to attempt to hide it in a psychiatric theory that more or less harmonized with the rest of medical knowledge, the first to follow its consequences with absolute rigor. Freud demystified all the other asylum structures: he abolished silence and observation; he eliminated madness's recognition of itself in the mirror of its own spectacle; he silenced the instances of condemnation. But, on the other hand, he exploited the structure that enveloped the medical personage; he amplified its thaumaturgical virtues, preparing for its omnipotence a quasi-divine status. He focused on this single presence—concealed behind the patient and above him, in an absence that is also a total presence—all the powers that had been distributed in the collective existence of the asylum; he transformed this into an absolute Observation, a pure and circumspect Silence, a Judge who punishes and rewards in a judgment that does not even condescend to language; he made it the Mirror in which madness, in an almost motionless movement, clings to and casts off itself.

To the doctor, Freud transferred all the structures Pinel and Tuke had set up within confinement. He did deliver the patient from the existence of the asylum within which his "liberators" had alienated him; but he did not deliver him from what was essential in this existence; he regrouped its powers, extended them to the maximum by uniting them in the doctor's hands; he created the psychoanalytic situation where, by an inspired short-circuit, alienation becomes disalienating because, in the doctor, it becomes a subject.

The doctor, as an alienating figure, remains the key to psychoanalysis. It is perhaps because it did not suppress this ultimate structure, and because it referred all the others to it, that psychoanalysis has not been able, will not be able, to hear the voices of unreason, nor to decipher in themselves the signs of the madman. Psychoanalysis can unravel some of the forms of madness; it remains a stranger to the sovereign enterprise of unreason. It can neither liberate nor transcribe, nor most certainly explain, what is essential in this enterprise.

Since the end of the eighteenth century, the life of unreason no longer manifests itself except in the lightning flash of such works as those of Hölderlin, of Nerval, of Nietzsche, or of Artaud—forever irreducible to those alienations that can be cured, resisting by their own strength that gigantic moral imprisonment which we are in the habit of calling, doubtless by antiphrasis, the liberation of the insane by Pinel and Tuke.

Notes

[1] Charles-Gaspard de la Rive, letter to the editors of the *Bibliothèque britannique* concerning a new establishment for the cure of the insane. This text appeared in the *Bibliothèque britannique*, then in a separate brochure. De la Rive's visit to the Retreat dates from 1798.

[2] Scipion Pinel, *Traité complet du régime sanitaire des aliénés* (Paris, 1836), p. 56.

[3] Samuel Tuke, *Description of the Retreat, an Institution near York for Insane Persons of the Society of Friends* (York, 1813), p. 50.

[4] Ibid., p. 23.

[5] Ibid., p. 121.

[6] Ibid., p. 141.

[7] Philippe Pinel, *Traité médico-philosophique sur l'aliénation mentale* (Paris, 1801), p. 265.

[8] Ibid., p. 141.

[9] Ibid., pp. 29–30.

[10] Pinel, *Traité*, p. 63.

[11] Cited in René Sémelaigne, *Aliénistes et philanthropes* (Paris, 1912), Appendix, p. 502.

[12] Philippe Pinel, *Traité*, p. 256.

[13] Ibid., pp. 207–8.

[14] Ibid., p. 205.

[15] Cited in Tuke, *Description of Retreat*, pp. 89–90.

[16] Philippe Pinel, *Traité*, pp. 292–3.

[17] John Haslam, *Observations on Insanity with Practical Remarks on This Disease* (London, 1798), cited by Philippe Pinel, *Traité*, pp. 253–4.

[18] *Ed.*: A discussion of Thomas Willis's work appears earlier in Foucault's *Madness and Civilization*.

[19] These structures still persist in nonpsychoanalytic psychiatry, and in many aspects of psychoanalysis itself.

DISCIPLINES AND
SCIENCES OF THE
INDIVIDUAL

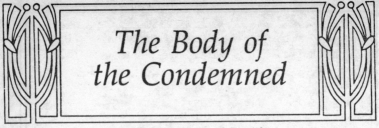

The Body of the Condemned

(FROM *Discipline and Punish*)

. . . This book [*Discipline and Punish*] is intended as a correlative history of the modern soul and of a new power to judge; a genealogy of the present scientifico-legal complex from which the power to punish derives its bases, justifications, and rules; from which it extends its effects and by which it masks its exorbitant singularity.

But from what point can such a history of the modern soul on trial be written? If one confined oneself to the evolution of legislation or of penal procedures, one would run the risk of allowing a change in the collective sensibility, an increase in humanization or the development of the human sciences to emerge as a massive, external, inert and primary fact. By studying only the general social forms, as Durkheim did, one runs the risk of positing as the principle of greater leniency in punishment processes of individualization that are, rather, one of the effects of the new tactics of power, among which are to be included the new penal mechanisms. This study obeys four general rules:

1. Do not concentrate the study of the punitive mechanisms on their "repressive" effects alone, on their "punishment" aspects alone, but situate them in a whole series of their possible positive effects, even if these seem marginal at first sight. As a consequence, regard punishment as a complex social function.

2. Analyze punitive methods not simply as consequences of legislation or as indicators of social structures, but as techniques possessing their own specificity in the more general field of other ways of exercising power. Regard punishment as a political tactic.

3. Instead of treating the history of penal law and the history of the human sciences as two separate series whose overlapping appears to have had, on one or the other, or perhaps on both, a disturbing or useful effect, according to one's point of view, see whether there is not some common matrix or whether they do not both derive from a single process of "epistemologico-juridical" formation; in short, make the technology of power the very principle both of the humanization of the penal system and of the knowledge of man.

4. Try to discover whether this entry of the soul onto the scene of penal justice, and with it the insertion in legal practice of a whole corpus of "scientific" knowledge, is not the effect of a transformation of the way in which the body itself is invested by power relations.

In short, try to study the metamorphosis of punitive methods on the basis of a political technology of the body, in which might be read a common history of power relations and object relations. Thus, by an analysis of penal leniency as a technique of power, one might understand both how man, the soul, the normal or abnormal individual have come to duplicate crime as objects of penal intervention; and in what way a specific mode of subjection was able to give birth to man as an object of knowledge for a discourse with a "scientific" status.

But I am not claiming to be the first to have worked in this direction.[1]

Rusche and Kirchheimer's great work, *Punishment and Social Structures*, provides a number of essential reference points. We must first rid ourselves of the illusion that penality is above all (if not exclusively) a means of reducing crime and that, in this role, according to the social forms, the political systems or beliefs, it may be severe or lenient, tend toward expiation of obtaining redress, toward the pursuit of individuals or the attribution of collective responsibility. We must analyze, rather, the "concrete systems of punishment," study them as social phenomena that cannot be accounted for by the juridical structure of society alone, nor by its fundamental ethical choices; we must situate them in their field of operation, in which the punishment of crime is not the sole element; we must show that punitive measures are not simply "negative" mechanisms that make it possible to repress, to prevent, to exclude, to eliminate; but that they are linked to a whole series of positive and useful effects which it is their task to support (and, in this sense, although legal punishment is carried out in order to punish offenses, one might say that the definition of offenses and their prosecution are carried out in turn in order to maintain the punitive mechanisms and their functions). From this point of view, Rusche and Kirchheimer relate the different systems of punishment with the systems of production within which they operate: thus, in a slave economy, punitive mechanisms serve to provide an additional labor force—and to constitute a body of "civil" slaves in addition to those provided by war or trading; with feudalism, at a time when money and production were still at an early stage of development, we find a sudden increase in corporal punishments—the body being in most cases the only property accessible; the penitentiary (the Hôpital Général, the Spinhuis, or the Rasphuis), forced labor, and the prison factory appear with the development of the mercantile economy. But the industrial system requires a free market in labor and, in the nineteenth century, the role of forced labor in the mechanisms of punishment diminishes accordingly and "corrective" detention takes its place. There are, no doubt, a number of observations to be made about such a strict correlation.

But we can surely accept the general proposition that, in our societies, the systems of punishment are to be situated in a certain "political economy" of the body: even if they do not make use of violent or bloody punishment, even when they use "lenient" methods involving confinement or correction, it is always the body that is at issue—the body and its forces, their utility and their docility, their distribution and their submission. It is certainly legitimate to write a history of punishment against the background of moral ideas or legal structures. But can one write such a history against the background of a history of bodies, when such systems of punishment claim to have only the secret souls of criminals as their objective?

Historians long ago began to write the history of the body.

They have studied the body in the field of historical demography or pathology; they have considered it as the seat of needs and appetites, as the locus of physiological processes and metabolisms, as a target for the attacks of germs or viruses; they have shown to what extent historical processes were involved in what might seem to be the purely biological base of existence; and what place should be given in the history of society to biological "events" such as the circulation of bacilli, or the extension of the lifespan.[2] But the body is also directly involved in a political field; power relations have an immediate hold upon it; they invest it, mark it, train it, torture it, force it to carry out tasks, to perform ceremonies, to emit signs. This political investment of the body is bound up, in accordance with complex reciprocal relations, with its economic use; it is largely as a force of production that the body is invested with relations of power and domination; but, on the other hand, its constitution as labor power is possible only if it is caught up in a system of subjection (in which need is also a political instrument meticulously prepared, calculated, and used); the body becomes a useful force only if it is both a productive body and a subjected body. This subjection is not only obtained by the instruments of violence or ideology; it can also be direct, physical, pitting force against force, bearing on material elements, and yet without involving violence; it may be calculated, organized, technically thought out; it may be subtle, make use neither of weapons nor of terror and yet remain of a physical order. That is to say, there may be a "knowledge" of the body that is not exactly the science of its functioning, and a mastery of its forces that is more than the ability to conquer them: this knowledge and this mastery constitute what might be called the political technology of the body. Of course, this technology is diffuse, rarely formulated in continuous, systematic discourse; it is often made up of bits and pieces; it implements a disparate set of tools or methods. In spite of the coherence of its results, it is generally no more than a multiform instrumentation. Moreover, it cannot be localized in a particular type of institution or state apparatus. For they have recourse to it; they use, select, or impose certain of its methods. But, in its mechanisms and its effects, it is situated at a quite different level. What the apparatuses and institutions operate is, in a sense, a microphysics of power, whose field of validity is situated, in a sense, between these great functionings and the bodies themselves with their materiality and forces.

Now, the study of this microphysics presupposes that the power exercised on the body is conceived not as a property, but as a strategy; that its effects of domination are attributed not to "appropriation," but to dispositions, maneuvers, tactics, techniques, functionings; that one should decipher in it a network of relations, constantly in tension, in activity, rather than a privilege that one might possess; that one should take as its model a perpetual battle, rather than a contract regulating a transaction or the conquest of a territory. In short, this power is exercised rather than possessed; it is not the "privilege," acquired or preserved, of the dominant class, but the overall effect of its strategic positions—an effect that is manifested and sometimes extended by the position of those who are dominated. Furthermore, this power is not exercised simply as an obligation or a prohibition on those who "do not have it"; it invests them, is transmitted by them and through them; it exerts pressure on them, just as they themselves, in their struggle against it, resist the grip it has on them. This means that these relations go right down into the depths of society; that they are not localized in the relations between the state and its citizens or on the frontier between classes and that they do not merely reproduce, at the level of individuals, bodies, gestures, and behavior, the general form of the law or government; that, although there is continuity (they are indeed articulated on this form through a whole series of complex mechanisms), there is neither analogy nor homology, but a specificity of mechanism and modality. Lastly, they are not univocal; they define innumerable points of confrontation, focuses of instability, each of which has its own risks of conflict, of struggles, and of an at least temporary inversion of the power relations. The overthrow of these "micropowers" does not, then, obey the law of all or nothing; it is not acquired once and for all by a new control of the apparatuses or by a new functioning or a destruction of the institutions; on the other hand, none of its localized episodes may be inscribed in history except by the effects that it induces on the entire network in which it is caught up.

Perhaps, too, we should abandon a whole tradition that allows us to imagine that knowledge can exist only where the power relations are suspended and that knowledge can develop only outside its injunctions, its demands, and its interests. Perhaps we should abandon the belief that power makes people mad and that, by the same token, the renunciation of power is one of the conditions of knowledge. We should admit, rather, that power produces knowledge (and not simply by encouraging it because it serves power or by applying it because it is useful); that power and knowledge directly imply one another; that there is no power relation without the correlative constitution of a field of knowledge, nor any knowledge that does not presuppose and constitute at the same time power relations. These "power-knowledge relations" are to be analyzed, therefore, not on the basis of a subject of knowledge who is or is not free in relation to the power system; but, on the contrary, the subject who knows, the objects to be known, and the modalities of knowledge must be regarded as so many effects of these fundamental implications of power-knowledge and their historical transformations. In short, it is not the activity of the subject of knowledge that produces a corpus of knowledge, useful or resistant to power, but power-knowledge, the processes and struggles that traverse it and of which it is made up, that determines the forms and possible domains of knowledge.

To analyze the political investment of the body and the microphysics of power presupposes, therefore, that one abandons—where power is concerned—the violence/ideology opposition, the metaphor of property, the model of the contract or of conquest; that—where knowledge is concerned—one abandons the opposition between what is "interested" and what is "disinterested," the model of knowledge and the primacy of the subject. Borrowing a word from Petty and his contemporaries, but giving it a different meaning from the one current in the seventeenth century, one might imagine a political "anatomy." This would not be the study of a state in terms of a "body" (with its elements, its resources, and its forces), nor would it be the study of the body and its surroundings in terms of a small state. One would be concerned with the "body politic," as a set of material elements and techniques that serve as weapons, relays, communication routes, and supports for the power and knowledge relations that invest human bodies and subjugate them by turning them into objects of knowledge.

It is a question of situating the techniques of punishment—whether they seize the body in the ritual of public torture and execution or whether they are addressed to the soul—in the history of this body politic; of considering penal practices less as a consequence of legal theories than as a chapter of political anatomy.

Kantorowitz gives a remarkable analysis of "The King's Body": a double body according to the juridical theology of the Middle Ages, since it involves not only the transitory element that is born and dies, but another that remains unchanged by time and is maintained as the physical yet intangible support of the kingdom; around this duality, which was originally close to the Christological model, are organized an iconography, a political theory of monarchy, legal mechanisms that distinguish between as well as link the person of the king and the demands of the crown, and a whole ritual that reaches its height in the coronation, the funeral, and the ceremonies of submission. At the opposite pole one might imagine placing the body of the condemned man; he, too, has his legal status; he gives rise to his own ceremonial and he calls forth a whole theoretical discourse, not in order to ground the "surplus power" possessed by the person of the sovereign, but in order to code the "lack of power" with which those subjected to punishment are marked. In the darkest region of the political field, the condemned man represents the symmetrical, inverted figure of the king. We should analyze what might be called, in homage to Kantorowitz, "the least body of the condemned man."

If the surplus power possessed by the king gives rise to the duplication of his body, has not the surplus power exercised on the subjected body of the condemned man given rise to another type of duplication? That of a "noncorporal," a "soul," as Mably called it. The history of this "microphysics" of the punitive power would then be a genealogy or an element in a genealogy of the modern "soul." Rather than seeing this soul as the reactivated remnants of an ideology, one would see it as the present correlative of a certain technology of power over the body. It would be wrong to say that the soul is an illusion, or an ideological effect. On the contrary, it exists; it has a reality; it is produced permanently around, on, within the body by the functioning of a power that is exercised on those punished—and, in a more general way, on those one supervises, trains, and corrects; over madmen, children at home and at school, the colonized; over those who are stuck at a machine and supervised for the rest of their lives. This is the historical reality of this soul, which, unlike the soul represented by Christian theology, is not born in sin and subject to punishment, but is born rather out of methods of punishment, supervision, and constraint. This real, noncorporal soul is not a substance; it is the element in which are articulated the effects of a certain type of power and the reference of a certain type of knowledge, the machinery by which the power relations give rise to a possible corpus of knowledge, and knowledge extends and reinforces the effects of this power. On this reality reference, various concepts have been constructed and domains of analysis carved out; psyche, subjectivity, personality, consciousness, etc.; on it have been built scientific techniques and discourses, and the moral claims of humanism. But let there be no misunderstanding: it is not that a real man, the object of knowledge, philosophical reflection, or technical intervention, has been substituted for the soul, the illusion of the theologians. The man described for us, whom we are invited to free, is already in himself the effect of a subjection much more profound than himself. A "soul" inhabits him and brings him to existence, which is itself a factor in the mastery that power exercises over the body. The soul is the effect and instrument of a political anatomy; the soul is the prison of the body.

That punishment in general and the prison is particular belong to a political technology of the body is a lesson that I have learned not so much from history as from the present. In recent years, prison revolts have occurred throughout the world. There was certainly something paradoxical about their aims, their slogans, and the way they took place. They were revolts against an entire state of physical misery that is over a century old: against cold, suffocation, and overcrowding; against decrepit walls, hunger, physical maltreatment. But they were also revolts against model prisons, tranquilizers, isolation, the medical or educational services. Were they revolts whose aims were merely material? Or contradictory revolts: against the obsolete, but also against comfort; against the warders, but also against the psychiatrists? In fact, all these movements—and the innumerable discourses that the prison has given rise to since the early nineteenth century—have been about the body and material things. What has sustained these discourses, these memories and invectives, are indeed those minute material details. One may, if one is so disposed, see them as no more than blind demands or suspect the existence behind them of alien strategies. In fact, they were revolts, at the level of the body, against the very body of the prison. What was at issue was not whether the prison environment was too harsh or too aseptic, too primitive or too efficient, but its very materiality as an instrument and vector of power; it is this whole technology of power over the body that the technology of the "soul"—that of the educationalists, psychologists, and psychiatrists—fails either to conceal or to compensate, for the simple reason that it is one of its tools. I would like to write the history of this prison, with all the political investments of the body that it gathers together in its closed architecture. Why? Simply because I am interested in the past? No, if one means by that writing a history of the past in terms of the present. Yes, if one means writing the history of the present.[3]

Notes

[1] In any case, I could give no notion by references or quotations what this book owes to Gilles Deleuze and the work he is undertaking with Félix Guattari. I should also have quoted a number of pages from R. Castell's *Psychanalysme* and say how much I am indebted to Pierre Nora.

[2] Cf. E. Le Roy-Ladurie, *Contrepoint* (Paris, 1973) and "L'Histoire immobile," *Annales* (May-June 1974).

[3] I shall study the birth of the prison only in the French penal system. Differences in historical developments and institutions would make a detailed comparative examination too burdensome and any attempt to describe the phenomenon as a whole too schematic.

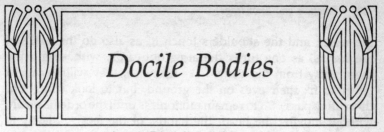

Docile Bodies

(FROM *Discipline and Punish*)

Let us take the ideal figure of the soldier as it was still seen in the early seventeenth century. To begin with, the soldier was someone who could be recognized from afar; he bore certain signs: the natural signs of his strength and his courage, the marks, too, of his pride; his body was the blazon of his strength and valor; and although it is true that he had to learn the profession of arms little by little—generally in actual fighting—movements like marching and attitudes like the bearing of the head belonged for the most part to a bodily rhetoric of honor; "The signs for recognizing those most suited to this profession are a lively, alert manner, an erect head, a taut stomach, broad shoulders, long arms, strong fingers, a small belly, thick thighs, slender legs and dry feet, because a man of such a figure could not fail to be agile and strong"; when he becomes a pike-bearer, the soldier "will have to march in step in order to have as much grace and gravity as possible, for the pike is an honorable weapon, worthy to be borne with gravity and boldness."[1] By the late eighteenth century, the soldier has become something that can be made; out of a formless clay, an inapt body, the machine required can be constructed; posture is gradually corrected; a calculated constraint runs slowly through each part of the body, mastering it, making it pliable, ready at all times, turning silently into the automatism of habit; in short, one has "got rid of the peasant" and given him "the air of a soldier." Recruits become accustomed to "holding their heads high and erect; to standing upright, without bending the back, to sticking out the belly, throwing out the chest and throwing back the shoulders; and, to help them acquire the habit, they are given this position while standing against a wall in such a way that the heels, the thighs,

179

the waist, and the shoulders touch it, as also do the backs of the hands, as one turns the arms outwards, without moving them away from the body. . . . Likewise, they will be taught never to fix their eyes on the ground, but to look straight at those they pass . . . to remain motionless until the order is given, without moving the head, the hands, or the feet . . . lastly to march with a bold step, with knee and ham taut, on the points of the feet, which should face outwards." [2]

The classical age discovered the body as object and target of power. It is easy enough to find signs of the attention then paid to the body—to the body that is manipulated, shaped, trained; which obeys, responds, becomes skillful, and increases its forces. The great book of Man-the-Machine was written simultaneously on two registers: the anatomico-metaphysical register, of which Descartes wrote the first pages and which the physicians and philosophers continued, and the technico-political register, which was constituted by a whole set of regulations and by empirical and calculated methods relating to the army, the school, and the hospital, for controlling or correcting the operations of the body. These two registers are quite distinct, since it was a question, on the one hand, of submission and use and, on the other, of functioning and explanation: there was a useful body and an intelligible body. And yet there are points of overlap from one to the other. La Mettrie's *L'Homme-machine* is both a materialist reduction of the soul and a general theory of *dressage*, at the center of which reigns the notion of "docility," which joins the analyzable body to the manipulable body. A body is docile that may be subjected, used, transformed, and improved. The celebrated automata, on the other hand, were not only a way of illustrating an organism; they were also political puppets, small-scale models of power: Frederick II, the meticulous king of small machines, well-trained regiments, and long exercises, was obsessed with them.

What was so new in those projects of docility that interested the eighteenth century so much? It was certainly not the first time that the body had become the object of such imperious and pressing investments; in every society, the body was in the grip of very strict powers, which imposed on it constraints, prohibitions, or obligations. However, there were several new things in these techniques. To begin with, there was the scale of the control: it was a question not of treating the body *en masse*, "wholesale," as if it were an indissociable unity, but of working it "retail," individually; of exercising upon it a subtle coercion, of obtaining holds upon it at the level of the mechanism itself— movements, gestures, attitudes, rapidity: an infinitesimal power over the active body. Then there was the object of the control: it was not or was no longer the signifying elements of behavior or the language of the body, but the economy, the efficiency of movements, their internal organization; constraint bears on the forces rather than on the signs; the only truly important ceremony is that of exercise. Lastly, there is the modality: it implies an uninterrupted, constant coercion, supervising the processes of the activity rather than its result, and it is exercised according to a codification that partitions as closely as possible time, space, movement. These methods, which made possible the meticulous control of the operations of the body, which assured the constant subjection of its forces and imposed on them a relation of docility-utility, might be called "disciplines." Many disciplinary methods had long been in existence—in monasteries, armies, workshops. But, in the course of the seventeenth and eighteenth centuries, the disciplines became general formulas of domination. They were different from slavery because they were not based on a relation of appropriation of bodies; indeed, the elegance of the discipline lay in the fact that it could dispense with this costly and violent relation by obtaining effects of utility at least as great. They were different, too, from "service," which was a constant, total, massive, nonanalytical, unlimited relation of domination, established in the form of the individual will of the master, his "caprice." They were different from vassalage, which was a highly coded, but distant relation of submission, which bore less on the operations of the body than on the products of labor and the ritual marks of allegiance. Again, they were different from asceticism and from "disciplines" of a monastic type, whose function was to obtain renunciations rather than increases of utility and which, although they involved obedience to others, had as their principal aim an increase of the mastery of each individual over his own body. The historical moment of the disciplines was the moment when an art of the human body was born, which was directed not only at the growth of its skills, or at the intensification of its subjection, but at the formation of a relation that in the mechanism itself makes it more obedient as it becomes more useful, and conversely. What was then being formed was a policy of coercions that act upon the body, a calculated manipulation of its elements, its gestures, its behavior. The human body was entering a machinery of power that explores it, breaks it down, and rearranges it. A "political anatomy," which was also a "mechanics of power," was being born; it defined how one may have a hold over others' bodies, not only so that they may do what one wishes, but so that they may operate as one wishes, with the techniques, the speed, and the efficiency that one determines. Thus discipline produces subjected and practiced bodies, "docile" bodies. Discipline increases the forces of the body (in economic terms of utility) and diminishes these same forces (in political terms of obedience). In short, it dissociates power from the body; on the one hand, it turns it into an "aptitude," a "capacity," which it seeks to increase; on the other hand, it reverses the course of the energy, the power that might result from it, and turns it into a relation of strict subjection. If economic exploitation separates the force and the product of labor, let us say that disciplinary coercion establishes in the body the constricting link between an increased aptitude and an increased domination.

The "invention" of this new political anatomy must not be seen as a sudden discovery. It is, rather, a multiplicity of often minor processes, of different origin and scattered location, which overlap, repeat, or imitate one another, support one another, distinguish themselves from one another according to their domain of application, converge, and gradually produce the blueprint of a general method. They were at work in secondary education at a very early date, later in primary schools; they slowly invested the space of the hospital; and, in a few decades, they restructured the military organization. They sometimes circulated very rapidly from one point to another (between the army and the technical schools or secondary schools), sometimes slowly and discreetly (the insidious militarization of the large workshops). On almost every occasion, they were adopted in response to particular needs: an industrial innovation, a renewed outbreak of certain epidemic diseases, the invention of the rifle, or the victories of Prussia. This did not prevent them from being totally inscribed in general and essential transformations, which we must now try to delineate.

There can be no question here of writing the history of the different disciplinary institutions, with all their individual differences. I simply intend to map, on a series of examples, some of the essential techniques that most easily spread from one to another. These were always meticulous, often minute, techniques, but they had their importance: because they defined a certain mode of detailed political investment of the body, a "new microphysics" of power; and because, since the seventeenth century, they had constantly reached out to ever-broader domains, as if they tended to cover the entire social body. Small acts of cunning endowed with a great power of diffusion; subtle arrangements, apparently innocent, but profoundly suspicious; mechanisms that obeyed economies too shameful to be acknowledged, or pursued petty forms of coercion—it was nevertheless they that brought about the mutation of the punitive system, at the threshold of the contemporary period. Describing them will require great attention to detail: beneath every set of figures, we must seek not a meaning, but a precaution; we must situate them not only in the inextricability of a functioning, but in the coherence of a tactic. They are the acts of cunning, not so much of the greater reason that works even in its sleep and gives meaning to the insignificant, as of the attentive "malevolence" that turns everything to account. Discipline is a political anatomy of detail.

Before we lose patience we would do well to recall the words of Marshal de Saxe: "Although those who concern themselves with details are regarded as folk of limited intelligence, it seems to me that this part is essential, because it is the foundation, and it is impossible to erect any building or establish any method without understanding its principles. It is not enough to have a liking for architecture. One must also know stone-cutting." [3] There is a whole history to be written about such "stone-cutting" —a history of the utilitarian rationalization of detail in moral accountability and political control. The classical age did not initiate it; rather, it accelerated it, changed its scale, gave it precise instruments, and perhaps found some echoes for it in the calculation of the infinitely small or in the description of the most detailed characteristics of natural beings. In any case, "detail" had long been a category of theology and asceticism: every detail is important since, in the sight of God, no immensity is greater than a detail, nor is anything so small that it was not willed by one of his individual wishes. In this great tradition of the eminence of detail, all the minutiae of Christian education, of scholastic or military pedagogy, all forms of "training" found their place easily enough. For the disciplined man, as for the true believer, no detail is unimportant, but not so much for the meaning that it conceals within it as for the hold it provides for the power that wishes to seize it. Characteristic is the great hymn to the "little things" and to their eternal importance, sung by Jean-Baptiste de La Salle in his *Traité sur les obligations des frères des Écoles chrétiennes*. The mystique of the everyday is joined here with the discipline of the minute. "How dangerous it is to neglect little things. It is a very consoling reflection for a soul like mine, little disposed to great actions, to think that fidelity to little things may, by an imperceptible progress, raise us to the most eminent sanctity: because little things lead to greater. . . . Little things; it will be said, alas, my God, what can we do that is great for you, weak and mortal creatures that we are. Little things; if great things presented themselves would we perform them? Would we not think them beyond our strength? Little things; and if God accepts them and wishes to receive them as great things? Little things; has one ever felt this? Does one judge according to experience? Little things; one is certainly guilty, therefore, if seeing them as such, one refuses them? Little things; yet it is they that in the end have made great saints! Yes, little things; but great motives, great feelings, great fervor, great ardor, and consequently great merits, great treasures, great rewards." [4] The meticulousness of the regulations, the fussiness of the inspections, the supervision of the smallest fragment of life and of the body will soon provide, in the context of the school, the barracks, the hospital, or the workshop, a laicized content, an economic or technical rationality for this mystical calculus of the infinitesimal and the infinite. And a History of Detail in the eighteenth century, presided over by Jean-Baptiste de La Salle, touching on Leibniz and Buffon, via Frederick II, covering pedagogy, medicine, military tactics, and economics, should bring us, at the end of the century, to the man who dreamt of being another Newton, not the Newton of the immensities of the heavens and the planetary masses, but a Newton of "small bodies," small movements, small actions; to the man who replied to Monge's remark, "there was only one world to discover": "What do I hear? But the world of details, who has never dreamt of that other world, what of that world? I have believed in it ever since I was fifteen. I was concerned with it then, and this memory lives within me, as an obsession never to be abandoned. . . . That other world is the most important of all that I flatter myself I have discovered: when I think of it, my heart aches" (these words are attributed to Bonaparte in the introduction to Saint-Hilaire's *Notions synthétiques et historiques de philosophie naturelle*). Napoleon did not discover this world; but we know that he set out to organize it; and he wished to arrange around him a mechanism of power that would enable him to see the smallest event that occurred in the state he governed; he intended, by means of the rigorous discipline that he imposed, "to embrace the whole of this vast machine without the slightest detail escaping his attention." [5]

A meticulous observation of detail and, at the same time, a political awareness of these small things, for the control and use of men, emerge through the classical age, bearing with them a whole set of techniques, a whole corpus of methods and knowledge, descriptions, plans, and data. And from such trifles, no doubt, the man of modern humanism was born. [6]

. . . It may be that war as strategy is a continuation of politics. But it must not be forgotten that "politics" has been conceived as a continuation, if not exactly and directly of war, at least of the military model as a fundamental means of preventing civil disorder. Politics, as a technique of internal peace and order, sought to implement the mechanism of the perfect army, of the disciplined mass, of the docile, useful troop, of the regiment in camp and in the field, on maneuvers and on exercises. In the great eighteenth-century states, the army guaranteed civil peace no doubt because it was a real force, an ever-threatening sword, but also because it was a technique and a body of knowledge that could project their schema over the social body. If there is a politics-war series that passes through strategy, there is an army-politics series that passes through tactics. It is strategy that makes it possible to understand warfare as a way of conducting politics between states; it is tactics that makes it possible to understand the army as a principle for maintaining the absence of warfare in civil society. The classical age saw the birth of the great political and military strategy by which nations confronted each other's economic and demographic forces; but it also saw the birth of meticulous military and political tactics by which the control of bodies and individual forces was exercised within states. The *"militaire"*—the military institution, military science, the *militaire* himself, so different from what was formerly characterized by the term *homme de guerre*—was specified, during this period, at the point of junction between war and the noise of battle, on the one hand, and order and silence, subservient to peace, on the other.

Historians of ideas usually attribute the dream of a perfect society to the philosophers and jurists of the eighteenth century; but there was also a military dream of society; its fundamental reference was not to the state of nature but to the meticulously subordinated cogs of a machine, not to the primal social contract but to permanent coercions, not to fundamental rights but to indefinitely progressive forms of training, not to the general will but to automatic docility.

"Discipline must be made national," said Guibert. "The state that I depict will have a simple, reliable, easily controlled administration. It will resemble those huge machines, which by quite uncomplicated means produce great effects; the strength of this state will spring from its own strength, its prosperity from its own prosperity. Time, which destroys all, will increase its power. It will disprove that vulgar prejudice by which we are made to imagine that empires are subjected to an imperious law of decline and ruin." [7] The Napoleonic regime was not far off and with it the form of state that was to survive it and, we must not forget, the foundations of which were laid not only by jurists but also by soldiers, not only councilors of state but also junior officers, not only the men of the courts but also the men of the camps. The Roman reference that accompanied this formation certainly bears with it this double index: citizens and legionaries, law and maneuvers. While jurists or philosophers were seeking in the pact a primal model for the construction or reconstruction of the social body, the soldiers and with them the technicians of discipline were elaborating procedures for the individual and collective coercion of bodies.

Notes

[1] J. de Montgommery, *La Milice française* (1636 ed.), pp. 6–7.

[2] Ordinance of 20 March 1764.

[3] Maréchal de Saxe, *Les Rêveries* (1756), p. 5.

[4] J.-B. de La Salle, *Traité sur les obligations des frères des Écoles chrétiennes* (1783 ed.), pp. 238–9.

[5] J. B. Treilhard, *Motifs du code d'instruction criminelle* (1808), p. 14.

[6] I shall choose examples from military, medical, educational, and industrial institutions. Other examples might have been taken from colonization, slavery, and child-rearing.

[7] J. A. de Guibert, "Discours préliminaire," *Essai général de tactique*, I (1772), pp. xxiii–xxiv. Cf. what Marx says about the army and forms of bourgeois society in his letter to Engels of September 25, 1857.

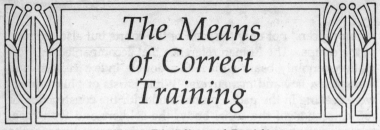

The Means of Correct Training

(FROM *Discipline and Punish*)

At the beginning of the seventeenth century, Walhausen spoke of "strict discipline" as an art of correct training. The chief function of the disciplinary power is to "train," rather than to select and to levy; or, no doubt, to train in order to levy and select all the more. It does not link forces together in order to reduce them; it seeks to bind them together in such a way as to multiply and use them. Instead of bending all its subjects into a single, uniform mass, it separates, analyzes, differentiates, carries its procedures of decomposition to the point of necessary and sufficient single units. It "trains" the moving, confused, useless multitudes of bodies and forces into a multiplicity of individual elements—small, separate cells; organic autonomies; genetic identities and continuities; combinatory segments. Discipline "makes" individuals; it is the specific technique of a power that regards individuals both as objects and as instruments of its exercise. It is not a triumphant power, which because of its own excess can pride itself on its omnipotence; it is a modest, suspicious power, which functions as a calculated but permanent economy. These are humble modalities, minor procedures, compared with the majestic rituals of sovereignty or the great apparatuses of the state. And it is precisely they that were gradually to invade the major forms, altering their mechanisms and imposing their procedures. The legal apparatus was not to escape this scarcely secret invasion. The success of disciplinary power derives no doubt from the use of simple instruments: hierarchical observation, normalizing judgment, and their combination in a procedure that is specific to it—the examination.

Hierarchical Observation

The exercise of discipline presupposes a mechanism that coerces by means of observation; an apparatus in which the techniques that make it possible to see induce effects of power and in which, conversely, the means of coercion make those on whom they are applied clearly visible. Slowly, in the course of the classical age, we see the construction of those "observatories" of human multiplicity for which the history of the sciences has so little good to say. Side by side with the major technology of the telescope, the lens, and the light beam, which were an integral part of the new physics and cosmology, there were the minor techniques of multiple and intersecting observations, of eyes that must see without being seen; using techniques of subjection and methods of exploitation, an obscure art of light and the visible was secretly preparing a new knowledge of man.

These "observatories" had an almost ideal model: the military camp—the short-lived, artificial city, built and reshaped almost at will; the seat of a power that must be all the stronger, but also all the more discreet, all the more effective and on the alert in that it is exercised over armed men. In the perfect camp, all power would be exercised solely through exact observation; each gaze would form a part of the overall functioning of power. The old, traditional square plan was considerably refined in innumerable new projects. The geometry of the paths, the number and distribution of the tents, the orientation of their entrances, the disposition of files and ranks were exactly defined; the network of gazes that supervised one another was laid down: "In the parade ground, five lines are drawn up; the first is sixteen feet from the second; the others are eight feet from one another; and the last is eight feet from the arms dépôts. The arms dépôts are ten feet from the tents of the junior officers, immediately opposite the first tentpole. A company street is fifty-one feet wide. . . . All tents are two feet from one another. The tents of the subalterns are opposite the alleys of their companies. The rear tentpole is eight feet from the last soldiers' tent and the gate is opposite the captains' tent. . . . The captains' tents are erected opposite the streets of their companies. The entrance is opposite the companies themselves." [1] The camp is the diagram of a power that acts by means of general visibility. For a long time this model of the camp, or at least its underlying principle, was found in urban development, in the construction of working-class housing estates, hospitals, asylums, prisons, schools: the spatial "nesting" of hierarchized surveillance. The principle was one of "embedding" (*encastrement*). The camp was to the rather shameful art of surveillance what the dark room was to the great science of optics.

A whole problematic then develops: that of an architecture that is no longer built simply to be seen (as with the ostentation of palaces), or to observe the external space (cf. the geometry of fortresses), but to permit an internal, articulated and detailed control—to render visible those who are inside it; in more general terms, an architecture that would operate to transform individuals: to act on those it shelters, to provide a hold on their conduct, to carry the effects of power right to them, to make it possible to know them, to alter them. Stones can make people docile and knowable. The old simple schema of confinement and enclosure—thick walls, a heavy gate that prevents entering or leaving—began to be replaced by the calculation of openings, of filled and empty spaces, passages and transparencies. In this way the hospital building was gradually organized as an instrument of medical action: it was to allow a better observation of patients, and therefore a better calibration of their treatment; the form of the buildings, by the careful separation of the patients, was to prevent contagions; lastly, the ventilation and the air that circulated around each bed were to prevent the deleterious vapors from stagnating around the patient, breaking down his humors and spreading the disease by their immediate effects. The hospital—which was to be built in the second half of the century and for which so many plans were drawn up after the Hôtel-Dieu burnt down for the second time—was no longer simply the roof under which penury and imminent death took shelter; it was, in its very materiality, a therapeutic operator.

Similarly, the school building was to be a mechanism for training. It was as a pedagogical machine that Pâris-Duverney conceived the École Militaire, right down to the minute details that he had imposed on the architect, Gabriel. Train vigorous bodies, the imperative of health; obtain competent officers, the imperative of qualification; create obedient soldiers, the imperative of politics; prevent debauchery and homosexuality, the imperative of morality. A fourfold reason for establishing sealed compartments between individuals, but also apertures for continuous surveillance. The very building of the École was to be an apparatus for observation; the rooms were distributed along a corridor like a series of small cells; at regular intervals, an officer's quarters was situated, so that "every ten pupils had an officer on each side"; the pupils were confined to their cells throughout the night; and Pâris had insisted that "a window be placed on the corridor wall of each room from chest level to within one or two feet of the ceiling. Not only is it pleasant to have such windows, but one would venture to say that it is useful, in several respects, not to mention the disciplinary reasons that may determine this arrangement." [2] In the dining rooms was "a slightly raised platform for the tables of the inspectors of studies, so that they may see all the tables of the pupils of their divisions during meals"; latrines had been installed with half-doors, so that the supervisor on duty could see the head and legs of the pupils, and also with side walls sufficiently high "that those inside cannot see one another." [3] This infinitely scrupulous concern with surveillance is expressed in the architecture by innumerable petty mechanisms. These mechanisms can only be seen as unimportant if one forgets the role of this instrumentation, minor but flawless, in the progressive objectification and the ever more subtle partitioning of individual behavior. The disciplinary institutions secreted a machinery of control that functioned like a microscope of conduct; the fine, analytical divisions that they created formed around men an apparatus of observation, recording, and training. How was one to subdivide the gaze in these observation machines? How was one to establish a network of communications between them? How was one so to arrange things that a homogeneous, continuous power would result from their calculated multiplicity?

The perfect disciplinary apparatus would make it possible for a single gaze to see everything constantly. A central point would be both the source of light illuminating everything and a locus of convergence for everything that must be known: a perfect eye that nothing would escape and a center toward which all gazes would be turned. This is what Ledoux had imagined when he built Arc-et-Senans; all the buildings were to be arranged in a circle, opening on the inside, at the center of which a high construction was to house the administrative functions of management, the policing functions of surveillance, the economic functions of control and checking, the religious functions of encouraging obedience and work; from here all orders would come, all activities would be recorded, all offenses perceived and judged; and this would be done immediately with no other aid than an exact geometry. Among all the reasons for the prestige that was accorded, in the second half of the eighteenth century, to circular architecture, one must no doubt include the fact that it expressed a certain political utopia. . . .

Hierarchized, continuous, and functional surveillance may not be one of the great technical "inventions" of the eighteenth century, but its insidious extension owed its importance to the mechanisms of power that it brought with it. By means of such surveillance, disciplinary power became an "integrated" system, linked from the inside to the economy and to the aims of the mechanism in which it was practiced. It was also organized as a multiple, automatic, and anonymous power; for although surveillance rests on individuals, its functioning is that of a network of relations from top to bottom, but also to a certain extent from bottom to top and laterally; this network "holds" the whole together and traverses it in its entirety with effects of power that derive from one another: supervisors, perpetually supervised. The power in the hierarchized surveillance of the disciplines is not possessed as a thing, or transferred as a property; it functions like a piece of machinery. And, although it is true that its pyramidal organization gives it a "head," it is the apparatus as a whole that produces "power" and distributes individuals in this permanent and continuous field. This enables the disciplinary power to be both absolutely indiscreet, since it is everywhere and always alert, since by its very principle it leaves no zone of shade and constantly supervises the very individuals who are entrusted with the task of supervising; and absolutely "discreet," for it functions permanently and largely in silence. Discipline makes possible the operation of a relational power that sustains itself by its own mechanism and which, for the spectacle of public events, substitutes the uninterrupted play of calculated gazes. Thanks to the techniques of surveillance, the "physics" of power, the hold over the body, operates according to the laws of optics and mechanics, according to a whole play of spaces, lines, screens, beams, degrees, and without recourse, in principle at least, to excess, force, or violence. It is a power that seems all the less "corporal" in that it is more subtly "physical."

Normalizing Judgment

1. At the orphanage of the Chevalier Paulet, the sessions of the tribunal that met each morning gave rise to a whole ceremonial: "We found all the pupils drawn up as if for battle, in perfect alignment, immobility, and silence. The major, a young gentleman of sixteen years, stood outside the ranks, sword in hand; at his command, the troop broke ranks at the double and formed a circle. The council met in the center; each officer made a report of his troop for the preceding twenty-four hours. The accused were allowed to defend themselves; witnesses were heard; the council deliberated and, when agreement was reached, the major announced the number of guilty, the nature of the offenses, and the punishments ordered. The troop then marched off in the greatest order." [4] At the heart of all disciplinary systems functions a small penal mechanism. It enjoys a kind of judicial privilege with its own laws, its specific offenses, its particular forms of judgment. The disciplines established an "infrapenality"; they partitioned an area that the laws had left empty; they defined and repressed a mass of behavior that the relative indifference of the great systems of punishment had allowed to escape. "On entering, the companions will greet one another . . . on leaving, they must lock up the materials and tools that they have been using and also make sure that their lamps are extinguished"; "it is expressly forbidden to amuse companions by gestures or in any other way"; they must "comport themselves honestly and decently"; anyone who is absent for more than five minutes without warning M. Oppenheim will be "marked down for a half-day"; and in order to be sure that

nothing is forgotten in this meticulous criminal justice, it is forbidden to do "anything that may harm M. Oppenheim and his companions."[5] The workshop, the school, the army were subject to a whole micropenality of time (latenesses, absences, interruptions of tasks), of activity (inattention, negligence, lack of zeal), of behavior (impoliteness, disobedience), of speech (idle chatter, insolence), of the body ("incorrect" attitudes, irregular gestures, lack of cleanliness), of sexuality (impurity, indecency). At the same time, by way of punishment, a whole series of subtle procedures was used, from light physical punishment to minor deprivations and petty humiliations. It was a question both of making the slightest departure from correct behavior subject to punishment, and of giving a punitive function to the apparently indifferent elements of the disciplinary apparatus: so that, if necessary, everything might serve to punish the slightest thing; each subject find himself caught in a punishable, punishing universality. "By the word punishment, one must understand everything that is capable of making children feel the offense they have committed, everything that is capable of humiliating them, of confusing them: . . . a certain coldness, a certain indifference, a question, a humiliation, a removal from office."[6]

2. But discipline brought with it a specific way of punishing that was not only a small-scale model of the court. What is specific to the disciplinary penality is nonobservance, that which does not measure up to the rule, that departs from it. The whole indefinite domain of the nonconforming is punishable: the soldier commits an "offense" whenever he does not reach the level required; a pupil's "offense" is not only a minor infraction, but also an inability to carry out his tasks. The regulations for the Prussian infantry ordered that a soldier who had not correctly learned to handle his rifle should be treated with the "greatest severity." Similarly, "when a pupil has not retained the catechism from the previous day, he must be forced to learn it, without making any mistake, and repeat it the following day; either he will be forced to hear it standing or kneeling, his hands joined, or he will be given some other penance."

The order that the disciplinary punishments must enforce

is of a mixed nature: it is an "artificial" order, explicitly laid down by a law, a program, a set of regulations. But it is also an order defined by natural and observable processes: the duration of an apprenticeship, the time taken to perform an exercise, the level of aptitude refer to a regularity that is also a rule. The children of the Christian Schools must never be placed in a "lesson" of which they are not yet capable, for this would expose them to the danger of being unable to learn anything; yet the duration of each stage is fixed by regulation and a pupil who, at the end of three examinations, has been unable to pass into the higher order must be placed, well in evidence, on the bench of the "ignorant." In a disciplinary regime punishment involves a double juridico-natural reference. . . .

In short, the art of punishing, in the regime of disciplinary power, is aimed neither at expiation, nor even precisely at repression. It brings five quite distinct operations into play: it refers individual actions to a whole that is at once a field of comparison, a space of differentiation, and the principle of a rule to be followed. It differentiates individuals from one another, in terms of the following overall rule: that the rule be made to function as a minimal threshold, as an average to be respected, or as an optimum toward which one must move. It measures in quantitative terms and hierarchizes in terms of value the abilities, the level, the "nature" of individuals. It introduces, through this "value-giving" measure, the constraint of a conformity that must be achieved. Lastly, it traces the limit that will define difference in relation to all other differences, the external frontier of the abnormal (the "shameful" class of the École Militaire). The perpetual penalty that traverses all points and supervises every instant in the disciplinary institutions compares, differentiates, hierarchizes, homogenizes, excludes. In short, it *normalizes*.

It is opposed, therefore, term by term, to a judicial penality whose essential function is to refer, not to a set of observable phenomena, but to a corpus of laws and texts that must be remembered; that operates not by differentiating individuals, but by specifying acts according to a number of general categories; not by hierarchizing, but quite simply by bringing into play the binary opposition of the permitted and the forbidden;

not by homogenizing, but by operating the division, acquired once and for all, of condemnation. The disciplinary mechanisms secreted a "penalty of the norm," which is irreducible in its principles and functioning to the traditional penalty of the law. The minor court that seems to sit permanently in the buildings of discipline, and which sometimes assumes the theatrical form of the great legal apparatus, must not mislead us: it does not bring, except for a few formal remnants, the mechanisms of criminal justice to the web of everyday existence; or at least that is not its essential role; the disciplines created—drawing on a whole series of very ancient procedures—a new functioning of punishment, and it was this that gradually invested the great external apparatus that it seemed to reproduce in either a modest or an ironic way. The juridico-anthropological functioning revealed in the whole history of modern penality did not originate in the superimposition of the human sciences on criminal justice and in the requirements proper to this new rationality or to the humanism that it appeared to bring with it; it originated in the disciplinary technique that operated these new mechanisms of normalizing judgment.

The power of the Norm appears through the disciplines. Is this the new law of modern society? Let us say rather that, since the eighteenth century, it has joined other powers—the Law, the Word (*Parole*), and the Text, Tradition—imposing new delimitations on them. The Normal is established as a principle of coercion in teaching with the introduction of a standardized education and the establishment of the *écoles normales* (teachers' training colleges); it is established in the effort to organize a national medical profession and a hospital system capable of operating general norms of health; it is established in the standardization of industrial processes and products.[7] Like surveillance and with it, normalization becomes one of the great instruments of power at the end of the classical age. For the marks that once indicated status, privilege, and affiliation were increasingly replaced—or at least supplemented—by a whole range of degrees of normality indicating membership of a homogeneous social body, but also playing a part in classification, hierarchization, and the distribution of rank. In a sense, the power of normalization imposes homogeneity; but it individualizes by making it possible to measure gaps, to determine levels, to fix specialties, and to render the differences useful by fitting them one to another. It is easy to understand how the power of the norm functions within a system of formal equality, since within a homogeneity that is the rule, the norm introduces, as a useful imperative and as a result of measurement, all the shading of individual differences.

The Examination

The examination combines the techniques of an observing hierarchy and those of a normalizing judgment. It is a normalizing gaze, a surveillance that makes it possible to qualify, to classify, and to punish. It establishes over individuals a visibility through which one differentiates them and judges them. That is why, in all the mechanisms of discipline, the examination is highly ritualized. In it are combined the ceremony of power and the form of the experiment, the deployment of force and the establishment of truth. At the heart of the procedures of discipline, it manifests the subjection of those who are perceived as objects and the objectification of those who are subjected. The superimposition of the power relations and knowledge relations assumes in the examination all its visible brilliance. It is yet another innovation of the classical age that the historians of science have left unexplored. People write the history of experiments on those born blind, on wolf-children or those under hypnosis. But who will write the more general, more fluid, but also more determinant history of the "examination"—its rituals, its methods, its characters and their roles, its play of questions and answers, its systems of marking and classification? For in this slender technique is to be found a whole domain of knowledge, a whole type of power. One often speaks of the ideology that the human "sciences" bring with them, in either discreet or prolix manner. But does their very technology, this tiny operational schema that has become so widespread (from psychiatry to pedagogy, from the diagnosis of diseases to the hiring of labor), this familiar method of the examination, implement, within a single mechanism, power relations that make it possible to extract and constitute knowledge? It is not simply at the level of consciousness, of representations and in what one thinks one knows, but at the level of what makes possible the knowledge that is transformed into political investment. . . .

The school became a sort of apparatus of uninterrupted examination that duplicated along its entire length the operation of teaching. It became less and less a question of jousts in which pupils pitched their forces against one another and increasingly a perpetual comparison of each and all that made it possible both to measure and to judge. The Brothers of the Christian Schools wanted their pupils to be examined every day of the week: on the first for spelling, on the second for arithmetic, on the third for catechism in the morning and for handwriting in the afternoon, etc. Moreover, there was to be an examination each month in order to pick out those who deserved to be submitted for examination by the inspector.[8] From 1775, there existed at the École des Ponts et Chaussées sixteen examinations a year: three in mathematics, three in architecture, three in drawing, two in writing, one in stone-cutting, one in style, one in surveying, one in leveling, one in quantity surveying. The examination did not simply mark the end of an apprenticeship; it was one of its permanent factors; it was woven into it through a constantly repeated ritual of power. The examination enabled the teacher, while transmitting his knowledge, to transform his pupils into a whole field of knowledge. Whereas the examinations with which an apprenticeship ended in the guild tradition validated an acquired aptitude—the "master-work" authenticated a transmission of knowledge that had already been accomplished—the examination in the school was a constant exchanger of knowledge; it guaranteed the movement of knowledge from the teacher to the pupil, but it extracted from the pupil a knowledge destined and reserved for the teacher. The school became the place of elaboration for pedagogy. And just as the procedure of the hospital examination made possible the epistemological "thaw" of medicine, the age of the "examining" school marked the beginnings of a pedagogy that functions as a science. The age of inspections and endlessly repeated movements in the army also marked the development of an immense tactical knowledge that had its effect in the period of the Napoleonic wars.

The examination introduced a whole mechanism that linked to a certain type of the formation of knowledge a certain form of the exercise of power.

1. *The examination transformed the economy of visibility into the exercise of power.* Traditionally, power was what was seen, what was shown, and what was manifested and, paradoxically, found the principle of its force in the movement by which it deployed that force. Those on whom it was exercised could remain in the shade; they received light only from that portion of power that was conceded to them, or from the reflection of it that for a moment they carried. Disciplinary power, on the other hand, is exercised through its invisibility; at the same time it imposes on those whom it subjects a principle of compulsory visibility. In discipline, it is the subjects who have to be seen. Their visibility assures the hold of the power that is exercised over them. It is the fact of being constantly seen, of being able always to be seen, that maintains the disciplined individual in his subjection. And the examination is the technique by which power, instead of emitting the signs of its potency, instead of imposing its mark on its subjects, holds them in a mechanism of objectification. In this space of domination, disciplinary power manifests its potency, essentially, by arranging objects. The examination is, as it were, the ceremony of this objectification.

Hitherto the role of the political ceremony had been to give rise to the excessive yet regulated manifestation of power; it was a spectacular expression of potency, an "expenditure," exaggerated and coded, in which power renewed its vigor. It was always more or less related to the triumph. The solemn appearance of the sovereign brought with it something of the consecration, the coronation, the return from victory; even the funeral ceremony took place with all the spectacle of power deployed. Discipline, however, had its own type of ceremony. It was not the triumph, but the review, the "parade," an ostentatious form of the examination. In it the "subjects" were presented as "objects" to the observation of a power that was manifested only by its gaze. They did not receive directly the image of the sovereign power; they only felt its effects—in replica, as it were—on their bodies, which had become precisely legible and docile.

On March 15, 1666, Louis XIV took his first military review: 18,000 men, "one of the most spectacular actions of the reign," which was supposed to have "kept all Europe in disquiet." Several years later, a medal was struck to commemorate the event.[9] It bears the exergue *Disciplina militaris restitua* and the legend *Prolusio ad victorias*. On the right, the king, right foot forward, commands the exercise itself with a stick. On the left, several ranks of soldiers are shown full-face and aligned in depth; they have raised their right arms to shoulder height and are holding their rifles exactly vertical; their right legs are slightly forward and their left feet turned outwards. On the ground, lines intersect at right angles to form, beneath the soldiers' feet, broad rectangles that serve as references for different phases and positions of the exercise. In the background is a piece of classical architecture. The columns of the palace extend those formed by the ranks of men and the erect rifles, just as the paving no doubt extends the lines of the exercise. But above the balustrade that crowns the building are statues representing dancing figures: sinuous lines, rounded gestures, draperies. The marble is covered with movements whose principle of unity is harmonic. The men, on the other hand, are frozen into a uniformly repeated attitude of ranks and lines: a tactical unity. The order of the architecture, which frees at its summit the figures of the dance, imposes its rules and its geometry on the disciplined men on the ground. The columns of power. "Very good," Grand Duke Mikhail once remarked of a regiment, after having kept it for one hour presenting arms, "only *they breathe*." [10]

Let us take this medal as evidence of the moment when, paradoxically but significantly, the most brilliant figure of sovereign power is joined to the emergence of the rituals proper to disciplinary power. The scarcely sustainable visibility of the monarch is turned into the unavoidable visibility of the subjects. And it is this inversion of visibility in the functioning of the disciplines that was to assure the exercise of power even in its lowest manifestations. We are entering the age of the infinite examination and of compulsory objectification.

2. *The examination also introduces individuality into the field of documentation*. The examination leaves behind it a whole meticulous archive constituted in terms of bodies and days. The examination that places individuals in a field of surveillance also situates them in a network of writing; it engages them in a whole mass of documents that capture and fix them. The procedures of examination were accompanied at the same time by a system of intense registration and of documentary accumulation. A "power of writing" was constituted as an essential part in the mechanisms of discipline. On many points, it was modeled on the traditional methods of administrative documentation, though with particular techniques and important innovations. Some concerned methods of identification, signaling, or description. This was the problem in the army, where it was necessary to track down deserters, avoid repeating enrollments, correct fictitious "information" presented by officers, know the services and value of each individual, establish with certainty the balance sheet of those who had disappeared or died. It was the problem of the hospitals, where it was necessary to recognize the patients, expel shammers, follow the evolution of diseases, study the effectiveness of treatments, map similar cases and the beginnings of epidemics. It was the problem of the teaching establishments, where one had to define the aptitude of each individual, situate his level and his abilities, indicate the possible use that might be made of them: "The register enables one, by being available in time and place, to know the habits of the children, their progress in piety, in catechism, in the letters, during the time they have been at the School." [11]

Hence the formation of a whole series of codes of disciplinary individuality that made it possible to transcribe, by means of homogenization, the individual features established by the examination: the physical code of signaling, the medical code of symptoms, the educational or military code of conduct or performance. These codes were still very crude, both in quality and quantity, but they marked a first stage in the "formalization" of the individual within power relations.

The other innovations of disciplinary writing concerned the correlation of these elements, the accumulation of documents, their seriation, the organization of comparative fields, making it possible to classify, to form categories, to determine averages, to fix norms. The hospitals of the eighteenth century, in particular, were great laboratories for scriptory and documentary methods. The keeping of registers, their specification, the modes of transcription from one to the other, their circulation during visits, their comparison during regular meetings of doctors and administrators, the transmission of their data to centralizing bodies (either at the hospital or at the central office of the poorhouses), the accountancy of diseases, cures, deaths, at the level of a hospital, a town, and even of the nation as a whole formed an integral part of the process by which hospitals were subjected to the disciplinary regime. Among the fundamental conditions of a good medical "discipline," in both senses of the word, one must include the procedures of writing that made it possible to integrate individual data into cumulative systems in such a way that they were not lost; so to arrange things that an individual could be located in the general register and that, conversely, each datum of the individual examination might affect overall calculations.

Thanks to the whole apparatus of writing that accompanied it, the examination opened up two correlative possibilities: first, the constitution of the individual as a describable, analyzable object, not in order to reduce him to "specific" features, as did the naturalists in relation to living beings, but in order to maintain him in his individual features, in his particular evolution, in his own aptitudes or abilities, under the gaze of a permanent corpus of knowledge; and, second, the constitution of a comparative system that made possible the measurement of overall phenomena, the description of groups, the characterization of collective facts, the calculation of the gaps between individuals, their distribution in a given "population."

These small techniques of notation, of registration, of constituting files, of arranging facts in columns and tables that are so familiar to us now, were of decisive importance in the epistemological "thaw" of the sciences of the individual. One is no doubt right to pose the Aristotelean problem: is a science of the individual possible and legitimate? A great problem needs great solutions perhaps. But there is the small historical problem of the emergence, toward the end of the eighteenth century, of what might generally be termed the "clinical" sciences; the problem of the entry of the individual (and no longer the species) into the field of knowledge; the problem of the entry of the individual description, of the cross-examination, of anamnesis, of the "file" into the general functioning of scientific discourse. To this simple question of fact, one must no doubt give an answer lacking in "nobility": one should look into these procedures of writing and registration; one should look into the mechanisms of examination, into the formation of the mechanisms of discipline, and of a new type of power over bodies. Is this the birth of the sciences of man? It is probably to be found in these "ignoble" archives, where the modern play of coercion over bodies, gestures, and behavior has its beginnings.

3. *The examination, surrounded by all its documentary techniques, makes each individual a "case"*: a case which at one and the same time constitutes an object for a branch of knowledge and a hold for a branch of power. The case is no longer, as in casuistry or jurisprudence, a set of circumstances defining an act and capable of modifying the application of a rule; it is the individual as he may be described, judged, measured, compared with others, in his very individuality; and it is also the individual who has to be trained or corrected, classified, normalized, excluded, etc.

For a long time ordinary individuality—the everyday individuality of everybody—remained below the threshold of description. To be looked at, observed, described in detail, followed from day to day by an uninterrupted writing, was a privilege. The chronicle of a man, the account of his life, his historiography, written as he lived out his life, formed part of the rituals of his power. The disciplinary methods reversed this relation, lowered the threshold of describable individuality, and made of this description a means of control and a method of domination. It is no longer a monument for future memory, but a document for possible use. And this new describability is all the more marked in that the disciplinary framework is a strict one: the child, the patient, the madman, the prisoner, were to become, with increasing ease from the eighteenth century and according to a curve which is that of the mechanisms of discipline, the object of individual descriptions and biographical accounts. This turning of real lives into writing is no longer a procedure of heroization; it functions as a procedure of objectification and subjection. The carefully collated life of mental patients or delinquents belongs, as did the chronicle of kings or the adventures of the great popular bandits, to a certain political function of writing; but in a quite different technique of power.

The examination as the fixing, at once ritual and "scientific," of individual differences, as the pinning down of each individual in his own particularity (in contrast to the ceremony in which status, birth, privilege, function are manifested with all the spectacle of their marks), clearly indicates the appearance of a new modality of power in which each individual receives as his status his own individuality, and in which he is linked by his status to the features, the measurements, the gaps, the "marks" that characterize him and make him a "case."

Finally, the examination is at the center of the procedures that constitute the individual as effect and object of power, as effect and object of knowledge. It is the examination which, by combining hierarchical surveillance and normalizing judgment, assures the great disciplinary functions of distribution and classification, maximum extraction of forces and time, continuous genetic accumulation, optimum combination of aptitudes, and, thereby, the fabrication of cellular, organic, genetic, and combinatory individuality. With it are ritualized those disciplines that may be characterized in a word by saying that they are a modality of power for which individual difference is relevant.

. . . It is often said that the model of a society that has individuals as its constituent elements is borrowed from the abstract juridical forms of contract and exchange. Mercantile society, according to this view, is represented as a contractual association of isolated juridical subjects. Perhaps. Indeed, the political theory of the seventeenth and eighteenth centuries often seems to follow this schema. But it should not be forgotten that there existed at the same period a technique for constituting individuals as correlative elements of power and knowledge. The individual is no doubt the fictitious atom of an "ideological" representation of society; but he is also a reality fabricated by this specific technology of power that I have called "discipline." We must cease once and for all to describe the effects of power in negative terms:

it "excludes," it "represses," it "censors," it "abstracts," it "masks," it "conceals." In fact, power produces; it produces reality; it produces domains of objects and rituals of truth. The individual and the knowledge that may be gained of him belong to this production.

Is it not somewhat excessive to derive such power from the petty machinations of discipline? How could *they* achieve effects of such scope?

Notes

[1] *Règlement pour l'infanterie prussienne* (French trans., Arsenal ms. 4067, fo. 144). For older plans, see Praissac, *Les Discours militaires* (1623), pp. 27–8; and J. de Montgommery, *La Milice française* (1636 ed.), p. 77. For the new plans, see Beneton de Morange, *Histoire de la guerre* (1741), pp. 61–4; and *Dissertations sur les tentes*; see also the many regulations such as the *Instruction sur le service des règlements de cavalerie dans les camps* (29 June 1753).

[2] Quoted in R. Laulau, *L'École militaire de Paris* (1950), pp. 117–8.

[3] Archives nationalistes, MM 666–9 (1763). Jeremy Bentham recounts that it was while visiting the École Militaire that his brother first had the idea of the panopticon.

[4] C. Pictet de Rochemont, in *Journal de Genève* (5 January 1788).

[5] M. Oppenheim, "Règlement provisoire pour la fabrique de M.S." (1809), in J. Hayem, *Memoires et documents pour revenir à l'histoire du commerce* (1911).

[6] J.-B. de La Salle, *Conduite des Écoles chrétiennes* (BN ms. 11759).

[7] On this topic one should refer to the important contribution of G. Canguilhem—*Le Normal et le pathologique* (Paris, 1966 ed.), pp. 179–91.

[8] La Salle, *Conduite*, pp. 204–5.

[9] See J. Jucquiot, *Le Club français de la medaille* (1970), pp. 50–4.

[10] P. Kropotkin, *Memoirs of a Revolutionist* (1906; Magnolia, Mass.: Peter Smith). I owe this reference to G. Canguilhem.

[11] MIDB (Batencourt), *Instruction méthodique pour l'école paroissiale* (1669), p. 64.

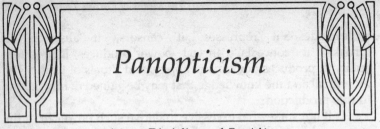

Panopticism

(FROM *Discipline and Punish*)

. . . "Discipline" may be identified neither with an institution nor with an apparatus; it is a type of power, a modality for its exercise, comprising a whole set of instruments, techniques, procedures, levels of application, targets; it is a "physics" or an "anatomy" of power, a technology. And it may be taken over either by "specialized" institutions (the penitentiaries or "houses of correction" of the nineteenth century), or by institutions that use it as an essential instrument for a particular end (schools, hospitals), or by preexisting authorities that find in it a means of reinforcing or reorganizing their internal mechanisms of power (one day we should show how intrafamilial relations, essentially in the parents-children cell, have become "disciplined," absorbing since the classical age external schemata, first educational and military, then medical, psychiatric, psychological, which have made the family the privileged locus of emergence for the disciplinary question of the normal and the abnormal), or by apparatuses that have made discipline their principle of internal functioning (the disciplinarization of the administrative apparatus from the Napoleonic period), or finally by state apparatuses whose major, if not exclusive, function is to assure that discipline reigns over society as a whole (the police).

On the whole, therefore, one can speak of the formation of a disciplinary society in this movement that stretches from the enclosed disciplines, a sort of social "quarantine," to an indefinitely generalizable mechanism of "panopticism." Not because the disciplinary modality of power has replaced all the others; but because it has infiltrated the others, sometimes undermining them, but serving as an intermediary between them, linking them together, extending them, and, above all, making it possible to bring the effects of power to the most minute and distant elements. It assures an infinitesimal distribution of the power relations. . . .

The formation of the disciplinary society is connected with a number of broad historical processes—economic, juridico-political, and, lastly, scientific—of which it forms part.

1. Generally speaking, it might be said that the disciplines are techniques for assuring the ordering of human multiplicities. It is true that there is nothing exceptional or even characteristic in this: every system of power is presented with the same problem. But the peculiarity of the disciplines is that they try to define in relation to the multiplicities a tactics of power that fulfills three criteria: first, to obtain the exercise of power at the lowest possible cost (economically, by the low expenditure it involves; politically, by its discretion, its low exteriorization, its relative invisibility, the little resistance it arouses); second, to bring the effects of this social power to their maximum intensity and to extend them as far as possible, without either failure or interval; third, to link this "economic" growth of power with the output of the apparatuses (educational, military, industrial, or medical) within which it is exercised; in short, to increase both the docility and the utility of all the elements of the system. This triple objective of the disciplines corresponds to a well-known historical conjuncture. One aspect of this conjuncture was the large demographic thrust of the eighteenth century; an increase in the floating population (one of the primary objects of discipline is to fix; it is an anti-nomadic technique); a change of quantitative scale in the groups to be supervised or manipulated (from the beginning of the seventeenth century to the eve of the French Revolution, the school population had been increasing rapidly, as had no doubt the hospital population; by the end of the eighteenth century, the peacetime army exceeded 200,000 men). The other aspect of the conjuncture was the growth in the apparatus of production, which was becoming more and more extended and complex; it was also becoming more costly and its profitability had to be increased. The development of the disciplinary methods corresponded to these two processes, or rather, no doubt, to the new need to adjust their correlation.

Neither the residual forms of feudal power nor the structures of the administrative monarchy, nor the local mechanisms of supervision, nor the unstable, tangled mass they all formed together, could carry out this role: they were hindered from doing so by the irregular and inadequate extension of their network, by their often conflicting functioning, but above all by the "costly" nature of the power that was exercised in them. It was costly in several senses: because directly it cost a great deal to the treasury; because the system of corrupt offices and farmed-out taxes weighted indirectly, but very heavily, on the population; because the resistance it encountered forced it into a cycle of perpetual reinforcement; because it proceeded essentially by levying (levying on money or products by royal, seigniorial, ecclesiastical taxation; levying on men or time by *corvées* of press-ganging, by locking up or banishing vagabonds). The development of the disciplines marks the appearance of elementary techniques belonging to a quite different economy: mechanisms of power which, instead of proceeding by deduction, are integrated into the productive efficiency of the apparatuses from within, into the growth of this efficiency and into the use of what it produces. For the old principle of "levying-violence," which governed the economy of power, the disciplines substitute the principle of "mildness-production-profit." These are the techniques that make it possible to adjust the multiplicity of men and the multiplication of the apparatuses of production (and this means not only "production" in the strict sense, but also the production of knowledge and skills in the school, the production of health in the hospitals, the production of destructive force in the army).

In this task of adjustment, discipline had to solve a number of problems for which the old economy of power was not sufficiently equipped. It could reduce the inefficiency of mass phenomena: reduce what, in a multiplicity, makes it much less manageable than a unity; reduce what is opposed to the use of each of its elements and of their sum; reduce everything that may counter the advantages of number. That is why discipline fixes; it arrests or regulates movements; it clears up confusion; it dissipates compact groupings of individuals wandering about the country in unpredictable ways; it establishes calculated distributions. It must also master all the forces that are formed from the very constitution of an organized multiplicity; it must neutralize the effects of counterpower that spring from them and which form a resistance to the power that wishes to dominate it: agitations, revolts, spontaneous organizations, coalitions—anything that may establish horizontal conjunctions. Hence the fact that the disciplines use procedures of partitioning and verticality; that they introduce, between the different elements at the same level, as solid separations as possible; that they define compact hierarchical networks; in short, that they oppose to the intrinsic, adverse force of multiplicity the technique of the continuous, individualizing pyramid. They must also increase the particular utility of each element of the multiplicity, but by means that are the most rapid and the least costly, that is to say, by using the multiplicity itself as an instrument of this growth. Hence, it order to extract from bodies the maximum time and force, the use of those overall methods known as timetables, collective training, exercises, total and detailed surveillance. Furthermore, the disciplines must increase the effect of utility proper to the multiplicities, so that each is made more useful than the simple sum of its elements: it is in order to increase the utilizable effects of the multiple that the disciplines define tactics of distribution; reciprocal adjustment of bodies, gestures, and rhythms; differentiation of capacities; reciprocal coordination in relation to apparatuses or tasks. Lastly, the disciplines have to bring into play the power relations, not above but inside the very texture of the multiplicity, as discreetly as possible, as well articulated on the other functions of these multiplicities and also in the least expensive way possible: to this correspond anonymous instruments of power, coextensive with the multiplicity that they regiment, such as hierarchical surveillance, continuous registration, perpetual assessment and classification. In short, to substitute for a power that is manifested through the brilliance of those who exercise it, a power that insidiously objectifies those on whom it is applied; to form a body of knowledge about these individuals, rather than to deploy the ostentatious signs of sovereignty. In a word, the disciplines are the ensemble of minute technical inventions that made it possible to increase the useful size of multiplicities by decreasing the inconveniences of the power which, in order to make them useful, most control them. A multiplicity, whether in a workshop or a nation, an army or a school, reaches the threshold of a discipline when the relation of the one to the other becomes favorable.

If the economic take-off of the West began with the techniques that made possible the accumulation of capital, it might perhaps be said that the methods for administering the accumulation of men made possible a political take-off in relation to the traditional, ritual, costly, violent forms of power, which soon fell into disuse and were superseded by a subtle, calculated technology of subjection. In fact, the two processes—the accumulation of men and the accumulation of capital—cannot be separated; it would not have been possible to solve the problem of the accumulation of men without the growth of an apparatus of production capable of both sustaining them and using them; conversely, the techniques that made the cumulative multiplicity of men useful accelerated the accumulation of capital. At a less general level, the technological mutations of the apparatus of production, the division of labor, and the elaboration of the disciplinary techniques sustained an ensemble of very close relations.[1] Each makes the other possible and necessary; each provides a model for the other. The disciplinary pyramid constituted the small cell of power within which the separation, coordination, and supervision of tasks were imposed and made efficient; and analytical partitioning of time, gestures, and bodily forces constituted an operational schema that could easily be transferred from the groups to be subjected to the mechanisms of production; the massive projection of military methods onto industrial organization was an example of this modeling of the division of labor following the model laid down by the schemata of power. But, on the other hand, the technical analysis of the process of production, its "mechanical" breaking-down, was projected onto the labor force, whose task it was to implement it: the constitution of those disciplinary machines in which the individual forces that they bring together are composed into a whole and therefore increased is the effect of this projection. Let us say that discipline is the unitary technique by which the body is reduced as a "political" force at the least cost and maximized as a useful force. The growth of a capitalist economy gave rise to the specific modality of disciplinary power, whose general formulas, techniques of submitting forces and bodies, in short, "political anatomy," could be operated in the most diverse political regimes, apparatuses, or institutions.

2. The panoptic modality of power—at the elementary, technical, merely physical level at which it is situated—is not under the immediate dependence or a direct extension of the great juridico-political structures of a society; it is nonetheless not absolutely independent. Historically, the process by which the bourgeoisie became, in the course of the eighteenth century, the politically dominant class was masked by the establishment of an explicit, coded, and formally egalitarian juridical framework, made possible by the organization of a parliamentary, representative regime. But the development and generalization of disciplinary mechanisms constituted the other, dark side of these processes. The general juridical form that guaranteed a system of rights that were egalitarian in principle was supported by these tiny, everyday, physical mechanisms, by all those systems of micropower that are essentially nonegalitarian and asymmetrical which we call the disciplines. And although, in a formal way, the representative regime makes it possible, directly or indirectly, with or without relays, for the will of all to form the fundamental authority of sovereignty, the disciplines provide, at the base, a guarantee of the submission of forces and bodies. The real, corporal disciplines constituted the foundation of the formal, juridical liberties. The contract may have been regarded as the ideal foundation of law and political power; panopticism constituted the technique, universally widespread, of coercion. It continued to work in depth on the juridical structures of society, in order to make the effective mechanisms of power function in opposition to the formal framework that it had acquired. The "Enlightenment," which discovered the liberties, also invented the disciplines.

In appearance, the disciplines constitute nothing more than an infra-law. They seem to extend the general forms defined by law to the infinitesimal level of individual lives; or they appear as methods of training that enable individuals to become integrated into these general demands. They seem to constitute the same type of law on a different scale, thereby making it more meticulous and more indulgent. The disciplines should be regarded as a sort of counterlaw. They have the precise role of introducing insuperable asymmetries and excluding reciprocities. First, because discipline creates between individuals a "private" link, which is a relation of constraints entirely different from contractual obligation; the acceptance of a discipline may be underwritten by contract; the way in which it is imposed, the mechanisms it brings into play, the nonreversible subordination of one group of people by another, the "surplus" power that is always fixed on the same side, in inequality of position of the different "partners" in relation to the common regulation, all these distinguish the disciplinary link from the contractual link, and make it possible to distort the contractual link systematically from the moment it has as its content a mechanism of discipline. We know, for example, how many real procedures undermine the legal fiction of the work contract: workshop discipline is not the least important. Moreover, whereas the juridical systems define juridical subjects according to universal norms, the disciplines characterize, classify, specialize; they distribute along a scale, around a norm, hierarchize individuals in relation to one another and, if necessary, disqualify and invalidate. In any case, in the space and during the time in which they exercise their control and bring into play the asymmetries of their power, they effect a suspension of the law that is never total, but is never annulled either. Regular and institutional as it may be, the discipline, in its mechanism, is a "counterlaw." And, although the universal juridicism of modern society seems to fix limits on the exercise of power, its universally widespread panopticism enables it to operate, on the underside of the law, a machinery that is both immense and minute, which supports, reinforces, multiplies the asymmetry of power and undermines the limits that are traced around the law. The minute disciplines, the panopticisms of everyday, may well be below the level of emergence of the great apparatuses and the great political struggles. But, in the genealogy of modern society, they have been, with the class domination that traverses it, the political counterpart of the juridical norms according to which power was redistributed. Hence, no doubt, the importance that has been given for so long to the small techniques of discipline, to those apparently insignificant tricks that it has invented, and even to those "sciences" that give it a respectable face; hence the fear of abandoning them if one cannot find any substitute; hence the affirmation that they are at the very foundation of society, and an element in its equilibrium, whereas they are a series of mechanisms for unbalancing power relations definitively and everywhere; hence the persistence in regarding them as the humble but concrete form of every morality, whereas they are a set of physico-political techniques.

To return to the problem of legal punishments, the prison with all the corrective technology at its disposal is to be resituated at the point where the codified power to punish turns into a disciplinary power to observe; at the point where the universal punishments of the law are applied selectively to certain individuals and always the same ones; at the point where the redefinition of the juridical subject by the penalty becomes a useful training of the criminal; at the point where the law is inverted and passes outside itself, and where the counterlaw becomes the effective and institutionalized content of the juridical forms. What generalizes the power to punish, then, is not the universal consciousness of the law in each juridical subject; it is the regular extension, the infinitely minute web of panoptic techniques. . . .

Notes

[1] See Karl Marx, *Das Kapital*, Vol. I (1867; New York: Random House, 1977), Chap. XIII; and the very interesting analysis in F. Guerry and D. Deleule, *Le Corps productif* (1973).

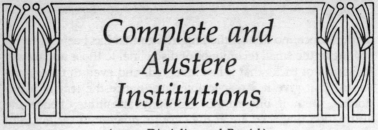

Complete and
Austere
Institutions

(FROM *Discipline and Punish*)

It would not be true to say that the prison was born with the new codes. The prison form antedates its systematic use in the penal system. It had already been constituted outside the legal apparatus when, throughout the social body, procedures were being elaborated for distributing individuals; fixing them in space; classifying them; extracting from them the maximum in time and forces; training their bodies; coding their continuous behavior; maintaining them in perfect visibility; forming around them an apparatus of observation, registration, and recording; constituting on them a body of knowledge that is accumulated and centralized. The general form of an apparatus intended to render individuals docile and useful, by means of precise work upon their bodies, indicated the prison institution, before the law ever defined it as the penalty *par excellence*. At the turn of the eighteenth and nineteenth centuries, there was, it is true, a penality of detention; and it was a new thing. But it was really the opening up of penality to mechanisms of coercion already elaborated elsewhere. The "models" of penal detention—Ghent, Gloucester, Walnut Street—marked the first visible points of this transition, rather than innovations or points of departure. The prison, an essential element in the punitive panoply, certainly marks an important moment in the history of penal justice: its access to "humanity." But it is also an important moment in the history of those disciplinary mechanisms that the new class power was developing: that in which they colonized the legal institution. At the turn of the century, a new legislation defined the power to punish as a general function of society that was exercised in the same manner over all its members, and in which each individual was equally represented: but in making detention the penalty *par excellence*, it introduced procedures of domination characteristic of a particular type of power. A justice that is supposed to be "equal," a legal machinery that is supposed to be "autonomous," but contains all the asymmetries of disciplinary subjection, this conjunction marked the birth of the prison, "the penalty of civilized societies." [1]

One can understand the self-evident character that prison punishment very soon assumed. In the first years of the nineteenth century, people were still aware of its novelty; and yet it appeared so bound up, and at such a deep level, with the very functioning of society that it banished into oblivion all the other punishments that the eighteenth-century reformers had imagined. It seemed to have no alternative, as if carried along by the very movement of history: "It is not chance, it is not the whim of the legislator that have made imprisonment the base and almost the entire edifice of our present penal scale: it is the progress of ideas and the improvement in morals." [2] And, although, in a little over a century, this self-evident character has become transformed, it has not disappeared. We are aware of all the inconveniences of prison, and that it is dangerous when it is not useless. And yet one cannot "see" how to replace it. It is the detestable solution, which one seems unable to do without.

This "self-evident" character of the prison, which we find so difficult to abandon, is based first of all on the simple form of "deprivation of liberty." How could prison not be the penalty *par excellence* in a society in which liberty is a good that belongs to all in the same way and to which each individual is attached, as Duport put it, by a "universal and constant" feeling? Its loss has therefore the same value for all; unlike the fine, it is an "egalitarian" punishment. The prison is the clearest, simplest, most equitable of penalties. Moreover, it makes it possible to quantify the penalty exactly according to the variable of time. There is a wages-form of imprisonment that constitutes, in industrial societies, its economic "self-evidence"—and enables it to appear as a reparation. By levying on the time of the prisoner, the prison seems to express in concrete terms the idea that the offense has injured, beyond the victim, society as a whole. There is an economico-moral self-evidence of a penality that metes out punishments in days, months, and years and draws up quantitative equivalences between offenses and durations. Hence the expression, so frequently heard, so consistent with the functioning of punishments, though contrary to the strict theory of penal law, that one is in prison in order to "pay one's debt." The prison is "natural," just as the use of time to measure exchanges is "natural" in our society.[3]

But the self-evidence of the prison is also based on its role, supposed or demanded, as an apparatus for transforming individuals. How could the prison not be immediately accepted when, by locking up, retraining, and rendering docile, it merely reproduces, with a little more emphasis, all the mechanisms that are to be found in the social body? The prison is like a rather disciplined barracks, a strict school, a dark workshop, but not qualitatively different. This double foundation—juridico-economic on the one hand, technico-disciplinary on the other—made the prison seem the most immediate and civilized form of all penalties. And it is this double functioning that immediately gave it its solidity. One thing is clear: the prison was not at first a deprivation of liberty to which a technical function of correction was later added; it was from the outset a form of "legal detention" entrusted with an additional corrective task, or an enterprise for reforming individuals that the deprivation of liberty allowed to function in the legal system. In short, penal imprisonment, from the beginning of the nineteenth century, covered both the deprivation of liberty and the technical transformation of individuals. . . .

The prison, the place where the penalty is carried out, is also the place of observation of punished individuals. This takes two forms: surveillance, of course, but also knowledge of each inmate, of his behavior, his deeper states of mind, his gradual improvement; the prisons must be conceived as places for the formation of clinical knowledge about the convicts; "the penitentiary system cannot be an *a priori* conception; it is an induction of the social state. There are moral diseases, as well as breakdowns in health, where the treatment depends on the site and direction of the illness."[4] This involves two essential mechanisms. It must be possible to hold the prisoner under permanent observation; every report that can be made about him must be recorded and computed. The theme of the panopticon—at once surveillance and observation, security and knowledge, individualization and totalization, isolation and transparency—found in the prison its privileged locus of realization. Although the panoptic procedures, as concrete forms of the exercise of power, have become extremely widespread, at least in their less concentrated forms, it was really only in the penitentiary institutions that Bentham's utopia could be fully expressed in a material form. In the 1830s, the panopticon became the architectural program of most prison projects. It was the most direct way of expressing "the intelligence of discipline in stone";[5] of making architecture transparent to the administration of power;[6] of making it possible to substitute for force or other violent constraints the gentle efficiency of total surveillance; of ordering space according to the recent humanization of the codes and the new penitentiary theory: "The authorities, on the one hand, and the architect, on the other, must know, therefore, whether the prisons are to be based on the principle of milder penalties or on a system of reforming convicts, in accordance with legislation which, by getting to the root cause of the people's vices, becomes a principle that will regenerate the virtues that they must practice."[7]

In short, its task was to constitute a prison-machine[8] with a cell of visibility in which the inmate will find himself caught as "in the glass house of the Greek philosopher"[9] and a central point from which a permanent gaze may control prisoners and staff. Around these two requirements, several variations were possible: the Benthamite panopticon in its strict form, the semicircle, the cross-plan, the star shape. In the midst of all these discussions, the Minister of the Interior in 1841 sums up the fundamental principles: "The central inspection hall is the pivot of the system. Without a central point of inspection, surveillance ceases to be guaranteed, continuous, and general; for it is impossible to have complete trust in the activity, zeal, and intelligence of the warder who immediately supervises the cells. . . . The architect must therefore bring all his attention to bear on this object; it is a question both of discipline and economy. The more accurate and easy the surveillance, the less need will there be to seek in the strength of the building guarantees against attempted escape and communication between the inmates. But surveillance will be perfect if from a central hall the director or head-warder sees, without moving and without being seen, not only the entrances of all the cells and even the inside of most of them when the unglazed door is open, but also the warders guarding the prisoners on every floor. . . . With the formula of circular or semicircular prisons, it would be possible to see from a single center all the prisoners in their cells and the warders in the inspection galleries." [10]

But the penitentiary panopticon was also a system of individualizing and permanent documentation. The same year in which variants of the Benthamite schema were recommended for the building of prisons, the system of "moral accounting" was made compulsory: and individual report of a uniform kind in every prison, on which the governor or head-warder, the chaplain, and the instructor had to fill in their observations on each inmate: "It is in a way the *vade mecum* of prison administration, making it possible to assess each case, each circumstance and, consequently, to know what treatment to apply to each prisoner individually." [11] Many other, much more complete systems of recording were planned or tried out.[12] The overall aim was to make the prison a place for the constitution of a body of knowledge that would regulate the exercise of penitentiary practice. The prison has not only to know the decision of the judges and to apply it in terms of the established regulations; it has to extract unceasingly from the inmate a body of knowledge that will make it possible to transform the penal measure into a penitentiary operation, which will make of the penalty required by the offense a modification of the inmate that will be of use to society. The autonomy of the carceral regime and the knowledge that it creates make it possible to increase the utility of the penalty, which the code had made the very principle of its punitive philosophy: "The governor must not lose sight of a single inmate, because in whatever part of the prison the inmate is to be found, whether he is entering or leaving, or whether he is staying there, the governor must also justify the motives for his staying in a particular classification or for his movement from one to another. He is a veritable accountant. Each inmate is for him, in the sphere of individual education, a capital invested with penitentiary interest." [13] As a highly efficient technology, penitentiary practice produces a return on the capital invested in the penal system and in the building of heavy prisons.

Similarly, the offender becomes an individual to know. This demand for knowledge was not, in the first instance, inserted into the legislation itself, in order to provide substance for the sentence and to determine the true degree of guilt. It is as a convict, as a point of application for punitive mechanisms, that the offender is constituted himself as the object of possible knowledge.

But this implies that the penitentiary apparatus, with the whole technological program that accompanies it, brings about a curious substitution: from the hands of justice, it certainly receives a convicted person; but what it must apply itself to is not, of course, the offense, nor even exactly the offender, but a rather different object, one defined by variables which at the outset at least were not taken into account in the sentence, for they were relevant only for a corrective technology. This other character, whom the penitentiary apparatus substitutes for the convicted offender, is the *delinquent*.

The delinquent is to be distinguished from the offender by the fact that it is not so much his act as his life that is relevant in characterizing him. The penitentiary operation, if it is to be a genuine reeducation, must become the sum total existence of the delinquent, making of the prison a sort of artificial and coercive theater in which his life will be examined from top to bottom. The legal punishment bears on an act, the punitive technique on a life; it falls to this punitive technique, therefore, to reconstitute all the sordid detail of a life in the form of knowledge, to fill in the gaps of that knowledge, and to act upon it by a practice of compulsion. It is a biographical knowledge and a technique for correcting individual lives. The observation of the delinquent "should go back not only to the circumstances, but also to the causes of his crime; they must be sought in the story of his life, from the triple point of view of psychology, social position, and upbringing, in order to discover the dangerous proclivities of the first, the harmful predispositions of the second, and the bad antecedents of the third. This biographical investigation is an essential part of the preliminary investigation for the classification of penalties before it becomes a condition for the classification of moralities in the penitentiary system. It must accompany the convict from the court to the prison, where the governor's task is not only to receive it, but also to complete, supervise, and rectify its various factors during the period of detention."[14] Behind the offender, to whom the investigation of the facts may attribute responsibility for an offense, stands the delinquent, whose slow formation is shown in a biographical investigation. The introduction of the "biographical" is important in the history of penality. Because it establishes the "criminal" as existing before the crime and even outside it. And, for this reason, a psychological causality, duplicating the juridical attribution of responsibility, confuses its effects. At this point one enters the "criminological" labyrinth from which we have certainly not yet emerged: any determining cause, because it reduces responsibility, marks the author of the offense with a criminality all the more formidable and demands penitentiary measures that are all the stricter. As the biography of the criminal duplicates in penal practice the analysis of circumstances used in gauging the crime, so one sees penal discourse and psychiatric discourse crossing each other's frontiers; and there, at their point of junction, is formed the notion of the "dangerous" individual, which makes it possible to draw up a network of causality in terms of an entire biography and to present a verdict of punishment-correction.[15]

The delinquent is also to be distinguished from the offender in that he is not only the author of his acts (the author responsible in terms of certain criteria of free, conscious will), but is linked to his offense by a whole bundle of complex threads (instincts, drives, tendencies, character). The penitentiary technique bears not on the relation between author and crime, but on the criminal's affinity with his crime. The delinquent, the strange manifestation of an overall phenomenon of criminality, is to be found in quasi-natural classes, each endowed with its own characteristics and requiring a specific treatment, what Marquet-Wasselot called in 1841 the "ethnography of the prisons"; "The convicts are . . . another people within the same people; with its own habits, instincts, morals." [16] We are still very close here to the "picturesque" descriptions of the world of the malefactors—an old tradition that goes back a long way and gained a new vigor in the early nineteenth century, at a time when the perception of another form of life was being articulated on that of another class and another human species. A zoology of social subspecies and an ethnology of the civilizations of malefactors, with their own rites and language, were beginning to emerge in a parody form. But an attempt was also being made to constitute a new objectivity in which the criminal belongs to a typology that is both natural and deviant. Delinquency, a pathological gap in the human species, may be analyzed as morbid syndromes or as great teratological forms. With Ferrus's classification, we probably have one of the first conversions of the old "ethnography" of crime into a systematic typology of delinquents. The analysis is slender, certainly, but it reveals quite clearly the principle that delinquency must be specified in terms not so much of the law as of the norm. There are three types of convict; there are those who are endowed "with intellectual resources above the average of intelligence that we have established," but who have been perverted either by the "tendencies of their organization" and a "native predisposition," or by "pernicious logic," an "iniquitous morality," a "dangerous attitude to social duties." Those that belong to this category require isolation day and night, solitary exercise, and, when one is forced to bring them into contact with the others, they should wear "a light mask made of metal netting, of the kind used for stone-cutting or fencing." The second category is made up of "vicious, stupid or passive convicts, who have been led into evil by indifference to either shame or honour, through cowardice, that is to say, laziness, and because of a lack of resistance to bad incitements"; the regime suitable to them is not so much that of punishment as of education, and if possible of mutual education: isolation at night, work in common during the day, conversations permitted provided they are conducted aloud, reading in common, followed by mutual questioning, for which rewards may be given. Lastly, there are the "inept or incapable convicts," who are "rendered incapable, by an incomplete organization, of any occupation requiring considered effort and consistent will, and who are therefore incapable of competing in work with intelligent workers and who, having neither enough education to know their social duties, nor enough intelligence to understand this fact or to struggle against their personal instincts, are led to evil by their very incapacity. For these, solitude would merely encourage their inertia; they must therefore live in common, but in such a way as to form small groups, constantly stimulated by collective operations, and subjected to rigid surveillance." [17] Thus a "positive" knowledge of the delinquents and their species, very different from the juridical definition of offenses and their circumstances, is gradually established; but this knowledge is also distinct from the medical knowledge that makes it possible to introduce the insanity of the individual and, consequently, to efface the criminal character of the act. Ferrus states the principle quite clearly: "Considered as a whole, criminals are nothing less than madmen; it would be unjust to the latter to confuse them with consciously perverted men." The task of this new knowledge is to define the act "scientifically" *qua* offense and above all the individual *qua* delinquent. Criminology is thus made possible.

The correlative of penal justice may well be the offender, but the correlative of the penitentiary apparatus is someone other; this is the delinquent, a biographical unity, a kernel of danger, representing a type of anomaly. And, although it is true that to a detention that deprives of liberty, as defined by law, the prison added the additional element of the penitentiary, this penitentiary element introduced in turn a third character who slipped between the individual condemned by the law and the individual who carries out this law. At the point that marked the disappearance of the branded, dismembered, burnt, annihilated body of the tortured criminal, there appeared the body of the prisoner, duplicated by the individuality of the "delinquent," by the little soul of the criminal, which the very apparatus of punishment fabricated as a point of application of the power to punish and as the object of what is still called today penitentiary science. It is said that the prison fabricated delinquents; it is true that it brings back, almost inevitably, before the courts those who have been sent there. But it also fabricates them in the sense that it has introduced into the operation of the law and the offense, the judge and the offender, the condemned man and the executioner, the noncorporal reality of the delinquency that links them together and, for a century and a half, has caught them in the same trap.

The penitentiary technique and the delinquent are in a sense twin brothers. It is not true that it was the discovery of the delinquent through a scientific rationality that introduced into our old prisons the refinement of penitentiary techniques. Nor is it true that the internal elaboration of penitentiary methods has finally brought to light the "objective" existence of a delinquency that the abstraction and rigidity of the law were unable to perceive. They appeared together, the one extending from the other, as a technological ensemble that forms and fragments the object to which it applies its instruments. And it is this delinquency, formed in the foundations of the judicial apparatus, among the "*basses œuvres*," the servile tasks, from which justice averts its gaze, out of the shame it feels in punishing those it condemns, it is this delinquency that now comes to haunt the untroubled courts and the majesty of the laws; it is this delinquency that must be known, assessed, measured, diagnosed, treated when sentences are passed. It is now this delinquency, this anomaly, this deviation, this potential danger, this illness, this form of existence, that must be taken into account when the codes are rewritten. Delinquency is the vengeance of the prison on justice. It is a revenge formidable enough to leave the judge speechless. It is at this point that the criminologists raise their voices.

But we must not forget that the prison, that concentrated and austere figure of all the disciplines, is not an endogenous element in the penal system as defined at the turn of the eighteenth and nineteenth centuries. The theme of a punitive society and of a general semio-technique of punishment that has sustained the "ideological" codes—Beccarian or Benthamite—did not itself give rise to the universal use of the prison. This prison came from elsewhere—from the mechanisms proper to a disciplinary power. Now, despite this heterogeneity, the mechanisms and effects of the prison have spread right through modern criminal justice; delinquency and the delinquents have become parasites on it through and through. One must seek the reason for this formidable "efficiency" of the prison. But one thing may be noted at the outset: the penal justice defined in the eighteenth century by the reformers traced two possible but divergent lines of objectification of the criminal: the first was the series of "monsters," moral or political, who had fallen outside the social pact; the second was that of the juridical subject rehabilitated by punishment. Now the "delinquent" makes it possible to join the two lines and to constitute under the authority of medicine, psychology, or criminology, an individual in whom the offender of the law and the object of a scientific technique are superimposed—or almost—one upon the other. That the grip of the prison on the penal system should not have led to a violent reaction of rejection is no doubt due to many reasons. One of these is that, in fabricating delinquency, it gave to criminal justice a unitary field of objects, authenticated by the "sciences," and thus enabled it to function on a general horizon of "truth."

The prison, that darkest region in the apparatus of justice, is the place where the power to punish, which no longer dares to manifest itself openly, silently organizes a field of objectivity in which punishment will be able to function openly as treatment and the sentence be inscribed among the discourses of knowledge. It is understandable that justice should have adopted so easily a prison that was not the offspring of its own thoughts. Justice certainly owed the prison this recognition.

Notes

1 P. Rossi, *Traité de droit pénal*, III (1829), p. 169.

2 P. Van Meenan, "Congrès pénitentiaire de Bruxelles," *Annales de la Charité* (1847), pp. 529–30.

3 The play between the two "natures" of the prison still continues. A few days ago [summer 1974] the head of state recalled the "principle" that detention ought to be no more than a "deprivation of liberty"— the pure essence of imprisonment, freed of the reality of prison; and added that the prison could be justified only by its "corrective" or rehabilitating effects.

[4] L. Faucher, *De la réforme des prisons* (1838), p. 6.

[5] C. Lucas, *De la réforme des prisons*, I (1836), p. 69.

[6] "If one treats of the administrative question by abstracting the question of buildings, one runs the risk of drawing up principles that are based on no reality; whereas, with a sufficient knowledge of administrative needs, an architect may accept a particular system of imprisonment that theory may have dismissed as utopian" (Abel Bouet, *Projet des prisons cellulaires* [1843], p. 1).

[7] L. Baltard, *Architectonographie des prisons* (1829), pp. 4–5.

[8] "The English reveal their genius for mechanics in everything they do . . . and they want their buildings to function as a machine subject to the action of a single motor" (Ibid., p. 18).

[9] N. P. Harou-Romain, *Projet de pénitencier* (1840), p. 8.

[10] Ducatel, *Instruction pour la construction des maisons d'arrêt* (1841), p. 9.

[11] E. Ducpétiaux, *De la réforme pénitentiaire*, III (1837), pp. 56–7.

[12] See, for example, G. de Grégory, *Projet de Code pénal universel* (1832), p. 199ff; and Grellet-Wammy, *Manuel des prisons*, II (1839), pp. 23–5, 199–203.

[13] Lucas, *De la réforme des prisons*, II, pp. 449–50.

[14] Ibid., pp. 440–2.

[15] One should study how the practice of biography became widespread at about the same time as the constitution of the individual delinquent in the punitive mechanisms: the biography or autobiography of prisoners in Appert; the drawing up of biographical files on the psychiatric model; the use of biography in the defense of accused persons. On the last point one might compare the great justificatory memoirs of the late eighteenth century written for the three men condemned to the wheel, or for Jeanne Salmon—and the defenses of criminals in the period of Louis Philippe. Chaix d'Est-Ange pleaded for La Roncière: "If long before the crime, long before the charge is laid, you can scrutinize the defendant's life, penetrate into his heart, find its most hidden corners, lay bare all his thoughts, his entire soul" (*Discours et plaidoyers*, III, p. 166).

[16] J. J. Marquet-Wasselot, *L'Ethnographie des prisons* (1841), p. 9.

[17] G. Ferrus, *Des prisonniers* (1850), pp. 182ff, 278ff.

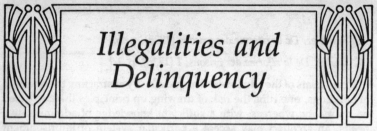

Illegalities and Delinquency

(FROM *Discipline and Punish*)

. . . The prison, in its reality and visible effects, was denounced at once as the great failure of penal justice. In a very strange way, the history of imprisonment does not obey a chronology in which one sees, in orderly succession, the establishment of a penality of detention; then the recognition of its failure; then the slow rise of projects of reform, seeming to culminate in the more or less coherent definition of penitentiary technique; then the implementation of this project; lastly, the recognition of its successes or its failure. There was in fact a telescoping or, in any case, a different distribution of these elements. And, just as the project of a corrective technique accompanied the principle of punitive detention, the critique of the prison and its methods appeared very early on, in those same years 1820–45; indeed, it was embodied in a number of formulations which—figures apart—are today repeated almost unchanged.

—Prisons do not diminish the crime rate: they can be extended, multiplied, or transformed; the quantity of crime and criminals remains stable or, worse, increases: "In France, one calculates at about 108,000 the number of individuals who are in a state of flagrant hostility to society. The means of repression at one's disposal are: the scaffold, the iron collar, three convict ships, 19 *maisons centrales*, 86 *maisons de justice*, 362 *maisons d'arrêt*, 2,800 cantonal prisons, 2,238 cells in police stations. Despite all these, vice goes unchecked. The number of crimes is not diminishing . . . the number of recidivists is increasing, rather than declining." [1]

—Detention causes recidivism; those leaving prison have more chance than before of going back to it; convicts are, in a very high proportion, former inmates; thirty-eight percent of those who left the *maisons centrales* were convicted again and thirty-three percent of those sent to convict ships (a figure given by G. de Rochefoucauld during the debate on the reform of the penal code, December 2, 1831);[2] between 1828 and 1834, out of almost 35,000 convicted of crime, about 7,400 were recidivists (that is, 1 out of 4.7 of those convicted); out of over 200,000 *correctionels*, or petty offenders, almost 35,000 were also recidivists (1 out of 6); in all, one recidivist out of 5.8 of those convicted;[3] in 1831, out of 2,174 of those condemned for recidivism, 350 had been in convict ships, 1,682 in *maisons centrales*, 142 in four *maisons de correction* that followed the same regime as the *centrales*.[4]

And the diagnosis became even more severe during the July monarchy: in 1835, out of 7,223 convicted criminals, 1,486 were recidivists; in 1839, 1,749 out of 7,858; in 1844, 1,821 out of 7,195. Among the 980 prisoners at Loos, there were 570 recidivists and, at Melun, 745 out of 1,008 prisoners.[5] Instead of releasing corrected individuals, then, the prison was setting loose a swarm of dangerous delinquents throughout the population: "7,000 persons handed back each year to society . . . they are 7,000 principles of crime or corruption spread throughout the social body. And, when one thinks that this population is constantly increasing, that it lives and moves around us, ready to seize every opportunity of disorder, to avail itself of every crisis in society to try out its strength, can one remain unmoved by such a spectacle?"[6]

—The prison cannot fail to produce delinquents. It does so by the very type of existence that it imposes on its inmates: whether they are isolated in cells or whether they are given useless work, for which they will find no employment, it is, in any case, not "to think of man in society; it is to create an unnatural, useless and dangerous existence"; the prison should educate its inmates, but can a system of education addressed to man reasonably have as its object to act against the wishes of nature?[7] The prison also produces delinquents by imposing violent constraints on its inmates; it is supposed to apply the law, and to teach respect for it; but all its functioning operates in the form of an abuse of power. The arbitrary power of administration: "The feeling of injustice that a prisoner has is one of the causes that may make his character untamable. When he sees himself exposed in this way to suffering, which the law has neither ordered nor envisaged, he becomes habitually angry against everything around him; he sees every agent of authority as an executioner; he no longer thinks that he was guilty: he accuses justice itself." [8] Corruption, fear, and the inefficiency of the warders: "Between 1,000 and 1,500 convicts live under the surveillance of between thirty and forty supervisors, who can preserve some kind of security only by depending on informers, that is to say, on the corruption that they carefully sow themselves. Who are these warders? Retired soldiers, men uninstructed in their task, making a trade of guarding malefactors." [9] Exploitation by penal labor, which can in these conditions have no educational character: "One inveighs against the slave trade. But are not our prisoners sold, like the slaves, by entrepreneurs and bought by manufacturers. . . . Is this how we teach our prisoners honesty? Are they not still more demoralized by these examples of abominable exploitation?" [10]

—The prison makes possible, even encourages, the organization of a milieu of delinquents, loyal to one another, hierarchized, ready to aid and abet any future criminal act: "Society prohibits associations of more than twenty persons . . . and it constitutes for itself associations of 200, 500, 1,200 convicts in the *maisons centrales*, which are constructed for them *ad hoc*, and which it divides up for their greater convenience into workshops, courtyards, dormitories, refectories, where they can all meet together. . . . And it multiplies them across France in such a way that, where there is a prison, there is an association . . . and as many anti-social clubs." [11] And it is in these clubs that the education of the young first offender takes place: "The first desire that is born within him will be to learn from his cleverer seniors how to escape the rigors of the law; the first lesson will be derived from the strict logic of thieves who regard society as an enemy; the morality will be the informing and spying honored in our prisons; the first passion to be aroused in him will be to frighten the young mind by these monsters that must have been born in the dungeon and which the pen refuses to name. . . . Henceforth he has broken with everything that has bound him to society." [12] Faucher spoke of "barracks of crime."

—The conditions to which the free inmates are subjected necessarily condemn them to recidivism: they are under the surveillance of the police; they are assigned to a particular residence, or forbidden others; "they leave prison with a passport that they must show everywhere they go and which mentions the sentence that they have served." [13] Being on the loose, being unable to find work, leading the life of a vagabond are the most frequent factors in recidivism. The *Gazette des tribunaux*, but also the workers' newspapers, regularly cited cases like that of the worker convicted of theft, placed under surveillance at Rouen, caught again for theft, and whom no lawyers would defend; so he took it upon himself to speak before the court, told the story of his life, explained how, on leaving prison and forced to reside in a particular place, he was unable to take up his trade as a gilder, since as an ex-convict he was turned down wherever he went; the police refused him the right to seek work elsewhere: he found himself unable to leave Rouen, with nothing to do but die of hunger and poverty as a result of this terrible surveillance. He went to the town hall and asked for work; for eight days he was given work in the cemeteries for fourteen sous a day: "But," he said, "I am young, I have a good appetite, I eat more than two pounds of bread a day at five sous a pound; what can I do with fourteen sous to feed myself, wash my clothes and find lodging? I was driven to despair, I wanted to become an honest man again; the surveillance plunged me back into misfortune. I became disgusted with everything; it was then that I met Lemaître, who was also a pauper; we had to live and wicked thoughts of thieving came back to us." [14]

—Lastly, the prison indirectly produces delinquents by throwing the inmate's family into destitution. "The same order that sends the head of the family to prison reduces each day the mother to destitution, the children to abandonment, the whole family to vagabondage and begging. It is in this way that crime can take root." [15]

It should be noted that this monotonous critique of the prison always takes one of two directions: either that the prison was insufficiently corrective, and that the penitentiary technique was still at the rudimentary stage; or that in attempting to be corrective it lost its power as punishment, [16] that the true penitentiary technique was rigor,[17] and that prison was a double economic error: directly, by its intrinsic cost, and, indirectly, by the cost of the delinquency that it did not abolish.[18] The answer to these criticisms was invariably the same: the reintroduction of the invariable principles of penitentiary technique. For a century and a half, the prison had always been offered as its own remedy: the reactivation of the penitentiary techniques as the only means of overcoming their perpetual failure; the realization of the corrective project as the only method of overcoming the impossibility of implementing it. . . .

One must not, therefore, regard the prison, its "failure," and its more or less successful reform as three successive stages. One should think, rather, of a simultaneous system that historically has been superimposed on the juridical deprivation of liberty; a fourfold system comprising: the additional, disciplinary element of the prison—the element of "super-power"; the production of an objectivity, a technique, a penitentiary "rationality"—the element of auxiliary knowledge; the *de facto* reintroduction, if not actual increase, of a criminality that the prison ought to destroy—the element of inverted efficiency; lastly, the repetition of a "reform" that is isomorphic, despite its "idealism," with the disciplinary functioning of the prison—the element of utopian duplication. It is this complex ensemble that constitutes the "carceral system," not only the institution of the prison, with its walls, its staff, its regulations, and its violence. The carceral system combines in a single figure discourses and architectures, coercive regulations and scientific propositions, real social effects and invincible utopias, programs for correcting delinquents and mechanisms that reinforce delinquency. Is not the supposed failure part of the functioning of the prison? Is it not to be included among those effects of power that discipline and the auxiliary technology of imprisonment have induced in the apparatus of justice, and in society in general, and which may be grouped together under the name of "carceral system"? If the prison institution has survived for so long, with such immobility, if the principle of penal detention has never seriously been questioned, it is no doubt because this carceral system was deeply rooted and carried out certain very precise functions. As evidence of this strength and immobility, let us take a recent fact: the model prison opened at Fleury-Mérogis in 1969 simply took over in its overall plan the panoptic star-shape that made such a stir in 1836 at the Petite-Roquette. It was the same machinery of power that assumed a real body and a symbolic form. But what role was it supposed to play?

. . . The prison, apparently "failing," does not miss its target; on the contrary, it reaches it, insofar as it gives rise to one particular form of illegality in the midst of others, which it is able to isolate, to place in full light, and to organize as a relatively enclosed, but penetrable, milieu. It helps to establish an open illegality, irreducible at a certain level and secretly useful, at once refractory and docile; it isolates, outlines, brings out a form of illegality that seems to sum up symbolically all the others, but which makes it possible to leave in the shade those that one wishes to—or must—tolerate. This form is, strictly speaking, delinquency. One should not see in delinquency the most intense, most harmful form of illegality, the form that the penal apparatus must try to eliminate through imprisonment because of the danger it represents; it is rather an effect of penality (and of the penality of detention) that makes it possible to differentiate, accommodate, and supervise illegalities. No doubt delinquency is a form of illegality; certainly it has its roots in illegality; but it is an illegality that the "carceral system," with all its ramifications, has invested, segmented, isolated, penetrated, organized, enclosed in a definite milieu, and to which it has given an instrumental role in relation to the other illegalities. In short, although the juridical opposition is between legality and illegal practice, the strategic opposition is between illegalities and delinquency.

For the observation that prison fails to eliminate crime, one should perhaps substitute the hypothesis that prison has succeeded extremely well in producing delinquency, a specific type, a politically or economically less dangerous—and, on occasion, usable—form of illegality; in producing delinquents, in an apparently marginal, but in fact centrally supervised, milieu; in producing the delinquent as a pathologized subject. The success of the prison, in the struggles around the law and illegalities, has been to specify a "delinquency." We have seen how the carceral system substituted the "delinquent" for the offender, and also superimposed on juridical practice a whole horizon of possible knowledge. Now this process that constitutes delinquency as an object of knowledge is one with the political operation that dissociates illegalities and isolates delinquency from them. The prison is the hinge of these two mechanisms; it enables them to reinforce one another perpetually, to objectify the delinquency behind the offense, to solidify delinquency in the movement of illegalities. So successful has the prison been that, after a century and a half of "failures," the prison still exists, producing the same results, and there is the greatest reluctance to dispense with it. . . .

Notes

[1] *La Fraternité*, No. 10 (February 1842).

[2] *Archives parlementaires*, Vol. 72 (1831), pp. 209–10.

[3] E. Ducpétiaux, *De la réforme pénitentiaire*, III (1837), p. 276ff.

[4] Ibid.

[5] G. Ferrus, *Des prisonniers* (1850).

[6] E. de Beaumont and A. de Tocqueville, *Note sur le système pénitentiaire* (1831), pp. 22–3.

[7] C. Lucas, *De la réforme des prisons*, I (1836), pp. 127, 130.

[8] F. Bigot Préameneu, *Rapport au conseil général de la société des prisons* (1819).

[9] *La Fraternité*, No. 10 (March 1842).

[10] Text addressed to *L'Atelier* (October 1842) by a worker imprisoned for joining a workers' association. He was able to note this protest at a time when the same newspaper was waging a campaign against competition from penal labor. The same issue carried a letter from another worker on the same subject. See also *La Fraternité*, No. 10 (March 1842).

[11] L. Moreau-Christophe, *De la mortalité et de la folie dans le régime pénitentiaire* (1839), p. 7.

[12] *L'Almanach populaire de France* (1839), pp. 49–56.

[13] F. de Barbé-Marbois, *Rapport sur l'état des prisons du Calvados, de l'Eure, la Manche et la Seine Inférieure* (1823), p. 17.

[14] *Gazette des tribunaux* (3 December 1829). See also *Gazette des tribunaux* (19 July 1839), the *Ruche populaire* (August 1840), *La Fraternité* (July-August 1847).

[15] Lucas, *De la réforme des prisons*, II, p. 64.

[16] This campaign was very vigorous before and after the passing of new regulations for the *maisons centrales* in 1839. The regulations were severe (silence, abolition of wine and tobacco, reduction in food) and they were followed by revolts. On October 3, 1840, *Le Moniteur* wrote: "It was scandalous to see prisoners gorging themselves with wine, meat, game, delicacies of all kinds and treating prison as a convenient hostelry where they could procure all the comforts that the state of liberty often refused them."

[17] In 1826, many of the General Councils demanded that deportation be substituted for constant and ineffective incarceration. In 1842, the General Council of the Hautes-Alpes demanded that the prisons become "truly expiatory"; those of Drôme, Eure-et-Loir, Nièvre, Rhône, and Seine-et-Oise made similar demands.

[18] According to an investigation carried out in 1839 among the directors of the *maisons centrales*. The director of the *maison centrale* of Embrun remarked: "The excessive comfort in the prisons probably contributes a great deal to the terrible increase in the number of recidivists." While the director at Eysses remarked: "The present regime is not severe enough, and if one thing is certain it is that for many of the inmates prison has its attractions and that they find in prison depraved pleasures that are entirely to their liking." The director of Limoges: "The present regime of the *maisons centrales* which, for the recidivists, are in fact little more than boarding houses, is in no way repressive" (see L. Moreau-Christophe, *Polémiques pénitentiaires* [1840], p. 86). Compare these remarks with declarations made, in July 1974, by the leaders of the union of prison workers concerning the effects of liberalization in prisons.

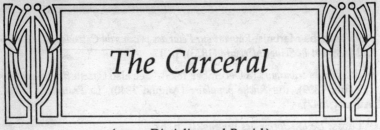

The Carceral

(FROM *Discipline and Punish*)

Were I to fix the date of completion of the carceral system, I would choose not 1810 and the penal code, nor even 1844, when the law laying down the principle of cellular internment was passed; I might not even choose 1838, when books on prison reform by Charles Lucas, Moreau-Christophe, and Faucher were published. The date I would choose would be January 22, 1840, the date of the official opening of Mettray. Or better still, perhaps, that glorious day, unremarked and unrecorded, when a child in Mettray remarked as he lay dying: "What a pity I left the colony so soon." [1] This marked the death of the first penitentiary saint. Many of the blessed no doubt went to join him, if the former inmates of the penal colonies are to be believed when, in singing the praises of the new punitive policies of the body, they remarked: "We preferred the blows, but the cell suits us better."

Why Mettray? Because it is the disciplinary form at its most extreme, the model in which are concentrated all the coercive technologies of behavior. In it were to be found "cloister, prison, school, regiment." The small, highly hierarchized groups, into which the inmates were divided, followed simultaneously five models: that of the family (each group was a "family" composed of "brothers" and two "elder brothers"); that of the army (each family, commanded by a head, was divided into two sections, each of which had a second in command; each inmate had a number and was taught basic military exercises; there was a cleanliness inspection every day, an inspection of clothing every week; a roll call was taken three times a day); that of the workshop, with supervisors and foremen, who were responsible for the regularity of the work and for the apprenticeship of the

234

younger inmates; that of the school (an hour or an hour and a half of lessons every day; the teaching was given by the instructor and by the deputy-heads); lastly, the judicial model (each day "justice" was meted out in the parlor: "The least act of disobedience is punished and the best way of avoiding serious offenses is to punish the most minor offenses very severely: at Mettray, a useless word is punishable"; the principal punishment inflicted was confinement to one's cell; for "isolation is the best means of acting on the moral nature of children; it is there above all that the voice of religion, even if it has never spoken to their hearts, recovers all its emotional power";[2] the entire parapenal institution, which is created in order not to be a prison, culminates in the cell, on the walls of which are written in black letters: "God sees you."

This superimposition of different models makes it possible to indicate, in its specific features, the function of "training." The chiefs and their deputies at Mettray had to be not exactly judges, or teachers, or foremen, or noncommissioned officers, or "parents," but something of all these things in a quite specific mode of intervention. They were in a sense technicians of behavior: engineers of conduct, orthopedists of individuality. Their task was to produce bodies that were both docile and capable; they supervised the nine or ten working hours of every day (whether in a workshop or in the fields); they directed the orderly movements of groups of inmates, physical exercises, military exercises, rising in the morning, going to bed at night, walks to the accompaniment of bugle and whistle; they taught gymnastics;[3] they checked cleanliness, supervised bathing. Training was accompanied by permanent observation; a body of knowledge was being constantly built up from the everyday behavior of the inmates; it was organized as an instrument of perpetual assessment: "On entering the colony, the child is subjected to a sort of interrogation as to his origins, the position of his family, the offense for which he was brought before the courts and all the other offenses that make up his short and often very sad existence. This information is written down on a board on which everything concerning each inmate is noted in turn, his stay at the colony and the place to which he is sent when he leaves."[4] The modeling of the body produces a knowledge of the individual, the apprenticeship of the techniques induces modes of behavior, and the acquisition of skills is inextricably linked with the establishment of power relations; strong, skilled agricultural workers are produced; in this very work, provided it is technically supervised, submissive subjects are produced and a dependable body of knowledge built up about them. This disciplinary technique exercised upon the body had a double effect: a "soul" to be known and a subjection to be maintained. One result vindicated this work of training: in 1848, at a moment when "the fever of revolution fired the imagination of all, when the schools at Angers, La Flèche, Alfort, even the boarding schools, rose up in rebellion, the inmates of Mettray were calmer than ever." [5]

Where Mettray was especially exemplary was in the specificity that it recognized in this operation of training. It was related to other forms of supervision, on which it was based: medicine, general education, religious direction. But it cannot be identified absolutely with them. Nor with administration in the strict sense. Heads or deputy-heads of "families," monitors, and foremen had to live in close proximity to the inmates; their clothes were "almost as humble" as those of the inmates themselves; they practically never left their side, observing them day and night; they constituted among them a network of permanent observation. And, in order to train them themselves, a specialized school had been organized in the colony. The essential element of its program was to subject the future cadres to the same apprenticeships and to the same coercions as the inmates themselves: they were "subjected as pupils to the discipline that, later, as instructors, they would themselves impose." They were taught the art of power relations. It was the first training college in pure discipline: the "penitentiary" was not simply a project that sought its justification in "humanity" or its foundations in a "science," but a technique that was learned, transmitted, and which obeyed general norms. The practice that normalized by compulsion the conduct of the undisciplined or dangerous could, in turn, by technical elaboration and rational reflection, be "normalized." The disciplinary technique became a "discipline" which also had its school.

It so happens that historians of the human sciences date

the birth of scientific psychology at this time: during these same years, it seems, Weber was manipulating his little compass for the measurement of sensations. What took place at Mettray (and in other European countries sooner or later) was obviously of a quite different order. It was the emergence or rather the institutional specification, the baptism as it were, of a new type of supervision—both knowledge and power—over individuals who resisted disciplinary normalization. And yet, in the formation and growth of psychology, the appearance of these professionals of discipline, normality, and subjection surely marks the beginning of a new stage. It will be said that the quantitative assessment of sensorial responses could at least derive authority from the prestige of the emerging science of physiology and that for this alone it deserves to feature in the history of the sciences. But the supervision of normality was firmly encased in a medicine or a psychiatry that provided it with a sort of "scientificity"; it was supported by a judicial apparatus which, directly or indirectly, gave it legal justification. Thus, in the shelter of these two considerable protectors, and, indeed, acting as a link between them, or a place of exchange, a carefully worked-out technique for the supervision of norms has continued to develop right up to the present day. The specific, institutional supports of these methods have proliferated since the founding of the small school at Mettray; their apparatuses have increased in quantity and scope; their auxiliary services have increased, with hospitals, schools, public administrations, and private enterprises; their agents have proliferated in number, in power, in technical qualification; the technicians of indiscipline have founded a family. In the normalization of the power of normalization, in the arrangement of a power-knowledge over individuals, Mettray and its school marked a new era. . . .

Notes

[1] E. Ducpétiaux, *Des colonies agricoles* (1851), p. 377.

[2] Ibid.

[3] "Anything that helps to tire the body helps to expel bad thoughts; so

care is taken that games consist of violent exercise. At night they fall asleep the moment they touch the pillow" (E. Ducpétiaux, *De la condition physique et morale des jeunes ouvriers*, II [1854], pp. 375–6).

4 Ducpétiaux, *Des colonies*, p. 61.

5 G. Ferrus, *Des prisonniers* (1850).

Space,
Knowledge,
and Power

Q. In your interview with geographers at *Herodote*, you said that architecture becomes[1] political at the end of the eighteenth century. Obviously, it was political in earlier periods, too, such as during the Roman Empire. What is particular about the eighteenth century?

M.F. My statement was awkward in that form. Of course I did not mean to say that architecture was not political before, becoming so only at that time. I only meant to say that in the eighteenth century one sees the development of reflection upon architecture as a function of the aims and techniques of the government of societies. One begins to see a form of political literature that addresses what the order of a society should be, what a city should be, given the requirements of the maintenance of order; given that one should avoid epidemics, avoid revolts, permit a decent and moral family life, and so on. In terms of these objectives, how is one to conceive of both the organization of a city and the construction of a collective infrastructure? And how should houses be built? I am not saying that this sort of reflection appears only in the eighteenth century, but only that in the eighteenth century a very broad and general reflection on these questions takes place. If one opens a police report of the times—the treatises that are devoted to the techniques of government—one finds that architecture and urbanism occupy a place of considerable importance. That is what I meant to say.

Q. Among the ancients, in Rome or Greece, what was the difference?

This interview with Michel Foucault was conducted by Paul Rabinow and translated by Christian Hubert.

239

M.F. In discussing Rome, one sees that the problem revolves around Vitruvius. Vitruvius was reinterpreted from the sixteenth century on, but one can find in the sixteenth century—and no doubt in the Middle Ages as well—many considerations of the same order as Vitruvius; if you consider them as *reflections upon*. The treatises on politics, on the art of government, on the manner of good government, did not generally include chapters or analyses devoted to the organization of cities or to architecture. The *Republic* of Jean Bodin does not contain extended discussions of the role of architecture, whereas the police treatises of the eighteenth century are full of them.[2]

Q. Do you mean there were techniques and practices, but the discourse did not exist?

M.F. I did not say that discourses upon architecture did not exist before the eighteenth century. Nor do I mean to say that the discussions of architecture before the eighteenth century lacked any political dimension or significance. What I wish to point out is that from the eighteenth century on, every discussion of politics as the art of the government of men necessarily includes a chapter or a series of chapters on urbanism, on collective facilities, on hygiene, and on private architecture. Such chapters are not found in the discussions of the art of government of the sixteenth century. This change is perhaps not in the reflections of architects upon architecture, but it is quite clearly seen in the reflections of political men.

Q. So it was not necessarily a change within the theory of architecture itself?

M.F. That's right. It was not necessarily a change in the minds of architects, or in their techniques—although that remains to be seen—but in the minds of political men in the choice and the form of attention that they bring to bear upon the objects that are of concern to them. Architecture became one of these during the seventeenth and eighteenth centuries.

Q. Could you tell us why?

M.F. Well, I think that it was linked to a number of phenomena, such as the question of the city and the idea that was clearly formulated at the beginning of the seventeenth century that the government of a large state like France should ultimately think of its territory on the model of the city. The city was no longer perceived as a place of privilege, as an exception in a territory of fields, forests, and roads. The cities were no longer islands beyond the common law. Instead, the cities, with the problems that they raised, and the particular forms that they took, served as the models for the governmental rationality that was to apply to the whole of the territory.

There is an entire series of utopias or projects for governing territory that developed on the premise that a state is like a large city; the capital is like its main square; the roads are like its streets. A state will be well organized when a system of policing as tight and efficient as that of the cities extends over the entire territory. At the outset, the notion of police applied only to the set of regulations that were to assure the tranquillity of a city, but at that moment the police become the very *type* of rationality for the government of the whole territory. The model of the city became the matrix for the regulations that apply to a whole state.

The notion of police, even in France today, is frequently misunderstood. When one speaks to a Frenchman about police, he can only think of people in uniform or in the secret service. In the seventeenth and eighteenth centuries, "police" signified a program of government rationality. This can be characterized as a project to create a system of regulation of the general conduct of individuals whereby everything would be controlled to the point of self-sustenance, without the need for intervention. This is the rather typically French effort of policing. The English, for a number of reasons, did not develop a comparable system, mainly because of the parliamentary tradition on one hand, and the tradition of local, communal autonomy on the other, not to mention the religious system.

One can place Napoleon almost exactly at the break between the old organization of the eighteenth-century police state (understood, of course, in the sense we have been discussing, not in the sense of the "police state" as we have come to know it) and the forms of the modern state, which he invented. At any rate, it seems that, during the eighteenth and nineteenth centuries, there appeared—rather quickly in the case of commerce and more slowly in all the other domains—this idea of a police that would manage to penetrate, to stimulate, to regulate, and to render almost automatic all the mechanisms of society.

This idea has since been abandoned. The question has been turned around. No longer do we ask: What is the form of governmental rationality that will be able to penetrate the body politic to its most fundamental elements? but rather: How is government possible? That is, what is the principle of limitation that applies to governmental actions such that things will occur for the best, in conformity with the rationality of government, and without intervention?

It is here that the question of liberalism comes up. It seems to me that at that very moment it became apparent that if one governed too much, one did not govern at all—that one provoked results contrary to those one desired. What was discovered at that time—and this was one of the great discoveries of political thought at the end of the eighteenth century—was the idea of *society*. That is to say, that government not only has to deal with a territory, with a domain, and with its subjects, but that it also has to deal with a complex and independent reality that has its own laws and mechanisms of reaction, its regulations as well as its possibilities of disturbance. This new reality is society. From the moment that one is to manipulate a society, one cannot consider it completely penetrable by police. One must take into account what it is. It becomes necessary to reflect upon it, upon its specific characteristics, its constants and its variables. . . .

Q. So there is a change in the importance of space. In the eighteenth century there was a territory and the problem of governing people in this territory: one can choose as an example *La Métropolite* (1682) of Alexandre LeMaitre—a utopian treatise on how to build a capital city—or one can understand a city as a metaphor or symbol for the territory and how to govern it. All of this is quite spatial, whereas after Napoleon, society is not necessarily so *spatialized*. . . .

M.F. That's right. On one hand, it is not so spatialized, yet at the same time a certain number of problems that are properly seen as spatial emerged. Urban space has its own dangers: disease, such as the epidemics of cholera in Europe from 1830 to about 1880; and revolution, such as the series of urban revolts that shook all of Europe during the same period. These spatial problems, which were perhaps not new, took on a new importance.

Second, a new aspect of the relations of space and power was the railroads. These were to establish a network of communication no longer corresponding necessarily to the traditional network of roads, but they nonetheless had to take into account the nature of society and its history. In addition, there are all the social phenomena that railroads gave rise to, be they the resistances they provoked, the transformations of population, or changes in the behavior of people. Europe was immediately sensitive to the changes in behavior that the railroads entailed. What was going to happen, for example, if it was possible to get married between Bordeaux and Nantes? Something that was not possible before. What was going to happen when people in Germany and France might get to know one another? Would war still be possible once there were railroads? In France a theory developed that the railroads would increase familiarity among people and that the new forms of human universality made possible would render war impossible. But what the people did not foresee—although the German military command was fully aware of it, since they were much cleverer than their French counterpart—was that, on the contrary, the railroads rendered war far easier to wage. The third development, which came later, was electricity.

So there were problems in the links between the exercise of political power and the space of a territory, or the space of cities—links that were completely new.

Q. So it was less a matter of architecture than before. These are sorts of technics of space. . . .

M.F. The major problems of space, from the nineteenth century on, were indeed of a different type. Which is not to say that problems of an architectural nature were forgotten. In terms of the first ones I referred to—disease and the political problems—architecture has a very important role to play. The reflections on urbanism and on the design of workers' housing—all of these questions—are an area of reflection upon architecture.

Q. But architecture itself, the École des Beaux-Arts, belongs to a completely different set of spatial issues.

M.F. That's right. With the birth of these new technologies and these new economic processes, one sees the birth of a sort of thinking about space that is no longer modeled on the police state of the urbanization of the territory, but that extends far beyond the limits of urbanism and architecture.

Q. Consequently, the École des Ponts et Chaussées. . . .

M.F. That's right. The École des Ponts et Chaussées and its capital importance in political rationality in France are part of this. It was not architects, but engineers and builders of bridges, roads, viaducts, railways, as well as the polytechnicians (who practically controlled the French railroads)—those are the people who thought out space.

Q. Has this situation continued up to the present, or are we witnessing a change in relations between the technicians of space?

M.F. We may well witness some changes, but I think that we have until now remained with the developers of the territory, the people of the Ponts et Chaussées, etc.

Q. So architects are not necessarily the masters of space that they once were, or believe themselves to be.

M.F. That's right. They are not the technicians or engineers of the three great variables—territory, communication, and speed. These escape the domain of architects.

Q. Do you see any particular architectural projects, either in the past or the present, as forces of liberation or resistance?

M.F. I do not think that it is possible to say that one thing is of the order of "liberation" and another is of the order of "oppression." There are a certain number of things that one can say with some certainty about a concentration camp to the effect that it is not an instrument of liberation, but one should still take into account—and this is not generally acknowledged—that, aside from torture and execution, which preclude any resistance, no matter how terrifying a given system may be, there always remain the possibilities of resistance, disobedience, and oppositional groupings.

On the other hand, I do not think that there is anything that is functionally—by its very nature—absolutely liberating. Liberty is a *practice*. So there may, in fact, always be a certain number of projects whose aim is to modify some constraints, to loosen, or even to break them, but none of these projects can, simply by its nature, assure that people will have liberty automatically, that it will be established by the project itself. The liberty of men is never assured by the institutions and laws that are intended to guarantee them. This is why almost all of these laws and institutions are quite capable of being turned around. Not because they are ambiguous, but simply because "liberty" is what must be exercised.

Q. Are there urban examples of this? Or examples where architects succeeded?

M.F. Well, up to a point there is Le Corbusier, who is described today—with a sort of cruelty that I find perfectly useless—as a sort of crypto-Stalinist. He was, I am sure, someone full of good intentions and what he did was in fact dedicated to liberating effects. Perhaps the means that he proposed were in the end less liberating than he thought, but, once again, I think that it can never be inherent in the structure of things to guarantee the exercise of freedom. The guarantee of freedom is freedom.

Q. So you do not think of Le Corbusier as an example of success. You are simply saying that his intention was liberating. Can you give us a successful example?

M.F. No. It *cannot* succeed. If one were to find a place, and perhaps there are some, where liberty is effectively exercised, one would find that this is not owing to the order of objects, but, once again, owing to the practice of liberty. Which is not to say that, after all, one may as well leave people in slums, thinking that they can simply exercise their rights there.

Q. Meaning that architecture in itself cannot resolve social problems?

M.F. I think that it can and does produce positive effects when the liberating intentions of the architect coincide with the real practice of people in the exercise of their freedom.

Q. But the same architecture can serve other ends?

M.F. Absolutely. Let me bring up another example: the *Familistère* of Jean-Baptiste Godin at Guise [1859]. The architecture of Godin was clearly intended for the freedom of people. Here was something that manifested the power of ordinary workers to participate in the exercise of their trade. It was a rather important sign and instrument of autonomy for a group of workers. Yet no one could enter or leave the place without being seen by everyone—an aspect of the architecture that could be totally oppressive. But it could only be oppressive if people were prepared to use their own presence in order to watch over others. Let's imagine a community of unlimited sexual practices that might be established there. It would once again become a place of freedom. I think it is somewhat arbitrary to try to dissociate the effective practice of freedom by people, the practice of social relations, and the spatial distributions in which they find themselves. If they are separated, they become impossible to understand. Each can only be understood through the other.

Q. Yet people have often attempted to find utopian schemes to liberate people, or to oppress them.

M.F. Men have dreamed of liberating machines. But there are no machines of freedom, by definition. This is not to say that the exercise of freedom is completely indifferent to spatial distribution, but it can only function when there is a certain convergence; in the case of divergence or distortion, it immediately becomes the opposite of that which had been intended. The panoptic qualities of Guise could perfectly well have allowed it to be used as a prison. Nothing could be simpler. It is clear that, in fact, the *Familistère* may well have served as an instrument for discipline and a rather unbearable group pressure.

Q. So, once again, the intention of the architect is not the fundamental determining factor.

M.F. Nothing is fundamental. That is what is interesting in the analysis of society. That is why nothing irritates me as much as these inquiries—which are by definition metaphysical—on the foundations of power in a society or the self-institution of a society, etc. These are not fundamental phenomena. There are only reciprocal relations, and the perpetual gaps between intentions in relation to one another.

Q. You have singled out doctors, prison wardens, priests, judges, and psychiatrists as key figures in the political configurations that involve domination. Would you put architects on this list?

M.F. You know, I was not really attempting to describe figures of domination when I referred to doctors and people like that, but rather to describe people through whom power passed or who are important in the fields of power relations. A patient in a mental institution is placed within a field of fairly complicated power relations, which Erving Goffman analyzed very well. The pastor in a Christian or Catholic church (in Protestant churches it is somewhat different) is an important link in a set of power relations. The architect is not an individual of that sort.

After all, the architect has no power over me. If I want to tear down or change a house he built for me, put up new partitions, add a chimney, the architect has no control. So the architect should be placed in another category—which is not to say that he is not totally foreign to the organization, the implementation, and all the techniques of power that are exercised in a society. I would say that one must take *him*—his mentality, his attitude—into account as well as his projects, in order to understand a certain number of the techniques of power that are invested in architecture, but he is not comparable to a doctor, a priest, a psychiatrist, or a prison warden.

Q. "Postmodernism" has received a great deal of attention recently in architectural circles. It is also being talked about in philosophy, notably by Jean-François Lyotard and Jurgen Habermas. Clearly, historical reference and language play an important role in the modern episteme. How do you see postmodernism, both as architecture and in terms of the historical and philosophical questions that are posed by it?

M.F. I think that there is a widespread and facile tendency, which one should combat, to designate that which has just occurred as the primary enemy, as if this were always the principal form of oppression from which one had to liberate oneself. Now this simple attitude entails a number of dangerous consequences: first, an inclination to seek out some cheap form of archaism or some imaginary past forms of happiness that people did not, in fact, have at all. For instance, in the areas that interest me, it is very amusing to see how contemporary sexuality is described as something absolutely terrible. To think that it is only possible now to make love after turning off the television! and in mass-produced beds! "Not like that wonderful time when . . ." Well, what about those wonderful times when people worked eighteen hours a day and there were six people in a bed, if one was lucky enough to have a bed! There is in this hatred of the present or the immediate past a dangerous tendency to invoke a completely mythical past. Second, there is the problem raised by Habermas: if one abandons the work of Kant or Weber, for example, one runs the risk of lapsing into irrationality.

I am completely in agreement with this, but at the same

time, our question is quite different: I think that the central issue of philosophy and critical thought since the eighteenth century has always been, still is, and will, I hope, remain the question: *What* is this Reason that we use? What are its historical effects? What are its limits, and what are its dangers? How can we exist as rational beings, fortunately committed to practicing a rationality that is unfortunately crisscrossed by intrinsic dangers? One should remain as close to this question as possible, keeping in mind that it is both central and extremely difficult to resolve. In addition, if it is extremely dangerous to say that Reason is the enemy that should be eliminated, it is just as dangerous to say that any critical questioning of this rationality risks sending us into irrationality. One should not forget—and I'm not saying this in order to criticize rationality, but in order to show how ambiguous things are—it was on the basis of the flamboyant rationality of social Darwinism that racism was formulated, becoming one of the most enduring and powerful ingredients of Nazism. This was, of course, an irrationality, but an irrationality that was at the same time, after all, a certain form of rationality. . . .

This is the situation that we are in and that we must combat. If intellectuals in general are to have a function, if critical thought itself has a function, and, even more specifically, if philosophy has a function within critical thought, it is precisely to accept this sort of spiral, this sort of revolving door of rationality that refers us to its necessity, to its indispensability, and at the same time, to its intrinsic dangers.

Q. All that being said, it would be fair to say that you are much less afraid of historicism and the play of historical references than someone like Habermas is; also, that this issue has been posed in architecture as almost a crisis of civilization by the defenders of modernism, who contend that if we abandon modern architecture for a frivolous return to decoration and motifs, we are somehow abandoning civilization. On the other hand, some postmodernists have claimed that historical references per se are somehow meaningful and are going to protect us from the dangers of an overly rationalized world.

M.F. Although it may not answer your question, I would say this: one should totally and absolutely suspect anything that claims to be a return. One reason is a logical one; there is in fact no such thing as a return. History, and the meticulous interest applied to history, is certainly one of the best defenses against this theme of the return. For me, the history of madness or the studies of the prison . . . were done in that precise manner because I knew full well—this is in fact what aggravated many people—that I was carrying out a historical analysis in such a manner that people *could* criticize the present, but it was impossible for them to say, "Let's go back to the good old days when madmen in the eighteenth century . . ." or, "Let's go back to the days when the prison was not one of the principal instruments. . . ." No; I think that history preserves us from that sort of ideology of the return.

Q. Hence, the simple opposition between reason and history is rather silly . . . choosing sides between the two. . . .

M.F. Yes. Well, the problem for Habermas is, after all, to make a transcendental mode of thought spring forth against any historicism. I am, indeed, far more historicist and Nietzschean. I do not think that there is a proper usage of history or a proper usage of intrahistorical analysis—which is fairly lucid, by the way—that works precisely against this ideology of the return. A good study of peasant architecture in Europe, for example, would show the utter vanity of wanting to return to the little individual house with its thatched roof. History protects us from historicism—from a historicism that calls on the past to resolve the questions of the present.

Q. It also reminds us that there is always a history; that those modernists who wanted to suppress any reference to the past were making a mistake.

M.F. Of course.

Q. Your next two books deal with sexuality among the Greeks and the early Christians. Are there any particular architectural dimensions to the issues you discuss?

M.F. I didn't find any; absolutely none. But what is interesting is that in imperial Rome there were, in fact, brothels, pleasure quarters, criminal areas, etc., and there was also one sort of quasi-public place of pleasure: the baths, the *thermes*. The baths were a very important place of pleasure and encounter, which slowly disappeared in Europe. In the Middle Ages, the baths were still a place of encounter between men and women as well as of men with men and women with women, although that is rarely talked about. What were referred to and condemned, as well as practiced, were the encounters between men and women, which disappeared over the course of the sixteenth and seventeenth centuries.

Q. In the Arab world it continues.

M.F. Yes; but in France it has largely ceased. It still existed in the nineteenth century. One sees it in *Les Enfants du Paradis*, and it is historically exact. One of the characters, Lacenaire, was—no one mentions it—a swine and a pimp who used young boys to attract older men and then blackmailed them; there is a scene that refers to this. It required all the naiveté and anti-homosexuality of the Surrealists to overlook that fact. So the baths continued to exist, as a place of sexual encounters. The bath was a sort of cathedral of pleasure at the heart of the city, where people could go as often as they want, where they walked about, picked each other up, met each other, took their pleasure, ate, drank, discussed. . . .

Q. So sex was not separated from the other pleasures. It was inscribed in the center of the cities. It was public; it served a purpose. . . .

M.F. That's right. Sexuality was obviously considered a social pleasure for the Greeks and the Romans. What is interesting about male homosexuality today—this has apparently been the case of female homosexuals for some time—is that their sexual relations are immediately translated into social relations and the social relations are understood as sexual relations. For the Greeks and the Romans, in a different fashion, sexual relations were located within social relations in the widest sense of the term. The baths were a place of sociality that included sexual relations.

One can directly compare the bath and the brothel. The brothel is in fact a place, and an architecture, of pleasure. There is, in fact, a very interesting form of sociality that was studied by Alain Corbin in *Les Filles de noces*.[3] The men of the city met at the brothel; they were tied to one another by the fact that the same women passed through their hands, that the same diseases and infections were communicated to them. There was a sociality of the brothel, but the sociality of the baths as it existed among the ancients—a new version of which could perhaps exist again—was completely different from the sociality of the brothel.

Q. We now know a great deal about disciplinary architecture. What about confessional architecture—the kind of architecture that would be associated with a confessional technology?

M.F. You mean religious architecture? I think that it has been studied. There is the whole problem of a monastery as xenophobic. There one finds precise regulations concerning life in common; affecting sleeping, eating, prayer, the place of each individual in all of that, the cells. All of this was programmed from very early on.

Q. In a technology of power, of confession as opposed to discipline, space seems to play a central role as well.

M.F. Yes. Space is fundamental in any form of communal life; space is fundamental in any exercise of power. To make a parenthetical remark, I recall having been invited, in 1966, by a group of architects to do a study of space, of something that I called at that time "heterotopias," those singular spaces to be found in some given social spaces whose functions are different or even the opposite of others. The architects worked on this, and at the end of the study someone spoke up—a Sartrean psychologist—who firebombed me, saying that *space* is reactionary and capitalist, but *history* and *becoming* are revolutionary. This absurd discourse was not at all unusual at the time. Today everyone would be convulsed with laughter at such a pronouncement, but not then.

Q. Architects in particular, if they do choose to analyze an institutional building such as a hospital or a school in terms of its disciplinary function, would tend to focus primarily on the walls. After all, that is what they design. Your approach is perhaps more concerned with space, rather than architecture, in that the physical walls are only one aspect of the institution. How would you characterize the difference between these two approaches, between the building itself and space?

M.F. I think there is a difference in method and approach. It is true that for me, architecture, in the very vague analyses of it that I have been able to conduct, is only taken as an element of support, to ensure a certain allocation of people in space, a *canalization* of their circulation, as well as the coding of their reciprocal relations. So it is not only considered as an element in space, but is especially thought of as a plunge into a field of social relations in which it brings about some specific effects.

For example, I know that there is a historian who is carrying out some interesting studies of the archaeology of the Middle Ages, in which he takes up the problem of architecture, of houses in the Middle Ages, in terms of the problem of the chimney. I think that he is in the process of showing that beginning at a certain moment it was possible to build a chimney inside the house—a chimney with a hearth, not simply an open room or a chimney outside the house; that at that moment all sorts of things changed and relations between individuals became possible. All of this seems very interesting to me, but the conclusion that he presented in an article was that the history of ideas and thoughts is useless.

What is, in fact, interesting is that the two are rigorously indivisible. Why did people struggle to find the way to put a chimney inside a house? Or why did they put their techniques to this use? So often in the history of techniques it takes years or even centuries to implement them. It is certain, and of capital importance, that this technique was a formative influence on new human relations, but it is impossible to think that it would have been developed and adapted had there not been in the play and strategy of human relations something which tended in that direction. What is interesting is always interconnection, not the primacy of this over that, which never has any meaning.

Q. In your book *The Order of Things* you constructed certain vivid spatial metaphors to describe structures of thought. Why do you think spatial images are so evocative for these references? What is the relationship between these spatial metaphors describing disciplines and more concrete descriptions of institutional spaces?

M.F. It is quite possible that since I was interested in the problems of space, I used quite a number of spatial metaphors in *The Order of Things*, but usually these metaphors were not ones that I advanced, but ones that I was studying as objects. What is striking in the epistemological mutations and transformations of the seventeenth century is to see how the spatialization of knowledge was one of the factors in the constitution of this knowledge as a science. If the natural history and the classifications of Linneas were possible, it is for a certain number of reasons: on the one hand, there was literally a spatialization of the very object of their analyses, since they gave themselves the rule of studying and classifying a plant only on the basis of that which was visible. They didn't even want to use a microscope. All the traditional elements of knowledge, such as the medical functions of the plant, fell away. The object was spatialized. Subsequently, it was spatialized insofar as the principles of classification had to be found in the very structure of the plant: the number of elements, how they were arranged, their size, etc., and certain other elements, like the height of the plant. Then there was the spatialization into illustrations within books, which was only possible with certain printing techniques. Then the spatialization of the reproduction of the plants themselves, which was represented in books. All of these are spatial techniques, not metaphors.

Q. Is the actual plan for a building—the precise drawing that becomes walls and windows—the same form of discourse as, say, a hierarchical pyramid that describes rather precisely relations between people, not only in space, but also in social life?

M.F. Well, I think there are a few simple and exceptional examples in which the architectural means reproduce, with more or less emphasis, the social hierarchies. There is the model of the military camp, where the military hierarchy is to be read in the ground itself, by the place occupied by the tents and the buildings reserved for each rank. It reproduces precisely through architecture a pyramid of power; but this is an exceptional example, as is everything military—privileged in society and of an extreme simplicity.

Q. But the plan itself is not always an account of relations or power.

M.F. No. Fortunately for human imagination, things are a little more complicated than that.

Q. Architecture is not, of course, a constant: it has a long tradition of changing preoccupations, changing systems, different rules. The *savoir* of architecture is partly the history of the profession, partly the evolution of a science of construction, and partly a rewriting of aesthetic theories. What do you think is particular about this form of *savoir*? Is it more like a natural science, or what you have called a "dubious science"?

M.F. I can't exactly say that this distinction between sciences that are certain and those that are uncertain is of no interest—that would be avoiding the question—but I must say that what interests me more is to focus on what the Greeks called the *techne*, that is to say, a practical rationality governed by a conscious goal. I am not even sure if it is worth constantly asking the question of whether government can be the object of an exact science. On the other hand, if architecture, like the practice of government and the practice of other forms of social organization, is considered as a *techne*, possibly using elements of sciences like physics, for example, or statistics, etc. . . . , that is what is interesting. But if one wanted to do a history of architecture, I think that it should be much more along the lines of that general history of the *techne*, rather than the histories of either the exact sciences or the inexact ones. The disadvantage of this word *techne*, I realize, is its relation to the word "technology," which has a very specific meaning. A very narrow meaning is given to "technology": one thinks of hard technology, the technology of wood, of fire, of electricity. Whereas government is also a function of technology: the government of individuals, the government of souls, the government of the self by the self, the government of families, the government of children, and so on. I believe that if one placed the history of architecture back in this general history of *techne*, in this wide sense of the word, one would have a more interesting guiding concept than by considering opposition between the exact sciences and the inexact ones.

Notes

1 See the article on Foucault in *Skyline* (March 1982), p. 14.

2 Jean Bodin, *Republic* (Paris, 1577).

3 Alain Corbin, *Les Filles de noces* (Aubier, 1978).

BIO-POWER

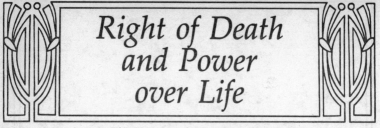

Right of Death and Power over Life

(FROM *The History of Sexuality*, Volume I)

For a long time, one of the characteristic privileges of sovereign power was the right to decide life and death. In a formal sense, it derived no doubt from the ancient *patria potestas* that granted the father of the Roman family the right to "dispose" of the life of his children and his slaves; just as he had given them life, so he could take it away. By the time the right of life and death was framed by the classical theoreticians, it was in a considerably diminished form. It was no longer considered that this power of the sovereign over his subjects could be exercised in an absolute and unconditional way, but only in cases where the sovereign's very existence was in jeopardy: a sort of right of rejoinder. If he was threatened by external enemies who sought to overthrow him or contest his rights, he could then legitimately wage war, and require his subjects to take part in the defense of the state; without "directly proposing their death," he was empowered to "expose their life": in this sense, he wielded an "indirect" power over them of life and death.[1] But if someone dared to rise up against him and transgress his laws, then he could exercise a direct power over the offender's life: as punishment, the latter could be put to death. Viewed in this way, the power of life and death was not an absolute privilege: it was conditioned by the defense of the sovereign, and his own survival. Must we follow Hobbes in seeing it as the transfer to the prince of the natural right possessed by every individual to defend his life even if this meant the death of others? Or should it be regarded as a specific right that was manifested with the formation of that new juridical being, the sovereign?[2] In any case, in its modern form—relative and limited—as in its ancient and absolute form, the right of life and death is a dissymmetrical one. The sovereign exercised his right of life only by exercising his right to kill, or by refraining from killing; he evidenced his power over life only through the death he was capable of requiring. The right which was formulated as the "power of life and death" was in reality the right to *take* life or *let* live. Its symbol, after all, was the sword. Perhaps this juridical form must be referred to a historical type of society in which power was exercised mainly as a means of deduction (*prélèvement*), a subtraction mechanism, a right to appropriate a portion of the wealth, a tax of products, goods and services, labor and blood, levied on the subjects. Power in this instance was essentially a right of seizure: of things, time, bodies, and ultimately life itself; it culminated in the privilege to seize hold of life in order to suppress it.

Since the classical age, the West has undergone a very profound transformation of these mechanisms of power. "Deduction" has tended to be no longer the major form of power but merely one element among others, working to incite, reinforce, control, monitor, optimize, and organize the forces under it: a power bent on generating forces, making them grow, and ordering them, rather than one dedicated to impeding them, making them submit, or destroying them. There has been a parallel shift in the right of death, or at least a tendency to align itself with the exigencies of a life-administering power and to define itself accordingly. This death that was based on the right of the sovereign is now manifested as simply the reverse of the right of the social body to ensure, maintain, or develop its life. Yet wars were never as bloody as they have been since the nineteenth century, and all things being equal, never before did regimes visit such holocausts on their own populations. But this formidable power of death—and this is perhaps what accounts for part of its force and the cynicism with which it has so greatly expanded its limits—now presents itself as the counterpart of a power that exerts a positive influence on life, that endeavors to administer, optimize, and multiply it, subjecting it to precise controls and comprehensive regulations. Wars are no longer waged in the name of a sovereign who must be defended; they are waged on behalf of the existence of everyone; entire populations are mobilized for the purpose of wholesale slaughter in the name of life necessity: massacres have become vital. It is as managers of life and survival, of bodies and the race, that so many regimes have been able to wage so many wars, causing so many men to be killed. And through a turn that closes the circle, as the technology of wars has caused them to tend increasingly toward all-out destruction, the decision that initiates them and the one that terminates them are in fact increasingly informed by the naked question of survival. The atomic situation is now at the end point of this process: the power to expose a whole population to death is the underside of the power to guarantee an individual's continued existence. The principle underlying the tactics of battle—that one has to be capable of killing in order to go on living—has become the principle that defines the strategy of states. But the existence in question is no longer the juridical existence of sovereignty; at stake is the biological existence of a population. If genocide is indeed the dream of modern powers, this is not because of a recent return of the ancient right to kill; it is because power is situated and exercised at the level of life, the species, the race, and the large-scale phenomena of population.

On another level, I might have taken up the example of the death penalty. Together with war, it was for a long time the other form of the right of the sword; it constituted the reply of the sovereign to those who attacked his will, his law, or his person. Those who died on the scaffold became fewer and fewer, in contrast to those who died in wars. But it was for the same reasons that the latter became more numerous and the former more and more rare. As soon as power gave itself the function of administering life, its reason for being and the logic of its exercise—and not the awakening of humanitarian feelings—made it more and more difficult to apply the death penalty. How could power exercise its highest prerogatives by putting people to death, when its main role was to ensure, sustain, and multiply life, to put this life in order? For such a power, execution was at the same time a limit, a scandal, and a contradiction. Hence capital punishment could not be maintained except by invoking less the enormity of the crime itself than the monstrosity of the criminal, his incorrigibility, and the safeguard of society. One had the right to kill those who represented a kind of biological danger to others.

One might say that the ancient right to *take* life or *let* live was replaced by a power to *foster* life or *disallow* it to the point of death. This is perhaps what explains that disqualification of death which marks the recent wane of the rituals that accompanied it. That death is so carefully evaded is linked less to a new anxiety which makes death unbearable for our societies than to the fact that the procedures of power have not ceased to turn away from death. In the passage from this world to the other, death was the manner in which a terrestrial sovereignty was relieved by another, singularly more powerful sovereignty; the pageantry that surrounded it was in the category of political ceremony. Now it is over life, throughout its unfolding, that power establishes its domination; death is power's limit, the moment that escapes it; death becomes the most secret aspect of existence, the most "private." It is not surprising that suicide—once a crime, since it was a way to usurp the power of death which the sovereign alone, whether the one here below or the Lord above, had the right to exercise—became, in the course of the nineteenth century, one of the first conducts to enter into the sphere of sociological analysis; it testified to the individual and private right to die, at the borders and in the interstices of power that was exercised over life. This determination to die, strange and yet so persistent and constant in its manifestations, and consequently so difficult to explain as being due to particular circumstances or individual accidents, was one of the first astonishments of a society in which political power had assigned itself the task of administering life.

In concrete terms, starting in the seventeenth century, this power over life evolved in two basic forms; these forms were not antithetical, however; they constituted, rather, two poles of development linked together by a whole intermediary cluster of relations. One of these poles—the first to be formed, it seems—centered on the body as a machine: its disciplining, the optimization of its capabilities, the extortion of its forces, the parallel increase of its usefulness and its docility, its integration into systems of efficient and economic controls, all this was ensured by the procedures of power that characterized the *disciplines:* an *anatomo-politics of the human body*. The second, formed somewhat later, focused on the species body, the body imbued with the mechanics of life and serving as the basis of the biological processes: propagation, births and mortality, the level of health, life expectancy and longevity, with all the conditions that can cause these to vary. Their supervision was effected through an entire series of interventions and *regulatory controls: a bio-politics of the population*. The disciplines of the body and the regulations of the population constituted the two poles around which the organization of power over life was deployed. The setting up, in the course of the classical age, of this great bipolar technology—anatomic and biological, individualizing and specifying, directed toward the performances of the body, with attention to the processes of life—characterized a power whose highest function was perhaps no longer to kill, but to invest life through and through.

The old power of death that symbolized sovereign power was now carefully supplanted by the administration of bodies and the calculated management of life. During the classical period, there was a rapid development of various disciplines—universities, secondary schools, barracks, workshops; there was also the emergence, in the field of political practices and economic observation, of the problems of birth rate, longevity, public health, housing, and migration. Hence there was an explosion of numerous and diverse techniques for achieving the subjugation of bodies and the control of populations, marking the beginning of an era of "bio-power." The two directions taken by its development still appeared to be clearly separate in the eighteenth century. With regard to discipline, this development was embodied in institutions such as the army and the schools, and in reflections on tactics, apprenticeship, education, and the nature of societies, ranging from the strictly military analyses of Marshal de Saxe to the political reveries of Guibert or Servan. As for population controls, one notes the emergence of demography, the evaluation of the relationship between resources and inhabitants, the constructing of tables analyzing wealth and its circulation: the work of Quesnay, Moheau, and Süssmilch. The philosophy of the "ideologists," as a theory of ideas, signs, and the individual genesis of sensations, but also a theory of the social composition of interests—ideology being a doctrine of apprenticeship, but also a doctrine of contracts and the regulated formation of the social body—no doubt constituted the abstract discourse in which one sought to coordinate these two techniques of power in order to construct a general theory of it. In point of fact, however, they were not to be joined at the level of a speculative discourse, but in the form of concrete arrangements *(agencement concrets)* that would go to make up the great technology of power in the nineteenth century: the deployment of sexuality would be one of them, and one of the most important.

This bio-power was, without question, an indispensable element in the development of capitalism; the latter would not have been possible without the controlled insertion of bodies into the machinery of production and the adjustment of the phenomena of population to economic processes. But this was not all it required; it also needed the growth of both these factors, their reinforcement as well as their availability and docility; it had to have methods of power capable of optimizing forces, aptitudes, and life in general without at the same time making them more difficult to govern. If the development of the great instruments of the state, as *institutions* of power, ensured the maintenance of production relations, the rudiments of anatomo- and bio-politics, created in the eighteenth century as *techniques* of power present at every level of the social body and utilized by very diverse institutions (the family and the army, schools and the police, individual medicine and the administration of collective bodies), operated in the sphere of economic processes, their development, and the forces working to sustain them. They also acted as factors of segregation and social hierarchization, exerting their influence on the respective forces of both these movements, guaranteeing relations of domination and effects of hegemony. The adjustment of the accumulation of men to that of capital, the joining of the growth of human groups to the expansion of the productive forces and the differential allocation of profit, was made possible in part by the exercise of bio-power in its many forms and modes of application. The investment of the body, its valorization, and the distributive management of its forces were at the time indispensable.

One knows how many times the question has been raised concerning the role of an ascetic morality in the first formation of capitalism; but what occurred in the eighteenth century in some Western countries, an event bound up with the development of capitalism, was a different phenomenon, having perhaps a wider impact than the new morality; this was nothing less than the entry of life into history, that is, the entry of phenomena peculiar to the life of the human species into the order of knowledge and power, into the sphere of political techniques. It is not a question of claiming that this was the moment when the first contact between life and history was brought about. On the contrary, the pressure exerted by the biological on the historical had remained very strong for thousands of years; epidemics and famine were the two great dramatic forms of this relationship that was always dominated by the menace of death. But through a circular process, the economic—and primarily agricultural—development of the eighteenth century, and an increase in productivity and resources even more rapid than the demographic growth it encouraged, allowed a measure of relief from these profound threats: despite some renewed outbreaks, the period of great ravages from starvation and plague had come to a close before the French Revolution; death was ceasing to torment life so directly. But at the same time, the development of the different fields of knowledge concerned with life in general, the improvement of agricultural techniques, and the observations and measures relative to man's life and survival contributed to this relaxation: a relative control over life averted some of the imminent risks of death. In the space for movement thus conquered, and broadening and organizing that space, methods of power and knowledge assumed responsibility for the life processes and undertook to control and modify them. Western man was gradually learning what it meant to be a living species in a living world, to have a body, conditions of existence, probabilities of life, an individual and collective welfare, forces that could be modified, and a space in which they could be distributed in an optimal manner. For the first time in history, no doubt, biological existence was reflected in political existence; the fact of living was no longer an inaccessible substrate that only emerged from time to time, amid the randomness of death and its fatality; part of it passed into knowledge's field of control and power's sphere of intervention. Power would no longer be dealing simply with legal subjects over whom the ultimate dominion was death, but with living beings, and the mastery it would be able to exercise over them would have to be applied at the level of life itself; it was the taking charge of life, more than the threat of death, that gave power its access even to the body. If one can apply the term *bio-history* to the pressures through which the movements of life and the processes of history interfere with one another, one would have to speak of *bio-power* to designate what brought life and its mechanisms into the realm of explicit calculations and made knowledge-power an agent of transformation of human life. It is not that life has been totally integrated into techniques that govern and administer it; it constantly escapes them. Outside the Western world, famine exists, on a greater scale than ever; and the biological risks confronting the species are perhaps greater, and certainly more serious, than before the birth of microbiology. But what might be called a society's "threshold of modernity" has been reached when the life of the species is wagered on its own political strategies. For millennia, man remained what he was for Aristotle: a living animal with the additional capacity for a political existence; modern man is an animal whose politics places his existence as a living being in question.

This transformation had considerable consequences. It would serve no purpose here to dwell on the rupture that occurred then in the pattern of scientific discourse and on the manner in which the twofold problematic of life and man disrupted and redistributed the order of the classical episteme. If the question of man was raised—insofar as he was a specific living being, and specifically related to other living beings—the reason for this is to be sought in the new mode of relation between history and life: in this dual position of life that placed it at the same time outside history, in its biological environment, and inside human historicity, penetrated by the latter's techniques of knowledge and power. There is no need either to lay further stress on the proliferation of political technologies that ensued, investing the body, health, modes of subsistence and habitation, living conditions, the whole space of existence.

Another consequence of this development of bio-power was the growing importance assumed by the action of the norm, at the expense of the juridical system of the law. Law cannot help but be armed, and its arm *par excellence* is death; to those who transgress it, it replies, at least as a last resort, with that absolute menace. The law always refers to the sword. But a power whose task is to take charge of life needs continuous regulatory and corrective mechanisms. It is no longer a matter of bringing death into play in the field of sovereignty, but of distributing the living in the domain of value and utility. Such a power has to qualify, measure, appraise, and hierarchize, rather than display itself in its murderous splendor; it does not have to draw the line that separates the enemies of the sovereign from his obedient subjects; it effects distributions around the norm. I do not mean to say that the law fades into the background or that the institutions of justice tend to disappear, but rather that the law operates more and more as a norm, and that the judicial institution is increasingly incorporated into a continuum of apparatuses (medical, administrative, and so on) whose functions are for the most part regulatory. A normalizing society is the historical outcome of a technology of power centered on life. We have entered a phase of juridical regression in comparison with the pre-seventeenth-century societies we are acquainted with; we should not be deceived by all the constitutions framed throughout the world since the French Revolution, the codes written and revised, a whole continual and clamorous legislative activity: these were the forms that made an essentially normalizing power acceptable.

Moreover, against this power that was still new in the nineteenth century, the forces that resisted relied for support on the very thing it invested, that is, on life and man as a living being. Since the last century, the great struggles that have challenged the general system of power were not guided by the belief in a return to former rights, or by the age-old dream of a cycle of time or a Golden Age. One no longer aspired toward the coming of the emperor of the poor, or the kingdom of the latter days, or even the restoration of our imagined ancestral rights; what was demanded and what served as an objective was life, understood as the basic needs, man's concrete essence, the realization of his potential, a plenitude of the possible. Whether or not it was utopia that was wanted is of little importance; what we have seen has been a very real process of struggle; life as a political object was in a sense taken at face value and turned back against the system that was bent on controlling it. It was life more than the law that became the issue of political struggles, even if the latter were formulated through affirmations concerning rights. The "right" to life, to one's body, to health, to happiness, to the satisfaction of needs, and, beyond all the oppressions or "alienations," the "right" to rediscover what one is and all that one can be, this "right"—which the classical juridical system was utterly incapable of comprehending—was the political response to all these new procedures of power which did not derive, either, from the traditional right of sovereignty.

This is the background that enables us to understand the importance assumed by sex as a political issue. It was at the pivot of the two axes along which developed the entire political technology of life. On the one hand, it was tied to the disciplines of the body: the harnessing, intensification, and distribution of forces, the adjustment and economy of energies. On the other hand, it was applied to the regulation of populations, through all the far-reaching effects of its activity. It fitted in both categories at once, giving rise to infinitesimal surveillances, permanent controls, extremely meticulous orderings of space, indeterminate medical or psychological examinations, to an entire micropower concerned with the body. But it gave rise as well to comprehensive measures, statistical assessments, and interventions aimed at the entire social body or at groups taken as a whole. Sex was a means of access both to the life of the body and the life of the species. It was employed as a standard for the disciplines and as a basis for regulations. This is why in the nineteenth century sexuality was sought out in the smallest details of individual existences; it was tracked down in behavior, pursued in dreams; it was suspected of underlying the least follies; it was traced back into the earliest years of childhood; it became the stamp of individuality—at the same time what enabled one to analyze the latter and what made it possible to master it. But one also sees it becoming the theme of political operations, economic interventions (through incitements to or curbs on procreation), and ideological campaigns for raising standards of morality and responsibility: it was put forward as the index of a society's strength, revealing of both its political energy and its biological vigor. Spread out from one pole to the other of this technology of sex was a whole series of different tactics that combined in varying proportions the objective of disciplining the body and that of regulating populations.

Whence the importance of the four great lines of attack along which the politics of sex advanced for two centuries. Each one was a way of combining disciplinary techniques with regulative methods. The first two rested on the requirements of regulation, on a whole thematic of the species, descent, and collective welfare, in order to obtain results at the level of discipline; the sexualization of children was accomplished in the form of a campaign for the health of the race (precocious sexuality was presented from the eighteenth century to the end of the nineteenth as an epidemic menace that risked compromising not only the future health of adults but the future of the entire society and species); the hysterization of women, which involved a thorough medicalization of their bodies and their sex, was carried out in the name of the responsibilty they owed to the health of their children, the solidity of the family institution, and the safeguarding of society. It was the reverse relationship that applied in the case of birth controls and psychiatrization of perversions: here the intervention was regulatory in nature, but it had to rely on the demand for individual disciplines and constraints (*dressages*). Broadly speaking, at the juncture of the "body" and the "population," sex became a crucial target of a power organized around the management of life rather than the menace of death.

The blood relation long remained an important element in the mechanisms of power, its manifestations, and its rituals. For a society in which the systems of alliance, the political form of the sovereign, the differentiation into orders and castes, and the value of descent lines were predominant; for a society in which famine, epidemics, and violence made death imminent, blood constituted one of the fundamental values. It owed its high value at the same time to its instrumental role (the ability to shed blood), to the way it functioned in the order of signs (to have a certain blood, to be of the same blood, to be prepared to risk one's blood), and also to its precariousness (easily spilled, subject to drying up, too readily mixed, capable of being quickly corrupted). A society of blood—I was tempted to say, of "sanguinity"—where power spoke *through* blood: the honor of war, the fear of famine, the triumph of death, the sovereign with his sword, executioners, and tortures; blood was *a reality with a symbolic function*. We, on the other hand, are in a society of "sex," or rather, a society "with a sexuality": the mechanisms of power are addressed to the body, to life, to what causes it to proliferate, to what reinforces the species, its stamina, its ability to dominate, or its capacity for being used. Through the themes of health, progeny, race, the future of the species, the vitality of the social body, power spoke *of* sexuality and *to* sexuality; the latter was not a mark or a symbol, it was an object and a target. Moreover, its importance was due less to its rarity or its precariousness than to its insistence, its insidious presence, the fact that it was everywhere an object of excitement and fear at the same time. Power delineated it, aroused it, and employed it as the proliferating meaning that had always to be taken control of again lest it escape; it was *an effect with a meaning-value*. I do not mean to say that a substitution of sex for blood was by itself responsible for all the transformations that marked the threshold of our modernity. It is not the soul of two civilizations or the organizing principle of two cultural forms that I am attempting to express; I am looking for the reasons for which sexuality, far from being repressed in the society of that period, on the contrary was constantly aroused. The new procedures of power that were devised during the classical age and employed in the nineteenth century were what caused our societies to go from *a symbolics of blood* to *an analytics of sexuality*. Clearly, nothing was more on the side of the law, death, transgression, the symbolic, and sovereignty than blood; just as sexuality was on the side of the norm, knowledge, life, meaning, the disciplines, and regulations.

Sade and the first eugenists were contemporary with this transition from "sanguinity" to "sexuality." But whereas the first dreams of the perfecting of the species inclined the whole problem toward an extremely exacting administration of sex (the art of determining good marriages, of inducing the desired fertilities, of ensuring the health and longevity of children), and while the new concept of race tended to obliterate the aristocratic particularities of blood, retaining only the controllable effects of sex, Sade carried the exhaustive analysis of sex over into the mechanisms of the old power of sovereignty and endowed it with the ancient but fully maintained prestige of blood; the latter flowed through the whole dimension of pleasure—the blood of torture and absolute power; the blood of the caste, which was respected in itself and which nonetheless was made to flow in the major rituals of parricide and incest; the blood of the people, which was shed unreservedly since the sort that flowed in its veins was not even deserving of a name. In Sade, sex is without any norm or intrinsic rule that might be formulated from its own nature; but it is subject to the unrestricted law of a power which itself knows no other law but its own; if by chance it is at times forced to accept the order of progressions carefully disciplined into successive days, this exercise carries it to a point where it is no longer anything but a unique and naked sovereignty: an unlimited right of all-powerful monstrosity.

While it is true that the analytics of sexuality and the symbolics of blood were grounded at first in two very distinct regimes of power, in actual fact the passage from one to the other did not come about (any more than did these powers themselves) without overlappings, interactions, and echoes. In different ways, the preoccupation with blood and the law has for nearly two centuries haunted the administration of sexuality. Two of these interferences are noteworthy, the one for its historical importance, the other for the problems it poses. Beginning in the second half of the nineteenth century, the thematic of blood was sometimes called on to lend its entire historical weight toward revitalizing the type of political power that was exercised through the devices of sexuality. Racism took shape at this point (racism in its modern, "biologizing," statist form): it was then that a whole politics of settlement (*peuplement*), family, marriage, education, social hierarchization, and property, accompanied by a long series of permanent interventions at the level of the body, conduct, health, and everyday life, received their color and their justification from the mythical concern with protecting the purity of the blood and ensuring the triumph of the race. Nazism was doubtless the most cunning and the most naive (and the former because of the latter) combination of the fantasies of blood and the paroxysms of a disciplinary power. A eugenic ordering of society, with all that implied in the way of extension and intensification of micropowers, in the guise of an unrestricted state control (*étatisation*), was accompanied by the oneiric exaltation of a superior blood; the latter implied both the systematic genocide of others and the risk of exposing oneself to a total sacrifice. It is an irony of history that the Hitlerite politics of sex remained an insignificant practice while the blood myth was transformed into the greatest blood bath in recent memory.

At the opposite extreme, starting from this same end of the nineteenth century, we can trace the theoretical effort to reinscribe the thematic of sexuality in the system of law, the symbolic order, and sovereignty. It is to the political credit of psychoanalysis—or, at least, of what was most coherent in it—that it regarded with suspicion (and this from its inception, that is, from the moment it broke away from the neuropsychiatry of degenerescence) the irrevocably proliferating aspects which might be contained in these power mechanisms aimed at controlling and administering the everyday life of sexuality: whence the Freudian endeavor (out of reaction, no doubt, to the great surge of racism that was contemporary with it) to ground sexuality in the law—the law of alliance, tabooed consanguinity, and the Sovereign-Father—in short, to surround desire with all the trappings of the old order of power. It was owing to this that psychoanalysis was—in the main, with a few exceptions—in theoretical and practical opposition to fascism. But this position of psychoanalysis was tied to a specific historical conjuncture. And yet, to conceive the category of the sexual in terms of the law, death, blood, and sovereignty—whatever the references to Sade and Bataille, and however one might gauge their "subversive" influence—is in the last analysis a historical "retroversion." We must conceptualize the deployment of sexuality on the basis of the techniques of power that are contemporary with it. . . .

Notes

1 Samuel von Pufendorf, *Le Droit de la nature* (French trans. 1734), p. 445.

2 "Just as a composite body can have properties not found in any of the simple bodies of which the mixture consists, so a moral body, by virtue of the very union of persons of which it is composed, can have certain rights which none of the individuals could expressly claim and whose exercise is the proper function of leaders alone" (Ibid., p. 452).

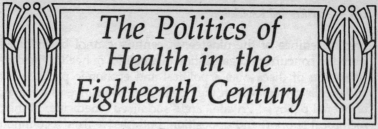

The Politics of Health in the Eighteenth Century

(FROM *Power/Knowledge*)

First of all, two preliminary remarks:

1. No doubt it is scarcely fruitful to look for a relation of anteriority or dependence between the two terms of a private, "liberal" medicine, subject to the mechanisms of individual initiative and laws of the market, and a medical politics, drawing support from structures of power and concerning itself with the health of a collectivity. It is somewhat mythical to suppose that Western medicine originated as a collective practice, endowed by magico-religious institutions with its social character and gradually dismantled through the subsequent organization of private clienteles.[1] But it is equally inadequate to posit the existence at the historical threshold of modern medicine of a singular, private, individual medical relation, "clinical" in its economic functioning and epistemological form, and to imagine that a series of corrections, adjustments, and constraints gradually came to socialize this relation, causing it to be to some degree taken charge of by the collectivity.

What the eighteenth century shows, in any case, is a double-sided process. The development of a medical market in the form of private clienteles; the extension of a network of personnel offering qualified medical attention; the growth of individual and family demand for health care; the emergence of a clinical medicine strongly centered on individual examination, diagnosis, and therapy; the explicitly moral and scientific—and secretly economic—exaltation of "private consultation"; in short, the progressive emplacement of what was to become the great

273

medical edifice of the nineteenth century cannot be divorced from the concurrent organization of a politics of health, the consideration of disease as a political and economic problem for social collectivities which they must seek to resolve as a matter of overall policy. "Private" and "socialized" medicine, in their reciprocal support and opposition, both derive from a common global strategy. No doubt there is no society which does not practice some kind of "noso-politics": the eighteenth century didn't invent this. But it prescribed new rules, and above all transposed the practice onto an explicit, concerted level of analysis such as had been previously unknown. At this point the age is entered not so much of social medicine as of a considered noso-politics.

2. The center of initiative, organization, and control for this politics should not be located only in the apparatuses of the state. In fact, there were a number of distinct health policies and various different methods for taking charge of medical problems: those of religious groups (the considerable importance, for example, of the Quakers and the various dissenting movements in England); those of charitable and benevolent associations, ranging from the parish *bureaux* to the philanthropic societies, which operated somewhat like organs of the surveillance of one class over those others which, precisely because they were less able to defend themselves, were sources of collective danger; those of the learned societies, the eighteenth-century academies and the early nineteenth-century statistics societies which endeavor to organize a global, quantifiable knowledge of morbid phenomena. Health and sickness, as characteristics of a group, a population, are problematized in the eighteenth century through the initiatives of multiple social instances, in relation to which the state itself plays various different roles. On occasion, it intervenes directly: a policy of free distribution of medicines was pursued in France on a varying scale from Louis XIV to Louis XVI. From time to time it also establishes bodies for purposes of consultation and information (the Prussian Sanitary Collegium dates from 1685; the Royal Society of Medicine was founded in France in 1776). Sometimes the state's projects for authoritarian medical organization are thwarted: the code of health

elaborated by Mai and accepted by the elector palatine in 1800 was never put into effect. Occasionally the state is also the object of solicitations which it resists.

Thus the eighteenth-century problematization of noso-politics does not correlate with a uniform trend of state intervention in the practice of medicine, but rather with the emergence at a multitude of sites in the social body of health and disease as problems requiring some form or other of collective control measures. Rather than being the product of a vertical initiative coming from above, noso-politics in the eighteenth century figures as a problem with a number of different origins and orientations, being the problem of the health of all as a priority for all, the state of health of a population as a general objective of policy.

The most striking trait of this noso-politics, concern with which extends throughout French and indeed European society in the eighteenth century, no doubt consists in the displacement of health problems relative to problems of assistance. Schematically, one can say that up to the end of the seventeenth century, institutions for assistance to the poor serve as the collective means of dealing with disease. Certainly there are exceptions to this: the regulations for times of epidemic, measures taken in plague towns, and the quarantines enforced in certain large ports, all constituted forms of authoritarian medicalization not organically linked to techniques of assistance. But outside these limit cases, medicine understood and practiced as a "service" operated simply as one of the components of "assistance." It was addressed to the category, so important despite the vagueness of its boundaries, of the "sick poor." In economic terms, this medical service was provided mainly thanks to charitable foundations. Institutionally, it was exercised within the framework of lay and religious organizations devoted to a number of ends: distribution of food and clothing, care of abandoned children, projects of elementary education and moral proselytism, provision of workshops and workrooms, and in some cases the surveillance of "unstable" or "troublesome" elements (in the cities, the hospital *bureaux* had a jurisdiction over vagabonds and beggars, and the parish *bureaux* and charitable societies also very explicitly adopted the role of denouncing "bad subjects"). From a technical point of view, the role of therapeutics in the working of the hospitals in the classical age was limited in extent in comparison with the scale of provision of material assistance, and with the administrative structure. Sickness is only one among a range of factors, including infirmity, old age, inability to find work, and destitution, which compose the figure of the "necessitous pauper" who deserves hospitalization.

The first phenomenon during the eighteenth century which should be noted is the progressive dislocation of these mixed and polyvalent procedures of assistance. This dismantling is carried out, or rather is called for (since it only begins to become effective late in the century), as the upshot of a general reexamination of modes of investment and capitalization. The system of "foundations," which immobilize substantial sums of money and whose revenues serve to support the idle and thus allow them to remain outside the circuits of production, is criticized by economists and administrators. The process of dismemberment is also carried out as a result of a finer grid of observation of the population and the distinctions which this observation aims to draw between the different categories of unfortunates to which charity confusedly addresses itself. In this process of the gradual attenuation of traditional social statuses, the "pauper" is one of the first to be effaced, giving way to a whole series of functional discriminations (the good poor and the bad poor, the willfully idle and the involuntarily unemployed, those who can do some kind of work and those who cannot). An analysis of idleness—and its conditions and effects—tends to replace the somewhat global charitable sacralization of "the poor." This analysis has as its practical objective at best to make poverty useful by fixing it to the apparatus of production, at worst to lighten as much as possible the burden it imposes on the rest of society. The problem is to set the "able-bodied" poor to work and transform them into a useful labor force, but it is also to assure the self-financing by the poor themselves of the cost of their sickness and temporary or permanent incapacitation, and further to render profitable in the short or long term the educating of orphans and foundlings. Thus, a complete utilitarian decomposition of poverty is marked out and the specific problem of the sickness of the poor begins to figure in the relationship of the imperatives of labor to the needs of production.

But one must also note another process which is more general than the first, and more than its simple elaboration. This is the emergence of the health and physical well-being of the population in general as one of the essential objectives of political power. Here it is not a matter of offering support to a particularly fragile, troubled and troublesome margin of the population, but of how to raise the level of health of the social body as a whole. Different power apparatuses are called upon to take charge of "bodies," not simply so as to exact blood service from them or levy dues, but to help and, if necessary, constrain them to ensure their own good health. The imperative of health: at once the duty of each and the objective of all.

Taking a longer perspective, one could say that from the heart of the Middle Ages power traditionally exercised two great functions: that of war and peace, which it exercised through the hard-won monopoly of arms, and that of the arbitration of lawsuits and punishments of crimes, which it ensured through its control of judicial functions. *Pax et justitia.* To these functions were added—from the end of the Middle Ages—those of the maintenance of order and the organization of enrichment. Now in the eighteenth century we find a further function emerging, that of the disposition of society as a milieu of physical well-being, health, and optimum longevity. The exercise of these three latter functions—order, enrichment, and health—is assured less through a single apparatus than by an ensemble of multiple regulations and institutions which in the eighteenth century take the generic name of "police." Down to the end of the *ancien régime*, the term "police" does not signify, at least not exclusively, the institution of police in the modern sense; "police" is the ensemble of mechanisms serving to ensure order, the properly channeled growth of wealth and the conditions of preservation of health "in general." Delamare's *Treatise* on police, the great charter of police functions in the classical period, is significant in this respect. The eleven headings under which it classifies police activities can readily be distinguished in terms of three main sets of aims: economic regulation (the circulation of commodities, manufacturing processes, the obligations of tradespeople both to one another and to their clientele), measures of public order (surveillance of dangerous individuals, expulsion of vagabonds and, if necessary, beggars, and the pursuit of criminals), and general rules of hygiene (checks on the quality of foodstuffs sold, the water supply, and the cleanliness of streets).

At the point when the mixed procedures of police are being broken down into these elements and the problem of sickness among the poor is identified in its economic specificity, the health and physical well-being of populations comes to figure as a political objective which the "police" of the social body must ensure along with those of economic regulation and the needs of order. The sudden importance assumed by medicine in the eighteenth century originates at the point of intersection of a new "analytical" economy of assistance with the emergence of a general "police" of health. The new noso-politics inscribes the specific question of the sickness of the poor within the general problem of the health of populations, and makes the shift from the narrow context of charitable aid to the more general form of a "medical police," imposing its constraints and dispensing its services. The texts of T. Rau (the *Medizinische Polizei ordnung* of 1764), and above all the great work of J. P. Frank, *System einer medizinische Polizei*, give this transformation its most coherent expression.

What is the basis for this transformation? Broadly, one can say that it has to do with the preservation, upkeep, and conservation of the "labor force." But no doubt the problem is a wider one. It arguably concerns the economico-political effects of the accumulation of men. The great eighteenth-century demographic upswing in Western Europe, the necessity for coordinating and integrating it into the apparatus of production, and the urgency of controlling it with finer and more adequate power mechanisms cause "population," with its numerical variables of space and chronology, longevity and health, to emerge not only as a problem but as an object of surveillance, analysis, intervention, modification, etc. The project of a technology of population begins to be sketched: demographic estimates, the calculation of the pyramid of ages, different life expectations and levels of mortality, studies of the reciprocal relations of growth of wealth and growth of population, various measures of incitement to marriage and procreation, the development of forms of education and professional training. Within this set of problems, the "body"—the body of individuals and the body of populations— appears as the bearer of new variables, not merely between the scarce and the numerous, the submissive and the restive, rich and poor, healthy and sick, strong and weak, but also between the more or less utilizable, more or less amenable to profitable investment, those with greater or lesser prospects of survival, death, and illness, and with more or less capacity for being usefully trained. The biological traits of a population become relevant factors for economic management, and it becomes necessary to organize around them an apparatus which will ensure not only their subjection but the constant increase of their utility.

This enables us to understand the main characteristics of eighteenth-century noso-politics as follows:

1. *The privilege of the child and the medicalization of the family.* The problem of "children" (that is, of their number at birth and the relation of births to mortalities) is now joined by the problem of "childhood" (that is, of survival to adulthood, the physical and economic conditions for this survival, the necessary and sufficient amount of investment for the period of child development to become useful, in brief the organization of this "phase" perceived as being both specific and finalized). It is no longer just a matter of producing an optimum number of children, but one of the correct management of this age of life.

New and highly detailed rules serve to codify relations between adults and children. The relations of filial submission and the system of signs that these entail certainly persist, with few changes. But they are to be henceforth invested by a whole series of obligations imposed on parents and children alike: obligations of a physical kind (care, contact, hygiene, cleanliness, attentive proximity), suckling of children by their mothers, clean clothing, physical exercise to ensure the proper development of the organism: the permanent and exacting corporal relation between adults and their children. The family is no longer to be just a system of relations inscribed in a social status, a kinship system, a mechanism for the transmission of property. It is to become a dense, saturated, permanent, continuous physical environment which envelops, maintains, and develops the child's body. Hence it assumes a material figure defined within a narrower compass; it organizes itself as the child's immediate environment, tending increasingly to become its basic framework for survival and growth. This leads to an effect of tightening, or at least intensification, of the elements and relations constituting the restricted family (the group of parents and children). It also leads to a certain inversion of axes: the conjugal bond no longer serves only, nor even perhaps primarily, to establish the junction of two lines of descent, but to organize the matrix of the new adult individual. No doubt it still serves to give rise to two lineages and hence produce a descent, but it serves also to produce—under the best possible conditions—a human being who will live to the state of adulthood. The new "conjugality" lies, rather, in the link between parents and children. The family, seen as a narrow, localized pedagogical apparatus, consolidates itself within the interior of the great traditional family-as-alliance. And at the same time health, and principally the health of children, becomes one of the family's most demanding objectives. The rectangle of parents and children must become a sort of homeostasis of health. At all events, from the eighteenth century onward, the healthy, clean, fit body; a purified, cleansed, aerated domestic space; the medically optimal siting of individuals, places, beds, and utensils; and the interplay of the "caring" and the "cared-for" figure among the family's essential laws. And from this period the family becomes the most constant agent of medicalization. From the second half of the eighteenth century, the family is the target for a great enterprise of medical acculturation. The first wave of this offensive bears on care of children, especially babies. Among the principal texts are Audrey's *L'Orthopédie* (1749); Vandermonde's *Essai sur la manière de perfectionner l'espèce humaine* (1756); Cadogan's *An Essay upon Nursing, and the Management of Children, from Their Birth to Three Years of Age* (1748; French translation, 1752); des Essartz's *Traité de l'éducation corporelle en bas age* (1760); Ballexsert's *Dissertation sur l'éducation physique des enfants* (1762); Raulin's *De la Conser-*

vation des enfants (1768); Nicolas's *Le Cri de la nature en faveur des enfants nouveaux-nés* (1775); Daignan's *Tableau des sociétés de la vie humaine* (1786); Saucerotte's *De la Conservation des enfants* (year IV); W. Buchan's *Advice to Mothers on the Subject of Their Own Health; and on the Means of Promoting the Health, Strength and Beauty of Their Offspring* (1803; French translation, 1804); J. A. Millot's *Le Nestor français* (1807), Laplace Chanvre's *Dissertation sur quelques points de l'éducation physique et morale des enfants* (1813); Leretz's *Hygiène des enfants* (1814); and Prévost Leygonie's *Essai sur l'éducation physique des enfants* (1813). This literature gains even further in extension in the nineteenth century with the appearance of a whole series of journals which address themselves directly to the lower classes.

The long campaign of inoculation and vaccination has its place in this movement to organize around the child a system of medical care for which the family is to bear the moral responsibility and at least part of the economic cost. Via different routes, the policy for orphans follows an analogous strategy. Special institutions are opened: the Foundling Hospital, the Enfants Trouvés in Paris; but there is also a system organized for placing children with nurses or in families, where they can make themselves useful by taking at least a minimal part in domestic life, and where, moreover, they will find a more favorable milieu of development at less cost than in a hsopital, where they would be barracked until adolescence.

The medical politics outlined in the eighteenth century in all European countries has as its first effect the organization of the family, or rather the family-children complex, as the first and most important instance for the medicalization of individuals. The family is assigned a linking role between general objectives regarding the good health of the social body and individuals' desire or need for care. This enables a "private" ethic of good health as the reciprocal duty of parents and children to be articulated onto a collective system of hygiene and scientific technique of cure made available to individual and family demand by a professional corps of doctors, qualified and, as it were, recommended by the state. The rights and duties of individuals respecting their health and that of others, the market where supply and demand for medical care meet, authoritarian interventions of power in the order of hygiene and illness accompanied at the same time by the institutionalizing and protection of the private doctor-patient relation, all these features in their multiplicity and coherence characterize the global functioning of the politics of health in the nineteenth century, yet they cannot be properly understood if one abstracts them from this central element formed in the eighteenth century, the medicalized and medicalizing family.

2. *The privilege of hygiene and the function of medicine as an instance of social control.* The old notion of the regime, understood at once as a rule of life and a form of preventive medicine, tends to become enlarged into that of the collective "regime" of a population in general, with the disappearance of the great epidemic tempests, the reduction of the death rate and the extension of the average lifespan and life expectation for every age group as its triple objective. This program of hygiene as a regime of health for populations entails a certain number of authoritarian medical interventions and controls.

First of all, control of the urban space in general: it is this space which constitutes perhaps the most dangerous environment for the population. The disposition of various quarters, their humidity and exposure, the ventilation of the city as a whole, its sewage and drainage systems, the siting of abattoirs and cemeteries, the density of population, all these are decisive factors for the mortality and morbidity of the inhabitants. The city with its principal spatial variables appears as a medicalizable object. Whereas the medical topographies of regions analyze climatic and geological conditions which are outside human control, and can only recommend measures of correction and compensation, the urban topographies outline, in negative at least, the general principles of a concerted urban policy. During the eighteenth century, the idea of the pathogenic city inspired a whole mythology and very real states of popular panic (the Charnel House of the Innocents in Paris was one of these high places of fear); it also gave rise to a medical discourse on urban morbidity and the placing under surveillance of a whole range of urban developments, constructions, and institutions.[2]

In a more precise and localized fashion, the needs of hygiene demand an authoritarian medical intervention in what are regarded as the privileged breeding grounds of disease: prisons; ships; harbor installations; the *hôpitaux généraux* where vagabonds, beggars, and invalids mingle together; the hospitals themselves, whose medical staffing is usually inadequate, and which aggravate or complicate the diseases of their patients, to say nothing of their diffusing of pathological germs into the outside world. Thus priority areas of medicalization in the urban environment are isolated and are destined to constitute so many points for the exercise and application of an intensified medical power. Doctors will, moreover, have the task of teaching individuals the basic rules of hygiene which they must respect for the sake of their own health and that of others: hygiene of food and habitat, exhortations to seek treatment in case of illness.

Medicine, as a general technique of health even more than as a service to the sick or an art of cures, assumes an increasingly important place in the administrative system and the machinery of power—a role which is constantly widened and strengthened throughout the eighteenth century. The doctor wins a footing within the different instances of social power. The administration acts as a point of support and sometimes a point of departure for the great medical inquiries into the health of populations, and conversely doctors devote an increasing amount of their activity to tasks, both general and administrative, assigned to them by power. A "medico-administrative" knowledge begins to develop concerning society, its health and sickness, its conditions of life, housing, and habits, which serves as the basic core for the "social economy" and sociology of the nineteenth century. And there is likewise constituted a politico-medical hold on a population hedged in by a whole series of prescriptions relating not only to disease but to general forms of existence and behavior (food and drink, sexuality and fecundity, clothing and the layout of living space).

A number of phenomena dating from the eighteenth century testify to this hygienist interpretation of political and medical questions and the "surplus of power" which it bestows on the doctor: the increasing presence of doctors in the academies and learned societies, the very substantial medical participation in the production of the Encyclopedias, their presence as coun-

selors to representatives of power, the organization of medical
societies officially charged with a certain number of administrative responsibilities and qualified to adopt or recommend authoritarian measures, the frequent role of doctors as programmers
of a well-ordered society (the doctor as social or political reformer
is a frequent figure in the second half of the eighteenth century),
and the superabundance of dotors in the Revolutionary Assemblies. The doctor becomes the great advisor and expert, if not
in the art of governing, at least in that of observing, correcting,
and improving the social "body" and maintaining it in a permanent state of health. And it is the doctor's function as hygienist, rather than his prestige as a therapist, that assures him
this politically privileged position in the eighteenth century, prior
to his accumulation of economic and social privileges in the
nineteenth century.

The challenge to the hospital institution in the eighteenth century can be understood on the basis of these three major phenomena: the emergence of "population," with its bio-medical
variables of longevity and health; the organization of the nar-
rowly parental family as a relay in a process of medicalization
for which it acts both as the permanent source and the ultimate
instrument; and the interlacing of medical and administrative
instances in organizing the control of collective hygiene.

The point is that in relation to these new problems the
hospital appears in many respects as an obsolete structure. A
fragment of space closed in on itself, a place of internment of
men and diseases, its ceremonious but inept architecture multiplying the ills in its interior without preventing their outward
diffusion, the hospital is more the seat of death for the cities
where it is sited than a therapeutic agent for the population as
a whole. Not only the difficulty of admission and the stringent
conditions imposed on those seeking to enter, but also the incessant disorder of comings and goings, inefficient medical surveillance, and the difficulty of effective treatment cause the hospital
to be regarded, from the moment the population in general is
specified as the object of medicalization and the overall improvement in its level of health as the objective, as an inadequate

instrument. The hospital is perceived as an area of darkness within the urban space that medicine is called upon to purify. And it acts as a deadweight on the economy since it provides a mode of assistance that can never make possible the diminution of poverty, but at best the survival of certain paupers—and hence their increase in number, the prolongation of their sicknesses, the consolidation of their ill health with all the consequent effects of contagion.

Hence there is the idea, which spreads during the eighteenth century, of a replacement of the hospital by three principal mechanisms. The first of these is the organization of a domestic form of "hospitalization." No doubt this has its risks where epidemics are concerned, but it has economic advantages in that the cost to society of the patient's upkeep is far less as he is fed and cared for at home in the normal manner. The cost to the social body is hardly more than the loss represented by his forced idleness, and then only where he had actually been working. The method also offers medical advantages, in that the family—given a little advice—can attend to the patient's needs in a constant and adjustable manner that would be impossible under hospital administration: each family will be enabled to function as a small, temporary, individual, and inexpensive hospital. But such a procedure requires the replacement of the hospital to be backed by a medical corps dispersed throughout the social body and able to offer treatment either free or as cheaply as possible. A medical staffing of the population, provided it is permanent, flexible, and easy to make use of, should render unnecessary a good many of the traditional hospitals. Lastly, it is possible to envisage the care, consultation, and distribution of medicaments already offered by certain hospitals to outpatients being extended on a general basis, without the need to hold or intern the patients: this is the method of the dispensaries which aim to retain the technical advantages of hospitalization without its medical and economic drawbacks.

These three methods gave rise, especially in the latter half of the eighteenth century, to a whole series of projects and programs. They inspired a number of experiments. In 1769 the Red Lion Square dispensary for poor children was opened in London. Thirty years later, almost every district of the city had its dispensary and the annual number of those receiving free treatment there was estimated at nearly 50,000. In France it seems that the main effort was toward the improvement, extension, and more or less homogeneous distribution of medical personnel in town and country. The reform of medical and surgical studies (in 1772 and 1784), the requirement of doctors to practice in boroughs and small towns before being admitted to certain of the large cities, the work of investigation and coordination performed by the Royal Society of Medicine, the increasing part occupied by control of health and hygiene in the responsibilities of the intendants, the development of free distribution of medicaments under the authority of doctors designated by the administration, all these measures are related to a health policy resting on the extensive presence of medical personnel in the social body. At the extreme point of these criticisms of the hospital and this project for its replacement, one finds under the Revolution a marked tendency toward "dehospitalization"; this tendency is already perceptible in the reports of the *Comité de mendicité*, with the project to establish a doctor or surgeon in each rural district to care for the indigent, supervise children under assistance, and practice inoculation. It becomes more clearly formulated under the Convention, with the proposal for three doctors in each district to provide the main health care for the whole population. However, the disappearance of the hospital was never more than the vanishing point of a utopian perspective. The real work lay in the effort to elaborate a complex system of functions in which the hospital comes to have a specialized role relative to the family (now considered as the primary instance of health), to the extensive and continuous network of medical personnel, and to the administrative control of the population. It is within this complex framework of policies that the reform of the hospitals is attempted.

The first problem concerns the spatial adaptation of the hospital, and in particular its adaptation to the urban space in which it is located. A series of discussions and conflicts arise between different schemes of implantation, respectively advocating massive hospitals capable of accommodating a sizable population, uniting and thus rendering more coherent the various forms of treatment, or alternatively smaller hospitals, where patients will receive better attention and the risks of contagion will be less grave. There was another, connected problem: should hospitals be sited outside the cities, where ventilation is better and there is no risk of hospital miasmas being diffused among the population—a solution which in general is linked to the planning of large architectural installations; or should a multiplicity of small hospitals be built at scattered points where they can most easily be reached by the population which is to use them—a solution which often involves the coupling of hospital and dispensary? In either case, the hospital is intended to become a functional element in an urban space where its effects must be subject to measurement and control.

It is also necessary to organize the internal space of the hospital so as to make it medically efficacious, a place no longer of assistance but of therapeutic action. The hospital must function as a "curing machine." First, in a negative manner, all the factors which make the hospital dangerous for its occupants must be suppressed, solving the problem of the circulation of air which must be constantly renewed without its miasmas or mephitic qualities being carried from one patient to another, solving as well the problem of the changing, transport, and laundering of bed linen. Second, in a positive manner, the space of the hospital must be organized according to a concerted therapeutic strategy, through the uninterrupted presence and hierarchical prerogatives of doctors, through systems of observation, notation, and record-taking which make it possible to fix the knowledge of different cases, to follow their particular evolution, and also to globalize the data which bear on the long-term life of a whole population, and finally through substituting better-adapted medical and pharmaceutical cures for the somewhat indiscriminate curative regimes which formed the essential part of traditional nursing. The hospital tends toward becoming an essential element in medical technology, not simply as a place for curing, but as an instrument which, for a certain number of serious cases, makes curing possible.

Consequently it becomes necessary in the hospital to articulate medical knowledge with therapeutic efficiency. In the eighteenth century there emerged specialized hospitals. If there existed certain establishments previously reserved for madmen or venereal patients, this was less for the sake of any specialized treatment than a measure of exclusion or out of fear. The new "unifunctional" hospital, on the other hand, comes to be organized only from the moment when hospitalization becomes the basis, and sometimes the condition, for a more or less complex therapeutic approach. The Middlesex Hospital, intended for the treatment of smallpox and the practice of vaccination, was opened in London in 1745; the London Fever Hospital dates from 1802, and the Royal Ophthalmic Hospital from 1804. The first Maternity Hospital was opened in London in 1749. In Paris, the Enfants Malades was founded in 1802. One sees the gradual constitution of a hospital system whose therapeutic function is strongly emphasized, designed, on the one hand, to cover with sufficient continuity the urban or rural space whose population it has charge of and, on the other, to articulate itself with medical knowledge and its classifications and techniques.

Lastly, the hospital must serve as the supporting structure for the permanent staffing of the population by medical personnel. Both for economic and medical reasons, it must be possible to make the passage from treatment at home to a hospital regime. By their visiting rounds, country and city doctors must lighten the burden of the hospitals and prevent their overcrowding, and in return the hospital must be accessible to patients on the advice and at the request of their doctors. Moreover, the hospital as a place of accumulation and development of knowledge must provide for the training of doctors for private practice. Clinical teaching in the hospital—the first rudiments of which appear in Holland with Sylvius and then Boerhaave, in Vienna with Van Swieten, and in Edinburgh through the linking of the School of Medicine with the Edinburgh Infirmary—becomes at the end of the eighteenth century the general principle around which the reorganization of medical studies is undertaken. The hospital, a therapeutic instrument for the patients who occupy it, contributes at the same time, through its clinical teaching and the quality of the medical knowledge acquired there, to the improvement of the population's health as a whole.

* * *

The return of the hospitals, and more particularly the projects for their architectural, institutional, and technical reorganization, owed its importance in the eighteenth century to this set of problems relating to the urban space, the mass of the population with its biological characteristics, the close-knit family cell, and the bodies of individuals. It is in the history of these materialities, which are at once political and economic, that the "physical" process of transformation of the hospitals is inscribed.

Notes

[1] Cf. George Rosen, *A History of Public Health* (New York: MD Publications, 1958).

[2] Cf. for example, J. P. L. Morel, *Dissertation sur les causes qui contribuent le plus à rendre cachectique et rachitique la constitution d'un grand nombre d'enfants de la ville de Lille* (A dissertation on the causes which most contribute to rendering the constitution of a great number of children in the city of Lille cachectic and rachitic), 1812.

SEX AND TRUTH

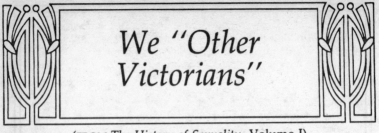

We "Other Victorians"

(FROM *The History of Sexuality*, Volume I)

For a long time, the story goes, we supported a Victorian regime, and we continued to be dominated by it even today. Thus the image of the imperial prude is emblazoned on our restrained, mute, and hypocritical sexuality.

At the beginning of the seventeenth century, a certain frankness was still common, it would seem. Sexual practices had little need of secrecy; words were said without undue reticence, and things were done without too much concealment; one had a tolerant familiarity with the illicit. Codes regulating the coarse, the obscene, and the indecent were quite lax compared to those of the nineteenth century. It was a time of direct gestures, shameless discourse, and open transgressions, when anatomies were shown and intermingled at will, and knowing children hung about amid the laughter of adults: it was a period when bodies "made a display of themselves."

But twilight soon fell upon this bright day, followed by the monotonous nights of the Victorian bourgeoisie. Sexuality was carefully confined; it moved into the home. The conjugal family took custody of it and absorbed it into the serious function of reproduction. On the subject of sex, silence became the rule. The legitimate and procreative couple laid down the law. The couple imposed itself as model, enforced the norm, safeguarded the truth, and reserved the right to speak while retaining the principle of secrecy. A single locus of sexuality was acknowledged in social space as well as at the heart of every household, but it was a utilitarian and fertile one: the parents' bedroom. The rest had only to remain vague; proper demeanor avoided contact with other bodies, and verbal decency sanitized one's speech. And sterile behavior carried the taint of abnormality; if

292

it insisted on making itself too visible, it would be designated accordingly and would have to pay the penalty.

Nothing that was not ordered in terms of generation or transfigured by it could expect sanction or protection. Nor did it merit a hearing. It would be driven out, denied, and reduced to silence. Not only did it not exist, it had no right to exist and would be made to disappear upon its least manifestation—whether in acts or in words. Everyone knew, for example, that children had no sex, which was why they were forbidden to talk about it, why one closed one's eyes and stopped one's ears whenever they came to show evidence to the contrary, and why a general and studied silence was imposed. These are the characteristic features attributed to repression, which serve to distinguish it from the prohibitions maintained by penal law: repression operated as a sentence to disappear, but also as an injunction to silence, an affirmation of nonexistence, and, by implication, an admission that there was nothing to say about such things, nothing to see, and nothing to know. Such was the hypocrisy of our bourgeois society with its halting logic. It was forced to make a few concessions, however. If it was truly necessary to make room for illegitimate sexualities, it was reasoned, let them take their infernal mischief elsewhere: to a place where they could be reintegrated, if not in the circuits of production, at least in those of profit. The brothel and the mental hospital would be those places of tolerance: the prostitute, the client, and the pimp, together with the psychiatrist and his hysteric—those "other Victorians," as Steven Marcus would say—seem to have surreptitiously transferred the pleasures that are unspoken into the order of things that are counted. Words and gestures, quietly authorized, could be exchanged there at the going rate. Only in those places would untrammeled sex have a right to (safely insularized) forms of reality, and only to clandestine, circumscribed, and coded types of discourse. Everywhere else, modern puritanism imposed its triple edict of taboo, nonexistence, and silence.

But have we not liberated ourselves from those two long centuries in which the history of sexuality must be seen first of all as the chronicle of an increasing repression? Only to a slight extent, we are told. Perhaps some progess was made by Freud;

but with such circumspection, such medical prudence, a scientific guarantee of innocuousness, and so many precautions in order to contain everything, with no fear of "overflow," in that safest and most discreet of spaces, between the couch and discourse: yet another round of whispering on a bed. And could things have been otherwise? We are informed that if repression has indeed been the fundamental link between power, knowledge, and sexuality since the classical age, it stands to reason that we will not be able to free ourselves from it except at a considerable cost: nothing less than a transgression of laws, a lifting of prohibitions, an irruption of speech, a reinstating of pleasure within reality, and a whole new economy in the mechanisms of power will be required. For the least glimmer of truth is conditioned by politics. Hence, one cannot hope to obtain the desired results simply from a medical practice, nor from a theoretical discourse, however rigorously pursued. Thus, one denounces Freud's conformism, the normalizing functions of psychoanalysis, the obvious timidity underlying Reich's vehemence, and all the effects of integration ensured by the "science" of sex and the barely equivocal practices of sexology.

This discourse on modern sexual repression holds up well, owing no doubt to how easy it is to uphold. A solemn historical and political guarantee protects it. By placing the advent of the age of repression in the seventeenth century, after hundreds of years of open spaces and free expression, one adjusts it to coincide with the development of capitalism: it becomes an integral part of the bourgeois order. The minor chronicle of sex and its trials is transposed into the ceremonious history of the modes of production; its trifling aspect fades from view. A principle of explanation emerges after the fact: if sex is so rigorously repressed, this is because it is incompatible with a general and intensive work imperative. At a time when labor capacity was being systematically exploited, how could this capacity be allowed to dissipate itself in pleasurable pursuits, except in those—reduced to a minimum—that enabled it to reproduce itself? Sex and its effects are perhaps not so easily deciphered; on the other hand, their repression, thus reconstructed, is easily analyzed. And the sexual cause—the demand for sexual freedom, but also for the knowledge to be gained from sex and the right to speak about it—becomes legitimately associated with the honor of a political cause: sex, too, is placed on the agenda for the future. A suspicious mind might wonder if taking so many precautions in order to give the history of sex such an impressive filiation does not bear traces of the same old prudishness: as if those valorizing correlations were necessary before such a discourse could be formulated or accepted.

But there may be another reason that makes it so gratifying for us to define the relationship between sex and power in terms of repression: something that one might call the speaker's benefit. If sex is repressed, that is, condemned to prohibition, nonexistence, and silence, then the mere fact that one is speaking about it has the appearance of a deliberate transgression. A person who holds forth in such language places himself to a certain extent outside the reach of power; he upsets established law; he somehow anticipates the coming freedom. This explains the solemnity with which one speaks of sex nowadays. When they had to allude to it, the first demographers and psychiatrists of the nineteenth century thought it advisable to excuse themselves for asking their readers to dwell on matters so trivial and base. But for decades now, we have found it difficult to speak on the subject without striking a different pose: we are conscious of defying established power, our tone of voice shows that we know we are being subversive, and we ardently conjure away the present and appeal to the future, whose day will be hastened by the contribution we believe we are making. Something that smacks of revolt, of promised freedom, of the coming age of a different law, slips easily into this discourse on sexual oppression. Some of the ancient functions of prophecy are reactivated therein. Tomorrow sex will be good again. Because this repression is affirmed, one can discreetly bring into coexistence concepts which the fear of ridicule or the bitterness of history prevent most of us from putting side by side: revolution and happiness; or revolution and a different body, one that is newer and more beautiful; or indeed, revolution and pleasure. What sustains our eagerness to speak of sex in terms of repression is doubtless this opportunity to speak out against the powers that be; to utter truths and promise bliss; to link together enlightenment, liberation, and manifold pleasures; to pronounce a discourse that combines the fervor of knowledge, the determination to change the laws, and the longing for the garden of earthly delights. This is perhaps what also explains the market value attributed not only to what is said about sexual repression, but also to the mere fact of lending an ear to those who would eliminate the effects of repression. Ours is, after all, the only civilization in which officials are paid to listen to all and sundry impart the secrets of their sex: as if the urge to talk about it, and the interest one hopes to arouse by doing so, had far surpassed the possibilities of being heard, so that some individuals had even offered their ears for hire.

But it appears to me that the essential thing is not this economic factor, but rather the existence in our era of a discourse in which sex, the revelation of truth, the overturning of global laws, the proclamation of a new day to come, and the promise of a certain felicity are linked together. Today it is sex that serves as a support for the ancient form—so familiar and important in the West—of preaching. A great sexual sermon—which has had its subtle theologians and its popular voices—has swept through our societies over the last decades; it has chastised the old order, denounced hypocrisy, and praised the rights of the immediate and the real; it has made people dream of a New City. The Franciscans are called to mind. And we might wonder how it is possible that the lyricism and religiosity that long accompanied the revolutionary project have, in Western industrial societies, been largely carried over to sex.

The notion of repressed sex is not, therefore, only a theoretical matter. The affirmation of a sexuality that has never been more rigorously subjugated than during the age of the hypocritical, bustling, and responsible bourgeoisie is coupled with the grandiloquence of a discourse purporting to reveal the truth about sex, modify its economy within reality, subvert law that governs it, and change its future. The statement of oppression and the form of the sermon refer back to one another; they are mutually reinforcing. To say that sex is not repressed, or rather that the relationship between sex and power is not characterized by repression, is to risk falling into a sterile paradox. It not only runs counter to a well-accepted argument; it goes against the whole economy and all the discursive "interests" that underlie this argument.

. . . Briefly, my aim is to examine the case of a society which has been loudly castigating itself for its hypocrisy for more than a century, which speaks verbosely of its own silence, takes great pains to relate in detail the things it does not say, denounces the powers it exercises, and promises to liberate itself from the very laws that have made it function. I would like to explore not only these discourses, but also the will that sustains them and the strategic intention that supports them. The question I would like to pose is not: Why are we repressed? but rather: Why do we say, with so much passion and so much resentment against our most recent past, against our present, and against ourselves, that we are repressed? By what spiral did we come to affirm that sex is negated? What led us to show, ostentatiously, that sex is something we hide, to say it is something we silence? And we do all this by formulating the matter in the most explicit terms, by trying to reveal it in its most naked reality, by affirming it in the positivity of its power and its effects. It is certainly legitimate to ask why sex was associated with sin for such a long time—although it would remain to be discovered how this association was formed, and one would have to be careful not to state in a summary and hasty fashion that sex was "condemned"—but we must also ask why we burden ourselves today with so much guilt for having once made sex a sin. What paths have brought us to the point where we are "at fault" with respect to our own sex? And how have we come to be a civilization so peculiar as to tell itself that, through an abuse of power which has not ended, it has long "sinned" against sex? How does one account for the displacement which, while claiming to free us from the sinful nature of sex, taxes us with a great historical wrong which consists precisely in imagining that nature to be blameworthy and in drawing disastrous consequences from that belief?

It will be said that if so many people today affirm this repression, the reason is that it is historically evident. And if they speak of it so abundantly, as they have for such a long time now, this is because repression is so firmly anchored, having solid roots and reasons, and weighs so heavily on sex that more than one denunciation will be required in order to free ourselves from it; the job will be a long one. All the longer, no doubt, as it is in the nature of power—particularly the kind of power that operates in our society—to be repressive, and to be especially careful in repressing useless energies, the intensity of pleasures, and irregular modes of behavior. We must not be surprised, then, if the effects of liberation vis-à-vis this repressive power are so slow to manifest themselves; the effort to speak freely about sex and accept it in its reality is so alien to a historical sequence that has gone unbroken for a thousand years now, and so inimical to the intrinsic mechanisms of power, that it is bound to make little headway for a long time before succeeding in its mission.

One can raise three serious doubts concerning what I shall term the "repressive hypothesis." First doubt: Is sexual repression truly an established historical fact? Is what first comes into view—and consequently permits one to advance an initial hypothesis—really the accentuation or even the establishment of a regime of sexual repression beginning in the seventeenth century? This is a properly historical question. Second doubt: Do the workings of power, and in particular those mechanisms that are brought into play in societies such as ours, really belong primarily to the category of repression? Are prohibition, censorship, and denial truly the forms through which power is exercised in a general way, if not in every society, most certainly in our own? This is a historico-theoretical question. A third and final doubt: Did the critical discourse that addresses itself to repression come to act as a roadblock to a power mechanism that had operated unchallenged up to that point, or is it not in fact part of the same historical network as the thing it denounces (and doubtless misrepresents) by calling it "repression"? Was there really a historical rupture between the age of repression and the critical analysis of repression? This is a historico-political question. My purpose in introducing these three doubts is not merely to construct counterarguments that are symmetrical and contrary to those outlined above; it is not a matter of saying that sexuality, far from being repressed in capitalist and bourgeois societies, has on the contrary benefited from a regime of unchanging liberty; nor is it a matter of saying that power in societies such as ours is more tolerant than repressive, and that the critique of repression, while it may give itself airs of a rupture with the past, actually forms part of a much older process and, depending on how one chooses to understand this process, will appear either as a new episode in the lessening of prohibitions, or as a more devious and discreet form of power.

The doubts I would like to oppose to the repressive hypothesis are aimed less at showing it to be mistaken than at putting it back within a general economy of discourses on sex in modern societies since the seventeenth century. Why has sexuality been so widely discussed, and what has been said about it? What were the effects of power generated by what was said? What are the links between these discourses, these effects of power, and the pleasures that were invested by them? What knowledge (*savoir*) was formed as a result of this linkage? The object, in short, is to define the regime of power-knowledge-pleasure that sustains the discourse on human sexuality in our part of the world. The central issue, then (at least in the first instance), is not to determine whether one says yes or no to sex, whether one formulates prohibitions or permissions, whether one asserts its importance or denies its effects, or whether one refines the words one uses to designate it; but to account for the fact that it is spoken about, to discover who does the speaking, the positions and viewpoints from which they speak, the institutions which prompt people to speak about it and which store and distribute the things that are said. What is at issue, briefly, is the overall "discursive fact," the way in which sex is "put into discourse." Hence, too, my main concern will be to locate the forms of power, the channels it takes, and the discourses it permeates in order to reach the most tenuous and individual modes of behavior, the paths that give it access to the rare or scarcely perceivable forms of desire, how it penetrates and controls everyday pleasure—all this entailing effects that may be those of refusal, blockage, and invalidation, but also incitement and intensification: in short, the "polymorphous techniques of power." And finally, the essential aim will not be to determine whether these discursive productions and these effects of power lead one to formulate the truth about sex or, on the contrary, falsehoods designed to conceal that truth, but rather to bring out the "will to knowledge" that serves as both their support and their instrument.

Let there be no misunderstanding: I do not claim that sex has not been prohibited or barred or masked or misapprehended since the classical age; nor do I even assert that it has suffered these things any less from that period on than before. I do not maintain that the prohibition of sex is a ruse; but it is a ruse to make prohibition into the basic and constitutive element from which one would be able to write the history of what has been said concerning sex starting from the modern epoch. All these negative elements—defenses, censorships, denials—which the repressive hypothesis groups together in one great central mechanism destined to say no, are doubtless only component parts that have a local and tactical role to play in a transformation into discourse, a technology of power, and a will to knowledge that are far from being reducible to the former.

In short, I would like to disengage my analysis from the privileges generally accorded the economy of scarcity and the principles of rarefaction, to search instead for instances of discursive production (which also administer silences, to be sure), of the production of power (which sometimes have the function of prohibiting), of the propagation of knowledge (which often cause mistaken beliefs or systematic misconceptions to circulate); I would like to write the history of these instances and their transformations. A first survey made from this viewpoint seems to indicate that since the end of the sixteenth century, the "putting into discourse of sex," far from undergoing a process of restriction, on the contrary has been subjected to a mechanism of increasing incitement; that the techniques of power exercised over sex have not obeyed a principle of rigorous selection, but rather one of dissemination and implantation of polymorphous sexualities; and that the will to knowledge has not come t a halt in the face of a taboo that must not be lifted, but has persisted in constituting— despite many mistakes, of course—a science of sexuality. It is these movements that I will now attempt to bring into focus in a schematic way, bypassing as it were the repressive hypothesis and the facts of interdiction or exclusion it invokes, and starting from certain historical facts that serve as guidelines for research.

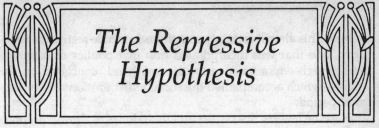

The Repressive Hypothesis

(FROM *The History of Sexuality*, Volume I)

I. The Incitement to Discourse

The seventeenth century, then, was the beginning of an age of repression emblematic of what we call the bourgeois societies, an age which perhaps we still have not completely left behind. Calling sex by its name thereafter became more difficult and more costly. As if in order to gain mastery over it in reality, it had first been necessary to subjugate it at the level of language, control its free circulation in speech, expunge it from the things that were said, and extinguish the words that rendered it too visibly present. And even these prohibitions, it seems, were afraid to name it. Without even having to pronounce the word, modern prudishness was able to ensure that one did not speak of sex, merely through the interplay of prohibitions that referred back to one another: instances of muteness which, by dint of saying nothing, imposed silence. Censorship.

Yet when one looks back over these last three centuries with their continual transformations, things appear in a very different light: around and apropos of sex, one sees a veritable discursive explosion. We must be clear on this point, however. It is quite possible that there was an expurgation—and a very rigorous one—of the authorized vocabulary. It may indeed be true that a whole rhetoric of allusion and metaphor was codified. Without question, new rules of propriety screened out some words: there was a policing of statements. A control over enunciations as well: where and when it was not possible to talk about such things became much more strictly defined; in which circumstances, among which speakers, and within which social relationships. Areas were thus established, if not of utter silence, at least of tact and discretion: between parents and children, for instance, or teachers and pupils, or masters and domestic servants. This almost certainly constituted a whole restrictive economy, one that was incorporated into that politics of language and speech—spontaneous on the one hand, concerted on the other—which accompanied the social redistributions of the classical period.

At the level of discourses and their domains, however, practically the opposite phenomenon occurred. There was a steady proliferation of discourses concerned with sex—specific discourses, different from one another both by their form and by their object: a discursive ferment that gathered momentum from the eighteenth century onward. Here I am thinking not so much of the probable increase in "illicit" discourses, that is, discourses of infraction that crudely named sex by way of insult or mockery of the new code of decency; the tightening up of the rules of decorum likely did produce, as a countereffect, a valorization and intensification of indecent speech. But more important was the multiplication of discourses concerning sex in the field of exercise of power itself: an institutional incitement to speak about it, and to do so more and more; a determination on the part of the agencies of power to hear it spoken about, and to cause *it* to speak through explicit articulation and endlessly accumulated detail.

Consider the evolution of the Catholic pastoral and the sacrament of penance after the Council of Trent. Little by little, the nakedness of the questions formulated by the confession manuals of the Middle Ages, and a good number of those still in use in the seventeenth century, was veiled. One avoided entering into that degree of detail which some authors, such as Sanchez or Tamburini, had for a long time believed indispensable for the confession to be complete: description of the respective positions of the partners, the postures assumed, gestures, places touched, caresses, the precise moment of pleasure—an entire painstaking review of the sexual act in its very unfolding. Discretion was advised, with increasing emphasis. The greatest reserve was counseled when dealing with sins against purity: "This matter is similar to pitch, for, however one might handle it, even to cast it far from oneself, it sticks nonetheless, and always soils." [1] And later, Alfonso de' Liguori prescribed starting—and possibly going no further, especially when dealing with children—with questions that were "roundabout and vague."[2]

But while the language may have been refined, the scope of the confession—the confession of the flesh—continually increased. This was partly because the Counter-Reformation busied itself with stepping up the rhythm of the yearly confession in the Catholic countries, and because it tried to impose meticulous rules of self-examination; but above all, because it attributed more and more importance in penance—and perhaps at the expense of some other sins—to all the insinuations of the flesh: thoughts, desires, voluptuous imaginings, delectations, combined movements of the body and the soul; henceforth all this had to enter, in detail, into the process of confession and guidance. According to the new pastoral, sex must not be named imprudently, but its aspects, its correlations, and its effects must be pursued down to their slenderest ramifications: a shadow in a daydream, an image too slowly dispelled, a badly exorcised complicity between the body's mechanics and the mind's complacency: everything had to be told. A twofold evolution tended to make the flesh into the root of all evil, shifting the most important moment of transgression from the act itself to the stirrings—so difficult to perceive and formulate—of desire. For this was an evil that afflicted the whole man, and in the most secret of forms: "Examine diligently, therefore, all the faculties of your soul: memory, understanding, and will. Examine with precision all your senses as well. . . . Examine, moreover, all your thoughts, every word you speak, and all your actions. Examine even unto your dreams, to know if, once awakened, you did not give them your consent. And finally, do not think that in so sensitive and perilous a matter as this, there is anything trivial or insignificant."[3] Discourse, therefore, had to trace the meeting line of the body and the soul, following all its meanderings: beneath the surface of the sins, it would lay bare the unbroken nervure of the flesh. Under the authority of a language that had been carefully expurgated so that it was no longer directly named, sex was taken charge of, tracked down as it were, by a discourse that aimed to allow it no obscurity, no respite.

It was here, perhaps, that the injunction, so peculiar to the

West, was laid down for the first time, in the form of a general constraint. I am not talking about the obligation to admit to violations of the laws of sex, as required by traditional penance; but of the nearly infinite task of telling—telling oneself and another, as often as possible, everything that might concern the interplay of innumerable pleasures, sensations, and thoughts which, through the body and the soul, had some affinity with sex. This scheme for transforming sex into discourse had been devised long before in an ascetic and monastic setting. The seventeenth century made it into a rule for everyone. It would seem in actual fact that it could scarcely have applied to any but a tiny elite; the great majority of the faithful who only went to confession on rare occasions in the course of the year escaped such complex prescriptions. But the important point, no doubt, is that this obligation was decreed, as an ideal at least, for every good Christian. An imperative was established: Not only will you confess to acts contravening the law, but you will seek to transform your desire, your every desire, into discourse. Insofar as possible, nothing was meant to elude this dictum, even if the words it employed had to be carefully neutralized. The Christian pastoral prescribed as a fundamental duty the task of passing everything having to do with sex through the endless mill of speech.[4] The forbidding of certain words, the decency of expressions, all the censorings of vocabulary, might well have been only secondary devices compared to that great subjugation: ways of rendering it morally acceptable and technically useful.

One could plot a line going straight from the seventeenth-century pastoral to what became its projection in literature, "scandalous" literature at that. "Tell everything," the directors would say time and again: "not only consummated acts, but sensual touchings, all impure gazes, all obscene remarks . . . all consenting thoughts."[5] Sade takes up the injunction in words that seem to have been retranscribed from the treatises of spiritual direction: "Your narrations must be decorated with the most numerous and searching details; the precise way and extent to which we may judge how the passion you describe relates to human manners and man's character is determined by your willingness to disguise no circumstance; and what is more, the least circumstance is apt to have an immense influence upon the procuring of that kind of sensory irritation we expect from your stories."[6] And again at the end of the nineteenth century, the anonymous author of *My Secret Life* submitted to the same prescription; outwardly, at least, this man was doubtless a kind of traditional libertine; but he conceived the idea of complementing his life—which he had almost totally dedicated to sexual activity—with a scrupulous account of every one of its episodes. He sometimes excuses himself by stressing his concern to educate young people, this man who had eleven volumes published, in a printing of only a few copies, which were devoted to the least adventures, pleasures, and sensations of his sex. It is best to take him at his word when he lets into his text the voice of a pure imperative: "I recount the facts, just as they happened, insofar as I am able to recollect them; this is all that I can do"; "a secret life must not leave out anything; there is nothing to be ashamed of . . . one can never know too much concerning human nature."[7] The solitary author of *My Secret Life* often says, in order to justify his describing them, that his strangest practices undoubtedly were shared by thousands of men on the surface of the earth. But the guiding principle for the strangest of these practices, which was the fact of recounting them all, and in detail, from day to day, had been lodged in the heart of modern man for over two centuries. Rather than seeing in this singular man a courageous fugitive from a "Victorianism" that would have compelled him to silence, I am inclined to think that, in an epoch dominated by (highly prolix) directives enjoining discretion and modesty, he was the most direct and in a way the most naive representative of a plurisecular injunction to talk about sex. The historical accident would consist, rather, of the reticences of "Victorian puritanism"; at any rate, they were a digression, a refinement, a tactical diversion in the great process of transforming sex into discourse.

This nameless Englishman will serve better than his queen as the central figure for a sexuality whose main features were already taking shape with the Christian pastoral. Doubtless, in contrast to the latter, for him it was a matter of augmenting the sensations he experienced with the details of what he said about them; like Sade, he wrote "for his pleasure alone," in the strongest sense of the expression; he carefully mixed the editing and rereading of his text with erotic scenes which that writer's activities repeated, prolonged, and stimulated. But, after all, the Christian pastoral also sought to produce specific effects on desire, by the mere fact of transforming it—fully and deliberately—into discourse: effects of mastery and detachment, to be sure, but also an effect of spiritual reconversion, of turning back to God, a physical effect of blissful suffering from feeling in one's body the pangs of temptation and the love that resists it. This is the essential thing: that Western man has been drawn for three centuries to the task of telling everything concerning his sex; that since the classical age there has been a constant optimization and an increasing valorization of the discourse on sex; and that this carefully analytical discourse was meant to yield multiple effects of displacement, intensification, reorientation, and modification of desire itself. Not only were the boundaries of what one could say about sex enlarged, and men compelled to hear it said; but more important, discourse was connected to sex by a complex organization with varying effects, by a deployment that cannot be adequately explained merely by referring it to a law of prohibition. A censorship of sex? There was installed, rather, an apparatus for producing an ever greater quantity of discourse about sex, capable of functioning and taking effect in its very economy.

This technique might have remained tied to the destiny of Christian spirituality if it had not been supported and relayed by other mechanisms. In the first place, by a "public interest." Not a collective curiosity or sensibility; not a new mentality; but power mechanisms that functioned in such a way that discourse on sex—for reasons that will have to be examined—became essential. Toward the beginning of the eighteenth century, there emerged a political, economic, and technical incitement to talk about sex. And not so much in the form of a general theory of sexuality as in the form of analysis, stocktaking, classification, and specification, of quantitative or causal studies. This need to take sex "into account," to pronounce a discourse on sex that would not derive from morality alone but from rationality as well, was sufficiently new that at first it wondered at itself and sought apologies for its own existence. How could a discourse based on reason speak of *that*? "Rarely have philosophers directed a steady gaze to these objects situated between disgust and ridicule, where one must avoid both hypocrisy and scandal."[8] And nearly a century later, the medical establishment, which one might have expected to be less surprised by what it was about to formulate, still stumbled at the moment of speaking: "The darkness that envelops these facts, the shame and disgust they inspire, have always repelled the observer's gaze. . . . For a long time I hesitated to introduce the loathsome picture into this study."[9] What is essential is not in all these scruples, in the "moralism" they betray, or in the hypocrisy one can suspect them of, but in the recognized necessity of overcoming this hesitation. One had to speak of sex; one had to speak publicly and in a manner that was not determined by the division between licit and illicit, even if the speaker maintained the distinction for himself (which is what these solemn and preliminary declarations were intended to show): one had to speak of it as of a thing to be not simply condemned or tolerated but managed, inserted into systems of utility, regulated for the greater good of all, made to function according to an optimum. Sex was not something one simply judged; it was a thing one administered. It was in the nature of a public potential; it called for management procedures; it had to be taken charge of by analytical discourses. In the eighteenth century, sex became a "police" matter—in the full and strict sense given the term at the time: not the repression of disorder, but an ordered maximization of collective and individual forces: "We must consolidate and augment, through the wisdom of its regulations, the internal power of the state; and since this power consists not only in the Republic in general, and in each of the members who constitute it, but also in the faculties and talents of those belonging to it, it follows that the police must concern themselves with these means and make them serve the public welfare. And they can only obtain this result through the knowledge they have of those different assets."[10] A policing of sex: that is, not the rigor of a taboo, but the necessity of regulating sex through useful and public discourses.

A few examples will suffice. One of the great innovations in the techniques of power in the eighteenth century was the emergence of "population" as an economic and political problem: population as wealth, population as manpower or labor capacity, population balanced between its own growth and the resources it commanded. Governments perceived that they were not dealing simply with subjects, or even with a "people," but with a "population," with its specific phenomena and its peculiar variables: birth and death rates, life expectancy, fertility, state of health, frequency of illnesses, patterns of diet and habitation. All these variables were situated at the point where the characteristic movements of life and the specific effects of institutions intersected: "States are not populated in accordance with the natural progression of propagation, but by virtue of their industry, their products, and their different institutions. . . . Men multiply like the yields from the ground and in proportion to the advantages and resources they find in their labors." [11] At the heart of this economic and political problem of population was sex: it was necessary to analyze the birth rate, the age of marriage, the legitimate and illegitimate births, the precocity and frequency of sexual relations, the ways of making them fertile and sterile, the effects of unmarried life or of the prohibitions, the impact of contraceptive practices—of those notorious "deadly secrets" which demographers on the eve of the Revolution knew were already familiar to the inhabitants of the countryside.

Of course, it had long been asserted that a country had to be populated if it hoped to be rich and powerful; but this was the first time that a society had affirmed, in a constant way, that its future and its fortune were tied not only to the number and the uprightness of its citizens, to their marriage rules and family organization, but to the manner in which each individual made use of his sex. Things went from ritual lamenting over the unfruitful debauchery of the rich, bachelors, and libertines to a discourse in which the sexual conduct of the population was taken both as an object of analysis and as a target of intervention; there was a progression from the crudely populationist arguments of the mercantilist epoch to the much more subtle and calculated attempts at regulation that tended to favor or discourage—according to the objectives and exigencies of the moment—an increasing birth rate. Through the political economy of population there was formed a whole grid of observations regarding sex. There emerged the analysis of the modes of sexual conduct, their determinations and their effects, at the boundary line of the biological and the economic domains. There also appeared those systematic campaigns which, going beyond the traditional means—moral and religious exhortations, fiscal measures—tried to transform the sexual conduct of couples into a concerted economic and political behavior. In time these new measures would become anchorage points for the different varieties of racism of the nineteenth and twentieth centuries. It was essential that the state know what was happening with its citizens' sex, and the use they made of it, but also that each individual be capable of controlling the use he made of it. Between the state and the individual, sex became an issue, and a public issue no less; a whole web of discourses, special knowledges, analyses, and injunctions settled upon it.

The situation was similar in the case of children's sex. It is often said that the classical period consigned it to an obscurity from which it scarcely emerged before the *Three Essays* or the beneficent anxieties of Little Hans. It is true that a longstanding "freedom" of language between children and adults, or pupils and teachers, may have disappeared. No seventeenth-century pedagogue would have publicly advised his disciple, as did Erasmus in his *Dialogues*, on the choice of a good prostitute. And the boisterous laughter that had accompanied the precocious sexuality of children for so long—and in all social classes, it seems—was gradually stifled. But this was not a plain and simple imposition of silence. Rather, it was a new regime of discourses. Not any less was said about it; on the contrary. But things were said in a different way; it was different people who said them, from different points of view, and in order to obtain different results. Silence itself—the things one declines to say, or is forbidden to name; the discretion that is required between different speakers—is less the absolute limit of discourse, the other side from which it is separated by a strict boundary, than an element that functions alongside the things said, with them and in relation to them within overall strategies. There is no binary division to be made between what one says and what one does not say; we must try to determine the different ways of not saying such things, how those who can and those who cannot speak of them are distributed, which type of discourse is authorized, or which form of discretion is required in either case. There is not one but many silences, and they are an integral part of the strategies that underlie and permeate discourses.

Take the secondary schools of the eighteenth century, for example. On the whole, one can have the impression that sex was hardly spoken of at all in these institutions. But one only has to glance over the architectural layout, the rules of discipline, and their whole internal organization: the question of sex was a constant preoccupation. The builders considered it explicitly. The organizers took it permanently into account. All who held a measure of authority were placed in a state of perpetual alert, which the fixtures, the precautions taken, the interplay of punishments and responsibilities, never ceased to reiterate. The space for classes, the shape of the tables, the planning of the recreation lessons, the distribution of the dormitories (with or without partitions, with or without curtains), the rules for monitoring bedtime and sleep periods—all this referred, in the most prolix manner, to the sexuality of children.[12] What one might call the internal discourse of the institution—the one it employed to address itself, and which circulated among those who made it function—was largely based on the assumption that this sexuality existed, that it was precocious, active, and ever-present. But this was not all: the sex of the schoolboy became in the course of the eighteenth century—and quite apart from that of adolescents in general—a public problem. Doctors counseled the directors and professors of educational establishments, but they also gave their opinions to families; educators designed projects which they submitted to the authorities; schoolmasters turned to students, made recommendations to them, and drafted for their benefit books of exhortation, full of moral and medical examples. Around the schoolboy and his sex there proliferated a whole literature of precepts, opinions, observations, medical advice, clinical cases, outlines for reform, and plans for ideal institutions. With Basedow and the German "philanthropic" movement, this transformation of adolescent sex into discourse grew to considerable dimensions. Salzmann even organized an experimental school which owed its exceptional character to a supervision and education of sex so well thought out that youth's universal sin would never need to be practiced there. And with all these measures taken, the child was not to be simply the mute and unconscious object of attentions prearranged between adults only; a certain reasonable, limited, canonical, and truthful discourse on sex was prescribed for him—a kind of discursive orthopedics. The great festival organized at the Philanthropinum in May of 1776 can serve as a vignette in this regard. Taking the form of an examination, mixed with floral games, the awarding of prizes, and a board of review, this was the first solemn communion of adolescent sex and reasonable discourse. In order to show the success of the sex education given students, Basedow had invited all the dignitaries that Germany could muster (Goethe was one of the few to decline the invitation). Before the assembled public, one of the professors, a certain Wolke, asked the students selected questions concerning the mysteries of sex, birth, and procreation. He had them comment on engravings that depicted a pregnant woman, a couple, and a cradle. The replies were enlightened, offered without shame or embarrassment. No unseemly laughter intervened to disturb them—except from the very ranks of an adult audience more childish than the children themselves, and whom Wolke severely reprimanded. At the end, they all applauded these cherub-faced boys who, in front of adults, had skillfully woven the garlands of discourse and sex.[13]

It would be less than exact to say that the pedagogical institution has imposed a ponderous silence on the sex of children and adolescents. On the contrary, since the eighteenth century it has multiplied the forms of discourse on the subject; it has established various points of implantation for sex; it has coded contents and qualified speakers. Speaking about children's sex, inducing educators, physicians, administrators, and parents to speak of it, or speaking to them about it, causing children themselves to talk about it, and enclosing them in a web of discourses which sometimes address them, sometimes speak about them, or impose canonical bits of knowledge on them, or use them as a basis for constructing a science that is beyond their grasp—all this together enables us to link an intensification of the interventions of power to a multiplication of discourse. The sex of children and adolescents has become, since the eighteenth century, an important area of contention around which innumerable institutional devices and discursive strategies have been deployed. It may well be true that adults and children themselves were deprived of a certain way of speaking about sex, a mode that was disallowed as being too direct, crude, or coarse. But this was only the counterpart of other discourses, and perhaps the condition necessary in order for them to function; discourses that were interlocking, heirarchized, and all highly articulated around a cluster of power relations.

One could mention many other centers which in the eighteenth or nineteenth century began to produce discourses on sex. First, there was medicine, via the "nervous disorders"; next psychiatry, when it set out to discover the etiology of mental illnesses, focusing its gaze first on "excess," then onanism, then frustration, then "frauds against procreation," but especially when it annexed the whole of the sexual perversions as its own province; criminal justice, too, which had long been concerned with sexuality, particularly in the form of "heinous" crimes and crimes against nature, but which, toward the middle of the nineteenth century, broadened its jurisdiction to include petty offenses, minor indecencies, insignificant perversions; and lastly, all those social controls, cropping up at the end of the last century, which screened the sexuality of couples, parents and children, dangerous and endangered adolescents—undertaking to protect, separate, and forewarn; signaling perils everywhere; awakening people's attention; calling for diagnoses; piling up reports; organizing therapies. These sites radiated discourses aimed at sex, intensifying people's awareness of it as a constant danger, and this in turn created a further incentive to talk about it.

One day in 1867, a farmhand from the village of Lapcourt, who was somewhat simple-minded, employed here then there, depending on the season, living hand-to-mouth from a little charity or in exchange for the worst sort of labor, sleeping in barns and stables, was turned in to the authorities. At the border of a field, he had obtained a few caresses from a little girl, just as he had done before and seen done by the village urchins round about him; for, at the edge of the wood, or in the ditch by the road leading to Saint-Nicolas, they would play the familiar game called "curdled milk." So he was pointed out by the girl's parents to the mayor of the village, reported by the mayor to the gendarmes, led by the gendarmes to the judge, who indicted him and turned him over first to a doctor, then to two other experts who not only wrote their report but also had it published.[14] What is the significant thing about this story? The pettiness of it all; the fact that this everyday occurrence in the life of village sexuality, these inconsequential bucolic pleasures, could become, from a certain time, the object not only of a collective intolerance but of a judicial action, a medical intervention, a careful clinical examination, and an entire theoretical elaboration. The thing to note is that they went so far as to measure the brainspan, study the facial bone structure, and inspect for possible signs of degenerescence the anatomy of this personage who up to that moment had been an integral part of village life; that they made him talk; that they questioned him concerning his thoughts, inclinations, habits, sensations, and opinions. And then, acquitting him of any crime, they decided finally to make him into a pure object of medicine and knowledge—an object to be shut away till the end of his life in the hospital at Maréville, but also one to be made known to the world of learning through a detailed analysis. One can be fairly certain that during this same period the Lapcourt schoolmaster was instructing the little villagers to mind their language and not talk about all these things aloud. But this was undoubtedly one of the conditions enabling the institutions of knowledge and power to overlay this everyday bit of theater with their solemn discourse. So it was that our society—and it was doubtless the first in history to take such measures—assembled around these timeless gestures, these barely furtive pleasures between simple-minded adults and alert children, a whole machinery for speechifying, analyzing, and investigating.

Between the licentious Englishman, who earnestly recorded for his own purposes the singular episodes of his secret life, and his contemporary, this village halfwit who would give a few pennies to the little girls for favors the older ones refused him, there was without doubt a profound connection: in any case, from one extreme to the other, sex became something to say, and to say exhaustively in accordance with deployments that were varied, but all, in their own way, compelling. Whether in the form of a subtle confession in confidence or an authoritarian interrogation, sex—be it refined or rustic—had to be put into words. A great polymorphous injunction bound the Englishman and the poor Lorrainese peasant alike. As history would have it, the latter was named Jouy.[15]

Since the eighteenth century, sex has not ceased to provoke a kind of generalized discursive erethism. And these discourses on sex did not multiply apart from or against power, but in the very space and as the means of its exercise. Incitements to speak were orchestrated from all quarters, apparatuses everywhere for listening and recording, procedures for observing, questioning, and formulating. Sex was driven out of hiding and constrained to lead a discursive existence. From the singular imperialism that compels everyone to transform his sexuality into a perpetual discourse, to the manifold mechanisms which, in the areas of economy, pedagogy, medicine, and justice, incite, extract, distribute, and institutionalize the sexual discourse, an immense verbosity is what our civilization has required and organized. Surely no other type of society has ever accumulated—and in such a relatively short span of time—a similar quantity of discourses concerned with sex. It may well be that we talk about sex more than anything else; we set our minds to the task; we convince ourselves that we have never said enough on the subject, that, through inertia or submissiveness, we conceal from ourselves the blinding evidence, and that what is essential always eludes us, so that we must always start out once again in search of it. It is possible that where sex is concerned, the most long-winded, the most impatient of societies is our own.

But as this first overview shows, we are dealing less with *a* discourse on sex than with a multiplicity of discourses produced by a whole series of mechanisms operating in different institutions. The Middle Ages had organized around the theme of the flesh and the practice of penance a discourse that was markedly unitary. In the course of recent centuries, this relative uniformity was broken apart, scattered, and multiplied in an explosion of distinct discursivities which took form in demography, biology, medicine, psychiatry, psychology, ethics, pedagogy, and political criticism. More precisely, the secure bond that held together the moral theology of concupiscence and the obligation of confession (equivalent to the theoretical discourse on sex and its first-person formulation) was, if not broken, at least loosened and diversified: between the objectification of sex in rational discourses, and the movement by which each individual was set to the task of recounting his own sex, there has occurred, since the eighteenth century, a whole series of tensions, conflicts, efforts at adjustment, and attempts at retranscription. So it is not simply in terms of a continual extension that we must speak of this discursive growth; it should be seen, rather, as a dispersion of centers from which discourses emanated, a diversification of their forms, and the complex deployment of the network connecting them. Rather than the uniform concern to hide sex, rather than a general prudishness of language, what distinguishes these last three centuries is the variety, the wide dispersion of devices that were invented for speaking about it, for having it be spoken about, for inducing it to speak of itself, for listening, recording, transcribing, and redistributing what is said about it: around sex, a whole network of varying, specific, and coercive transpositions into discourse. Rather than a massive censorship, beginning with the verbal proprieties imposed by the Age of Reason, what was involved was a regulated and polymorphous incitement to discourse.

The objection will doubtless be raised that if so many stimulations and constraining mechanisms were necessary in order to speak of sex, this was because there reigned over everyone a certain fundamental prohibition; only definite necessities—economic pressures, political requirements—were able to lift this prohibition and open a few approaches to the discourse on sex, but these were limited and carefully coded; so much talk about sex, so many insistent devices contrived for causing it to be talked about—but under strict conditions: Does this not prove that it was an object of secrecy, and more important, that there is still an attempt to keep it that way? But this oft-stated theme, that sex is outside of discourse and that only the removing of an obstacle, the breaking of a secret, can clear the way leading to it, is precisely what needs to be examined. Does it not partake of the injunction by which discourse is provoked? Is it not with the aim of inciting people to speak of sex that it is made to mirror, at the outer limit of every actual discourse, something akin to a secret whose discovery is imperative, a thing abusively reduced to silence, and at the same time difficult and necessary, dangerous and precious to divulge? We must not forget that by making sex into that which, above all else, had to be confessed, the Christian pastoral always presented it as the disquieting enigma: not a thing which stubbornly shows itself, but one which always hides, the insidious presence that speaks in a voice so muted and often disguised that one risks remaining deaf to it. Doubtless the secret does not reside in that basic reality in relation to which all the incitements to speak of sex are situated—whether they try to force the secret, or whether in some obscure way they reinforce it by the manner in which they speak of it. It is a question, rather, of a theme that forms part of the very mechanics of these incitements: a way of giving shape to the requirement to speak about the matter, a fable that is indispensable to the endlessly proliferating economy of the discourse on sex. What is peculiar to modern societies, in fact, is not that they consigned sex to a shadow existence, but that they dedicated themselves to speaking of it *ad infinitum*, while exploiting it as *the* secret.

II. The Perverse Implantation

A possible objection: it would be a mistake to see in this proliferation of discourses merely a quantitative phenomenon, something like a pure increase, as if what was said in them were immaterial, as if the fact of speaking about sex were of itself more important than the forms of imperatives that were imposed on it by speaking about it. For was this transformation of sex into discourse not governed by the endeavor to expel from reality the forms of sexuality that were not amenable to the strict economy of reproduction: to say no to unproductive activities, to banish casual pleasures, to reduce or exclude practices whose object was not procreation? Through the various discourses, legal sanctions against minor perversions were multiplied; sexual irregularity was annexed to mental illness; from childhood to old age, a norm of sexual development was defined and all the possible deviations were carefully described; pedagogical controls and medical treatments were organized; around the least fantasies, moralists, but especially doctors, brandished the whole emphatic vocabulary of abomination. Were these anything more than means employed to absorb, for the benefit of a genitally centered sexuality, all the fruitless pleasures? All this garrulous attention which has us in a stew over sexuality, is it not motivated by one basic concern: to ensure population, to reproduce labor capacity, to perpetuate the form of social relations: in short, to constitute a sexuality that is economically useful and politically conservative?

I still do not know whether this is the ultimate objective. But this much is certain: reduction has not been the means employed for trying to achieve it. The nineteenth century and our own have been, rather, the age of multiplication: a dispersion of sexualities, a strengthening of their disparate forms, a multiple implantation of "perversions." Our epoch had initiated sexual heterogeneities.

Up to the end of the eighteenth century, three major explicit codes—apart from the customary regularities and constraints of opinion—governed sexual practices: canonical law, the Christian pastoral, and civil law. They determined, each in its own way, the division between licit and illicit. They were all centered on matrimonial relations: the marital obligation, the ability to fulfill it, the manner in which one complied with it, the requirements and violences that accompanied it, the useless or unwarranted caresses for which it was a pretext, its fecundity or the way one went about making it sterile, the moments when one demanded it (dangerous periods of pregnancy or breast-feeding, forbidden times of Lent or abstinence), its frequency or infrequency, and so on. It was this domain that was especially saturated with prescriptions. The sex of husband and wife was beset by rules and recommendations. The marriage relation was the most intense focus of constraints; it was spoken of more than anything else; more than any other relation, it was required to give a detailed accounting of itself. It was under constant surveillance: if it was found to be lacking, it had to come forward and plead its case before a witness. The "rest" remained a good deal more confused: one only has to think of the uncertain status of "sodomy," or the indifference regarding the sexuality of children.

Moreover, these different codes did not make a clear dis-

tinction between violations of the rules of marriage and deviations with respect to genitality. Breaking the rules of marriage
or seeking strange pleasures brought an equal measure of condemnation. On the list of grave sins, and separated only by
their relative importance, there appeared debauchery (extra-
marital relations), adultery, rape, spiritual or carnal incest, but
also sodomy, or the mutual "caress." As to the courts, they
could condemn homosexuality as well as infidelity, marriage
without parental consent, or bestiality. What was taken into
account in the civil and religious jurisdictions alike was a general
unlawfulness. Doubtless acts "contrary to nature" were stamped
as especially abominable, but they were perceived simply as an
extreme form of acts "against the law"; they were infringements
of decrees which were just as sacred as those of marriage, and
which had been established for governing the order of things
and the plan of beings. Prohibitions bearing on sex were essentially of a juridical nature. The "nature" on which they were
based was still a kind of law. For a long time hermaphrodites
were criminals, or crime's offspring, since their anatomical disposition, their very being, confounded the law that distinguished the sexes and prescribed their union.

The discursive explosion of the eighteenth and nineteenth
centuries caused this system centered on legitimate alliance to
undergo two modifications. First, a centrifugal movement with
respect to heterosexual monogamy. Of course, the array of practices and pleasures continued to be referred to it as their internal
standard; but it was spoken of less and less, or in any case with
a growing moderation. Efforts to find out its secrets were abandoned; nothing further was demanded of it than to define itself
from day to day. The legitimate couple, with its regular sexuality, had a right to more discretion. It tended to function as
a norm, one that was stricter, perhaps, but quieter. On the
other hand, what came under scrutiny was the sexuality of children, mad men and women, and criminals; the sensuality of
those who did not like the opposite sex; reveries, obsessions,
petty manias, or great transports of rage. It was time for all
these figures, scarcely noticed in the past, to step forward and
speak, to make the difficult confession of what they were. No
doubt they were condemned all the same; but they were listened

to; and if regular sexuality happened to be questioned once again, it was through a reflux movement, originating in these peripheral sexualities.

Whence the setting apart of the "unnatural" as a specific dimension in the field of sexuality. This kind of activity assumed an autonomy with regard to the other condemned forms such as adultery or rape (and the latter were condemned less and less): to marry a close relative or practice sodomy, to seduce a nun or engage in sadism, to deceive one's wife or violate cadavers, became things that were essentially different. The area covered by the Sixth Commandment began to fragment. Similarly, in the civil order, the confused category of "debauchery," which for more than a century had been one of the most frequent reasons for administrative confinement, came apart. From the debris, there appeared, on the one hand, infractions against the legislation (or morality) pertaining to marriage and the family, and on the other, offenses against the regularity of a natural function (offenses which, it must be added, the law was apt to punish). Here we have a likely reason, among others, for the prestige of Don Juan, which three centuries have not erased. Underneath the great violator of the rules of marriage—stealer of wives, seducer of virgins, the shame of families, and an insult to husbands and fathers—another personage can be glimpsed: the individual driven, in spite of himself, by the somber madness of sex. Underneath the libertine, the pervert. He deliberately breaks the law, but at the same time, something like a nature gone awry transports him far from all nature; his death is the moment when the supernatural return of the crime and its retribution thwart the flight into counternature. There were two great systems conceived by the West for governing sex: the law of marriage and the order of desires—and the life of Don Juan overturned them both. We shall leave it to psychoanalysts to speculate whether he was homosexual, narcissistic, or impotent.

Although not without delay and equivocation, the natural laws of matrimony and the immanent rules of sexuality began to be recorded on two separate registers. There emerged a world of perversion which partook of that of legal or moral infraction, yet was not simply a variety of the latter. An entire subrace race was born, different—despite certain kinship ties—from the libertines of the past. From the end of the eighteenth century to our own, they circulated through the pores of society; they were always hounded, but not always by laws; were often locked up, but not always in prisons; were sick perhaps, but scandalous, dangerous victims, prey to a strange evil that also bore the name of vice and sometimes crime. They were children wise beyond their years, precocious little girls, ambiguous schoolboys, dubious servants and educators, cruel or maniacal husbands, solitary collectors, ramblers with bizarre impulses; they haunted the houses of correction, the penal colonies, the tribunals, and the asylums; they carried their infamy to the doctors and their sickness to the judges. This was the numberless family of perverts who were on friendly terms with delinquents and akin to madmen. In the course of the century they successively bore the stamp of "moral folly," "genital neurosis," "aberration of the genetic instinct," "degenerescence," or "physical imbalance."

What does the appearance of all these peripheral sexualities signify? Is the fact that they could appear in broad daylight a sign that the code had become more lax? Or does the fact that they were given so much attention testify to a stricter regime and to its concern to bring them under close supervision? In terms of repression, things are unclear. There was permissiveness, if one bears in mind that the severity of the codes relating to sexual offenses diminished considerably in the nineteenth century and that law itself often deferred to medicine. But an additional ruse of severity, if one thinks of all the agencies of control and all the mechanisms of surveillance that were put into operation by pedagogy or therapeutics. It may be the case that the intervention of the Church in conjugal sexuality and its rejection of "frauds" against procreation had lost much of its insistence over the previous two hundred years. But medicine made a forceful entry into the pleasures of the couple: it created an entire organic, functional, or mental pathology arising out of "incomplete" sexual practices; it carefully classified all forms of related pleasures; it incorporated them into the notions of "development" and instinctual "disturbances"; and it undertook to manage them.

Perhaps the point to consider is not the level of indulgence or the quantity of repression, but the form of power that was exercised. When this whole thicket of disparate sexualities was labeled, as if to disentangle them from one another, was the object to exclude them from reality? It appears, in fact, that the function of the power exerted in this instance was not that of interdiction, and that it involved four operations quite different from simple prohibition.

1. Take the ancient prohibitions of consanguine marriages (as numerous and complex as they were) or the condemnation of adultery, with its inevitable frequency of occurrence; or, on the other hand, the recent controls through which, since the nineteenth century, the sexuality of children has been subordinated and their "solitary habits" interfered with. It is clear that we are not dealing with one and the same power mechanism. Not only because in the one case it is a question of law and penality and, in the other, medicine and regimentation; but also because the tactics employed are not the same. On the surface, what appears in both cases is an effort at elimination that was always destined to fail and always constrained to begin again. But the prohibition of "incests" attempted to reach its objective through an asymptotic decrease in the thing it condemned, whereas the control of infantile sexuality hoped to reach it through a simultaneous propagation of its own power and of the object on which it was brought to bear. It proceeded in accordance with a twofold increase extended indefinitely. Educators and doctors combatted children's onanism like an epidemic that needed to be eradicated. What this actually entailed, throughout this whole secular campaign that mobilized the adult world around the sex of children, was using these tenuous pleasures as a prop, constituting them as secrets (that is, forcing them into hiding so as to make possible their discovery), tracing them back to their source, tracking them from their origins to their effects, searching out everything that might cause them or simply enable them to exist. Wherever there was the chance they might appear, devices of surveillance were installed; traps were laid for compelling admissions; inexhaustible and corrective discourses were imposed; parents and teachers were alerted, and left with the suspicion that all children were guilty, and with the fear of being

themselves at fault if their suspicions were not sufficiently strong; they were kept in readiness in the face of this recurrent danger; their conduct was prescribed and their pedagogy recodified; an entire medico-sexual regime took hold of the family milieu. The child's "vice" was not so much an enemy as a support; it may have been designated as the evil to be eliminated, but the extraordinary effort that went into the task that was bound to fail leads one to suspect that what was demanded of it was to persevere, to proliferate to the limits of the visible and the invisible, rather than to disappear for good. Always relying on this support, power advanced, multiplied its relays and its effects, while its target expanded, subdivided, and branched out, penetrating further into reality at the same pace. In appearance, we are dealing with a barrier system; but in fact, all around the child, indefinite *lines of penetration* were disposed.

2. This new persecution of the peripheral sexualities entailed an *incorporation of perversions* and a new *specification of individuals*. As defined by the ancient civil or canonical codes, sodomy was a category of forbidden acts; their perpetrator was nothing more than the juridical subject of them. The nineteenth-century homosexual became a personage, a past, a case history, and a childhood, in addition to being a type of life, a life form, and a morphology, with an indiscreet anatomy and possibly a mysterious physiology. Nothing that went into his total composition was unaffected by his sexuality. It was everywhere present in him: at the root of all his actions because it was their insidious and indefinitely active principle; written immodestly on his face and body because it was a secret that always gave itself away. It was consubstantial with him, less as a habitual sin than as a singular nature. We must not forget that the psychological, psychiatric, medical category of homosexuality was constituted from the moment it was characterized—Westphal's famous article of 1870 on "contrary sexual sensations" can stand as its date of birth[16]—less by a type of sexual relation than by a certain quality of sexual sensibility, a certain way of inverting the masculine and the feminine in oneself. Homosexuality appeared as one of the forms of sexuality when it was transposed from the practice of sodomy onto a kind of interior androgyny, a her-

maphrodism of the soul. The sodomite had been a temporary aberration; the homosexual was now a species.

So, too, were all those minor perverts whom nineteenth-century psychiatrists entomologized by giving them strange baptismal names: there were Krafft-Ebing's zoophiles and zooerasts, Rohleder's auto-monosexualists; and later, mixo-scopophiles, gynecomasts, presbyophiles, sexoesthetic inverts, and dyspareunist women. These fine names for heresies referred to a nature that was overlooked by the law, but not so neglectful of itself that it did not go on producing more species, even where there was no order to fit them into. The machinery of power that focused on this whole alien strain did not aim to suppress it, but rather to give it an analytical, visible, and permanent reality: it was implanted in bodies, slipped in beneath modes of conduct, made into a principle of classification and intelligibility, established as a *raison d'être* and a natural order of disorder. Not the exclusion of these thousand aberrant sexualities, but the specification, the regional solidification of each one of them. The strategy behind this dissemination was to strew reality with them and incorporate them into the individual.

3. More than the old taboos, this form of power demanded constant, attentive, and curious presences for its exercise; it presupposed proximities; it proceeded through examination and insistent observation; it required an exchange of discourses, through questions that extorted admissions, and confidences that went beyond the questions that were asked. It implied a physical proximity and an interplay of intense sensations. The medicalization of the sexually peculiar was both the effect and the instrument of this. Embedded in bodies, becoming deeply characteristic of individuals, the oddities of sex relied on a technology of health and pathology. And conversely, since sexuality was a medical and medicalizable object, one had to try and detect it—as a lesion, a dysfunction, or a symptom—in the depths of the organism, or on the surface of the skin, or among all the signs of behavior. The power which thus took charge of sexuality set about contacting bodies, caressing them with its eyes, intensifying areas, electrifying surfaces, dramatizing troubled moments. It wrapped the sexual body in its embrace. There

was undoubtedly an increase in effectiveness and an extension of the domain controlled; but also a sensualization of power and a gain of pleasure. This produced a twofold effect: an impetus was given to power through its very exercise; an emotion rewarded the overseeing control and carried it further; the intensity of the confession renewed the questioner's curiosity; the pleasure discovered fed back to the power that encircled it. But so many pressing questions singularized the pleasures felt by the one who had to reply. They were fixed by a gaze, isolated and animated by the attention they received. Power operated as a mechanism of attraction; it drew out those peculiarities over which it kept watch. Pleasure spread to the power that harried it; power anchored the pleasure it uncovered.

The medical examination, the psychiatric investigation, the pedagogical report, and family controls may have the overall and apparent objective of saying no to all wayward or unproductive sexualities, but the fact is that they function as mechanisms with a double impetus: pleasure and power. The pleasure that comes of exercising a power that questions, monitors, watches, spies, searches out, palpates, brings to light; and on the other hand, the pleasure that kindles at having to evade this power, flee from it, fool it, or travesty it. The power that lets itself be invaded by the pleasure it is pursuing; and opposite it, power asserting itself in the pleasure of showing off, scandalizing, or resisting. Capture and seduction, confrontation and mutual reinforcement: parents and children, adults and adolescents, educators and students, doctors and patients, the psychiatrist with his hysteric and his perverts, all have played this game continually since the nineteenth century. These attractions, these evasions, these circular incitements have traced around bodies and sexes, not boundaries not to be crossed, but *perpetual spirals of power and pleasure*.

4. Whence those *devices of sexual saturation* so characteristic of the space and the social rituals of the nineteenth century. People often say that modern society has attempted to reduce sexuality to the couple—the heterosexual and, insofar as possible, legitimate couple. There are equal grounds for saying that it has, if not created, at least outfitted and made to proliferate, groups with multiple elements and a circulating sexuality: a distribution of points of power, hierarchized and placed opposite to one another; "pursued" pleasures, that is, both sought after and searched out; compartmental sexualities that are tolerated or encouraged; proximities that serve as surveillance procedures, and function as mechanisms of intensification; contacts that operate as inductors. This is the way things worked in the case of the family, or rather the household, with parents, children, and in some instances, servants. Was the nineteenth-century family really a monogamous and conjugal cell? Perhaps to a certain extent. But it was also a network of pleasures and powers linked together at multiple points and according to transformable relationships. The separation of grown-ups and children, the polarity established between the parents' bedroom and that of the children (it became routine in the course of the century when working-class housing construction was undertaken), the relative segregation of boys and girls, the strict instructions as to the care of nursing infants (maternal breast-feeding, hygiene), the attention focused on infantile sexuality, the supposed dangers of masturbation, the importance attached to puberty, the methods of surveillance suggested to parents, the exhortations, secrets, and fears, the presence—both valued and feared—of servants: all this made the family, even when brought down to its smallest dimensions, a complicated network, saturated with multiple, fragmentary, and mobile sexualities. To reduce them to the conjugal relationship, and then to project the latter, in the form of a forbidden desire, onto the children, cannot account for this apparatus which, in relation to these sexualities, was less a principle of inhibition than an inciting and multiplying mechanism. Educational or psychiatric institutions, with their large populations, their hierarchies, their spatial arrangements, their surveillance systems, constituted, alongside the family, another way of distributing the interplay of powers and pleasures; but they, too, delineated areas of extreme sexual saturation, with privileged spaces or rituals such as the classroom, the dormitory, the visit, and the consultation. The forms of a nonconjugal, nonmonogamous sexuality were drawn there and established.

Nineteenth-century "bourgeois" society—and it is doubtless still with us—was a society of blatant and fragmented perversion. And this was not by way of hypocrisy, for nothing was more manifest and more prolix, or more manifestly taken over by discourses and institutions. Not because, having tried to erect too rigid or too general a barrier against sexuality, society succeeded only in giving rise to a whole perverse outbreak and a long pathology of the sexual instinct. At issue, rather, is the type of power it brought to bear on the body and on sex. In point of fact, this power had neither the form of the law, nor the effects of the taboo. On the contrary, it acted by multiplication of singular sexualities. It did not set boundaries for sexuality; it extended the various forms of sexuality, pursuing them according to lines of indefinite penetration. It did not exclude sexuality, but included it in the body as a mode of specification of individuals. It did not seek to avoid it; it attracted its varieties by means of spirals in which pleasure and power reinforced one another. It did not set up a barrier; it provided places of maximum saturation. It produced and determined the sexual mosaic. Modern society is perverse, not in spite of its puritanism or as if from a backlash provoked by its hypocrisy; it is in actual fact, and directly, perverse.

In actual fact. The manifold sexualities—those which appear with the different ages (sexualities of the infant or the child); those which become fixated on particular tastes or practices (the sexuality of the invert, the gerontophile, the fetishist); those which, in a diffuse manner, invest relationships (the sexuality of doctor and patient, teacher and student, psychiatrist and mental patient); those which haunt spaces (the sexuality of the home, the school, the prison)—all form the correlate of exact procedures of power. We must not imagine that all these things that were formerly tolerated attracted notice and received a pejorative designation when the time came to give a regulative role to the one type of sexuality that was capable of reproducing labor power and the form of the family. These polymorphous conducts were actually extracted from people's bodies and from their pleasures; or rather, they were solidified in them; they were drawn out, revealed, isolated, intensified, incorporated, by multifarious power devices. The growth of perversions is not a moralizing theme that obsessed the scrupulous minds of the Victorians. It is the real product of the encroachment of a type of power on bodies and their pleasures. It is possible that the West has not been capable of inventing any new pleasures, and it has doubtless not discovered any original vices. But it has defined new rules for the game of powers and pleasures. The frozen countenance of the perversions is a fixture of this game.

Directly. This implantation of multiple perversions is not a mockery of sexuality taking revenge on a power that has thrust on it an excessively repressive law. Neither are we dealing with paradoxical forms of pleasure that turn back on power and invest it in the form of a "pleasure to be endured." The implantation of perversions is an instrument effect: it is through the isolation, intensification, and consolidation of peripheral sexualities that the relations of power to sex and pleasure branched out and multiplied, measured the body, and penetrated modes of conduct. And accompanying this encroachment of powers, scattered sexualities rigidified, became stuck to an age, a place, a type of practice. A proliferation of sexualities through the extension of power; an optimization of the power to which each of these local sexualities gave a surface of intervention: this concatenation, particularly since the nineteenth century, has been ensured and relayed by the countless economic interests which, with the help of medicine, psychiatry, prostitution, and pornography, have tapped into both this analytical multiplication of pleasure and this optimization of the power that controls it. Pleasure and power do not cancel or turn back against one another; they seek out, overlap, and reinforce one another. They are linked together by complex mechanisms and devices of excitation and incitement.

We must therefore abandon the hypothesis that modern industrial societies ushered in an age of increased sexual repression. We have not only witnessed a visible explosion of unorthodox sexualities; but—and this is the important point—a deployment quite different from the law, even if it is locally dependent on procedures of prohibition, has ensured, through a network of interconnecting mechanisms, the proliferation of specific pleasures and the multiplication of disparate sexualities. It is said that no society has been more prudish; never have the agencies of power taken such care to feign ignorance of the thing they prohibited, as if they were determined to have nothing to do with it. But it is the opposite that has become apparent, at least after a general review of the facts: never have there existed more centers of power; never more attention manifested and verbalized; never more circular contacts and linkages; never more sites where the intensity of pleasures and the persistency of power catch hold, only to spread elsewhere.

Notes

[1] Paolo Segneri, *L'Instruction du pénitent* (French trans. 1695), p. 301.

[2] Alfonso de' Liguori, *Pratique des confesseurs* (French trans. 1854), p. 140.

[3] Segneri, *L'Instruction*, pp. 301–2.

[4] The reformed pastoral also laid down rules, albeit in a more discreet way, for putting sex into discourse. This notion will be developed in the second volume of *The History of Sexuality*.

[5] Alfonso de' Liguori, *Préceptes sur le sixième commandement* (French trans. 1835), p. 5.

[6] Donatien-Alphonse de Sade, *The 120 Days of Sodom*, trans. Austryn Wainhouse and Richard Seaver (1785; New York: Grove Press, 1966), p. 271.

[7] Anonymous, *My Secret Life* (New York: Grove Press, 1966).

[8] Condorcet, cited by Jean-Louis Flandrin, *Familles: parenté, maison, sexualité dans l'ancienne société* (Paris: Hachette, 1976).

[9] Auguste Tardieu, *Étude médico-légale sur les attentats aux moeurs* (1857), p. 114.

[10] Johann von Justi, *Éléments généraux de police* (French trans. 1769), p. 20.

[11] Claude-Jacques Herbert, *Essai sur la police générale des grains* (1753), pp. 320–1.

[12] *Règlement de police pour les lycées* (1809), Art. 67: "There shall always be, during class and study hours, an instructor watching the exterior, so as to prevent students who have gone out to relieve themselves from stopping and congregating." Art. 68: "After the evening prayer, the students will be conducted back to the dormitory, where the school-masters will put them to bed at once." Art. 69: "The masters will not retire except after having made certain that every student is in bed."

Art. 70: "The beds shall be separated by partitions two meters in height. The dormitories shall be illuminated during the night."

[13] Johann Gottlieb Schummel, *Fritizens Reise nach Dessau* (1776), cited by Auguste Pinloche, *La Réforme de l'éducation en Allemagne au XVIIIe siècle* (1889), pp. 125–9.

[14] H. Bonnet and J. Bulard, *Rapport médico-légal sur l'état mental de Ch.-J. Jouy* (4 January 1968).

[15] *Trans.*: "Jouy" sounds like the past participle of *jouir*, the French verb meaning "to enjoy, to delight in (something)" but also "to have an orgasm, to come."

[16] Carl Westphal, in *Archiv für Neurologie* (1870).

PRACTICES
AND SCIENCES
OF THE SELF

Preface to *The History of Sexuality,* Volume II

. . . In this series of researches on sexuality it was not my aim to reconstitute the history of sexual behavior—by studying its successive forms, their respective models, how they spread, how they conflicted or agreed with laws, rules, customs, or conventions. Nor did I intend to analyze religious, moral, medical, or biological ideas about sexuality. Not that such inquiries should be considered illegitimate, impossible, or sterile; plenty of work has proved otherwise. But I wanted to confront this very everyday notion of sexuality, step away from it, monitor its familiar evidence, and analyze the theoretical and practical content in which it made its appearance and with which it is still associated.

I wanted to undertake a history in which sexuality would not be conceived as a general type of behavior whose particular elements might vary according to demographic, economic, social, or ideological conditions, anymore than it would be seen as a collection of (scientific, religious, moral) representations which, though diverse and changeable, are joined to an invariant reality. My object was to analyze sexuality as a historically singular form of experience. Taking this historical singularity into account does not mean overinterpreting the recent emergence of the term "sexuality," or taking it for granted that the word has brought in its trail the reality to which it refers. Rather, it means an effort to treat sexuality as the correlation of a domain of knowledge, a type of normativity and a mode of relation to the self; it means trying to decipher how, in Western societies, a complex experience is constituted from and around certain forms of behavior: an experience which conjoins a field of study (*connaissance*) (with its own concepts, theories, diverse disci-

Translated by William Smock.

333

plines), a collection of rules (which differentiate the permissible from the forbidden, natural from monstrous, normal from pathological, what is decent from what is not, etc.), a mode of relation between the individual and himself (which enables him to recognize himself as a sexual subject amid others).

To study forms of experience in this way—in their history—is an idea that originated with an earlier project, in which I made use of the methods of existential analysis in the field of psychiatry and in the domain of "mental illness." For two reasons, not unrelated to each other, this project left me unsatisfied: its theoretical weakness in elaborating the notion of experience, and its ambiguous link with a psychiatric practice which it simultaneously ignored and took for granted. One could deal with the first problem by referring to a general theory of the human being, and treat the second altogether differently by turning, as is so often done, to the "economic and social context"; one could choose, by doing so, to accept the resulting dilemma of a philosophical anthropology and a social history. But I wondered whether, rather than playing on this alternative, it would not be possible to consider the very historicity of forms of experience. This entailed two negative tasks: first, a "nominalist" reduction of philosophical anthropology and the notions which it serves to promote, and second, a shift of domain to the concepts and methods of the history of societies. On the positive side, the task was to bring to light the domain where the formation, development, and transformation of forms of experience can situate themselves: that is, a history of thought. By thought, I mean what establishes, in a variety of possible forms, the play of true and false, and which as a consequence constitutes the human being as a subject of learning (*connaissance*); in other words, it is the basis for accepting or refusing rules, and constitutes human beings as social and juridical subjects; it is what establishes the relation with oneself and with others, and constitutes the human being as ethical subject.

"Thought," understood in this way, is not, then, to be sought only in theoretical formulations such as those of philosophy or science; it can and must be analyzed in every manner of speaking, doing, or behaving in which the individual appears and acts as subject of learning, as ethical or juridical subject, as subject conscious of himself and others. In this sense, thought is understood as the very form of action—as action insofar as it implies the play of true and false, the acceptance or refusal of rules, the relation to oneself and others. The study of forms of experience can thus proceed from an analysis of "practices"— discursive or not—as long as one qualifies that word to mean the different systems of action *insofar as* they are inhabited by thought as I have characterized it here.

Posing the question in this way brings into play certain altogether general principles. Singular forms of experience may perfectly well harbor universal structures; they may well not be independent from the concrete determinations of social existence. However, neither those determinations nor those structures can allow for experiences (that is, for understandings of a certain type, for rules of a certain form, for certain modes of consciousness of oneself and of others) except through thought. There is no experience which is not a way of thinking, and which cannot be analyzed from the point of view of the history of thought; this is what might be called the principle of irreducibility of thought. According to a second principle, this thought has a historicity which is proper to it. That it should have this historicity does not mean it is deprived of all universal form, but instead that the putting into play of these universal forms is itself historical. And that this historicity should be proper to it does not mean that it is independent of all the other historical determinations (of an economic, social, or political order), but that it has complex relations with them which always leave their specificity to the forms, transformations, and events of thought. This is what could be called the principle of singularity of the history of thought: there are events of thought. There is a third and final principle implied by this enterprise: an awareness that criticism—understood as analysis of the historical conditions which bear on the creation of links to truth, to rules, and to the self— does not mark out impassable boundaries or describe closed systems; it brings to light transformable singularities. These transformations could not take place except by means of a working of thought upon itself; that is the principle of the history of thought as critical activity. All of this bears upon the work and teaching I have labeled "the history of systems of thought"; it infers a double reference: to philosophy, which must be asked to explain how thought could have a history, and to history, which must be asked to produce the various forms of thought in whatever concrete forms they may assume (system of representations, institutions, practices). What is the price to philosophy of a history of thought? What is the effect, within history, of thought and the events which are proper to it? In what way do individual or collective experiences arise from singular forms of thought—that is, from what constitutes the subject in its relations to the true, to rules, to itself? It is easy to see how the reading of Nietzsche in the early '50s has given access to these kinds of questions, by breaking with the double tradition of phenomenology and Marxism.

I know that this rereading is schematic: things did not really unfold so neatly, and there were many obscurities and hesitations along the way. But in *Madness and Civilization* I was trying, after all, to describe a locus of experience from the point of view of the history of thought, even if my usage of the word "experience" was very floating. Looking at practices of internment, on the one hand, and medical procedures, on the other, I tried to analyze the genesis, during the seventeenth and eighteenth centuries, of a system of thought as the matter of possible experiences: first, the formation of a domain of recognitions (*connaissances*) which constitute themselves as specific knowledge of "mental illness"; second, the organization of a normative system built on a whole technical, administrative, juridical, and medical apparatus whose purpose was to isolate and take custody of the insane; and finally, the definition of a relation to oneself and to others as possible subjects of madness. It is also these three axes and the play between types of understanding, forms of normality, and modes of relation to oneself and others which seemed to me to give individual cases the status of significant experiences—cases such as those of Pierre Rivière or Alexina B.—and to assign a like importance to that permanent dramatization of family affairs which one finds in the *lettres de cachet* (whereby people committed their relatives to asylums) in the eighteenth century.

But the relative importance of these three axes is not always the same for all forms of experience. And, moreover, it was necessary to elaborate the analysis of each a little more precisely, starting with the problem of the formation of domains of knowledge. The work was directed along two lines: first, in the "vertical" dimension, taking the example of sickness, and studying how an institutional organization for therapy, instruction, and research is related to the constitution of a clinical medicine articulated on the development of pathological anatomy. The object was to bring out the complex causalities and reciprocal determinations affecting, on the one hand, the development of a certain kind of medical knowledge and, on the other, the transformations of an institutional field linked directly to social and political changes. Then, once scientific knowledge was endowed with its own rules for which external determinations could not account—its own structure as discursive practice—I tried to show what common, but transformable, criteria—what *epistemes*—governed those bodies of knowledge which, from the seventeenth to the early nineteenth centuries, had been charged with explaining certain aspects of human activity or existence: the wealth which men produce, exchange, and circulate; the linguistic signs they use to communicate; and the collectivity of living things to which they belong.

It is the second axis—the relation to rules—which I wanted to explore using the example of punitive practices. It was a matter not of studying the theory of penal law in itself, or the evolution of such and such penal institution, but of analyzing the formation of a certain "punitive rationality" whose appearance might seem that much more surprising in that it offered, as its principal means of action, a practice of imprisonment which had long been and still was criticized at the time. Instead of seeking the explanation in a general conception of the Law, or in the evolving modes of industrial production (as Rusche and Kirchheimer did), it seemed to me far wiser to look at the workings of Power. I was concerned not with some omnipresent power, almighty and above all clairvoyant, diffusing itself throughout the social body in order to control it down to the tiniest detail, but with the refinement, the elaboration and installation since the seventeenth century, of techniques for "governing" individuals—that is, for "guiding their conduct"—in domains as different as the school, the army, and the workshop. The new punitive rationality must be relocated in the context of this technology, itself linked to the demographic, economic, and political changes which accompany the development of industrial states. Accordingly, the analysis does not revolve around the general principle of the Law or the myth of Power, but concerns itself with the complex and multiple practices of a "governmentality" which presupposes, on the one hand, rational forms, technical procedures, instrumentations through which to operate and, on the other hand, strategic games which subject the power relations they are supposed to guarantee to instability and reversal. Starting from an analysis of these forms of "government," one can see how criminality was constituted as an object of knowledge, and how a certain "consciousness" of criminality could be formed (including the image which criminals might have of themselves, and the representation of criminals which the rest of us might entertain).

The project of a history of sexuality was linked to a desire on my part to analyze more closely the third of the axes which constitute any matrix of experience: the modality of relation to the self. Not that sexuality cannot and should not—like madness, sickness, or criminality—be envisaged as a locus of experience, one which includes a domain of knowledge, a system of rules, and a model for relations to the self. Indeed, relative importance of the last element recommends it as a guiding thread for the very history of this experience and its formation; my planned study of children, women, and "perverts" as sexual subjects was to have followed those lines.

I found myself confronted with a choice which was a long time in unraveling: a choice between fidelity to the chronological outline which I had originally imagined, and a different line of inquiry in which the modes of relation to the self took precedence. The period when this singular form of experience, sexuality, took shape is particularly complex: the very important role played at the end of the eighteenth and in the nineteenth centuries by the formation of domains of knowledge about sexuality from the points of view of biology, medicine, psycho-pathology, sociology, and ethnology; the determining role also played by the normative systems imposed on sexual behavior through the intermediary of education, medicine, and justice made it hard to distinguish the form and effects of the relation to the self as particular elements in the constitution of this experience. There was always the risk of reproducing, with regard to sexuality, forms of analysis focused on the organization of a domain of learning or on the techniques of control and coercion, as in my previous work on sickness or criminality. In pursuing my analysis of the forms of relation to the self, in and of themselves, I found myself spanning eras in a way that took me farther and farther from the chronological outline I had first decided on, both in order to address myself to periods when the effect of scientific knowledge and the complexity of normative systems were less, and in order eventually to make out forms of relation to the self different from those characterizing the experience of sexuality. And that is how, little by little, I ended up placing the work's emphasis on what was to have been simply the point of departure or historical background; rather than placing myself at the threshold of the formation of the experience of sexuality, I tried to analyze the formation of a certain mode of relation to the self in the experience of the flesh. This called for a marked chronological displacement, because it became obvious that I should study the period in late antiquity when the principal elements of the Christian ethic of the flesh were being formulated. And it led in turn to a rearrangement of my original plan, a considerable delay in publication, and the hazards of studying material which I had barely heard of six or seven years ago. But I reflected that, after all, it was best to sacrifice a definite program to a promising line of approach. I also reminded myself that it would probably not be worth the trouble of making books if they failed to teach the author something he hadn't known before, if they didn't lead to unforeseen places, and if they didn't disperse one toward a strange and new relation with himself. The pain and pleasure of the book is to be an experience.

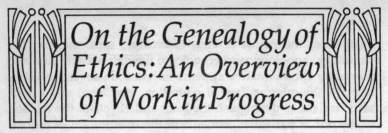

On the Genealogy of Ethics: An Overview of Work in Progress

(FROM *Michel Foucault: Beyond Structuralism and Hermeneutics*)

History of the Project

Q. The first volume of *The History of Sexuality* was published in 1976, and none has appeared since. Do you still think that understanding sexuality is central for understanding who we are?

M.F. I must confess that I am much more interested in problems about techniques of the self and things like that than sex . . . sex is boring.

Q. It sounds like the Greeks were not too interested either.

M.F. No, they were not much interested in sex. It was not a great issue. Compare, for instance, what they say about the place of food and diet. I think it is very, very interesting to see the move, the very slow move, from the privileging of food, which was overwhelming in Greece, to interest in sex. Food was still much more important during the early Christian days than sex. For instance, in the rules for monks, the problem was food, food, food. Then you can see a very slow shift during the Middle Ages, when they were in a kind of equilibrium . . . and after the seventeenth century it was sex.

The following is the result of a series of working sessions with Michel Foucault conducted by Paul Rabinow and Hubert Dreyfus at Berkeley in April 1983. Although we have retained the interview form, the material has been jointly reedited. We should emphasize that Foucault has generously allowed us to publish these preliminary formulations, which are the product of oral interviews and free conversations in English and therefore lack the precision and supporting scholarship found in Foucault's written texts.

Q. Yet Volume II of *The History of Sexuality*, *L'Usage des plaisirs*, is concerned almost exclusively with, not to put too fine a point on it, sex.

M.F. Yes. One of the numerous reasons I had so much trouble with that book was that I first wrote a book about sex, which I put aside. Then I wrote a book about the self and the techniques of the self; sex disappeared, and for the third time I was obliged to rewrite a book in which I tried to keep the equilibrium between one and the other.

You see, what I wanted to do in Volume II of *The History of Sexuality* was to show that you have nearly the same restrictive, the same prohibition code in the fourth century B.C. and in the moralists and doctors at the beginning of the Empire. But I think that the way they integrate those prohibitions in relation to oneself is completely different. I don't think one can find any normalization in, for instance, the Stoic ethics. The reason is, I think, that the principal aim, the principal target of this kind of ethics was an aesthetic one. First, this kind of ethics was only a problem of personal choice. Second, it was reserved for a few people in the population; it was not a question of giving a pattern of behavior for everybody. It was a personal choice for a small elite. The reason for making this choice was the will to live a beautiful life, and to leave to others memories of a beautiful existence. I don't think that we can say that this kind of ethics was an attempt to normalize the population.

The continuity of the themes of this ethics is something very striking, but I think that behind, below this continuity, there were some changes, which I have tried to acknowledge.

Q. So the equilibrium in your work has shifted from sex to techniques of the self?

M.F. I wondered what the technology of the self before Christianity was, or where the Christian technology of the self came from, and what kind of sexual ethics was characteristic of the ancient culture. And then I was obliged after I finished *Les Aveux de la chair*, the book about Christianity, to reexamine what I said in the introduction to *L'Usage des plaisirs* about the supposed pagan ethics, because what I had said about pagan ethics were only clichés borrowed from secondary texts. And then I discovered, first, that this pagan ethics was not at all liberal, tolerant, and so on, as it was supposed to be; second, that most of the themes of Christian austerity were very clearly present nearly from the beginning, but that also in pagan culture the main problem was not the rules for austerity, but much more the techniques of the self.

Reading Seneca, Plutarch, and all those people, I discovered that there were a very great number of problems or themes about the self, the ethics of the self, the technology of the self, and I had the idea of writing a book composed of a set of separate studies, papers about such and such aspects of ancient, pagan technology of the self.

Q. What is the title?

M.F. *Le Souci de soi*. So in the series about sexuality: the first one is *L'Usage des plaisirs*, and in this book there is a chapter about the technology of the self, since I think it's not possible to understand clearly what Greek sexual ethics was without relating it to this technology of the self. Then, a second volume in the same sex series, *Les Aveux de la chair*, deals with Christian technologies of the self. And then, *Le Souci de soi*, a book separate from the sex series, is composed of different papers about the self—for instance, a commentary on Plato's *Alcibiades* in which you find the first elaboration of the notion of *epimeleia heautou*, "care of the self," about the role of reading and writing in constituting the self, maybe the problem of the medical experience of the self, and so on. . . .

Q. And what will come next? Will there be more on the Christians when you finish these three?

M.F. Well, I am going to take care of myself! . . . I have more than a draft of a book about sexual ethics in the sixteenth century, in which also the problem of the techniques of the self, self-examination, the cure of souls, is very important, both in the Protestant and Catholic churches.

What strikes me is that in Greek ethics people were concerned with their moral conduct, their ethics, their relations to themselves and to others much more than with religious problems. For instance, what happens to us after death? What are the gods? Do they intervene or not?—these are very, very unimportant problems for them, and they are not directly related to ethics, to conduct. The second thing is that ethics was not related to any social—or at least to any legal—institutional system. For instance, the laws against sexual misbehavior were very few and not very compelling. The third thing is that what they were worried about, their theme, was to constitute a kind of ethics which was an aesthetics of existence.

Well, I wonder if our problem nowadays is not, in a way, similar to this one, since most of us no longer believe that ethics is founded in religion, nor do we want a legal system to intervene in our moral, personal, private life. Recent liberation movements suffer from the fact that they cannot find any principle on which to base the elaboration of a new ethics. They need an ethics, but they cannot find any other ethics than an ethics founded on so-called scientific knowledge of what the self is, what desire is, what the unconscious is, and so on. I am struck by this similarity of problems.

Q. Do you think that the Greeks offer an attractive and plausible alternative?

M.F. No! I am not looking for an alternative; you can't find the solution of a problem in the solution of another problem raised at another moment by other people. You see, what I want to do is not the history of solutions, and that's the reason why I don't accept the word *alternative*. I would like to do the genealogy of problems, of *problématiques*. My point is not that everything is bad, but that everything is dangerous, which is not exactly the same as bad. If everything is dangerous, then we always have something to do. So my position leads not to apathy but to a hyper- and pessimistic activism.

I think that the ethico-political choice we have to make every day is to determine which is the main danger. Take as an example Robert Castel's analysis of the history of the anti-psychiatry movement (*La Gestion des risques*). I agree completely with what Castel says, but that does not mean, as some people suppose, that the mental hospitals were better than anti-psychiatry; that does not mean that we were not right to criticize those mental hospitals. I think it was good to do that, because *they* were the danger. And now it's quite clear that the danger has changed. For instance, in Italy they have closed all the mental hospitals, and there are more free clinics, and so on—and they have new problems.

Q. Isn't it logical, given these concerns, that you should be writing a genealogy of bio-power?

M.F. I have no time for that now, but it could be done. In fact, I have to do it.

Why the Ancient World Was Not a Golden Age, But What We Can Learn from It Anyway

Q. So Greek life may not have been altogether perfect; still, it seems an attractive alternative to endless Christian self-analysis.

M.F. The Greek ethics were linked to a purely virile society with slaves, in which the women were underdogs whose pleasure had no importance, whose sexual life had to be only oriented toward, determined by, their status as wives, and so on.

Q. So the women were dominated, but surely homosexual love was better than now?

M.F. It might look that way. Since there is an important and large literature about loving boys in Greek culture, some historians say, "Well, that's the proof that they loved boys." But I say that proves that loving boys was a problem. Because if there were no problem, they would speak of this kind of love in the same terms as love between men and women. The problem was that they couldn't accept that a young boy who was supposed to become a free citizen could be dominated and used as an object for someone's pleasure. A woman, a slave, could be passive: such was their nature, their status. All this reflection, philosophizing about the love of boys—with always the same conclusion: please, don't treat a boy as a woman—is proof that they could not integrate this real practice in the framework of their social selves.

You can see through a reading of Plutarch how they couldn't even imagine reciprocity of pleasure between a boy and a man. If Plutarch finds problems in loving boys, it is not at all in the sense that loving boys was anti-natural or something like that. He says, "It's not possible that there could be any reciprocity in the physical relations between a boy and a man."

Q. There seems to be an aspect of Greek culture, that we are told about in Aristotle, that you don't talk about, but that seems very important—friendship. In classical literature, friendship is the locus of mutual recognition. It's not traditionally seen as the highest virtue, but both in Aristotle and in Cicero, you could read it as really being the highest virtue because it's selfless and enduring, it's not easily bought, it doesn't deny the utility and pleasure of the world, but yet it seeks something more.

M.F. But don't forget *L'Usage des plaisirs* is a book about sexual ethics; it's not a book about love, or about friendship, or about reciprocity. And it's very significant that when Plato tries to integrate love for boys and friendship, he is obliged to put aside sexual relations. Friendship is reciprocal, and sexual relations are not reciprocal: in sexual relations, you can penetrate or you are penetrated. I agree completely with what you say about friendship, but I think it confirms what I say about Greek sexual ethics: if you have friendship, it is difficult to have sexual relations. If you look at Plato, reciprocity is very important in a friendship, but you can't find it on the physical level; one of the reasons why they needed a philosophical elaboration in order to justify this kind of love was that they could not accept a physical reciprocity. You find in Xenophon, in the *Banquet*, Socrates saying that between a man and a boy it is obvious that the boy is only the spectator of the man's pleasure. What they say about this beautiful love of boys implies that the pleasure of the boy was not to be taken into account; moreover, that it was dishonorable for the boy to feel any kind of physical pleasure in a relation with a man.

What I want to ask is: Are we able to have an ethics of acts and their pleasures which would be able to take into account the pleasure of the other? Is the pleasure of the other something which can be integrated in our pleasure, without reference either to law, to marriage, to I don't know what?

Q. It looks like nonreciprocity was a problem for the Greeks all right, but it seems to be the kind of problem that one could straighten out. Why does sex have to be virile? Why couldn't women's pleasure and boys' pleasure be taken account of without any big change to the general framework? Or is it that it's not just a little problem, because if you try to bring in the pleasure of the other, the whole hierarchical, ethical system would break down?

M.F. That's right. The Greek ethics of pleasure is linked to a virile society, to dissymmetry, exclusion of the other, an obsession with penetration, and a kind of threat of being dispossessed of your own energy, and so on. All that is quite disgusting!

Q. OK, granted that sexual relations were both nonreciprocal and a cause of worry for the Greeks, at least pleasure itself seems unproblematic for them.

M.F. Well, in *L'Usage des plaisirs* I try to show, for instance, that there is a growing tension between pleasure and health. When you take the physicians and all the concern with diet, you see first that the main themes are very similiar during several centuries. But the idea that the sex has its dangers is much stronger in the second century A.D. than in the fourth century B.C. I think that you can show that, for Hippocrates, the sexual act was already dangerous, so you had to be very careful with it and not have sex all the time, only in certain seasons and so on. But in the first and second centuries it seems that, for a physician, the sexual act is much closer to *pathos*. And I think the main shift is this one: that in the fourth century B.C., the sexual act was an activity, and for the Christians it is a passivity. You have a very interesting analysis by Augustine which is, I think, quite typical concerning the problem of erection. The erection was, for the Greek of the fourth century, the sign of activity, the main activity. But since, for Augustine and the Christians, the erection is not something which is voluntary, it is a sign of a passivity—it is a punishment for the first sin.

Q. So the Greeks were more concerned with health than with pleasure?

M.F. Yes, about what the Greeks had to eat in order to be in good health, we have thousands of pages. And there are comparatively few things about what to do when you have sex with someone. Concerning food, it was the relation between the climate, the seasons, the humidity or dryness of the air and the dryness of the food, and so on. There are very few things about the way they had to cook it; much more about these qualities. It's not a cooking art; it's a matter of choosing.

Q. So, despite the German Hellenists, classical Greece was not a Golden Age. Yet surely we can learn something from it?

M.F. I think there is no exemplary value in a period which is not our period . . . it is not anything to get back to. But we do have an example of an ethical experience which implied a very strong connection between pleasure and desire. If we compare that to our experience now, where everybody—the philosopher or the psychoanalyst—explains that what is important is desire, and pleasure is nothing at all, we can wonder whether this disconnection wasn't a historical event, one which was not at all necessary, not linked to human nature, or to any anthropological necessity.

Q. But you already illustrated that in *The History of Sexuality* by contrasting our science of sexuality with the oriental *ars erotica*.

M.F. One of the numerous points where I was wrong in that book was what I said about this *ars erotica*. I should have opposed our science of sex to a contrasting practice in our own culture. The Greeks and Romans did not have any *ars erotica* to be compared with the Chinese *ars erotica* (or at least it was not something very important in their culture). They had a *techne tou biou* in which the economy of pleasure played a very large role. In this "art of life" the notion of exercising a perfect mastery over oneself soon became the main issue. And the Christian hermeneutics of the self constituted a new elaboration of this *techne*.

Q. But, after all you have told us about nonreciprocity and obsession with health, what can we learn from this third possibility?

M.F. What I want to show is that the general Greek problem was not the *techne* of the self, it was the *techne* of life, the *techne tou biou*, how to live. It's quite clear from Socrates to Seneca or Pliny, for instance, that they didn't worry about the afterlife, what happened after death, or whether God exists or not. That was not really a great problem for them; the problem was: which *techne* do I have to use in order to live as well as I ought to live? And I think that one of the main evolutions in ancient culture has been that this *techne tou biou* became more and more a *techne* of the self. A Greek citizen of the fifth or fourth century would have felt that his *techne* for life was to take care of the city, of his companions. But for Seneca, for instance, the problem is to take care of himself.

With Plato's *Alcibiades*, it's very clear: you have to take care of yourself because you have to rule the city. But taking care of yourself for its own sake starts with the Epicureans—it becomes something very general with Seneca, Pliny, and so on: everybody has to take care of himself. Greek ethics is centered on a problem of personal choice, of aesthetics of existence.

The idea of the *bios* as a material for an aesthetic piece of art is something which fascinates me. The idea also that ethics can be a very strong structure of existence, without any relation with the juridical per se, with an authoritarian system, with a disciplinary structure. All that is very interesting.

Q. How, then, did the Greeks deal with deviance?

M.F. The great difference in sexual ethics for the Greeks was not between people who prefer women or boys or have sex in this way or another, but was a question of quantity and of activity and passivity. Are you a slave of your own desires or their master?

Q. What about someone who had sex so much he damaged his health?

M.F. That's hubris, that's excess. The problem is not one of deviancy but of excess or moderation.

Q. What did they do with these people?

M.F. They were considered ugly; they had a bad reputation.

Q. They didn't try to cure or reform such people?

M.F. There were exercises in order to make one master of oneself. For Epictetus, you had to be able to look at a beautiful girl or a beautiful boy without having any desire for her or him. You have to become completely master of yourself.

Sexual austerity in Greek society was a trend or movement, a philosophical movement coming from very cultivated people in order to give to their life much more intensity, much more beauty. In a way it's the same in the twentieth century when people, in order to get a more beautiful life, tried to get rid of all the sexual repression of their society, of their childhood. Gide in Greece would have been an austere philosopher.

Q. In the name of a beautiful life they were austere, and now in the name of psychological science we seek self-fulfillment.

M.F. Exactly. My idea is that it's not at all necessary to relate ethical problems to scientific knowledge. Among the cultural inventions of mankind there is a treasury of devices, techniques, ideas, procedures, and so on, that cannot exactly be reactivated, but at least constitute, or help to constitute, a certain point of view which can be very useful as a tool for analyzing what's going on now—and to change it.

We don't have to choose between our world and the Greek world. But since we can see very well that some of the main principles of our ethics have been related at a certain moment to an aesthetics of existence, I think that this kind of historical analysis can be useful. For centuries we have been convinced that between our ethics, our personal ethics, our everyday life, and the great political and social and economic structures, there were analytical relations, and that we couldn't change anything, for instance, in our sex life or our family life, without ruining our economy, our democracy, and so on. I think we have to get rid of this idea of an analytical or necessary link between ethics and other social or economic or political structures.

Q. So what kind of ethics can we build now, when we know that between ethics and other structures there are only historical coagulations and not a necessary relation?

M.F. What strikes me is the fact that in our society, art has become something which is related only to objects and not to individuals, or to life. That art is something which is specialized or which is done by experts who are artists. But couldn't everyone's life become a work of art? Why should the lamp or the house be an art object, but not our life?

Q. Of course, that kind of project is very common in places like Berkeley where people think that eveything from the way they eat breakfast, to the way they have sex, to the way they spend their day, should itself be perfected.

M.F. But I am afraid in most of those cases, most of the people think if they do what they do, if they live as they live, the reason is that they know the truth about desire, life, nature, body, and so on.

Q. But if one is to create oneself without recourse to knowledge or universal rules, how does your view differ from Sartrean existentialism?

M.F. I think that from the theoretical point of view, Sartre avoids the idea of the self as something which is given to us, but through the moral notion of authenticity, he turns back to the idea that we have to be ourselves—to be truly our true self. I think that the only acceptable practical consequence of what Sartre has said is to link his theoretical insight to the practice of creativity—and not of authenticity. From the idea that the self is not given to us, I think that there is only one practical consequence: we have to create ourselves as a work of art. In his analyses of Baudelaire, Flaubert, etc., it is interesting to see that Sartre refers the work of creation to a certain relation to oneself— the author to himself—which has the form of authenticity or of inauthenticity. I would like to say exactly the contrary: we should not have to refer the creative activity of somebody to the kind of relation he has to himself, but should relate the kind of relation one has to oneself to a creative activity.

Q. That sounds like Nietzsche's observation in *The Gay Science* [no. 290] that one should create one's life by giving style to it through long practice and daily work.

M.F. Yes. My view is much closer to Nietzsche's than to Sartre's.

The Structure of Genealogical Interpretation

Q. How do the next two books after *The History of Sexuality* Volume I, *L'Usage des plaisirs* and *Les Aveux de la chair*, fit into the structure of your genealogy project?

M.F. Three domains of genealogy are possible. First, a historical ontology of ourselves in relation to truth through which we constitute ourselves as subjects of knowledge; second, a historical ontology of ourselves in relation to a field of power through which we constitute ourselves as subjects acting on others; third, a historical ontology in relation to ethics through which we constitute ourselves as moral agents.

So, three axes are possible for genealogy. All three were present, albeit in a somewhat confused fashion, in *Madness and Civilization*. The truth axis was studied in *The Birth of the Clinic* and *The Order of Things*. The power axis was studied in *Discipline and Punish*, and the ethical axis in *The History of Sexuality*.

The general framework of the book about sex is a history of morals. I think, in general, we have to distinguish, where the history of morals is concerned, acts and moral code. The acts (*conduites*) are the real behavior of people in relation to the moral code (*prescriptions*) which is imposed on them. I think we have to distinguish between the code which determines which acts are permitted or forbidden and the code which determines the positive or negative value of the different possible behaviors—you're not allowed to have sex with anyone but your wife, that's an element of the code. And there is another side to the moral prescriptions, which most of the time is not isolated as such but is, I think, very important: the kind of relationship you ought to have with yourself, *rapport à soi*, which I call ethics, and which determines how the individual is supposed to constitute himself as a moral subject of his own actions.

This relationship to oneself has four major aspects. The first aspect answers the question: which is the aspect or the part of myself or my behavior which is concerned with moral conduct? For instance, you can say, in general, that in our society the main field of morality, the part of ourselves which is most relevant for morality, is our feelings. (You can have a girl in the street or anywhere, if you have very good feelings toward your wife.) Well, it's quite clear that from the Kantian point of view, intention is much more important than feelings. And from the Christian point of view, it is desire—well, we could discuss that, because in the Middle Ages it was not the same as the seventeenth century. . . .

Q. But, roughly, for the Christians it was desire, for Kant it was intentions, and for us now it's feelings?

M.F. Well, you can say something like that. It's not always the same part of ourselves, or of our behavior, which is relevant for ethical judgment. That's the aspect I call the ethical substance (*substance éthique*).

Q. The ethical substance is like the material that's going to be worked over by ethics?

M.F. Yes, that's it. And, for instance, when I describe the *aphrodisia* in *L'Usage des plaisirs*, it is to show that the part of sexual behavior which is relevant in Greek ethics is something different from concupiscence, from flesh. For the Greeks, the ethical substance was acts linked to pleasure and desire in their unity. And it is very different from flesh, Christian flesh. Sexuality is a third kind of ethical substance.

Q. What is the difference ethically between flesh and sexuality?

M.F. I cannot answer because all that can only be analyzed through a precise inquiry. Before I studied Greek or Greco-Roman ethics, I couldn't answer the question: What exactly is the ethical substance of Greco-Roman ethics? Now I think that I know, through the analysis of what they mean by *aphrodisia*, what the Greek ethical substance was.

For the Greeks, when a philosopher was in love with a boy, but did not touch him, his behavior was valued. The problem was: does he touch the boy or not? That's the ethical substance: the act linked with pleasure and desire. For Augustine, it's very clear that when he remembers his relationship to his young friend when he was eighteen years old, what bothers him is what exactly was the kind of desire he had for him. So you see that the ethical substance has changed.

The second aspect is what I call the mode of subjection (*mode d'assujettissement*), that is, the way in which people are invited or incited to recognize their moral obligations. Is it, for instance, divine law, which has been revealed in a text? Is it natural law, a cosmological order, in each case the same for every living being? Is it a rational rule? Is it the attempt to give your existence the most beautiful form possible?

Q. When you say "rational," do you mean scientific?

M.F. No, Kantian, universal. You can see, for instance, in the Stoics, how they move slowly from an idea of an aesthetics of existence to the idea that we have to do such and such things because we are rational beings—as members of the human community we have to do them. For example, you find in Isocrates a very interesting discourse, which is supposed to be held with Nicocles, who was the ruler of Cyprus. There he explains why he has always been faithful to his wife: "Because I am the king, and because as somebody who commands others, who rules others, I have to show that I am able to rule myself." And you can see that this rule of faithfulness has nothing to do with the universal and Stoic formulation: "I have to be faithful to my wife because I am a human and rational being." In the former case, it is because I am the king! And you can see that the way the same rule is accepted by Nicocles and by a Stoic is quite different. And that's what I call the *mode d'assujettissement*, the second aspect of ethics.

Q. When the king says, "because I am the king," is that a form of the beautiful life?

M.F. Both aesthetic and political, which were directly linked. Because if I want people to accept me as a king, I must have a kind of glory which will survive me, and this glory cannot be dissociated from aesthetic value. So political power, glory, immortality, and beauty are all linked at a certain moment. That's the *mode d'assujettissement*, the second aspect of ethics.

The third one is: What are the means by which we can change ourselves in order to become ethical subjects?

Q. How we work on this ethical substance?

M.F. Yes. What are we to do, either to moderate our acts, or to decipher what we are, or to eradicate our desires, or to use our sexual desire in order to obtain certain aims like having children, and so on—all this elaboration of ourselves in order to behave ethically? In order to be faithful to your wife, you can do different things to the self. That's the third aspect, which

I call the self-forming activity (*pratique de soi*) or *l'ascétisme—asceticism* in a very broad sense.

The fourth aspect is: Which is the kind of being to which we aspire when we behave in a moral way? For instance, shall we become pure, or immortal, or free, or masters of ourselves, and so on? So that's what I call the telos (*téléologie*). In what we call morals, there is the effective behavior of people, there are the codes, and there is this kind of relationship to oneself with the above four aspects.

Q. Which are all independent?

M.F. There are both relationships between them and a certain kind of independence. For instance, you can very well understand why, if the goal is an absolute purity of being, then the type of techniques of self-forming activity, the techniques of asceticism you are to use, is not exactly the same as when you try to be master of your own behavior. In the first place you are inclined to a kind of deciphering technique, or purification technique.

Now, if we apply this general framework to pagan or early Christian ethics, what would we say? First, if we take the code—what is forbidden and what is not—you see that, at least in the philosophical code of behavior, you find three main prohibitions or prescriptions: one about the body—that is, you have to be very careful with your sexual behavior since it is very costly, so do it as infrequently as possible. The second is: when you are married, please don't have sex with anybody else but your wife. And with boys—please don't touch boys. And you find this in Plato, in Isocrates, in Hippocrates, in late Stoics, and so on—and you find it also in Christianity, and even in our own society. So I think you can say that the codes in themselves didn't change a great deal. Some of those interdictions changed; some of the prohibitions are much stricter and much more rigorous in Christianity than in the Greek period. But the themes are the same. So I think that the great changes which occurred between Greek society, Greek ethics, Greek morality, and how the Christians viewed themselves are not in the code, but are in what I call the "ethics," which is the relation to oneself. In *L'Usage des plaisirs*

I analyze those four aspects of the relation to oneself, through the three austerity themes of the code: health, wives or women, and boys.

Q. Would it be fair to say that you're not doing the genealogy of morals, because you think the moral codes are relatively stable, but that what you're doing is a genealogy of ethics?

M.F. Yes, I'm writing a genealogy of ethics. The genealogy of the subject as a subject of ethical actions, or the genealogy of desire as an ethical problem. So, if we take ethics in classical Greek philosophy or medicine, what is the ethical substance? It is the *aphrodisia*, which are at the same time acts, desire, and pleasure. What is the *mode d'assujettissement?* It is that we have to build our existence as a beautiful existence; it is an aesthetic mode. You see, what I tried to show is that nobody is obliged in classical ethics to behave in such a way as to be truthful to their wives, to not touch boys, and so on. But if they want to have a beautiful existence, if they want to have a good reputation, if they want to be able to rule others, they have to do that. So they accept those obligations in a conscious way for the beauty or glory of existence. The choice, the aesthetic choice or the political choice, for which they decide to accept this kind of existence—that's the *mode d'assujettissement*. It's a choice, it's a personal choice.

In late Stoicism, when they start saying, "Well, you are obliged to do that because you are a human being," something changes. It's not a problem of choice; you have to do it because you are a rational being. The *mode d'assujettissement* is changing.

In Christianity what is very interesting is that the sexual rules for behavior were, of course, justified through religion. The institutions by which they were imposed were religious institutions. But the form of the obligation was a legal form. There was a kind of the internal juridification of religious law inside Christianity. For instance, all the casuistic practice was typically a juridical practice.

Q. After the Enlightenment, though, when the religious drops out, is the juridical what's left?

M.F. Yes, after the eighteenth century, the religious framework of those rules disappears in part, and then between a medical or scientific approach and a juridical framework there was competition, with no resolution.

Q. Could you sum this up?

M.F. Well, the *substance éthique* for the Greeks was the *aphrodisia;* the *mode d'assujettissement* was a politico-aesthetic choice; the *form d'ascèse* was the *techne* which was used—and there we find, for example, the *techne* about the body, or economics as the rules by which you define your role as husband, or the erotic as a kind of asceticism toward oneself in loving boys, and so on—and the *téléologie* was the mastery of oneself. So that's the situation I describe in the two first parts of *L'Usage des plaisirs.*

Then there is a shift within this ethics. The reason for the shift is the change of the role of men within society, both in their homes toward their wives and also in the political field, since the city disappears. So, for those reasons, the way they can recognize themselves as subjects of political, economic behavior changes. We can say roughly that along with these sociological changes something is changing also in classical ethics—that is, in the elaboration of the relationship to oneself. But I think that the change doesn't affect the ethical substance: it is still *aphrodisia.* There are some changes in the *mode d'assujettissement*, for instance, when the Stoics recognize themselves as universal beings. And there are also very important changes in the *asceticism*, the kind of techniques you use in order to recognize, to constitute yourself as a subject of ethics. And also a change in the goal. I think that the difference is that in the classical perspective, to be master of oneself meant, first, taking into account only oneself and not the other, because to be master of oneself meant that you were able to rule others. So the mastery of oneself was directly related to a dissymmetrical relation to others. You should be master of yourself in a sense of activity, dissymmetry, and nonreciprocity.

Later on, due to the changes in marriage, society, and so on, mastery of oneself is something which is not primarily related to power over others: you have to be master of yourself not only in order to rule others, as it was in the case of Alcibiades or Nicocles, but you have to be master of yourself because you are a rational being. And in this mastery of yourself, you are related to other people, who are also masters of themselves. And this new kind of relation to the other is much less nonreciprocal than before.

So those are the changes, and I try to show those changes in the three last chapters, the fourth part of *L'Usage des plaisirs*. I take the same themes—the body, wives or women, and boys— and I show that these same three austerity themes are linked to a partially new ethics. I say "partially" because some of the parts of this ethics do not change: for instance, the *aphrodisia*. On the other hand, others do: for instance, the techniques. According to Xenophon, the way to become a good husband is to know exactly what your role is inside your home or outside, what kind of authority you have to exercise on your wife, what are your expectations of your wife's behavior, and so on. All this calculation gives you the rules for behavior, and defines the way you have to be toward yourself. But for Epictetus, or for Seneca, for instance, in order to be really master of yourself, you don't have to know what your role in society or in your home is, but you do have to do some exercises like depriving yourself of eating for two or three days, in order to be sure that you can control yourself. If one day you are in prison, you won't suffer from being deprived of food, and so on. And you have to do that for all the pleasures—that's a kind of asceticism you can't find in Plato or Socrates or Aristotle.

There is no complete and identical relation between the techniques and the *tele*. You can find the same techniques in different *tele*, but there are privileged relations, some privileged techniques related to each telos.

In the Christian book—I mean the book about Christianity!—I try to show that all this ethics has changed. Because the telos has changed: the telos is immortality, purity, and so on. The asceticism has changed, because now self-examination takes the form of self-deciphering. The *mode d'assujettissement* is now divine law. And I think that even the ethical substance has changed, because it is not *aphrodisia*, but desire, concupiscence, flesh, and so on.

Q. It seems, then, that we have a grid of intelligibility for desire as an ethical problem?

M.F. Yes, we now have this scheme. If, by sexual behavior, we understand the three poles—acts, pleasure, and desire—we have the Greek "formula," which is the same at the first and at the second stage. In this Greek formula what is underscored is "acts," with pleasure and desire as subsidiary: *acte—plaisir—[désir]*. I have put desire in brackets because I think that in the Stoic ethics you start a kind of elision of desire; desire begins to be condemned.

The Chinese "formula" would be *plaisir—désir—[acte]*. Acts are put aside because you have to restrain acts in order to get the maximum duration and intensity of pleasure.

The Christian "formula" puts an accent on desire and tries to eradicate it. Acts have to become something neutral; you have to act only to produce children, or to fulfill your conjugal duty. And pleasure is both practically and theoretically excluded: *[désir]—acte—[plaisir]*. Desire is practically excluded— you have to eradicate your desire—but theoretically very important.

And I could say that the modern "formula" is desire, which is theoretically underlined and practically accepted, since you have to liberate your own desire. Acts are not very important, and pleasure—nobody knows what it is!

From the Classical Self to the Modern Subject

Q. What is the care of the self which you have decided to treat separately in *Le Souci de soi*?

M.F. What interests me in the Hellenistic culture, in the Greco-Roman culture, starting from about the third century B.C. and continuing until the second or third century after Christ, is a precept for which the Greeks had a specific word, *epimeleia heautou*, which means taking care of one's self. It does not mean simply being interested in oneself, nor does it mean having a certain tendency to self-attachment or self-fascination. *Epimeleia heautou* is a very powerful word in Greek which means working on or being concerned with something. For example, Xenophon used the word *epimeleia heautou* to describe agricultural management. The responsibility of a monarch for his fellow citizens was also *epimeleia heautou*. That which a doctor does in the course of caring for a patient is *epimeleia heautou*. It is therefore a very powerful word; it describes a sort of work, an activity; it implies attention, knowledge, technique.

Q. But isn't the application of knowledge and technology to the self a modern invention?

M.F. Knowledge played a different role in the classical care of the self. There are very interesting things to analyze about relations between scientific knowledge and the *epimeleia heautou*. The one who cared for himself had to choose among all the things that you can know through scientific knowledge only those kinds of things which were relative to him and important to life.

Q. So theoretical understanding, scientific understanding, was secondary to and guided by ethical and aesthetic concerns?

M.F. Their problem and their discussion concerned what limited sorts of knowledge were useful for *epimeleia*. For instance, for the Epicureans, the general knowledge of what is the world, of what is the necessity of the world, the relation between world, necessity, and the gods—all that was very important for the care of the self. Because it was first a matter of meditation: if you were able exactly to understand the necessity of the world, then you could master passions in a much better way, and so on. So, for the Epicureans, there was a kind of adequation between all possible knowledge and the care of the self. The reason that one had to become familiar with physics or cosmology was that one had to take care of the self. For the Stoics, the true self is defined only by what I can be master of.

Q. So knowledge is subordinated to the practical end of mastery?

M.F. Epictetus is very clear on that. He gives as an exercise to walk every morning in the streets looking, watching. And if you meet a consular figure you say, "Is the consul something I can master?" No, so I have nothing to do. If I meet a beautiful girl or beautiful boy, is their beauty, their desirability, something which depends on me, and so on? For the Christians, things are quite different; for Christians, the possibility that Satan can get inside your soul and give you thoughts you cannot recognize as satanic, but that you might interpret as coming from God, leads to uncertainty about what is going on inside your soul. You are unable to know what the real root of your desire is, at least without hermeneutic work.

Q. So, to what extent did the Christians develop new techniques of self-mastery?

M.F. What interests me about the classical concept of care of the self is that we see here the birth and development of a certain number of ascetic themes ordinarily attributed to Christianity. Christianity is usually given credit for replacing the generally tolerant Greco-Roman lifestyle with an austere lifestyle marked by a series of renunciations, interdictions, or prohibitions. Now, we can see that in this activity of the self on itself, the ancients developed a whole series of austerity practices that the Christians later directly borrowed from them. So we see that this activity became linked to a certain sexual austerity which was subsumed directly into the Christian ethic. We are not talking about a moral rupture between tolerant antiquity and austere Christianity.

Q. In the name of what does one choose to impose this lifestyle upon oneself?

M.F. In antiquity, this work on the self with its attendant austerity is not imposed on the individual by means of civil law or religious obligation, but is a choice about existence made by the individual. People decide for themselves whether or not to care for themselves.

I don't think it is to attain eternal life after death, because they were not particularly concerned with that. Rather, they acted so as to give to their life certain values (reproduce certain examples, leave behind them an exalted reputation, give the maximum possible brilliance to their lives). It was a question of making one's life into an object for a sort of knowledge, for a *techne*—for an art.

We have hardly any remnant of the idea in our society, that the principal work of art which one has to take care of, the main area to which one must apply aesthetic values, is oneself, one's life, one's existence. We find this in the Renaissance, but in a slightly academic form, and yet again in nineteenth-century dandyism, but those were only episodes.

Q. But isn't the Greek concern with the self just an early version of our self-absorption, which many consider a central problem in our society?

M.F. You have a certain number of themes—and I don't say that you have to reutilize them in this way—which indicate to you that in a culture to which we owe a certain number of our most important constant moral elements, there was a practice of the self, a conception of the self, very different from our present culture of the self. In the Californian cult of the self, one is supposed to discover one's true self, to separate it from that which might obscure or alienate it, to decipher its truth thanks to psychological or psychoanalytic science, which is supposed to be able to tell you what your true self is. Therefore, not only do I not identify this ancient culture of the self with what you might call the Californian cult of the self, I think they are diametrically opposed.

What happened in between is precisely an overtuning of the classical culture of the self. This took place when Christianity substituted the idea of a self which one had to renounce, because clinging to the self was opposed to God's will, for the idea of a self which had to be created as a work of art.

Q. We know that one of the studies for *Le Souci de soi* concerns the role of writing in the formation of the self. How is the question of the relation of writing and the self posed by Plato?

M.F. First, to bring out a certain number of historical facts which are often glossed over when posing this problem of writing, we must look into the famous question of the *hypomnemata*. Current interpreters see in the critique of the *hypomnemata* in the *Phaedrus* a critique of writing as a material support for memory. Now, in fact, *hypomnemata* has a very precise meaning. It is a copybook, a notebook. Precisely this type of notebook was coming into vogue in Plato's time for personal and administrative use. This new technology was as disrupting as the introduction of the computer into private life today. It seems to me the question of writing and the self must be posed in terms of the technical and material framework in which it arose.

Second, there are problems of interpretation concerning the famous critique of writing as opposed to the culture of memory in the *Phaedrus*. If you read the *Phaedrus*, you will see that this passage is secondary with respect to another one, which is fundamental and which is in line with the theme which runs throughout the end of the text. It does not matter whether a text is written or oral—the problem is whether or not the discourse in question gives access to truth. Thus the written/oral question is altogether secondary with respect to the question of truth.

Third, what seems remarkable to me is that these new instruments were immediately used for the constitution of a permanent relationship to oneself—one must manage oneself as a governor manages the governed, as a head of an enterprise manages his enterprise, a head of household manages his household. This new idea that virtue consists essentially in perfectly governing oneself, that is, in exercising upon oneself as exact a mastery as that of a sovereign against whom there would no longer be revolts, is something very important which we will find, for centuries—practically until Christianity. So, if you will, the point at which the question of the *hypomnemata* and the culture of the self comes together in a remarkable fashion is the point at which the culture of the self takes as its goal the perfect government of the self—a sort of permanent political relationship between self and self. The ancients carried on this politics of themselves with these notebooks just as governments and those who manage enterprises administered by keeping registers. This is how writing seems to me to be linked to the problem of the culture of the self.

Q. Can you tell us more about the *hypomnemata*?

M.F. In the technical sense, the *hypomnemata* could be account books, public registers, individual notebooks serving as memoranda. Their use as books of life, guides for conduct, seems to have become a current thing among a whole cultivated public. Into them one entered quotations, fragments of works, examples, and actions to which one had been witness or of which one had read the account, reflections or reasonings which one had heard or which had come to mind. They constituted a material memory of things read, heard, or thought, thus offering these as an accumulated treasure for rereading and later meditation. They also formed a raw material for the writing of more systematic treatises in which were given arguments and means by which to struggle against some defect (such as anger, envy, gossip, flattery) or to overcome some difficult circumstance (a mourning, an exile, downfall, disgrace).

Q. But how does writing connect up with ethics and the self?

M.F. No technique, no professional skill can be acquired without exercise; neither can one learn the art of living, the *techne tou biou*, without an *askesis* which must be taken as a training of oneself by oneself: this was one of the traditional principles to which the Pythagoreans, the Socratics, the Cynics had for a long time attributed great importance. Among all the forms this training took (and which included abstinences, memorizations, examinations of conscience, meditations, silence, and listening to others), it seems that writing—the fact of writing for oneself and for others—came quite late to play a sizable role.

Q. What specific role did the notebooks play when they finally became influential in late antiquity?

M.F. As personal as they were, the *hypomnemata* must nevertheless not be taken for intimate diaries or for those accounts of spiritual experience (temptations, struggles, falls, and victories) which can be found in later Christian literature. They do not constitute an "account of oneself"; their objective is not to bring the *arcana conscientiae* to light, the confession of which—be it oral or written—has a purifying value. The movement that they seek to effect is the inverse of this last one. The point is not to pursue the indescribable, not to reveal the hidden, not to say the non-said, but, on the contrary, to collect the already-said, to reassemble that which one could hear or read, and this to an end which is nothing less than the constitution of oneself.

The *hypomnemata* are to be resituated in the context of a very sensitive tension of that period. Within a culture very affected by traditionality, by the recognized value of the already-said, by the recurrence of discourse, by the "citational" practice under the seal of age and authority, an ethic was developing which was very explicitly oriented to the care of oneself, toward definite objectives such as retiring into oneself, reaching oneself, living with oneself, being sufficient to oneself, profiting by and enjoying oneself. Such is the objective of the *hypomnemata*: to make of the recollection of the fragmentary *logos* transmitted by teaching, listening, or reading a means to establish as adequate and as perfect a relationship of oneself to oneself as possible.

Q. Before we turn to the role of these notebooks in early Christianity, could you tell us something about how Greco-Roman austerity differs from Christian austerity?

M.F. One thing that has been very important is that in Stoic ethics the question of purity was nearly nonexistent or rather marginal. It was important in Pythagorean circles and also in the neo-Platonic schools and became more and more important through their influence and also through religious influences. At a certain moment, the problem of an aesthetics of existence is covered over by the problem of purity, which is something else and which requires another kind of technique. In Christian ascetism the question of purity becomes more and more important; the reason why you have to take control of yourself is to keep yourself pure. The problem of virginity, this model of feminine integrity, becomes much more important in Christianity. The theme of virginity has nearly nothing to do with sexual ethics in Greco-Roman ascetism. There the problem is a problem of self-domination. It was a virile model of self-domination and a woman who was temperate was as virile to herself as a man. The paradigm of sexual self-restraint becomes a feminine paradigm through the theme of purity and virginity, based on the model of physical integrity. Physical integrity rather than self-regulation became important. So the problem of ethics as an aesthetics of existence is covered over by the problem of purification.

This new Christian self had to be constantly examined because in this self were lodged concupiscence and desires of the flesh. From that moment on, the self was no longer something to be made but something to be renounced and deciphered. Consequently, between paganism and Christianity, the opposition is not between tolerance and austerity, but between a form of austerity which is linked to an aesthetics of existence and other forms of austerity which are linked to the necessity of renouncing the self and deciphering its truth.

Q. So Nietzsche, then, must be wrong, in *The Genealogy of Morals*, when he credits Christian asceticism for making us the kind of creatures that can make promises?

M.F. Yes, I think he has given mistaken credit to Christianity, given what we know about the evolution of pagan ethics from the fourth century B.C. to the fourth century after.

Q. How was the role of the notebooks transformed when the technique of using them to relate oneself to oneself was taken over by the Christians?

M.F. One important change is that the writing down of inner movements appears, according to Athanase's text on the life of Saint Anthony, as an arm in spiritual combat: while the demon is a force which deceives and which makes one be deceived about oneself (one great half of the *Vita Antonii* is devoted to these ploys), writing constitutes a test and something like a touchstone: in bringing to light the movements of thought, it dissipates the inner shadow where the enemy's plots are woven.

Q. How could such a radical transformation take place?

M.F. There is, indeed, a dramatic change between the *hypomnemata* evoked by Xenophon, where it was only a question of remembering the elements of a diet, and the description of the nocturnal temptations of Saint Anthony. An interesting place to look for a transitional set of techniques seems to be the description of dreams. Almost from the beginning one had to have a notebook beside one's bed upon which to write one's dreams in order either to interpret them oneself the next morning or to show them to someone who would interpret them. By means of this nightly description, an important step is taken toward the description of the self.

Q. But surely the idea that the contemplation of the self allows the self to dissipate shadows and arrive at truth is already present in Plato?

M.F. Yes, but this is an ontological and not a psychological form of contemplation. This ontological knowledge of the self takes shape, at least in certain texts and in particular in the *Alcibiades*, in the form of the contemplation of the soul by itself in terms of the famous metaphor of the eye. Plato asks, "How can the eye see itself?" The answer is apparently very simple, but in fact it is very complicated. For Plato, one cannot simply look at oneself in a mirror. One has to look into another eye, that is, one *in* oneself, however in oneself in the shape of the eye of the other. And there, in the other pupil, one will see oneself: the pupil serves as a mirror. And, in the same manner, the soul contemplating itself in another soul (or in the divine element of the other soul), which is like its pupil, will recognize its divine element.

You see that this idea that one must know oneself, i.e., gain ontological knowledge of the soul's mode of being, is independent of what one could call an exercise of the self upon the self. When grasping the mode of being of your soul, there is no need to ask yourself what you have done, what you are thinking, what the movements of your ideas or your representations are, to what you are attached. That's why you can perform this technique of contemplation using as your object the soul of an other. Plato never speaks of the examination of conscience—never!

Q. It is a commonplace in literary studies that Montaigne was the first great autobiographer, yet you seem to trace writing about the self to much earlier sources.

M.F. It seems to me that in the religious crisis of the sixteenth century—the great rejection of the Catholic confessional practices—new modes of relationship to the self were being developed. We can see the reactivation of a certain number of ancient Stoic practices. The notion, for example, of proofs of oneself seems to me thematically close to what we find among the Stoics, where the experience of the self is not a discovering of a truth hidden inside the self, but an attempt to determine what one can and cannot do with one's available freedom. Among both the Catholics and Protestants, the reactivation of these ancient techniques in the form of Christian spiritual practices is quite marked.

Let me take as an example the walking exercise recommended by Epictetus. Each morning, while taking a walk in the city, one should try to determine with respect to each thing (a public official or an attractive woman), one's motives, whether one is impressed by or drawn to it, or whether one has sufficient self-mastery so as to be indifferent.

In Christianity one has the same sort of exercises, but they serve to test one's dependence on God. I remember having found in a seventeenth-century text an exercise reminiscent of Epictetus, where a young seminarist, when he is walking,.does certain exercises which show in what way each thing shows his dependence vis-à-vis God—which permit him to decipher the presence of divine providence. These two walks correspond to the extent that you have a case with Epictetus of a walk during which the individual assures himself of his own sovereignty over himself and shows that he is dependent on nothing. While in the Christian case the seminarist walks and before each thing he sees, says, "Oh, how God's goodness is great! He who made this, holds all things in his power, and me, in particular," thus reminding himself that he is nothing.

Q. So discourse plays an important role but always serves other practices even in the constitution of the self.

M.F. It seems to me, that all the so-called literature of the self—private diaries, narratives of the self, etc.—cannot be understood unless it is put into the general and very rich framework of these practices of the self. People have been writing about themselves for two thousand years, but not in the same way. I have the impression—I may be wrong—that there is a certain tendency to present the relationship between writing and the narrative of the self as a phenomenon particular to European modernity. Now, I would not deny it is modern, but it was also one of the first uses of writing.

So it is not enough to say that the subject is constituted in a symbolic system. It is not just in the play of symbols that the subject is constituted. It is constituted in real practices—historically analyzable practices. There is a technology of the constitution of the self which cuts across symbolic systems while using them.

Q. If self-analysis is a cultural invention, why does it seem so natural and pleasurable to us?

M.F. It may have been an extremely painful exercise at first and required many cultural valorizations before ending up transformed into a positive activity. Techniques of the self, I believe, can be found in all cultures in different forms. Just as it is necessary to study and compare the different techniques of the production of objects and the direction of men by men through government, one must also question techniques of the self. What makes the analysis of the techniques of the self difficult is two things. First, the techniques of the self do not require the same material apparatus as the production of objects; therefore they are often invisible techniques. Second, they are frequently linked to the techniques for the direction of others. For example, if we take educational institutions, we realize that one is managing others and teaching them to manage themselves.

Q. Let's move on to the history of the modern subject. To begin with, was the classical culture of the self completely lost, or was it, rather, incorporated and transformed by Christian techniques?

M.F. I do not think that the culture of the self disappeared or was covered up. You find many elements which have simply been integrated, displaced, reutilized in Christianity. From the moment that the culture of the self was taken up by Christianity, it was, in a way, put to work for the exercise of a pastoral power to the extent that the *epimeleia heautou* became essentially *epimeleia tonallon*—the care of others—which was the pastor's job. But insofar as individual salvation is channeled—to a certain extent at least—through a pastoral institution which has the care of souls as its object, the classical care of the self disappeared, that is, was integrated and lost a large part of its autonomy.

What is interesting is that during the Renaissance you see a whole series of religious groups (whose existence is, moreover, already attested to in the Middle Ages) which resist this pastoral power and which claim the right to make their own statutes for themselves. According to these groups, the individual should take care of his own salvation independently of the ecclesiastical institution and of the ecclesiastical pastorate. We can see, therefore, a reappearance, up to a certain point, not of the culture of the self, which had never disappeared, but a reaffirmation of its autonomy.

In the Renaissance you also see—and here I refer to Burck-hardt's text on the famous aesthetics of existence—the hero as his own work of art. The idea that from one's own life one can make a work of art is an idea which was undoubtedly foreign to the Middle Ages and which reappears at the moment of the Renaissance.

Q. So far you have been treating various degrees of appropriation of ancient techniques of self-mastery. In your own writing, you always show a big break between the Renaissance and the classical age. Was there an equally significant change in the way self-mastery was related to other social practices?

M.F. That is very interesting, but I won't answer you immediately. Let us start by saying that the relationship between Montaigne, Pascal, and Descartes could be rethought in terms of this question. First, Pascal was still in a tradition in which practices of the self, the practice of asceticism, were tied up to the knowledge of the world. Second, we must not forget that Descartes wrote "meditations"—and meditations are a practice of the self. But the extraordinary thing in Descartes's texts is that he succeeded in substituting a subject as founder of practices of knowledge, for a subject constituted through practices of the self.

This is very important. Even if it is true that Greek philosophy founded rationality, it always held that a subject could not have access to the truth if he did not first operate upon himself a certain work which would make him susceptible to knowing the truth—a work of purification, conversion of the soul by contemplation of the soul itself. You also have the theme of the Stoic exercise by which a subject first ensures his autonomy and independence—and he ensures it in a rather complex relationship to the knowledge of the world, since it is this knowledge which allows him to ensure his independence and it is only once he has ensured it that he is able to recognize the order of the world as it stands. In European culture up to the sixteenth century, the problem remains: What is the work which I must effect upon myself so as to be capable and worthy of acceding to the truth? To put it another way: truth always has a price; no access to truth without ascesis. In Western culture up to the sixteenth century, asceticism and access to truth are always more or less obscurely linked.

Descartes, I think, broke with this when he said, "To accede to truth, it suffices that I be *any* subject which can see what is evident." Evidence is substituted for ascesis at the point where the relationship to the self intersects the relationship to others and the world. The relationship to the self no longer needs to be ascetic to get into relation to the truth. It suffices that the relationship to the self reveals to me the obvious truth of what I see for me to apprehend that truth definitively. Thus, I can be immoral and know the truth. I believe that this is an idea which, more or less explicitly, was rejected by all previous culture. Before Descartes, one could not be impure, immoral, and know the truth. With Descartes, direct evidence is enough. After Descartes, we have a nonascetic subject of knowledge. This change makes possible the institutionalization of modern science.

I am obviously schematizing a very long history, which is, however, fundamental. After Descartes, we have a subject of knowledge which poses for Kant the problem of knowing the relationship between the subject of ethics and that of knowledge. There was much debate in the Enlightenment as to whether these two subjects were completely different or not. Kant's solution was to find a universal subject, which, to the extent that it was universal, could be the subject of knowledge, but which demanded, nonetheless, an ethical attitude—precisely the relationship to the self which Kant proposes in *The Critique of Practical Reason*.

Q. You mean that once Descartes had cut scientific rationality loose from ethics, Kant reintroduced ethics as an applied form of procedural rationality?

M.F. Right. Kant says, "I must recognize myself as universal subject, that is, I must constitute myself in each of my actions as a universal subject by conforming to universal rules." The old questions were reinterpreted: How can I constitute myself as a subject of ethics? Recognize myself as such? Are ascetic exercises needed? Or simply this Kantian relationship to the universal which makes me ethical by conformity to practical reason? Thus Kant introduces one more way in our tradition whereby the self is not merely given but is constituted in relationship to itself as subject.

Politics
and Ethics:
An Interview

Q. There is much talk in America these days comparing your work to that of Jurgen Habermas. It has been suggested that your work is more concerned with ethics and his with politics. Habermas, for example, grew up reading Heidegger as a politically disastrous heir of Nietzsche. He associates Heidegger with German neo-conservatism. He thinks of these people as the conservative heirs of Nietzsche and of you as the anarchistic heir. You don't read the philosophical tradition this way at all, do you?

M.F. That's right. When Habermas was in Paris, we talked at some length, and in fact I was quite struck by his observation of the extent to which the problem of Heidegger and of the political implications of Heidegger's thought was quite a pressing and important one for him. One thing he said to me has left me musing, and it's something I'd like to mull over further. After explaining how Heidegger's thought indeed constituted a political disaster, he mentioned one of his professors who was a great Kantian, very well-known in the '30s, and he explained how astonished and disappointed he had been when, while looking through card catalogues one day, he found some texts from around 1934 by this illustrious Kantian that were thoroughly Nazi in orientation.

I have just recently had the same experience with Max Pohlenz, who heralded the universal values of Stoicism all his life. I came across a text of his from 1934 devoted to *Führertum* in

This is an edited version of interviews with Michel Foucault conducted in Berkeley, in April 1983, by Paul Rabinow, Charles Taylor, Martin Jay, Richard Rorty, and Leo Lowenthal.

Translated by Catherine Porter.

373

Stoicism. You should reread the introductory page and the book's closing remarks on the *Führersideal* and on the true humanism constituted by the Volk under the inspiration of the leader's direction—Heidegger never wrote anything more disturbing. Nothing in this condemns Stoicism or Kantianism, needless to say.

But I think that we must reckon with several facts: there is a very tenuous "analytic" link between a philosophical conception and the concrete political attitude of someone who is appealing to it; the "best" theories do not constitute a very effective protection against disastrous political choices; certain great themes such as "humanism" can be used to any end whatever—for example, to show with what gratitude Pohlenz would have greeted Hitler.

I do not conclude from this that one may say just anything within the order of theory, but, on the contrary, that a demanding, prudent, "experimental" attitude is necesary; at every moment, step by step, one must confront what one is thinking and saying with what one is doing, with what one is. I have never been too concerned about people who say: "You are borrowing ideas from Nietzsche; well, Nietzsche was used by the Nazis, therefore . . ."; but, on the other hand, I have always been concerned with linking together as tightly as possible the historical and theoretical analysis of power relations, institutions, and knowledge, to the movements, critiques, and experiences that call them into question in reality. If I have insisted on all this "practice," it has not been in order to "apply" ideas, but in order to put them to the test and modify them. The key to the personal poetic attitude of a philosopher is not to be sought in his ideas, as if it could be deduced from them, but rather in his philosophy-as-life, in his philosophical life, his ethos.

Among the French philosophers who participated in the Resistance during the war, one was Cavaillès, a historian of mathematics who was interested in the development of its internal structures. None of the philosophers of *engagement*—Sartre, Simone de Beauvoir, Merleau-Ponty—none of them did a thing.

Q. And would this apply also to your own historical work? It seems to me that you're read as a more political thinker than you want to be, or is this going too far? To call you an anarchistic heir of Nietzsche seems all wrong; it's placing your work in the wrong context.

M.F. I would more or less agree with the idea that in fact what interests me is much more morals than politics or, in any case, politics as an ethics.

Q. Would that be true, though, of your work five or ten years ago; in other words, when you were considered more a philosopher or a historian of power than a historian of the self or subject? This is certainly the reason why you were perceived as essentially advocating an alternative view of politics rather than no view of politics at all. This is the reason why Marxists or Habermasians or whatever saw you as a figure to contend with.

M.F. If you like, what strikes me is the fact that from the beginning I have been considered an enemy by the Marxists, an enemy by the right wing, an enemy by the people in the center. I think that if my work were essentially political, it would end up finding its place somewhere in the long run.

Q. Where?

M.F. I don't know . . . if it were political it would inevitably be localized in the political arena. In fact, I have especially wanted to question politics, and to bring to light in the political field, as in the field of historical and philosophical interrogation, some problems that had not been recognized there before. I mean that the questions I am trying to ask are not determined by a preestablished political outlook and do not tend toward the realization of some definite political project.

This is doubtless what people mean when they reproach me for not presenting an overall theory. But I believe precisely that the forms of totalization offered by politics are always, in fact, very limited. I am attempting, to the contrary, apart from any *totalization*—which would be at once *abstract* and *limiting*—

to *open up* problems that are as *concrete* and *general* as possible, problems that approach politics from behind and cut across societies on the diagonal, problems that are at once constituents of our history and constituted by that history: for example, the problem of the relation between sanity and insanity; the question of illness, of crime, or of sexuality. And it has been necessary to try to raise them both as present-day questions and as historical ones, as moral, epistemological, and political problems.

Q. And this is hard to situate within a struggle that is already under way, because the lines are drawn by others. . . .

M.F. It is difficult to project these questions, which have several dimensions, several sides, onto a personal political space. There have been Marxists who said I was a danger to Western democracy—that has been written; there was a socialist who wrote that the thinker who resembled me most closely was Adolf Hitler in *Mein Kampf*. I have been considered by liberals as a technocrat, an agent of the Gaullist government; I have been considered by people on the right, Gaullists or otherwise, as a dangerous left-wing anarchist; there was an American professor who asked why a crypto-Marxist like me, manifestly a KGB agent, was invited to American universities; and so on. Fine, none of this matters; we have all been exposed to the same thing—you, too, I imagine. It's not at all a matter of making a particular issue of my own situation; but, if you like, I think that by asking this sort of ethico-epistemologico-political question, one is not taking up a position on a chessboard.

Q. The ethics label seems fine to me, very interesting, but it has to be said that you are not purely contemplative. You have undeniably been acting for years in very specific sectors of French society, and what is interesting and perhaps also a major challenge to the political parties is the way in which you've done it, that is, linking an analysis with a type of action that is not ideological in itself, and thus which is harder to name . . . and you help other people get their own struggles going in specific areas; but that is certainly an ethics, if I may say so, of the interaction between theory and practice; it consists in linking the two. Thinking and acting are connected in an ethical sense, but one which has results that have to be called political.

M.F. Yes, but I think that ethics is a practice; ethos is a manner of being. Let's take an example that touches us all, that of Poland. If we raise the question of Poland in strictly political terms, it's clear that we quickly reach the point of saying that there's nothing we can do. We can't dispatch a team of paratroopers, and we can't send armored cars to liberate Warsaw. I think that, politically, we have to recognize this, but I think we also agree that, for ethical reasons, we have to raise the problem of Poland in the form of a nonacceptance of what is happening there, and a nonacceptance of the passivity of our own governments. I think this attitude is an ethical one, but it is also political; it does not consist in saying merely, "I protest," but in making of that attitude a political phenomenon that is as substantial as possible, and one which those who govern, here or there, will sooner or later be obliged to take into account.

Q. There is a vision of politics associated in America with Hannah Arendt, and now Jurgen Habermas, which sees the possibility of power as acting in concert, acting together, rather than power as a relation of domination. The idea that power can be a consensus, a realm of intersubjectivity, common action is one that your work seems to undermine. It is hard to find a vision in it of alternative politics. Perhaps, in this sense, you can be read as anti-political.

M.F. Let me take some very simple examples, but which, I think, will not fall outside the theme you've chosen. If we take the penal system, the questions that are currently being raised, we are well aware that in many democratic countries efforts are being made to put penal justice to work in another form, called "informal justice" in the United States, "societal form" in France. This means in reality that a certain form of authority is given to groups, to group leaders. This authority obeys other rules and requires other instruments, but it also produces power effects that are not necessarily valid, owing to the simple fact that they are not state-sanctioned, that they do not pass through the same network of authority. Now to come back to your question, the idea of a consensual politics may indeed at a given moment serve either as regulatory principle, or better yet as critical principle with respect to other political forms; but I do not believe that that liquidates the problem of the power relation.

Q. But may I ask you a question on this point, starting from Hannah Arendt? Arendt reserved the word *power* for just one of the two sides, but let us use the term more broadly, let us say that she saw two possible sides of power. There are relations among people that allow them to accomplish things they would not have been able to do otherwise; people are linked by power relations in the sense that together they have a capacity that they would not have otherwise, and this supposes a certain common understanding, and so on, that may also include relations of subordination, because one of the necessary conditions of this common action may be that of having heads, or leaders—but, according to Arendt, these would not be in any way relations of domination; and there is another side of power that may be implied in the same relations in a sense, in which there are, unequivocally, relations of domination of certain people over others. Do you recognize these two aspects of power; or do you define power, rather, in terms of the second facet?

M.F. Here I think you are entirely right to bring up the problem of the relation of domination because in fact it seems to me that in many of the analyses that have been made by Arendt, or in any case from her perspective, the relation of domination has been constantly dissociated from the relation of power. Yet I wonder whether this distinction is not something of a verbal one; for we can recognize that certain power relations function in such a way as to constitute, globally, an effect of domination, but the network constituted by the power relations hardly allows for a decisive distinction.

I think that starting from this general theme, we have to be both extremely prudent and extremely empirical. For example, with regard to the pedagogical relation—I mean the relation of teaching, that passage from the one who knows the most to the one who knows the least—it is not certain that self-management is what produces the best results; nothing proves, on the contrary, that that approach isn't a hindrance. So I would say yes, on the whole, with the reservation that all the details have to be examined.

Q. If one can perhaps assume that the consensus model is a fictional possibility, people might nonetheless act according to that fiction in such a way that the results might be superior to the action that would ensue from the rather bleaker view of politics as essentially domination and repression, so that although in an empirical way you may be correct and although the utopian possibility may never be achievable, nonetheless, pragmatically, it might in some sense be better, healthier, freer, whatever positive value one uses, if we assume that the consensus is a goal still to be sought rather than one that we simply throw away and say it's impossible to achieve.

M.F. Yes, I think that as, let us say, a critical principle . . .

Q. As a regulatory principle?

M.F. I perhaps wouldn't say regulatory principle, that's going too far, because starting from the point where you say regulatory principle, you grant that it is indeed under its governance that the phenomenon has to be organized, within limits that may be defined by experience or the context. I would say, rather, that it is perhaps a critical idea to maintain at all times: to ask oneself what proportion of nonconsensuality is implied in such a power relation, and whether that degree of nonconsensuality is necessary or not, and then one may question every power relation to that extent. The farthest I would go is to say that perhaps one must not be for consensuality, but one must be against nonconsensuality.

Q. The problem of subjugation is not the same as the problem of ordering. At the present time we very often see, in the name of consensus, of liberation, of self-expression and all that, an entirely different sort of operation of power fields, which is not strictly domination, but which is nevertheless not very attractive.

In my opinion, one of the advances made by the analyses of power was that of showing that certain ideas of a subjugation that was not strictly ordering could nevertheless be very dangerous.

M.F. Power of the disciplinary type such as the one that is exercised, that has been exercised, at least in a certain number of institutions, at bottom something like the ones Erving Goffman calls total institutions—this sort of power is absolutely localized, it's a formula invented at a given moment; it has produced a certain number of results, has been experienced as totally intolerable or partially intolerable, and so on; but it is clear that it does not adequately represent all power relations and all possibilities of power relations. Power is not discipline; discipline is a possible procedure of power.

Q. But aren't there relations of discipline which are not necessarily relations of domination?

M.F. Of course, there are consensual disciplines. I have tried to indicate the limits of what I wanted to achieve, that is, the analysis of a specific historical figure, of a precise technique of government of individuals, and so forth. Consequently these analyses can in no way, to my mind, be equated with a general analytics of every possible power relation.

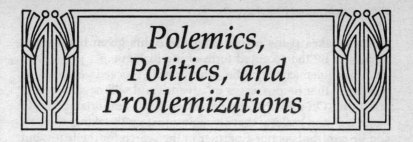

Polemics, Politics, and Problemizations

An Interview with Michel Foucault

Q. Why is it that you don't engage in polemics?

M.F. I like discussions, and when I am asked questions, I try to answer them. It's true that I don't like to get involved in polemics. If I open a book and see that the author is accusing an adversary of "infantile leftism," I shut it again right away. That's not my way of doing things; I don't belong to the world of people who do things that way. I insist on this difference as something essential: a whole morality is at stake, the morality that concerns the search for the truth and the relation to the other.

In the serious play of questions and answers, in the work of reciprocal elucidation, the rights of each person are in some sense immanent in the discussion. They depend only on the dialogue situation. The person asking the questions is merely exercising the right that has been given him: to remain unconvinced, to perceive a contradiction, to require more information, to emphasize different postulates, to point out faulty reasoning, etc. As for the person answering the questions, he too exercises a right that does not go beyond the discussion itself; by the logic of his own discourse he is tied to what he has said earlier, and by the acceptance of dialogue he is tied to the questioning of the other. Questions and answers depend on a game—a game that is at once pleasant and difficult—in which each of the two

This interview was conducted by Paul Rabinow in May, 1984, just before Foucault's death, to answer questions frequently asked by American audiences. It was translated by Lydia Davis. Special thanks are due Thomas Zummer for his help in preparing it.

partners takes pains to use only the rights given him by the other and by the accepted form of the dialogue.

The polemicist, on the other hand, proceeds encased in privileges that he possesses in advance and will never agree to question. On principle, he possesses rights authorizing him to wage war and making that struggle a just undertaking; the person he confronts is not a partner in the search for the truth, but an adversary, an enemy who is wrong, who is harmful and whose very existence constitutes a threat. For him, then, the game does not consist of recognizing this person as a subject having the right to speak, but of abolishing him, as interlocutor, from any possible dialogue; and his final objective will be, not to come as close as possible to a difficult truth, but to bring about the triumph of the just cause he has been manifestly upholding from the beginning. The polemicist relies on a legitimacy that his adversary is by definition denied.

Perhaps, someday, a long history will have to be written of polemics, polemics as a parasitic figure on discussion and an obstacle to the search for the truth. Very schematically, it seems to me that today we can recognize the presence in polemics of three models: the religious model, the judiciary model, and the political model. As in heresiology, polemics sets itself the task of determining the intangible point of dogma, the fundamental and necessary principle that the adversary has neglected, ignored, or transgressed; and it denounces this negligence as a moral failing; at the root of the error, it finds passion, desire, interest, a whole series of weaknesses and inadmissible attachments that establish it as culpable. As in judiciary practice, polemics allows for no possibility of an equal discussion: it examines a case; it isn't dealing with an interlocutor, it is processing a suspect; it collects the proofs of his guilt, designates the infraction he has committed, and pronounces the verdict and sentences him. In any case, what we have here is not on the order of a shared investigation; the polemicist tells the truth in the form of his judgment and by virtue of the authority he has conferred on himself. But it is the political model that is the most powerful today. Polemics defines alliances, recruits partisans, unites interests or opinions, represents a party; it establishes the other as an enemy, an upholder of opposed interests, against which one must fight until the moment this enemy is defeated and either surrenders or disappears.

Of course, the reactivation, in polemics, of these political, judiciary, or religious practices is nothing more than theater. One gesticulates: anathemas, excommunications, condemnations, battles, victories, and defeats are no more than ways of speaking, after all. And yet, in the order of discourse, they are also ways of acting which are not without consequence. There are the sterilizing effects: Has anyone ever seen a new idea come out of a polemic? And how could it be otherwise, given that here the interlocutors are incited, not to advance, not to take more and more risks in what they say, but to fall back continually on the rights that they claim, on their legitimacy, which they must defend, and on the affirmation of their innocence? There is something even more serious here: in this comedy, one mimics war, battles, annihilations, or unconditional surrenders, putting forward as much of one's killer instinct as possible. But it is really dangerous to make anyone believe that he can gain access to the truth by such paths, and thus to validate, even if in a merely symbolic form, the real political practices that could be warranted by it. Let us imagine, for a moment, that a magic wand is waved and one of the two adversaries in a polemic is given the ability to exercise all the power he likes over the other. One doesn't even have to imagine it: one has only to look at what happened during the debates in the USSR over linguistics or genetics not long ago. Were these merely aberrant deviations from what was supposed to be the correct discussion? Not at all: they were the real consequences of a polemic attitude whose effects ordinarily remain suspended.

Q. You have been read as an idealist, as a nihilist, as a "new philosopher," an anti-Marxist, a new conservative, and so on. . . . Where *do* you stand?

M.F. I think I have in fact been situated in most of the squares on the political checkerboard, one after another and sometimes simultaneously: as anarchist, leftist, ostentatious or disguised Marxist, nihilist, explicit or secret anti-Marxist, technocrat in the service of Gaullism, new liberal, etc. An American professor complained that a crypto-Marxist like me was invited to the U.S.A., and I was denounced by the press in Eastern European countries for being an accomplice of the dissidents. None of these descriptions is important by itself; taken together, on the other hand, they mean something. And I must admit that I rather like what they mean.

It's true that I prefer not to identify myself and that I'm amused by the diversity of the ways I've been judged and classified. Something tells me that by now a more or less approximate place should have been found for me, after so many efforts in such various directions; and since I obviously can't suspect the competence of the people who are getting muddled up in their divergent judgments, since it isn't possible to challenge their inattention or their prejudices, I have to be convinced that their inability to situate me has something to do with me.

And no doubt fundamentally it concerns my way of approaching political questions. It is true that my attitude isn't a result of the form of critique that claims to be a methodical examination in order to reject all possible solutions except for the one valid one. It is more on the order of "problemization"— which is to say, the development of a domain of acts, practices, and thoughts that seem to me to pose problems for politics. For example, I don't think that in regard to madness and mental illness there is any "politics" that can contain the just and definitive solution. But I think that in madness, in derangement, in behavior problems, there are reasons for questioning politics; and politics must answer these questions, but it never answers them completely. The same is true for crime and punishment: naturally it would be wrong to imagine that politics has nothing to do with the prevention and punishment of crime, and therefore nothing to do with a certain number of elements that modify its form, its meaning, its frequency; but it would be just as wrong to think that there is a political formula likely to resolve the question of crime and put an end to it. The same is true of sexuality: it doesn't exist apart from a relationship to political structures, requirements, laws, and regulations that have a primary importance for it; and yet one can't expect politics to provide the forms in which sexuality would cease to be a problem.

It is a question, then, of thinking about the relations of these different experiences to politics, which doesn't mean that one will seek in politics the main constituent of these experiences or the solution that will definitively settle their fate. The problems that experiences like these pose to politics have to be elaborated. But it is also necessary to determine what "posing a problem" to politics really means. R. Rorty points out that in these analyses I do not appeal to any "we"—to any of those "we's" whose consensus, whose values, whose traditions constitute the framework for a thought and define the conditions in which it can be validated. But the problem is, precisely, to decide if it is actually suitable to place oneself within a "we" in order to assert the principles one recognizes and the values one accepts; or if it is not, rather, necessary to make the future formation of a "we" possible, by elaborating the question. Because it seems to me that the "we" must not be previous to the question; it can only be the result—and the necessarily temporary result—of the question as it is posed in the new terms in which one formulates it. For example, I'm not sure that at the time when I wrote the history of madness, there was a preexisting and receptive "we" to which I would only have had to refer in order to write my book, and of which this book would have been the spontaneous expression. Laing, Cooper, Basaglia, and I had no community, nor any relationship. But the problem posed itself to those who had read us, as it also posed itself to some of us, of seeing if it was possible to establish a "we" on the basis of the work that had been done, a "we" that would also be likely to form a community of action.

I have never tried to analyze anything whatsoever from the point of view of politics, but always to ask politics what it had to say about the problems with which it was confronted. I question it about the positions it takes and the reasons it gives for this; I don't ask it to determine the theory of what I do. I am neither an adversary nor a partisan of Marxism; I question it about what it has to say about experiences that ask questions of it.

As for the events of May 1968, it seems to me they depend on another problematic. I wasn't in France at that time; I only returned several months later. And it seemed to me one could recognize completely contradictory elements in it: on the one hand, an effort that was very widely asserted, to ask politics a whole series of questions that were not traditionally a part of its statutory domain (questions about women, about relations between the sexes, about medicine, about mental illness, about the environment, about minorities, about delinquency); and on the other hand, a desire to rewrite all these problems in the vocabulary of a theory that was derived more or less directly from Marxism. But the process that was evident at that time led, not to taking over the problems posed by the Marxist doctrine, but on the contrary to a more and more manifest powerlessness on the part of Marxism to confront these problems. So that one found oneself faced with interrogations that were addressed to politics but that had not themselves sprung from a political doctrine. From this point of view, such a liberation of the act of questioning seemed to me to have played a positive role: now there was a plurality of questions posed to politics rather than the reinscription of the act of questioning in the framework of a political doctrine.

Q. Would you say that your work centers on the relations among ethics, politics, and the genealogy of truth?

M.F. No doubt one could say that in some sense I try to analyze the relations among science, politics, and ethics. But I don't think that would be an entirely accurate representation of the work I set out to do. I don't want to remain at that level; rather, I am trying to see how these processes may have interfered with one another in the formation of a scientific domain, a political structure, a moral practice. Let's take psychiatry as an example: no doubt one can analyze it today in its epistemological structure—even if that is still rather loose; one can also analyze it within the framework of the political institutions in which it operates; one can also study it in its ethical implications, as regards the person who is the object of the psychiatry as much as the psychiatrist himself. But my goal hasn't been to do this. Rather, I have tried to see how the formation of psychiatry as a science, the limitation of its field, and the definition of its object implicated a political structure and a moral practice: in the twofold sense that they were presupposed by the progressive organization of psychiatry as a science and that they were also changed by this development. Psychiatry as we know it couldn't have existed without a whole interplay of political structures and without a set of ethical attitudes; but inversely, the establishment of madness as a domain of knowledge changed the political practices and the ethical attitudes that concerned it. It was a matter of determining the role of politics and ethics in the establishment of madness as a particular domain of scientific knowledge, and also of analyzing the effects of the latter on political and ethical practices.

The same is true in relation to delinquency. It was a question of seeing which political strategy had, by giving its status to criminality, been able to appeal to certain forms of knowledge and certain moral attitudes; it was also a question of seeing how these modalities of knowledge and these forms of morality could have been reflected in and changed by these disciplinary techniques. In the case of sexuality, it was the development of a moral attitude that I wanted to isolate; but I tried to reconstruct it through the play that it engaged in with political structures (essentially in the relation between self-control and domination of others) and with the modalities of knowledge (self-knowledge and knowledge of different areas of activity).

So that in these three areas—madness, delinquency, and sexuality—I emphasized a particular aspect each time: the establishment of a certain objectivity, the development of a politics and a government of the self, and the elaboration of an ethics and a practice in regard to oneself. But each time I also tried to point out the place occupied here by the other two components necessary for constituting a field of experience. It is basically a matter of different examples in which the three fundamental elements of any experience are implicated: a game of truth, relations of power, and forms of relation to oneself and to others. And if each of these examples emphasizes, in a certain way, one of these three aspects—since the experience of madness was recently organized as primarily a field of knowledge, that of crime as an area of political intervention, while that of sexuality was defined as an ethical position—each time I have tried to show how the two other elements were present, what roles they played, and how each one was affected by the transformations in the other two.

Q. You have recently been talking about a "history of problematics." What is a history of problematics?

M.F. For a long time I have been trying to see if it would be possible to describe the history of thought as distinct both from the history of ideas—by which I mean the analysis of systems of representation—and from the history of mentalities—by which I mean the analysis of attitudes and types of action (*schémas de comportement*). It seemed to me there was one element that was capable of describing the history of thought: this was what one could call the element of problems or, more exactly, problemizations. What distinguishes thought is that it is something quite different from the set of representations that underlies a certain behavior; it is also something quite different from the domain of attitudes that can determine this behavior. Thought is not what inhabits a certain conduct and gives it its meaning; rather, it is what allows one to step back from this way of acting or reacting, to present it to oneself as an object of thought and question it as to its meaning, its conditions, and its goals. Thought is freedom in relation to what one does, the motion by which one detaches oneself from it, establishes it as an object, and reflects on it as a problem.

To say that the study of thought is the analysis of a freedom does not mean one is dealing with a formal system that has reference only to itself. Actually, for a domain of action, a behavior, to enter the field of thought, it is necessary for a certain number of factors to have made it uncertain, to have made it lose its familiarity, or to have provoked a certain number of difficulties around it. These elements result from social, economic, or political processes. But here their only role is that of instigation. They can exist and perform their action for a very long time, before there is effective problemization by thought. And when thought intervenes, it doesn't assume a unique form that is the direct result or the necessary expression of these difficulties; it is an original or specific response—often taking many forms, sometimes even contradictory in its different aspects—to these difficulties, which are defined for it by a situation or a context and which hold true as a possible question.

To one single set of difficulties, several responses can be made. And most of the time different responses actually are proposed. But what has to be understood is what makes them simultaneously possible: it is the point in which their simultaneity is rooted; it is the soil that can nourish them all in their diversity and sometimes in spite of their contradictions. To the different difficulties encountered by the practice regarding mental illness in the eighteenth century, diverse solutions were proposed: Tuke's and Pinel's are examples; in the same way, a whole group of solutions was proposed for the difficulties encountered in the second half of the eighteenth century by the penal practice; or again, to take a very remote example, the diverse schools of philosophy of the Hellenistic period proposed different solutions to the difficulties of traditional sexual ethics.

But the work of a history of thought would be to rediscover at the root of these diverse solutions the general form of problemization that has made them possible—even in their very opposition; or what has made possible the transformations of the difficulties and obstacles of a practice into a general problem for which one proposes diverse practical solutions. It is problemization that responds to these difficulties, but by doing something quite other than expressing them or manifesting them: in connection with them it develops the conditions in which possible responses can be given; it defines the elements that will constitute what the different solutions attempt to respond to. This development of a given into a question, this transformation of a group of obstacles and difficulties into problems to which the diverse solutions will attempt to produce a response, this is what constitutes the point of problemization and the specific work of thought.

It is clear how far one is from an analysis in terms of deconstruction (any confusion between these two methods would be unwise). Rather, it is a question of a movement of critical analysis in which one tries to see how the different solutions to a problem have been constructed; but also how these different solutions result from a specific form of problemization. And it then appears that any new solution that might be added to the others would arise from current problemization, modifying only several of the postulates or principles on which one bases the responses that one gives. The work of philosophical and historical reflection is put back into the field of the work of thought only on condition that one clearly grasps problemization not as an arrangement of representations but as a work of thought.

FOR THE BEST IN PAPERBACKS, LOOK FOR THE 🐧

In every corner of the world, on every subject under the sun, Penguin represents quality and variety – the very best in publishing today.

For complete information about books available from Penguin – including Puffins, Penguin Classics and Arkana – and how to order them, write to us at the appropriate address below. Please note that for copyright reasons the selection of books varies from country to country.

In the United Kingdom: Please write to *Dept E.P., Penguin Books Ltd, Harmondsworth, Middlesex, UB7 0DA.*

If you have any difficulty in obtaining a title, please send your order with the correct money, plus ten per cent for postage and packaging, to *PO Box No 11, West Drayton, Middlesex*

In the United States: Please write to *Dept BA, Penguin, 299 Murray Hill Parkway, East Rutherford, New Jersey 07073*

In Canada: Please write to *Penguin Books Canada Ltd, 2801 John Street, Markham, Ontario L3R 1B4*

In Australia: Please write to the *Marketing Department, Penguin Books Australia Ltd, P.O. Box 257, Ringwood, Victoria 3134*

In New Zealand: Please write to the *Marketing Department, Penguin Books (NZ) Ltd, Private Bag, Takapuna, Auckland 9*

In India: Please write to *Penguin Overseas Ltd, 706 Eros Apartments, 56 Nehru Place, New Delhi, 110019*

In the Netherlands: Please write to *Penguin Books Netherlands B.V., Postbus 3507, 1001 AH, Amsterdam*

In West Germany: Please write to *Penguin Books Ltd, Friedrichstrasse 10–12, D–6000 Frankfurt/Main 1*

In Spain: Please write to *Alhambra Longman S.A., Fernandez de la Hoz 9, E–28010 Madrid*

In Italy: Please write to *Penguin Italia s.r.l., Via Como 4, I-20096 Pioltello (Milano)*

In France: Please write to *Penguin Books Ltd, 39 Rue de Montmorency, F-75003 Paris*

In Japan: Please write to *Longman Penguin Japan Co Ltd, Yamaguchi Building, 2–12–9 Kanda Jimbocho, Chiyoda-Ku, Tokyo 101*

BY THE SAME AUTHOR

A History of Sexuality: Volume 1
An Introduction

Here one of France's greatest intellectuals explores the evolving social, economic and political forces that have shaped our attitudes to sex. In a book that is at once controversial and seductive, Foucault describes how we are in the process of making a science of sex which is devoted to the analysis of desire rather than the increase of pleasure.

'Foucault is at his polemical best. He brilliantly succeeds in turning commonplaces on their heads (or sides), permitting us to see that, like any notion that has become a part of conventional wisdom, they can be viewed in at least two ways' – Hayden White in *The Times Literary Supplement*

The History of Sexuality: Volume 2
The Use of Pleasure

The Use of Pleasure offers a startlingly original account of the emergence of Christianity from the Ancient World. The book abounds in extraordinary insights into the differences – and the continuities – between the Ancient, Christian and Modern worlds. But Foucault does far more than merely re-create a vanished era when sex was not a major moral issue (only Plato, like Saint Paul, saw puritanical restraint as the way of wisdom): he makes us rethink all our assumptions about sex.

The History of Sexuality: Volume 3
The Care of the Self

'It is the transformation of discourse about *aphrodisia* from the Hellenistic to the Roman world which dominates the third volume of Foucault's enquiry.

'Foucault's reconstruction of Roman sexual discourse as defined by techniques for self-enhancement and self-respect constitutes a remarkable achievement ... At the peak of his powers, Foucault abandoned his protracted war against everyday intelligibility and familiar intellectual forms, and revealed himself as a superb practitioner of conventional intellectual history' – Roy Porter in the *London Review of Books*